THE LIFE & TIMES OF
MORRIS K. UDALL

DONALD W. CARSON & JAMES W. JOHNSON

THE UNIVERSITY OF ARIZONA PRESS
TUCSON

First printing
The University of Arizona Press
© 2001 Donald W. Carson and James W. Johnson
♻ This book is printed on acid-free, archival-quality paper.
Manufactured in the United States of America
06 05 04 03 02 01   6 5 4 3 2 1

Library of Congress Cataloging-in-Publication Data
Carson, Donald W. (Donald Winslow), 1933–
Mo : the life and times of Morris K. Udall / Donald W. Carson and James W. Johnson.
p. cm.
Includes bibliographical references and index.
ISBN 0-8165-2049-6 (acid-free paper)
1. Udall, Morris K. 2. United States—Politics and government—1945–1989.
3. Legislators—United States—Biography. 4. United States. Congress. House—
Biography.
I. Johnson, James W., 1938–
II. Title.
E840.8.U3 C37 2001   00-009255
973.925′092—dc21

British Library Cataloguing-in-Publication Data
A catalogue record for this book is available from the British Library.

Publication of this book is made possible in part by grants from the Provost's Support
Fund of the University of Arizona and members of the Circle of Friends of the
University of Arizona Press.

To Helen Carson
For her support, patience, love

To Marilyn Johnson
For her loving encouragement and advice

CONTENTS

ILLUSTRATIONS

following page 20

Young Mo practicing in St. Johns around 1935.
Soldier Mo at the Holbrook train station.
The family in St. Johns in about 1945.
University of Arizona basketball days.
The 1961 swearing-in with Speaker Sam Rayburn.
The family in Tucson in the early 1960s.
A visit with Speaker John W. McCormack in the early 1960s.
Arizona power: Rhodes, Goldwater, Fannin, Mo Udall, Hayden, &
    Stewart Udall.
A firsthand look at strip mining in the early 1970s.
Stewart and Lee Udall and Ella and Mo in 1976.
Spreading the presidential gospel in the 1976 campaign.
A campaign pause with some nonvoters.
Mo and Ella at a Udall roast.
Checking out Three Mile Island, March 1979.
Keynoting the 1980 Democratic National Convention.
Mo and Norma on their wedding day in 1989.

All photographs are courtesy of Special Collections, The University of
Arizona Library

FOREWORD

*M*o Udall was the best public servant I ever knew. I have known hundreds of public men, and admired a few of them, but the late Arizona congressman and one-time serious presidential candidate is judged "best of breed" because of a combination of factors: a rare intelligence, prodigious energy, the ability to persuade and explain, a sense of humor that eased tensions and made friends, an instinctive understanding of process, an innate sense of justice, a good heart, and uncommon courage. When healthy and at the top of his game, he never ran from a fight.

Morris "Mo" Udall was not perfect, as this honest book documents. A workaholic, he often distanced himself from family and friends. Ambitious, he would go to the mat with those standing in his way. He did not forget those who had politically wronged him, though he would likely appear more affable on the surface than might be the case within. But he was not a man of ill will, nor was he a kamikaze legislator bent on suicide missions just to grab a headline or embarrass a colleague for partisan gain. He knew the value of honorable compromise in the political arena—that half a loaf was better than no bread at all, to paraphrase Lyndon B. Johnson. Yet he was not afraid to do battle when he thought his cause just, as when he early opposed the Vietnam War, tried to make procedural reforms in Congress, and reduced abuses and corruption in political funding. Often he proved ahead of his time, but he lived to see some improvements in areas where, for years, he had been almost a lone voice crying in the wilderness. I pay him the highest compliment I know: He was fair-minded, and he cared.

I had the good fortune to meet and get to know Mo Udall from his first day in Washington, in 1961, when he came to the U.S. House of Representatives—where I then worked for Texas congressman J. T. Rutherford—to replace his older brother, Stewart, newly named secretary of the interior in President Kennedy's cabinet. Somehow we connected almost like brothers ourselves—a rarity in the congressional pecking order, where each person in Congress runs his or her own grand duchy and mere staff members are often considered little more than instruments of convenience.

Even after I left Capitol Hill in 1964, to write for magazines and newspapers while trying to craft books, Mo Udall continued to confide in me and I helped him when and where I could. When I taught a course in politics and the media at Princeton, he came to speak to my students, perhaps shocking some of the dewy-eyed young theorists with wry examples of Realpolitik as played at the national level. And when my friend ran for the Democratic presidential nomination in 1976, I held fundraisers, made media contacts for him, and wrote favorably of him at every opportunity. Not once did I write anything I didn't believe, because I truly *believed* in Mo Udall. I still do.

James W. Johnson and Donald W. Carson have done a magnificent job in this book of detailing Udall's life and career almost from cradle to grave. Here you will see his values shaped as a young man in Arizona, as an army air corps officer during World War II and after, as a college man and basketball player, as a young lawyer and county prosecutor. And here you will find the best and most complete record of Mo Udall's congressional career ever published.

You will find, too, the sad tale of the debilitating disease that robbed Mo Udall of his vigor at too early an age, and his proud and stubborn fight against it, of—yes—his uncommon courage even after he was confined to a wheelchair and then to a bed, where his voice was stilled for far too long a cruel time until death claimed him in December 1998. I regret that I didn't see as much of Mo Udall in his final years as I should have, because I had trouble keeping my composure as I watched him waste away. He was more courageous than I was, and tougher, simply a better man. But I knew that a long time before events proved it.

R.I.P., Ol' Mo. I think this book is worthy of you.

—*Larry L. King*
Washington, D.C.

ACKNOWLEDGMENTS

*T*he authors had no trouble finding people who wanted to talk about Mo Udall. There were scores of them. To those who gave us their valuable time, we thank them. We could not have written the book without them.

We encountered worry about how Mo Udall would be presented by those who knew and loved him. We tried to be fair and honest. We hope we did not disappoint.

The Udall family was exceptional in its willingness to help. Mo's brothers and sisters, his former wife, his widow, and his children welcomed us to their homes to share candid and heartfelt stories. One arranged to meet at a roadside rest area for an interview.

Our deepest gratitude goes to Mo's brother Stewart, who helped beyond the call of duty. No one knew Mo better. This book is about Mo Udall, but at times it was difficult to separate the two, so close were they.

Brother D. Burr Udall and sisters Elma Udall and Eloise Whiting were exceedingly gracious in their time and warmth. Eloise even provided homemade root beer for a lunch table discussion of life in St. Johns.

Mo's children, Representative Mark E. Udall, J. Randolph Udall, Bradley H. Udall, Anne J. Udall, Judith K. "Dodie" Udall, and Katherine L. "Kate" Udall, are scattered about the country, but all found time to talk. Sometimes they felt deep pain when they reminisced, but all have come to love and accept their father for who and what he was.

Mo's first wife, Patricia, and his widow, Norma, willingly talked about the joys and the sorrows. We are grateful for their patience and candor when we had to ask that tough question, often more times than we felt comfortable in doing.

Librarians in Special Collections at the University of Arizona Library, particularly archivists Peter L. Steere and J. Roger Myers, were of significant help. Librarians always were cheerful when we asked for yet another of the 770 boxes of Udall Papers. Jan Davis, in particular, was a joy to work with in selecting and copying most of the photographs.

We especially thank our wives, Helen Carson and Marilyn Johnson, for sharing our joys, our frustrations, our times away from home, our long hours at the computer, and for listening to us go on and on about Mo. Their editing suggestions were always thoughtful and helpful. Many thanks to Susan Carson Cormier, who transcribed hours of taped interviews.

Thanks also to Jim D. Patten, the head of the University of Arizona Department of Journalism, who supported the book project with his encouragement and financial resources.

A special thanks to the director of the University of Arizona Press, Christine R. Szuter, for her faith, encouragement, and enthusiasm, to our editor, Debra Makay, whose eye for consistency and detail helped make this a better book, and to the assistant managing editor of the press, Alan M. Schroder, for coaxing the book into final form.

INTRODUCTION

*A*s we drove from Tucson to Mo Udall's birthplace in St. Johns, Arizona, we approached the town of Globe. Crossing into the city limits, we spotted a sign noting that Globe was the hometown of Rose P. Mofford, the Democrat who was Arizona's governor from 1988 to 1991.

We then wound through the Salt River Canyon, through Show Low, and headed northeast to Udall's hometown of St. Johns, situated in an isolated section of Apache County, an hour's drive from the nearest large community.

As we approached the town of 3,800 people, we saw no mention that it was the hometown of two of the nation's best-known and most respected politicians, the brothers Morris K. and Stewart L. Udall, and two Arizona Supreme Court justices, their father, Levi S. Udall, and their uncle Jesse Udall. If you didn't know that the Udalls were born in this predominantly Mormon community, it was unlikely that you would discover it on your own.

We stopped at a Mormon family history center. No references to those Udalls were available. Why? we wondered. Could it be because Mo and Stewart had left the church years ago? A visit to the Apache County Museum produced only one small folder that referred to the brothers, one a U.S. congressman for thirty years and a presidential candidate and the other a U.S. congressman and then secretary of the interior in the Kennedy and Johnson administrations.

Just as puzzling was the failure to acknowledge Mo Udall in a history of the Mormon presence in northeastern Arizona that was sanctioned by the St. Johns stake of the Church of Jesus Christ of Latter-day Saints. The 1982 book *A History of the St. Johns Arizona Stake,* written by C. LeRoy and Mabel R. Wilhelm, refers to Mo almost as an afterthought in the brief biography of his brother.

The reference refers to the swamp, river, and Blue Hills that lay in a three-mile-square area behind the Udall family home in St. Johns. It says, "Here could be observed that balance of nature and the chain of life. It was here that Stewart Udall and his brother, Morris, spent countless hours learning of the environment and man's relationship to it."[1] The book fails to mention that Mo Udall by that time had served twenty-one years in Congress, that he had sought the Democratic nomination for president in 1976, and that he was a nationally recognized environmentalist. The omission seemed deliberate. Such accomplishments would be difficult to overlook.

Few people remain in St. Johns who remember the Udalls as young boys. Both left to attend the University of Arizona and returned only for infrequent family gatherings after their careers soared in Washington, D.C.

The best answers for the lack of recognition are that the Mormons are disinclined to brag about themselves and that perhaps the Udall family was not as well liked as people may have thought. Mo's sister Eloise describes it this way: "How would you like to be in St. Johns stake under the Udall sponsorship for fifty years if you didn't like the Udalls?"[2]

David K. Udall, grandfather to Stewart and Mo, helped establish the Mormon presence in St. Johns and was president of the Church of Jesus Christ of Latter-day Saints stake for thirty-five years until his son Levi took over and reigned for twenty-three more years. Stewart Udall said there was an undercurrent of Udall resentment because, by the town's standards, "we were well-to-do" during the depression because his father was a judge.[3]

Stewart and Mo left St. Johns when they were in their late teens, so most people did not get a chance to know them well. Stewart went on a two-year Mormon mission, but Mo never did, nor did his other brother, Burr.

Mormons generally are conservative in their politics. The vast majority of the Udalls outside the Levi Udall family were Republicans. The town might be less than willing to recognize the accomplishments of two

Democratic brothers—and liberal ones, at that. On at least three occasions in the 1970s and 1980s, the Udalls were honored in their hometown, but the lasting tributes are missing.

If they are not readily acknowledged in St. Johns, both still are remembered and respected across the nation. As Terrence L. Bracy, Mo Udall's former aide, put it: "In many ways [Stewart and Mo's] legacy is one." When Mo was in the House and Stewart was interior secretary, they conferred "all the time," Bracy said.[4] It's fair to say that despite their sibling rivalry they were both seeking the same end and worked together to achieve it, even long after Stewart left government service.

With this book, we hope to shed light on one of those brothers, Mo Udall. In researching the book, we rarely encountered anyone who disliked Mo. People may have disliked his liberal politics, but they genuinely liked and respected the man, often drawn to him by his humor, his humanity, and his courage.

That's the way it was with Mo. In the bleakest moment, Udall could crack a joke that would lift everyone's spirits, even when he was at the lowest point—and he had his share. His brother Stewart cautioned that too much emphasis has been placed on Mo's humor. He said the story of Mo Udall was one of "guts rather than laughter."[5]

Mo Udall, by the sheer force of his personality, could persuade others to see his point of view. Lyndon Johnson's personality also bent others to his wishes, but he did it by threat and cajole. Mo accomplished the same things because people liked and respected him. As political analyst Mark Shields said, "Mo Udall has been a gentle giant with laughter in his soul and integrity in his bones."[6]

Perhaps that's why he never made it to the White House. As much as he sought the presidency, he "lacked that all-consuming conviction that the fate, fortune, and future of the planet depended upon his being elected."[7]

A political writer once asked him if he were sob enough to be president, a question that stunned him. Maybe he was too nice or, as the title of his humorous semiautobiography put it, he was "too funny to be president." He never understood why it would be a shortcoming for a president to have a sense of humor. Certainly, John F. Kennedy and Ronald Reagan found it useful.

One can only wonder what kind of a nation it would have become under a Udall administration. It has been said that Mo Udall might have been the best candidate never to become president. His House colleague Henry S. Reuss, a Wisconsin Democrat, wrote in his memoirs that "Udall could have ended the cold war in 1979 rather than ten years later—by agreeing to help the Russians reconstruct their society and economy in return for their dissolution of communism and their empire. He could have avoided the heavyhanded money tightening, tax cutting, military spending, and poor-people bashing of the Reagan years."[8]

Udall was a reformer and reformation takes courage, something that he had in abundance. It is one thing to be smart, and Mo Udall was extremely intelligent. It is another to have the courage to take risks. That separates potential from achievement.

Stewart Udall said his brother operated with a sense of audacity. From challenging the seniority system in the House to running for president from the unlikely position of U.S. representative, Udall liked to reform the system. He took a relatively obscure committee, the House Insular and Interior Committee, and turned it into a powerful panel that did as much to protect the environment as any organization in the twentieth century.

Nevertheless, his political actions at times were incongruous. Often the same policies that he felt were good for the rest of the nation he gave short shrift in Arizona. For example, his support of the environmentally unfriendly Central Arizona Project, newspaper monopolies, and right-to-work laws seemed to clash with his liberal ideology.

Udall also had a personal side that few people saw. He had his shortcomings as a husband and a father, although his six children are mature, responsible, and loving kin. The first of his marriages ended in divorce and the second in his wife's suicide.

He also was a loner, from his early days when he had few close friends to his later years when his life was filled with acquaintances and associates. He was a workaholic, whose focus was politics to the detriment of other aspects of his life, but he left an impact on this country, a nation that is better for his efforts.

This book will explore the paradoxes and the man behind them. It is filled with dedication, admiration, sadness, humor, and, most of all, his love of country.

Most biographies are written in cradle-to-grave order. We strayed from that, mostly by grouping key issues into separate chapters. The book is organized in chronological order from the first chapter through Udall's election to Congress. Then it focuses on issues such as his opposition to the Vietnam War, his fight to gain House leadership, his efforts to attain passage of the Central Arizona Project, and his run for the presidency. Although Udall's humor is evident throughout the book, we have devoted a separate chapter to exploring how it came to be, how he used it, and what results it brought. The last chapters look at his life as a husband and father and his long struggle with Parkinson's disease.

END OF A DREAM

*M*o Udall was exhausted. He was returning from a grueling weekend in California, traveling from Los Angeles, where he met with political backers, to Sacramento for the state Democratic Party Convention. The January 20, 1983, convention was seen as a major stop at the beginning of the campaign trail. He had received a warm welcome, perhaps better than any of the other hopefuls preparing for the 1984 presidential race. That reception gave him hope that he could make another run at the presidency, as his attempt in 1976 had come close to wresting the nomination from Jimmy Carter.

He had made a masterful speech and in his jovial manner complained about having to limit himself to ten minutes. "A great orator, Cicero—or perhaps it was [former U.S. senator from California] Sam Hayakawa—once said, 'I can't even clear my throat in ten minutes,'" he joked with the 2,100 convention delegates. He had made the obligatory round of receptions to gauge his support, and at the end of the day he was physically fatigued. One political reporter described Udall's skin as waxy and his gait slowed by Parkinson's disease.[1]

Now he was flying to Washington, D.C., after meeting with friends and supporters in Phoenix and Tucson about whether he should seek the Democratic nomination. He was flying first class, but his lanky six-foot, five-inch frame made it difficult to stretch his achy arthritic back, and his Parkinson's disease was exacerbated by having to cram himself into his seat.

Traveling with Udall was Marvin S. Cohen, a friend dating back to their law years in the 1950s in Tucson. Udall had called in a favor with President Carter, who appointed Cohen to the Civil Aeronautics Board in 1978. Now Udall had asked Cohen to think about becoming his campaign manager if he decided to run.

But, at age sixty, Udall knew he lacked the stamina for an eighteen-month presidential campaign. That weekend in California proved it to him. He looked over at Cohen and said, "I can't do it, can I?" Cohen replied, "No, you can't, Mo."

Cohen later said, "This, to me, was the moment that he finally acknowledged that he could never be president."[2]

Although he would withhold announcement of his plans for two weeks, it was clear he would abandon his long-held dream of residing in the White House. Nonetheless, he had come a long way, this whip-smart, witty liberal from hearty pioneer Mormon stock in Arizona's outback.

MORMON PIONEERS

*T*he agricultural lifestyle in the arid highlands of northeastern Arizona played as much a role in shaping Morris King Udall as did the values of his parents and the Mormon church. He would say about his ancestral home: "Of the places the Mormons picked, this was probably as harsh and as unproductive a land as they tried. They were willing to try most anything, but the growing season was short, water was scarce, the soil wasn't all that good and your fruit trees would freeze; always had these late May freezes that would ruin your fruit trees. They stuck it out and made a pretty community out of it. Life was pretty good."[1]

It was in that climate that Mo Udall learned to love and cherish the land. If he appreciated the starkness of such land at 5,730 feet on an isolated plateau, he could all the more appreciate the wonders of Alaska's wilderness, the beauty of the Everglades, the peaks of the Rocky Mountains. The land taught him to preserve and conserve. Every drop of water was precious, every tree was cherished, and everything had a use and reuse.

The town is a day's wagon drive from the New Mexico border, lying 40 miles southeast of what is now the Petrified Forest National Park, and is tucked between the Navajo and the Apache reservations.

The land is barren, dry, and huge. Apache County, of which St. Johns is the county seat, is bigger than Massachusetts, New Jersey, New

Hampshire, Vermont, or Maryland and nearly twice as large as the combined states of Connecticut, Delaware, and Rhode Island.

Udall remembered his mother's reaction when he took her up in a plane in 1946. Eight to twelve inches of rain had fallen during the previous two months, an unusual amount. "We cruised around. There were natural lakes all over, places where the water had settled. The grass was green. It looked something like a garden of Eden. And she said to me as we landed, 'Something comes clear to me now.' And I said, 'What do you mean?' She said, 'I always wondered why they started these settlements here in St. Johns with this rugged dry climate and cold winter, hot summer, with the wind blowing. Now I understand.' "[2]

Mo's sister Eloise noted that "the wind blows all year long and crops freeze but the Lord sent us there, so that's where we stayed. But it does grow good people."[3]

St. Johns rests a mile high and lies hard by the Little Colorado River. It was founded in 1873 as a way station by wagoners hauling supplies for the U.S. Cavalry from Santa Fe, New Mexico, to Fort Apache, Arizona.[4] Seven years later a group of settlers from Kanab, Utah, near the Arizona border, established the Mormon presence in St. Johns. They were led by Mo Udall's grandfather David King Udall, born on September 7, 1851, in St. Louis, Missouri, and when they first saw the hostile, barren landscape they called it "the land God forgot."[5]

David Udall had married Eliza Luella "Ella" Stewart, a "fair, slender girl with clear blue eyes [who] took my heart away,"[6] on February 1, 1875, six weeks before he was to go on his two-year mission to England. Ella had moved from Salt Lake City to Kanab, where her father was the bishop. Before she left Utah, Brigham Young asked that she learn Morse code so she could be a telegraph operator. Her first assignment, in December 1871, was at Pipe Springs, the first telegraph office in Arizona Territory, and now a national monument. It was there that Ella cabled reports of Major John Wesley Powell's Grand Canyon expedition to Washington, D.C.

After Udall returned from England, he received a letter from Mormon president John Taylor in June 1880 telling him that he was to move to St. Johns, where he would become bishop of the Latter-day Saints ward.[7] The Udalls left Kanab for St. Johns on Udall's twenty-ninth birthday in two wagons and with $100 in his pocket.[8] The trip from

Kanab to Glen Canyon was relatively easy, but crossing the Colorado River presented a foreboding obstacle. The travelers had to painstakingly lower their wagons down the sheer cliffs at Lee's Ferry, ford the treacherous Colorado, and then raise the wagons up the other side of the canyon, crossing the rocky ridge called "Lee's Backbone."

When the settlers arrived in St. Johns to establish a Mormon stake, an ecclesiastical subdivision of the church—only the third in Arizona—on October 6, 1880, all they found were Indians and Mexican Americans. "The Mexicans resented us and we did not blame them very much," David Udall wrote in his memoirs. "Their 'squatters' rights had not been properly respected by those who [would sell] the land to our people."[9] The Mexicans had founded the community as San Juan but when a post office was sought in 1880, an assistant postmaster general named it St. Johns, adding the letter s to make it more "euphonious."[10]

The Udalls noted waving fields of grama grass, called the best range grass, nurtured by several years of unusual rainfall. The fields would not remain bountiful without help. Mo's grandfather wrote: "As the years passed, it proved to be a land of extremes, with alternating periods of drouths [sic] and floods, undependable seasons, and devastating spring winds. Washes and gullies grew deeper and deeper from the forces of erosion."[11]

The Mormons were less than welcome in St. Johns. They faced harassment at every turn. On May 30, 1884, for example, the anti-Mormon newspaper, the *Apache Chief,* editorialized, "How did Missouri and Illinois get rid of the Mormons? By use of the shotgun and rope. Apache County can rid herself of them also. . . . He has no rights and should be allowed none. Down with them. Grind out their very existence."[12]

A year and a half after their arrival, despite increasing hostility toward polygamous marriages, David King Udall married his second wife, Ida Hunt, the daughter of Lois and John Hunt, bishop of Snowflake Ward.

David had hired Ida in the fall of 1881 as a clerk in the co-op and married her after John Taylor urged church leaders to take plural wives. He loved his first wife and apparently took Ida as his second wife only at Taylor's urging.[13]

David King Udall fathered fifteen children with two wives, nine by

Ella (four died before the age of two) and six by Ida. Not widely known is that in March 1903 he married a third woman, the wife of a friend who had died, at the urging of the church's governing body. Council members told him it was his duty to raise and educate the widow's three sons.[14] For fifty-eight years David Udall served as the religious leader of the region, and he labored hard to provide for his family in this dry, hard land.

While David King Udall tended to three families and battled the harsh environment, hostilities arose between the Mormons and the Catholics over entitlement to land. In 1885 Udall and nine other Mormons were arrested for unlawful assembly but were acquitted. Later that year, Udall was charged with perjury by a federal grand jury for testimony he had given on a fellow Mormon's land claim. He was freed on bail while he awaited trial, the bond put up by Prescott merchant Michel Goldwater, the grandfather of 1964 Republican presidential candidate Barry M. Goldwater.[15]

What the non-Mormon townspeople really wanted Udall prosecuted for was polygamy. But Ida, for most of her married life, lived in exile in remote areas of Apache County to avoid prosecution. She could not be subpoenaed for her testimony and instead Udall was tried for perjury on the land claim of Miles P. Romney, the grandfather of George W. Romney, who served from 1963 to 1969 as governor of Michigan and was a Republican presidential candidate in 1968.

Udall was convicted on August 6, 1885. For four days he was held in a Prescott jail, 250 miles from St. Johns, and then was sentenced to three years in prison. On August 29 he was moved to the federal penitentiary in Detroit, Michigan. He was imprisoned until December 12 when he was pardoned by President Grover Cleveland, who, after being petitioned by Udall's attorney, decided that there had been a miscarriage of justice. Later Udall would name one of his sons Grover Cleveland Udall.

Udall returned to St. Johns, declaring, "I was fired with carrying out the work of redeeming the desert," and he would admonish his kin, "Be good to the ground. It is holy. It is origin, possession, sustenance, destiny."[16] No doubt Mo Udall recalled those words years later while he pressed his legislation in Congress to protect the environment.

Over the years the Mormons purchased land, surveyed, and established a town site on which several small homes were built. They also surveyed and fenced an area of 820 acres, divided it into plots, and irrigated the fields with water from the Little Colorado River. They established a school, a grist mill, a sawmill, an assembly hall, and the Arizona Cooperative Mercantile Institution.

It was difficult in those early years. As Stewart Udall, Mo's older brother, put it, "The Colorado plateau has never been a land flowing with milk and honey. This high desert area is essentially cow-country; grass and water are its two most important resources."[17] The land can best be described as scrubland, with native trees of cedar and juniper.

As they had done in the Salt Lake valley, the Mormons dammed the river and created irrigation ditches to water their meager crops. "Every boy in St. Johns learned to work with water at an early age," Stewart Udall remembered. "I can still hear my father [Levi] telling me earnestly, 'Irrigation is a science, son.' "[18]

The public political history of the Udalls began when David King Udall was elected to the senate of the Twentieth Territorial Legislature, which convened on January 16, 1899. Barry Goldwater's grandfather was president and among those serving in the body were Henry F. Ashurst, later to become a U.S. senator, and George W. P. Hunt, a future governor of Arizona. Another future Arizona governor, Sidney P. Osborn, was a senate page.

David Udall was a lifelong Republican who became more conservative toward national politics as he grew older. Ten-year-old Mo Udall remembered his grandfather's anger the night in 1932 when the report came over their radio that Roosevelt was beating Hoover.[19]

David King Udall died on February 18, 1938, at the age of eighty-six in his bed at home after a brief illness. His wife Ida had died on April 26, 1915, and his wife Ella died on May 28, 1937.

THEY STOOD ON HIS
SHOULDERS

*W*hen Levi S. Udall was chief justice of the Arizona Supreme Court, he would attend conferences around the nation. When the law graduates of Harvard, Yale, or Michigan asked him where he obtained his degree, they were surprised when Udall replied that he had earned it by correspondence from the LaSalle Institute of Chicago.[1] Hobnobbing with judges from across the country was a long way from his agricultural upbringing in tiny St. Johns at the end of the nineteenth century.

Levi Stewart Udall was born on January 20, 1891, to Ella Udall, the third son and the tenth child that David King Udall fathered in his polygamous marriages. He was named for his mother's father.

As a young boy, Levi labored tirelessly in that hardscrabble life, working on the farm and in the family's store. When he was sixteen, he served as a "mail puncher" with his brothers, helping their father deliver the mail by buckboard across the wide expanse of northeastern Arizona and western New Mexico. "It gave my boys work and splendid training in dependability and resourcefulness," David K. Udall said. "It encouraged initiative in them too, and played a part in developing their character. They carried the responsibility of men while they were only in their middle teens."[2]

Years later, after Levi became a judge, he kept a family farm in the old Mormon belief that work was the best cure for all problems. When they were in high school, sons Stewart and Morris ran the farm.[3] It was common to see the judge helping out when hay baling time came around.[4]

In those days, St. Johns provided only two years of high school, so in 1909 Levi went to Thatcher, Arizona, to attend St. Joseph Academy. There he met a comely schoolgirl, Louise Lee, two years his junior. She was born on March 30, 1893, in Luna, New Mexico, and moved to Thatcher as a young girl. One of her grandfathers was John David Lee, who began operating a ferry system across the Colorado River in 1872; the location was later named Lee's Ferry. The other was Jacob Hamblin, for whom Jacob Lake near the north rim of the Grand Canyon is named.

Levi was twenty when he graduated from St. Joseph in a class of four boys and ten girls. He was older than most students because he had spent so much time delivering the mail and working on the family farm. He received a $125 scholarship to the University of Arizona, where he studied agriculture and helped establish the social fraternity, Sigma Alpha Epsilon. He supplemented the scholarship with a job as a janitor in the dormitories.[5] He dropped out after a year. Louise taught second grade in Pima, Arizona, for a year before attending Northern Arizona Normal School, now Northern Arizona University, in Flagstaff.

On June 14, 1914, Levi, twenty-three, and Louise, twenty-one, were married in Salt Lake City in a Mormon temple, then returned to St. Johns to live with his family. They had six children: Inez, born on November 28, 1915; Elma, on December 23, 1917; Stewart Lee, on January 31, 1920; Morris King, on June 15, 1922; Eloise, on November 14, 1924; and David Burr, on January 20, 1929. They had twenty-five grandchildren.

In 1915, the newlyweds moved into the "Air Castle," so named because the winter winds poured into the pioneer home from the many cracks in the walls.[6]

Levi Udall's political career began in 1914 when he lost by one vote to his half brother, John H. Udall, a Republican, for clerk of the superior court in Apache County. During that time, he began a three-year study of the law through correspondence from LaSalle and under the tutelage of Apache County superior court judge A. S. Gibbons.

"We had three little children [when Levi was studying law]," said Louise, "and it was my duty to shoo them out of the room so their father could work."[7] He was admitted to practice in 1922 after finishing second on the state bar exam by a quarter point behind an attorney who had been practicing for two years in Illinois.[8] In 1923, he was elected county attorney.

In 1930, he was elected a superior court judge, defeating mentor Gibbons 847–596. It could not be learned why Udall challenged Gibbons, who then moved from the county. Udall served on the superior court until 1946.

Levi traveled throughout the county as a judge and as president of the St. Johns Mormon stake. His family remembers him being home only about half of the time. "He was not an at-home father," said daughter Elma.[9] Once he presided in Tucson for six months, returning to St. Johns on weekends. Even then, he had church duties to attend to.[10] But when he held court in the Apache County courthouse—"Daddy's Courthouse," as the Udall children called it—he would walk home every day for lunch.

In 1946, Udall decided to seek a seat on the state supreme court. "He had had it in his mind all the time," Louise said. "We'd saved up $5,000, and, by cracky, that's all we spent. It was a tough decision to make at the time—but it was what he wanted. He'd say, 'I'm just a country boy—in the Supreme Court.' I'd say, 'Where do you think our presidents come from?' "[11]

Levi was the first person from Apache County ever elected statewide. He had far more difficulty winning the Democratic primary than he did the general election. During his thirteen years on the high court, he wrote 401 opinions.

According to Levi's daughter Elma, "One time my mother was complaining about all the things my father was involved in—in church and politics—and my father said, 'If good men don't run for office and try to make things go, the bad men will.' "[12] It was a philosophy similar to that of Edmund Burke, the eighteenth-century British statesman, orator, and writer, who said: "The only thing necessary for the triumph of evil is for good men to do nothing." Levi never called it politics; he called it public service.[13] Morris said he learned from his father "that public service was an honorable and satisfying career, that if you have leadership ability, you owe it to yourself and the community to use it."[14]

Although Morris said his father was a major influence on his life, they "were never close or chummy. Looking back, I can see that he was a very busy man, traveling much and without a great deal of time for father and son activities." Morris said that he absorbed much of his philosophy and outlook from his father. "Levi was impatient with those who insisted on doing things the same way simply because that was the pattern. On the family farm, in court, in the legal profession, and elsewhere he was always seeking a new and better way, although he was usually cautious and judging consequences before he made a major move."[15]

Morris would follow that pattern as well throughout his life with his workaholic habits and having little time for his family. His contributions to reforming the system no doubt grew from Levi's philosophy of "seeking a new and better way."

Morris said he admired the fact that his father could bring people together. "I never heard him bad-mouth anyone, put somebody down. He was a peacemaker."[16] He also noted, "We knew our father was somebody big in the community and he was there and he would talk to you. He was not a stern disciplinarian. I don't think I ever got spanked or whacked, or anything like that. He taught more by example and exhortation and that kind of thing."[17]

Stewart Udall said that when he was asked how he first got started in politics, he would say, "I was Levi Udall's boy. He was in some ways the most respected man in the state."[18] He said Levi's attitude toward public service established the foundation for his and Morris's success. "I stood on my father's shoulders," he said. "Morris stood on his shoulders."[19]

Louise Udall possessed a deep intellectual curiosity and was continually raising questions that caused her children to think. "I'm sure that she thought that she never had much influence on me," Morris said, "but she was constantly subscribing to magazines or buying books or raising issues at the family table that required us to think things through. She was really quite more liberal than Levi on many political matters. On economics, deficit spending, and things of this kind he tended to be quite a conservative Democrat whereas Mother was more interested in the human problems of the poor and the sick."[20]

Both Stewart and Morris said growing up during Roosevelt's New Deal had an enormous impact on them. Morris said that his heroes in high school and college were the liberals like Franklin Roosevelt and members of his administration.

The same year that Levi was admitted to the bar, he succeeded his father as president of the St. Johns stake. At age thirty-one, he was the youngest stake president in the Mormon church by five years.[21] It was also the same year his second son and fourth child, Morris King Udall, was born. He served as stake president until he moved to Phoenix to sit on the supreme court in 1947. The Mormon religion was an important part of the Udall household, although the three sons broke from the church in their early years.

Levi Udall's manner of being aloof, taciturn, and even pompous separated people from him, but nevertheless he was held in great regard. His wife, Louise, was much beloved. Neighbors said she tried to keep the Udalls from becoming pompous. She was active in community and church affairs, was an expert seamstress and horsewoman and a talented singer, and was nana to her twenty-five grandchildren.

If Levi was often absent during his children's formative years, Louise was not, and the youngsters thrived. Morris described his mother as "a much more lively person [than Levi]. . . . I think a lot of my humor—much more of my humor came from Mother than from Dad." Morris noted that Mormon women were not viewed as being liberated, but Louise was an exception. "She was extremely so [liberated] in a very real sense. She was an independent person. She'd argue politics and things with my father. She had strong views."[22]

When Levi was elected to the supreme court, they moved to Phoenix. By that time, their children had scattered. For the first time, Louise Udall was at a loss with what to do with herself with no children at home and living in a new city.

"I sat around for a while, eating my crust of bread at lunch, feeling sorry for myself, remembering the days when I was busy in St. Johns with the Red Cross, the Mormon youth organization, the little theater," she said. "Then I realized that Levi had accepted this challenge and I had to accept mine. I started going to the mission at Maricopa once a week; began to quilt for the Indians, teach them how to work the treadle machine. I was the dime store's best customer—I bought material by the bolt."[23]

Louise wound up serving from 1951 to 1958 as president of the Relief Society of Maricopa Indian Branch. In 1969, she wrote the book *Me and Mine,* a story of the Hopi woman Helen Sekaquaptewa, who achieved a successful compromise between her culture and the conflicting ways of the American mainstream. It was published when Louise was seventy-six years old.

Levi also looked out for the Indian. Perhaps his most significant supreme court opinion assured Native Americans in Arizona the right to vote. The opinion was handed down on July 22, 1948. He wrote, "In a democracy, suffrage is the most basic civil right and [its] exercise is the chief means whereby other rights may be safe. To deny the right to vote where one is legally entitled to does violence to the principles of freedom and equality." Levi deplored the treatment of the Navajos, noting that Americans were willing to help the underprivileged and downtrodden of European countries while ignoring the Navajos. "That should cause every one of us to hang his head in shame," he wrote.[24]

Louise knew she had to keep busy during those Phoenix years because it was difficult for Levi to slow down. Work was his consuming passion and there was little time for leisurely pursuits. Louise had trouble getting her husband to take a vacation. "The Udalls aren't the vacation-type," she said, "but I learned to ride horseback as a child, and I'd tell him I'd like to go to the mountains. My happiest memories are those vacations. It was the only time Levi ever got away from his work. He'd bring a briefcase home at night, read until he fell asleep, and when he'd wake up in the middle of the night he'd read another case. The calendar was so crowded. . . . I'd always had a dream to go down the Grand Canyon to Supai. I told him I wanted to go before we got old. It was wonderful, when the judge finally said he'd go. We had a great time."[25] The joy was short-lived.

Two weeks later, on Memorial Day 1960, Levi Stewart Udall died of a cerebral hemorrhage on a family picnic beside the Hassayampa River in Wickenburg, Arizona. Levi had not lived long enough to see Stewart become secretary of the interior or Morris be elected to the House to replace his brother. Louise lived fourteen years after Levi's death, and saw Morris begin his pursuit of the Democratic nomination for president.

Stewart said Levi left a modest estate because he did not expect wealth, but "he left us the best name in Arizona."[26]

GROWING UP

*T*he early years in the life of Morris Udall were, as they are for most people, years lived and years that faded from memory. Recollections probably were artificial ones, created by the oft-told family story or the photograph that somehow seemed to slip into the mind as a real event.

He broke an arm when he fell from a horse at the age of five,[1] but for Morris, the quasi-memories may have begun at the age of six with an event that marked him for life: the loss of his right eye. So forgotten were the details that after his mother wrote a chronology in 1946, he responded, "I was so young that most of it is just vague impression."[2]

The incident occurred on January 13, 1929, as he and best friend Fenton Overson played with a knife and string. His mother, Louise Lee Udall, recorded this story: "They were playing bottle horses, making little harnesses of string fastened to coke bottles for the horses and a sardine can was the wagon. I had bought a cheap little pocket knife for Morris for Christmas. Morris held the string tight in his hands and Fenton cut up with the knife and when the string cut, the knife went into Morris's eye. I phoned Dad to come and bring the doctor, and in a short time he came with Doctor Bouldin. The Dr. didn't seem to think it was serious. Just had us lay a wet boric acid pack upon his eye, not bandaged nor taped."[3] Udall said years later that "an alcoholic physician [Bouldin] botched the injury."[4]

A week later, Morris's father, Levi, took him to a Mesa physician, "who it proved to be, was a second-rater. That doctor operated, putting the iris back in place in the kitchen of Grandma Udall's house in Mesa."[5]

By Easter, Morris had lost sight in the eye and could see only light. In May, a respected ophthalmologist in Miami, Arizona, recommended removal of the bad eye, saying its infection had sent symptoms of blindness to the good eye. Two specialists in Phoenix agreed, and the eye was removed within forty-eight hours.[6]

His sister Elma recalled her brother's first comment after surgery: "I can still see everything there is." She added, "Maybe in a way that's how he saw the world. I'm sure it left its mark on him and all, but he carried on as if nothing had happened."[7]

Louise and Levi Udall were determined that Morris would not feel self-pity. His siblings all say that he was never treated differently, and over the years, the episode became the stuff of which family legends are made. For example, the whole family would gather in the living room to provide advice when a replacement was needed for a broken or damaged glass eye. Louise played the major role in the decision-making.

Morris later described the process this way: "In those days, we would send to the Denver Optical Company and you would give them the rough size and color and then they'd send you pre-made glass eyes, two dozen of the damn things. And you'd put them in and the one that was the right shade of blue was too big—your eye would bulge. And the one that was the right size would look over to the left instead of to the right. And we'd all sit around and have these testings." Ultimately, two—one as a backup—would be selected and the others returned.[8]

Younger brother Burr Udall shared a double bed with Morris for several years and recalled: "When I go to bed I take a glass of water with me and I put it by the side of the bed and if I wake up in the middle of the night I have a drink of water and I remember there was only one night stand and he would take a glass of water and put salt in it and put that eye in it and I'd wake up in the middle of the night with an eye in my mouth." Burr also said, "My biggest boast was that my brother can take his eye out."[9]

Just a year and six days after the knife accident, the alcoholic physician was called again when life-threatening spinal meningitis struck Morris. This time, the only doctor in town performed well. "We are so thankful that he was not drunk and that he was able to recognize the disease before he had had it long," Louise Udall wrote. "Dr. Bouldin had been sober for about one week. Had been drunk for four weeks. I had worried over this dreaded disease as all other mothers must have and am surely glad that we live now instead of 35 years ago or it would surely have been different with us now than it is."[10]

Morris King Udall was born at home in St. Johns, Arizona, on June 15, 1922. "He was the biggest of my babies (eight pounds), born at 9 a.m.," Louise Udall wrote.[11]

The early life of Morris Udall was simple and diverse. St. Johns was then a community of about 1,400 people, essentially divided into two groups: 900 Anglo Mormons and 500 Mexican-American Catholics. The young were educated in separate elementary schools until a mid-1950s merger of the two districts; they were united in high school, although few Hispanics continued beyond the elementary years.

The Mormons developed their community in orderly fashion as was their tradition. Each family farmed forty to a hundred acres outside of town with an acre in town on which they maintained vegetable gardens, fruit trees, and animals, including milk cows, pigs, and chickens. It was the foundation for self-sufficiency. The larger acreage was used primarily to grow alfalfa hay, which fed the cattle and could sometimes be sold to dairies in nearby Winslow or in Gallup, New Mexico.[12]

It was a typical "Mormon village," Stewart Udall said. "The villagers lived in a close-knit town (with gardens and cows) and traveled each day in wagons or on horseback out to their farms."[13]

Crime was almost nonexistent. "If somebody did something, they were always given a suspended sentence and you had a thousand pair of eyes watching them all the time," Morris recalled. "You were really put on probation and the whole community was your parole officer."[14] Houses were left unlocked and car keys were left in the ignition. If a car was missing, the owner knew someone had needed it and it would be returned.[15]

Siblings Elma and Stewart called it a nineteenth-century existence. Cousin Calvin H. Udall described it as "more like 1830 than 1930. Every family had one or more milk cows, a kerosene lamp, a Coleman lamp, pigs, a pasture, chickens, an orchard, an outhouse, and lots of mason jars."[16]

People helped one another. When a truckload of peaches arrived, families would work together to preserve and seal the fruit for the winter. In the appropriate season, youngsters stripped beehives of their honey, picked wild grapes for jelly, and made molasses from sugar cane.[17] Morris once noted: "I remember people would die and someone would ask what can I do to help? The answer was go dig the grave."[18] Conrad Overson, a town handyman, taught Stewart and Morris how to dress a hog, fix a roof, and practice the craft of stone masonry.[19]

Erratic electricity and undependable 8 A.M. to 8 P.M. telephone service came to St. Johns in the early 1920s. Most energy came from cedar wood, which was in ready supply in the immediate area. Heavy farmwork was done by horses or humans. Water came from wells. St. Johns had two or three mercantile stores and no bank.[20]

Unlike most families, the Udalls had a steady income. Levi earned a regular salary, first as clerk of the superior court after winning on his second try, then as county attorney, and finally when he won election as a superior court judge. His office was in the courthouse, constructed in 1917 and still in use. Despite the salary, the Udall standard of living was not much higher than that of other families. They did have running water, but like others, used an outhouse. They kept their perishable canned and bottled items in a cool cupboard on the dark side of the house.

They also owned a Buick. The car was a necessity for Levi, who was on the road often in his capacities as Latter-day Saints stake president, watching over wards in northeastern Arizona and a bit of western New Mexico, and as a judge who conducted court in other counties.

Life had a regularity and a predictability in the Mormon town. It centered on family, work, church, and school activities. "You got up at 5:30 or 5:45, made sure the fire was going, milked the cow, and slopped the pig, got the wood, and all that stuff," Burr recalled. Such responsibilities had first been handed to Inez, then to Elma, Stewart, and Morris. Burr said Morris was delighted when his younger brother became old enough and strong enough to take over the early-morning chores.[21] Explained Elma: "The boys saddled up the horses, they plowed, they did it all."[22]

Working the land was a way of life that early on instilled quality conservation and environmental values in Morris and all the young of St.

Johns. Elma called it "the Mormon heritage," saying: "We lived very close to nature. Nature was part of him. You had to work with nature to exist."[23] Burr added: "It was a community goal to conserve. We never threw anything away."[24] Warren G. Whiting, who went on Boy Scout camping trips with Morris and later married Eloise, the youngest Udall daughter, said: "You cleaned up. It was automatic."[25]

School and chores monopolized much of the day. At night, Levi led dinner-table conversations that focused on politics and current events. Afterward, the discussion might continue by the living room fireplace or Louise might play the piano while the family sang. Schoolwork was done at the dining room table. The evening might conclude with everyone reading or listening to radio broadcasts from Albuquerque, Phoenix, Salt Lake City, Denver, or Laredo, Texas. It was not until 1934 that the first town movie theater opened.

"In St. Johns, you made your own fun," Eloise said.[26] Added Elma: "The world was ours. We walked out the door and there it was. I remember Mother saying once, 'My children never came to me and said, What can I do?' "[27]

Eloise also noted: "In St. Johns, there's a saying that your friends are your family. The boys did boys' things and the girls did girls' things." The Udall family ate together and sat around the living room, she said, but interrelations tended to be by gender.[28]

In the pre–high school years, the Udall boys found plenty to do in addition to their regular chores and schoolwork, and the brothers were invariably the leaders when playing with the other children in town. They had watched their father preside over court trials, so they established their own court in the garage. An elevated area was set aside for the judge. "Here were little kids out with coal oil lamps in the garage having trials, both civil and criminal," Morris recalled.[29] "And we'd convict some kid and confine him in the chicken coop for three hours with the sheriff standing guard to see that the sentence was carried out."[30]

At one time, Louise Udall said, a "Udall, Udall & Greer" shingle was posted by their bedroom door. The Greer was friend Dick L. Greer, who also became a lawyer and later a superior court judge in Apache County.[31]

Stewart and Morris staged a kids' rodeo every year by rounding up neighborhood calves, and they would have roping and cow-milking contests. An open field next to the Udall home and behind the high school served for both baseball and football, depending on the season. Half-court basketball was played in front of the house.

Always there was the work.

"Every boy in town milked, chopped wood, fed the pigs, fed the chickens," said brother-in-law Whiting. "That was just part of your life. And you did it or else your dad would take a stick to you. None of us liked it."[32]

Morris said his own father "believed, like the old Mormons, that work is the best cure for all your problems. He was a lawyer and a judge, but he wanted his boys to learn to farm. So Stew and I from the time we were in high school really ran Dad's farm. . . . We'd have to irrigate at night when it became our turn in the community to use water out of the ditch. You'd use it solidly for three days, and you'd have to take a blanket and sleep out there and change the water every three or four hours from one field to the next. And you'd get together a baler crew and bring in the hay. You learned how to bring in the hay and repair harnesses and mowing machines and simple farm equipment."[33]

The church scheduled religious and social activities several times a week, and Mormon students left school during a study hall period to attend forty-five-minute religion classes. Morris later explained: "The Mormons believe in keeping you busy, you know. On Sunday you'd go to Sunday School in the morning and church services at night. On Tuesday it's the young people's organization with dances and classes in self-improvement and everything else. Wednesday the relief society meets and there's other church activity on Thursday and Friday. They keep you busy all the time."[34]

No one remembers exactly when, but Morris stopped attending religious classes and services at an early age. Morris always joked a lot, Stewart recalled, and one Sunday when he was eleven or twelve, the teacher "tossed him out and he never went back. He didn't participate." Stewart said the only time their mother ever scolded Morris was for shooting baskets outside the classroom where she was teaching Sunday school. Morris respected her wishes and never shot baskets again when classes were under way.[35]

The surviving siblings agreed that their parents remained open-minded and did not force anyone to participate, despite their father's prominence in the church. They emphasized that the basic values were instilled through the home and the community. There may have been more than one maternal crack in the freedom, however. In a letter to his mother, Morris wrote: "If you are still having trouble with Burr and Sunday school, let me repeat my oft given advice. Never, never, never beg him to go, or lay out his clothes for him to go. Let him feel that he is going because *he* feels that he ought to. Nuff said."[36]

Sister Elma remembered that Morris put his religious education to profitable use during his time in the military: He won bets from unsuspecting acquaintances who doubted that he could name all the books in the Bible. The memory work had been a part of his early church education.[37] His absence from Sunday services also allowed him to develop another moneymaking skill: Morris organized traveling Sunday poker parties that began at the Udall house, then moved about. At one time, Burr said, Morris held a third mortgage on the newspaper printing press.[38] Later, in the military, he won small amounts playing poker at Fort Douglas, Utah, and larger sums while being transferred to a Pacific assignment by ship. Elma speculated that Morris was a winning player partly because "you couldn't look him in the eye."[39]

The high school years were a contrast in style for Morris. On one hand, he walked a few fine behavioral lines; on the other, he was a constant leader in traditional activities.

The most frequently chronicled of Morris's questionable activities was the joyride he and a friend took in "Brother Lillywhite's new flivver." Lillywhite, "a stuffy, sanctimonious type," customarily parked on a hill so he could get a jump start by letting the car roll down it. Morris and his friend pirated the vehicle when Lillywhite went into church, but Morris missed a turn and ran into an irrigation ditch. Only then did the two realize that Lillywhite had left his eighteen-month-old daughter asleep in the back seat. Morris and his companion appeared before Judge Levi Udall. "I toiled for two long summers in the fields to pay off my fine," Morris wrote.[40]

Judge Udall conducted an unofficial juvenile court at 2 P.M. on Sundays at home, the poker players having cleared out before the judge returned from church services. Burr described his father's juvenile proceedings this way: "Dad handled juvenile problems with slavery; no trial, no hearing, the adult always was right."[41]

Young Mo practicing in St. Johns around 1935. (Photograph by Elma Udall)

Below:
Soldier Mo at the Holbrook train station.

Above: The family in St. Johns in about 1945: Inez, Eloise, Elma, Levi, Louise, Burr, Mo, and Stew.

University of Arizona basketball days.

The 1961
swearing-in with
Speaker Sam
Rayburn.

Below: The family
in Tucson in the
early 1960s:
Dodie, Pat, Anne,
Mo, Kate, Mark,
Brad, and Randy.
(Photograph by
Kew Photocenter,
Tucson)

A visit with Speaker John W. McCormack in the early 1960s. (Photograph by National Publishing Co., Div. of McCall Corp.)

Below:
Arizona power: Republicans John Rhodes, Barry Goldwater, and Paul Fannin; Democrats Mo Udall, Carl Hayden, and Stewart Udall.

A firsthand look at strip mining in the early 1970s.

Below: Stewart and Lee Udall and Ella and Mo in 1976. (Photograph © Shepard Sherbell/ SABA)

Spreading the presidential gospel in the 1976 campaign. (Photograph © Shepard Sherbell/ SABA)

A campaign pause with some non-voters. (Photograph © Shepard Sherbell/ SABA)

Mo and Ella at a Udall roast.

Below:
Checking out Three Mile Island, March 1979.

Keynoting the 1980 Democratic National Convention.

Mo and Norma on their wedding day in 1989. (Photograph courtesy of Norma Udall)

Small towns provide big opportunities, and Morris began to increase his leadership experience and to grow intellectually during his high school years, despite internal feelings of insecurity. "Kids can be cruel, and the inevitable jokes about 'Cyclops' and 'here comes Ol' One Eye' hit hard," he said. "My glass eye, coupled with my gawky frame and lack of confidence, made me an extremely self-conscious boy. Fortunately, the 'up' side was also present, in the form of a loving family who inspired me to compensate by excelling in athletics and academics."[42] He noted that "most all of the national leaders come from little towns. You get something in those little towns from the standpoint of leadership. You got a smattering of everything, and it was really very good preparation."[43]

High school provided a hint of the individual he was to become—he was well on his way to becoming a workaholic. As a junior, he was a starter in both football and basketball, sports editor of the mimeographed student newspaper, an actor in school plays, and leader of a dance band. He capped the year by defeating longtime chum Fenton Overson for student body president and being selected as editor of the newspaper.

At six feet, five inches tall, he was certainly the tallest quarterback around in an era when a height of six feet was considered unusual. At 165 pounds, he also was the heaviest player on the team. The *St. Johns Herald-Observer* reported before the 1939 season started that "Morris Udall, rangy passer and field strategist, is returning with the distinction of being chosen All-Northern quarterback in 1938."[44] In that final season, he played both quarterback and fullback as the Apaches finished at 4–2–1. In the final game, a 14–0 Thanksgiving victory over Round Valley, the twenty-member St. Johns High School marching band took the field at halftime for the first time, and that meant Morris and three others had to trade their football helmets for band caps and instruments.[45] They returned for the second half, and Morris broke an ankle. Nonetheless, his injury had healed by basketball season, and he scored 20 points when the team defeated Payson 45–27 just before Christmas. Cousin Calvin often slept over after games and recalled that he would wake up in the morning to find Morris already departed for the bus station to see if his name had been printed in the incoming big-city papers.[46]

Fenton Overson played both sports, too, and the two were named basketball co-captains their final year. If Fenton was not the high scorer, then Morris was. They ended up as consolation champions at the state tournament in Tucson, defeating, among others, big school Phoenix Union. Fenton was selected first-team all-state and Morris was named to the second team.

About midway through high school, Morris began writing for local newspapers, and once reported that four students had been selected to compete in English and algebra at an academic contest in Flagstaff; one of the four: Morris K. Udall.[47]

Among his greatest pleasures, however, were the foreign affairs columns he wrote for the *Apache County Independent News.* He regularly criticized Columbus Giragi, editor of the similarly titled *Apache County News.* In August 1939, Udall called him a "warmonger" and predicted that there would be "no general war in Europe for at least ten years." The newspaper containing his column was delivered a day after "the German Army launched its Blitzkrieg."[48]

The next month, he attacked Giragi again, this time in a 1,500-word letter to the editor in the *Herald-Observer,* declaring that entry into the war would mean sending "the cream of our younger generation—the leaders of tomorrow—5000 miles to have their brains blown out, their lives ruined, and their bodies maimed permanently by guns manufactured, possibly, in their own country."[49]

A few years later, Udall would be trying to conceal his glass eye to sneak his way in for active duty. And much later when he was running for Congress, he was seeking—and receiving—editorial backing from Giragi.

Udall's school newspaper, the *Redskin,* provided a different sort of outlet for his intellect, imagination, and humor. One week it might call itself "the best weakly in Arizona," and the next it would announce: "If you read it in the *Redskin,* it's the truth," a declaration that may have overstated a bit inasmuch as it also carried a column labeled "Scandal Sheet" with the byline of "A. Nony Mouse."

As graduation neared, he defeated junior Leonard Isaacson for the school tennis championship. A summer before, he had placed second in the 54-hole city golf tournament, posting a 30-over-par 256. Brother Stewart finished seventh at 297.

Throughout his junior and senior years, he also served as leader of a dance band. A friend organized the band, then was killed when a tractor overturned. "Morris came in, took over, and we didn't mind," Whiting said. "Whatever it was, he was the leader and you wanted him to be. He made it fun."[50] The band used Levi's Buick to travel to gigs in nearby Concho, Sanders, or Snowflake.

Cousin Calvin laughed as he reminisced about the band. "It was an extremely untalented and very unmusical group of people. . . . They were good if you had a tin ear."[51]

Whatever the quality, the band may have given Udall an excuse to avoid the dance floor. They played at after-game dances, and the tall and skinny trumpet player preferred playing to dancing.

Virgene Jarvis Farr recalled that Morris on two occasions drew her lottery number for a Sadie Hawkins type of affair. He liked her food, went off to eat it by himself, and would not ask her to dance. Nonetheless, she added: "Whenever Morris was around, it was fun."[52] Sister Eloise said he even refused to dance with her, noting that there was no such thing as Morris thinking, "She's my little sister. I'll make her feel good and dance with her."[53]

After a summer of running the farm with Stewart, Morris was off to the University of Arizona. "I remember feeling rather inferior coming to the university from St. Johns High School and here were all these graduates from Tucson High and Phoenix Union—the biggest schools west of the Mississippi," he said.[54] Intellectual worries vanished early when he realized how well he had been educated: "I got command of the English language from two good English teachers, and learned some really fundamental things about writing that stood me in good stead both in law and in politics."[55] As a first-semester college student, Morris earned eight units of A, three units of B, and six units of C. He later worked his way onto the dean's list.

Morris found housing and employment quickly. Throughout his time on the Tucson campus, he lived in the basement of the infirmary, fetching meals for the half dozen or so patients, emptying bedpans, and providing general janitorial service. Morris had been the family barber in St. Johns, and when the price of haircuts jumped from 25 cents to 35 cents, he opened a cheapie barber shop in the infirmary.

Morris majored in pre-law and was an honors student his second year. He met Robert W. Pickrell, son of one of his father's friends, in freshman Latin and invited him home for the 1941 spring break. Years later, when Republican Pickrell, a former attorney general, was unsuccessfully seeking the governorship of Arizona, Democrat Udall dug out a photo of the two of them cleaning a cowpen and wrote: "In cleaning out some old files the other day, I came across the enclosed picture which depicts you engaged in shoveling a substance—an activity which you apparently have not ceased through the years." Udall threatened to release the photo to the press with the following caption: "Attention Voters of Arizona: The man on the left was shoveling manure 25 years ago and he is still at it."[56]

Morris joined the freshman basketball squad and invited basketball teammate George F. Genung to St. Johns during a Christmas break. Genung, now retired after thirty-five years as a high school basketball coach, had taken a bath in a room attached to the house, then pulled the plug. Morris and Stewart were shocked, and told Genung he was supposed to soap, rinse quickly, and get out so more hot water could be added for the next bather.[57]

Genung praised Udall's intellect, recalling that when he would get behind in his humanities reading, "Mo would prep me. I'd get almost as good a grade as Morris and he would get mad and say he wouldn't tutor me anymore."[58] Genung, who later was named to the Arizona Sports Hall of Fame for his softball ability, reciprocated by giving pitching lessons to Udall, a fact Udall mentioned more than once in letters home when he was winning games for military teams.

George Miller, a Reserve Officers' Training Corps (ROTC) classmate, remembered Morris for both his intellect and his integrity. The university was a land grant school and thus all male freshmen and sophomores were required to take ROTC regardless of their physical disabilities. Miller, who later served fourteen years as a city councilman and eight years as mayor of Tucson, and Udall were the same height, so they sat next to each other and marched together. On test days, the teacher, usually a captain, would pass out exams, announce that the honor system was in force, and walk out of the room. Miller told of one occasion when "everyone jumped for their books. Nobody studied except Morris, and he just began writing. I was too ashamed to go into the books because I sat next to him. I think I passed."[59]

Udall was not much of a ladies' man in college, Genung said. Basketball team members used to hang out together, and "a big evening was going to the Fox Theater or to the Rialto." Genung also recounted how the two were pushing Genung's old Ford to a gas station when it picked up speed and they ran it through a stop sign. A policeman stopped them, and "Morris talked him out of a ticket. I knew then that he would be a pretty good lawyer. He was a politician from the day he woke up."[60]

Freshmen were not allowed to play varsity basketball, but Udall made the team as a sophomore. The Wildcats won 9 and lost 13, with Udall averaging 2.4 points as he saw limited action in 18 games.

The military draft prevented his enrollment as a junior in the fall of 1942.

Pearl Harbor had been bombed on December 7, 1941, and "the next day I'm down trying to enlist in the Army, Navy, Marine Corps," he recalled. "Nobody wants me. I've got a glass eye. So I was in the ROTC and they had a special deal that you could continue your ROTC and two years later you'd be commissioned a second lieutenant and also get your degree. So I thought 'That's a hell of a deal. That's the way I'm going to get in and help my country.' So I took the eye test for ROTC. They said, 'Cover your right eye.' So I covered my right eye. Then they said, 'Cover your left eye,' and I covered my right eye again (with the other hand). It was an old trick, but they hadn't heard of it. I was OK until a guy who was washed out for flat feet told the colonel that they were accepting a guy with a glass eye, why not flat feet. And they gave me another eye test—this time they held the hand in front of the eyes. And that was that. Anyhow, I figured I am 4-F and am going to stay at home and can't be in this great war." Later, however, Udall was drafted. "There's a gap in the law; you couldn't enlist, but you could be drafted. So they sent me off to a special limited service. They didn't want us guys in combat, but they figured we could type, do intelligence stuff, and administration."[61]

Udall spent the summer of 1942 as a laborer for the Atkinson Construction Company in Bellemont, Arizona, and was inducted into the army in September.

OFF TO THE MILITARY

*T*he scene was typical of that played out in rural and urban America during World War II. A young man was departing for military service, putting his dreams on hold for a future unknown.

Morris K. Udall, age twenty, two years of college behind him and his bank account fattened by a seven-day, $76-a-week, summer construction job, left his home in the early fall of 1942 for a job that would pay him $50 a month. First destination: the Atchison, Topeka & Santa Fe railroad station at Holbrook, fifty-five miles northwest of St. Johns. Second stop: Fort MacArthur, twenty-five miles south of Los Angeles. Final assignment in the zigzag trip: Fort Douglas, just outside of Salt Lake City.

In an undated letter home ("Dear People," it began), buck private Udall wrote: "After many a sob by the young brides we left S.J. at 1:30, and waited in Holbrook until 5:00. It took 21 miserable hours by chair car to get to L.A. at 2 p.m. the next day."[1]

The letter from Fort Douglas was the first in a string of letters that were filed away by father Levi and passed on to sister Elma, who became the family historian. Morris wrote at least 120 times during his October 22, 1942, to June 26, 1946, tour with the army and army air corps. At times, he wrote every Sunday, although the schedule depended on where he was and what he was doing. It worked out to an average of one letter every two weeks. In addition to Fort Douglas, letters were mailed from officer candidate school in Fargo, North Dakota; Lake Charles Army Air Field, Louisiana; adjutant general school at Fort Sam Houston, Texas; and a variety of locations in the Pacific, including Saipan, Iwo Jima, and Honolulu.

They chronicled his military doings, and they also provided glimpses into his intellectual development. Their value may best have been described in an April 28, 1971, memorandum Morris wrote to his son Randy: "Stew was 2 ½ years older than I, and was more sensitive and I guess more intellectual. He was always reading something new, getting into a new philosophy or a new field, and I tended as a younger brother to follow onto those interests. During that period we were exchanging regular letters, long essays on the state of the world, evil and justice, and all of the rest. A major portion of my philosophy when I later went into politics developed out of that period and that correspondence."[2] Unfortunately, most of the letters exchanged between the brothers were not preserved.

Morris spent six months in Utah before moving to officer candidate school in Fargo. The Utah assignment was in a unit composed of individuals marred by some physical defect that the army said barred them from battlefield service but still allowed them to provide administrative support. Morris undertook his jobs as he always had and always would: with enthusiasm.

He combined a basic knowledge of shorthand, learned in high school, and an interest in the law, developed from his father, to become a legal assistant. "They are starting a series of trials in desertion, larceny, etc cases," he wrote in an early letter, "and the captain is defense counsel in all of them. He is having a hard time preparing them and called me in three times in the last week for consultation and method of attack. He was really grateful when I uncovered a technicality by which we can foil the prosecution and get about 5 years knocked off a boy's sentence. Work like this could really get to be interesting."[3]

By November 19, 1942, he had been promoted to private first class, and used the occasion to write the phrase "which reminds me" as an introduction to the tale of a not-so-bright soldier "who returned his issue shirts and said he wanted some of 'them with the stripes on.'"[4] The words "that reminds me" or "I am reminded of" were to become the trademark introductions for his future political jokes.

In a December 10, 1942, letter, he wrote, "I'm getting a little opportunity now and then to accept a little responsibility and getting to do jobs on my own, which is all I ask of any work." The captain, he said, was letting him draw up stipulations and briefs, "and accepts them as very good." He worried about getting "stuck in one place," and for that reason rejected his father's suggestion to take additional shorthand in night school. "To save being shunted into such a position I shall not become too proficient," he declared.[5]

By early December Udall had become coach of a basketball team and had been given responsibility for most of the defense's court-martial investigative work. His energy and curiosity were leading him to the happy state of workaholism. "The past two weeks, I have no further complaints of boredom," he wrote, "but with basketball and my added work, have more than I can handle, which is just what I like."[6]

He showed an occasional inclination to tell his parents what to do, saying: "You mention Burr's delinquency after mutual [the word Mormons use to describe youth activities]; for gad's sake please ignore it—I might go into the twisted workings of an adolescent's mind, but will leave the psychology of it to your imagination." Christmas was nearing, and he advised: "As for me, don't worry. I guess I'm one of the family's most adjustable personalities, and can get along in most any society. Christmas will find me happy, well fed, busy, and interested in many things."[7]

Poker returned to his life: "Christmas and all cut my finances quite badly, and last night I got in a poker game, and dropped the five I had left, so will be a pauper until Thursday."[8] His father responded: "I am sorry that you lost your $5, but am hoping that you will quit playing poker and if you don't I hope you lose all of the time."[9] Shortly thereafter, Morris wrote about another game in which he "damn near thought I was going to have to wire home, before I learned how it was done. The sum I had lost at one time would shock you so it shall remain undesignated. I did come back and turned a neat profit, some of which shall go to Eloise, in remembrance of the sums Elma used to give me."[10]

He took over as sports editor of the post newspaper, and he coached one basketball team and played on others, often seeing action in three or four games a week. He remembered his team as being "composed entirely of men on noncombatant status due to various handicaps. Our starting five had a grand total of seven good eyes."[11] The club occasionally played in the preliminary to college games.

His opportunity for legal work declined as the duties of one officer were changed and another was transferred. Shortly thereafter, Udall was accepted for administrative officer candidate school and scheduled for departure. On April 1, 1943, he began a two-and-a-half-day train trip from Utah to Fargo, connecting with the Great Northern in Butte, Montana. Young Udall was starting to see more of the world.

He described officer candidate school as "about the roughest thing I ever got into" and said he undoubtedly was the youngest in the class of 333 men, pegging the average age at thirty with many between thirty-eight and forty-two. He described it as a sixteen-hour day that included cleaning and polishing, classes, drill, calisthenics, and study hall. Success, he said, would depend on academics, "which won't be any trouble, especially with my valuable experience at Fort Douglas," and leadership, "which is mainly your ability to give drill orders. We march in formation to all classes, meals and study halls, usually at double time [running]. My ROTC training will be valuable in this connection."[12] His prediction on academics proved out as he scored the highest grade on the first of three major exams. With four weeks to go, he had posted ten A's out of twelve tests. At the end, he was one of a dozen selected for command posts in a four-day operation designed to evaluate administrative skills.

Despite his earlier parental criticism, Morris, in a Father's Day letter, told Levi: "I'm sure that all and any industry, success, or compassion for my fellow men or tolerance I've had has been due in large degree to your example. I've fallen short, in many particulars of your standards, but I don't think I could have hand-picked a better provider, man and father than you have been to all of us."[13] In a subsequent letter, he wrote: "I've come to appreciate my family more and more all the time. Maybe I'll turn out to be a little more human character after all some day."[14]

On June 23, 1943, eight days after turning twenty-one, Morris Udall graduated from officer candidate school. He was transferred from the army to the army air corps and began wearing the single gold bar that identifies a second lieutenant. He was dispatched to the 3rd Air Force Headquarters Replacement Depot in Tampa, Florida, to await a permanent assignment. It was another train trip and a new part of the country.

He wrote: "I was particularly amazed by the swampy jungle lands of Louisiana and South Texas."[15] From Tampa, he was sent to the B-26 training facility at Lake Charles, Louisiana.

"The difference in cultures from Arizona Mormon to Old Deep South was alarming, and events would make it difficult for me to adapt," he said. "My first superior was a bigoted major whose primary pleasure in life seemed to be abusing anyone who was black or Jewish. When I introduced myself, the major scowled as he looked me up and down. 'Morris? What kind of a name is that?' he asked. His worst suspicions were confirmed at mail call when he saw a letter to me from one 'Judge Levi Udall.' For six long months he treated me as he did his Jewish officers—badly. It proved a painful but eye-opening experience."[16]

The young lieutenant was learning firsthand the impact of the prejudice his Mormon ancestors had lived with on a daily basis. He would learn much more a few months later when he was selected to command a black squadron. "In time I grew to love the Cajun country," Udall wrote, "but I never grew accustomed to the segregation of the Deep South. While the Mormon religion also discriminated against blacks, at home I had rarely seen a black person."[17]

Udall spent three months as a squadron adjutant, then was assigned command of the 75th Aviation Squadron, a black unit that was authorized to have five white officers, but usually numbered no more than two. The outfit totaled 120 men when he took over and ultimately grew to 300. The squadron supplied men to operate base refueling units and operated a bombing and gunnery range, rifle ranges, the officers' mess, the base motor pool, and its own mess, supply, and administrative sections. "The job of being commanding officer is the one task few get in the army because it has such responsibilities, and I feel highly complimented," he said. "You have to be father, chaplain, foreman, and everything else to the men—and especially with the emotional Negro. There is so much that a good CO can do for an outfit that I want to give it a try."[18]

The command was a significant responsibility for a young second lieutenant with a Mormon upbringing. And he wrote his family: "As you may or may not know, the company or squadron CO is called 'the old man' in GI parlance—my friends get quite a bang out of it. . . . This job is the last thing from a bed of roses. I have spent the last three months getting the 82nd from an untrained outfit with no up-to-date records to one in which practically every man is set to go overseas. Now they throw me in here where things are worse than they ever were there. No training has been had, and the records are in impossible shape. To top it off my men are scattered all over this area for duty. Most of them go out into the gunnery ranges in the swamps at 0700 and don't get back until dark. In addition there has been some Negro rioting in this sector which makes the acute disciplinary problem worse. These colored boys are hard to handle, believe me. I'm just getting to the point where they don't all look just alike."[19] He worked day and night, he reported, adding: "I find that I thrive on hard sustained work and the more of it the better."[20]

As always, Udall moved ahead in positive fashion. He established a service club and filled it with sofas, overstuffed chairs, lamps, rugs, and magazine racks. "I raided a Special Service warehouse and have really fixed the place up ritzier than most living rooms in white homes," he wrote. "These poor fellows haven't seen anything like it. We have hired a full time hostess, and will have dances, a short order restaurant, and all the trimmings in the place."[21] He arranged for a black preacher to provide a service at the base chapel. "We had 55 men out, more than three times as many as had ever attended a colored service before," he said.[22] And he instituted a regular drill and training regimen, scheduling overnight bivouacs that required a six-mile march with full pack, the pitching of camp and a field kitchen, and instruction on camouflage, foxholes, and other battlefield information.

Udall's speaking style was developing, and he now saw the need to fit the humor to the audience. He gave many of the training lectures himself, and at the outset encountered some rough going. What had worked with the 82nd did not go over with the 75th. "My type of dry humor which went over so well," he said, "just doesn't even penetrate. Maybe they'll get to know me eventually."[23]

He worked at it, and within months, he actually was in demand as a speaker. "I picked up ten dollars acting as MC at a big bingo party at the Off club last evening, and had a delightful evening at the expense of various and sundry dignitaries," he wrote on July 6, 1944. "One major asked me how many years experience I had had as an MC, stating that my repartee was unusually acute."[24]

The squadron included eight men who "sang spirituals and Negro songs like real professionals," so Udall landed them a fifteen-minute New

Year's Eve spot with station KPLC. "They were a bit frightened, and didn't quite know the score, so I wrote a script and announced the show for them," he said. When he submitted the script to higher authorities for approval, "they immediately discovered that I'd studiously omitted any reference to race" and ordered that the fact be included. "I howled 'discrimination' and took the matter to the base executive," who said the men would feel slighted if race was not identified. "However, I was not to be outdone and finally won my point with the colonel. The whole thing went off well, and the boys in the chorus are local heroes now."[25] In early 1944, the racial education of Morris Udall appeared to have moved beyond Mormon discrimination and the white man's stereotypes he had demonstrated with phrases such as "I'm just getting to the point where they don't all look just alike" and references such as "the emotional Negro."

The evidence came in a March 24, 1944, letter that told of a squadron meeting in which "one soldier, who I believe had been drinking, stood up and fired the following hot potato: 'Sir, do you think a white soldier is better than a colored one?'" Udall noted that the War Department frowned on such discussions, and the base commander would probably take away his commission for discussing such subjects, then wrote: "I parried the inquiry by telling him that, and adding that I wasn't afraid to discuss anything, and that if he or anyone else would come into the orderly room I would be happy to give them my ideas. I closed by stating that I always tried to treat anybody as a person, a human being, and a soldier—regardless of any other consideration."[26]

In a May 30, 1944, letter home, Morris inserted a note to his brother Stewart: "I've finished Nehru, and found it extremely interesting reading. It is refreshing to get the Asiatic perspective, and an Indian view of Britain. I have passed it on to a colored private (BS, MA) who is always bringing me liberal literature. Sorry I can't be as idealistic and humane as you, but I can't agree with your main point in entirety [in a recent essay]. Material rewards and the esteem of my fellow men have always been the most powerful of incentives with me, and it is probably unfortunate but true that many are like me."[27]

Morris continued to suggest parental action. He wrote that the mother of a friend was "dashing down madly" to Lake Charles to try to talk her son out of a planned marriage. "Such interference disgusts me," he said, "and although I disagree with him about getting married now and think he is making a mistake, I'm trying to give him the backbone to tell his family off and do what he wants to do."[28]

He said he enjoyed reading a speech his father had written: "There is only one criticism—probably not well-founded. I don't believe in speeches prepared word for word; even under the best conditions they tend to be dull. I have had much better luck preparing an outline, and then talking from it after carefully rehearsing in my mind what I am to say."[29] Throughout his political career, Morris would often discard a prepared speech in favor of a seemingly extemporaneous presentation.

Court-martial work at Fort Douglas had been mostly for the defense. At Lake Charles, it consisted primarily of prosecutions. He figured he handled two hundred cases, winning all but two. One case involved Udall, the grandson of a polygamist, successfully prosecuting a white soldier for polygamy.

He served as defense counsel for at least two black men who asked for his help. One was a murder case. He lost, and it left a lifetime impact. Client Clarence Gibson, he wrote, was one of two "colored prisoners being taken to breakfast before it was light by a white guard whose habits they knew. Outside the colored mess hall door there was a piece of two-inch pipe about 18-in long which was used to prop the door open. As they reached the door, the one prisoner grabbed his stomach and began moaning on the ground. When the guard stooped down to see what was the matter, my client (allegedly) grabbed the pipe and delivered a mortal blow on the head."[30]

Death by firing squad was ordered, and Udall wrote letters to President Truman and the man's senators "to get a commutation if possible, though he is guilty, undoubtedly, though I doubt if he deserves to be shot."[31] Udall learned of the execution while serving in the Pacific and wrote brother Stewart: "His intrepidity in the 'crime,' and in its punishment, stemmed from his association with a family, a society, and, finally, an Army that had no concern for him as an individual. His reaction to such an environment—a go-to-hell attitude of complete irresponsibility—was perhaps the only possible mental-set he could have been expected to emerge with! That he killed with premeditation I do not doubt; that he deserved to die is questionable."[32]

Morris wrote that the attitude of that military court, "and most white men, toward murder is:

"1) White who kills white is a murderer, a wrongdoer. . . .

"2) White who kills Negro is a regrettably temperamental person who should know better;

"3) Negro who kills Negro is a primitive berserk of about as much sinister interest (to society at large) as a renegade horse;

"4) Negro who kills white is a murderous beast to be tracked down like the man-eating Tiger . . . and strung up out of hand if possible."

He continued: "I have often wondered if capital punishment won't sometime be abandoned: there is something basically incongruous in taking a man's life from him because he hasn't been properly instructed in its use. We correct [Clarence] Gibson's mistake by taking away his opportunity to make another, and not by a process that would obviate future errors."[33]

In 1962, Congressman Udall, still bothered by the case, asked the Department of the Army whether the firing squad had bungled its assignment and an officer had administered a fatal bullet in the head. The response said only that "certain details concerning the execution are not available," but Private Clarence D. Gibson had been executed on September 8, 1945, and proper procedure would have required such action if he had survived the firing squad barrage.[34] For years, Udall carried a yellowed, tattered, undated newspaper clipping about the execution in his wallet. The headline said: "Firing Squad to Shoot Negro Here." In 1988, Udall wrote: "For a brief period when I was a prosecutor, I believed that the death penalty was a deterrent and therefore justifiable; I no longer hold that view."[35]

Udall won an acquittal for one of his own men, who was accused of attempted murder. It was an eye-opening episode of law enforcement and racism in the Deep South. In a March 24, 1944, letter to his family, he described the case this way:

> Pvt. Myers is a 30 yr old meek typical southern Negro. He has been a preacher for 8 years, is a good soldier, and never gets in any kind of trouble. He was going home on furlough last May (Tampa) and at 1:30 in the night he was on a bus about 60 miles from home when the bus stopped at a service station

(white). He was asleep in the very back Jim Crow seat. All the white passengers were having cokes and sandwiches, and just after he awoke some white lady dropped her empty bottle out onto the pavement breaking same and almost hitting a white man standing out there. This bounder immediately stormed into the bus, and the first one he sees is Pvt. Myers, so he says "you black SOB you tried to kill me." After an exchange of words the sheriff, a close friend of the first white man, was called to the scene, and he told Myers to get off the bus and go with him.

Myers had been in that country before, and he testified to several lynchings there, and to the fact that a colored person couldn't even walk down the streets of the small town. In the meantime a crowd had gathered around and were crying "kill the black ——," etc. He was pretty scared, and told the sheriff that he wouldn't go with him, but would go with an MP. After getting very insulted, the sheriff with the aid of others pulled him off the bus, beat him severely, and threw him in the county jail on charges of everything from first degree murder (believe it or not) on down. Where they were going to get the corpus delecti [body] I don't know. Anyway, the sheriff claimed that during the scuffle on the bus, Myers had grabbed his gun and threatened to kill him. Myers languished in jail for over a week, and finally the military authorities in Tampa had him released. After an impartial investigation the whole case was dropped. However when the sheriff came up for this summer's election, I presume this thing was mentioned, and he then put the bee on 3AF [the 3rd Air Force] to have the man tried.

I spent about an hour on each of the prosecution's three witnesses, and succeeded in breaking their testimony, both individually and collectively. They had made affidavits last summer, statements to the investigating officer in February, and then I would question them closely on the stand. In many instances there were variances between the three, and I would pull out the old paper, make them identify their signature, and then have them read the contradicting statement. They were particularly inconsistent on just who dragged the man off the bus, just how he got ahold of the pistol, and just where he was when he was alleged to have thrown the bottle. The testimony included these exchanges:

U—"Now then, sheriff, you have made three different statements as to just where Myers had your gun. As a matter of fact, you can't positively state that he ever had his hand on your gun at all, can you?"

A—"Well, yes he did, but I can't state just where."

U—"You keep the colored people pretty well in their place in your county, don't you sheriff?"

A—"You mean the niggers, yes, we do our best."

U—"And sometimes you don't even let them walk on the streets in your town do you?"

A—"That's right."

U—"And you certainly wouldn't serve drinks and sandwiches to a Negro at a white filling station would you?"

A—"We certainly wouldn't."

Udall said he made "a brief and passionate plea for racial justice," and the panel returned in about fifteen minutes with acquittals on assault with intent to murder and resisting an officer. "He was really a happy man. I wrote him out a fifteen day furlough and sent him home."[36]

Early in January of 1945, Udall was assigned to the six-week adjutant general school at Fort Sam Houston, Texas, and the squadron made clear he had earned their complete respect. He wrote his parents: "My boys gave me a very touching farewell party, with piles of refreshments and a . . . Parker pen and pencil set plus a new shaving kit. I shook hands with each one and most or all made the usual flattering comments. Two I remember particularly: (1) 'Lt, they say an outfit is only as good as its CO, and you've got the best outfit I've ever been in' and (2) 'You sure have done a lot for us, sir—you're the best white man I've ever seen.'"[37]

Morris found the adjutant general course easy. He took solace on the basketball court and there was time for contemplation. When he thanked his mother for recording the history of his eye injury, he wrote: "I felt rather repentant when I realized what you went through and it occurred to me later that you must have felt me a coarse ingrate in the

Lillywhite days,"[38] a reference to the time he took Lillywhite's car—and the owner's sleeping baby—for a joyride. On Mother's Day, he elaborated: "Let it suffice to say that I am increasingly thankful as I become more mature for the great good fortune I have had in having such an intelligent, vigorous, charming, and above all Christian tolerant and liberal parent."[39]

Throughout his time at Fargo and Lake Charles, Udall had unsuccessfully sought an overseas assignment. The war in Europe concluded on May 7, 1945, and the Japanese surrendered on August 14, a month after he finally received an overseas order, but a month before he reached the Pacific. On July 6, 1945, he was assigned to the overseas replacement depot at Kearns, Utah, thus returning to the area where he had begun his military career in earnest.

SEEING THE WORLD

ieutenant Morris K. Udall waited seven weeks when he returned to Utah. It was not until August 30, 1945, that the U.S.S. *Baxter*, a naval attack transport, would depart Seattle en route to Saipan in the Mariana Islands in the Pacific.

He occupied some of his idle time with his uncle Don T. Udall, who was awaiting his discharge at Fort Douglas. Morris wrote his mother about one session, indicating that his experience at Lake Charles had fortified his resolve to treat people as individuals: "Had a discussion with Aunt Pearl and Uncle Don last Sunday on various political topics, particularly 'communism' and the Negro-Jew questions," he wrote. "They were (not too surprisingly) mildly liberal in outlook on most points and accepted my argument for tolerance and for individual evaluation as opposed to group condemnation; but I was not a little disappointed that both Aunt P and Uncle Don justified the almost universal intolerance toward the Jews by some damn passage of scripture which avers that the race will be 'hated and reviled' or a similar phrase. If scripture contradicts humanitarianism and tolerance (the real basis of Christianity), I want none of the former."[1]

Life on the *Baxter* was "extremely uncomfortable in our compartment in the bow of the ship, where they have some 40 of us sleeping in an unusually hot and unventilated hole the size of your living room. The food is good, however, and I manage to pass the long days with reading, writing, conversation and occasional forays at the poker table." The ship's library was limited, but "Shakespeare, a book of John Dewey's philosophy, and *Wind, Sand and Stars* by [Antoine de] Saint-Exupéry have occupied most of my time on the reading deck."[2]

The concluding months of his air corps career were less hectic and provided more time for thinking, reading, and writing—and, of course, basketball. He was selected for the 20th Air Force all-star team after its athletics officer watched him score 35 points in three quarters against a team "of dubious quality."[3]

His primary job was to help process soldiers who were being discharged. He spent most of the time in Saipan and Iwo Jima. He lived his first days on Saipan in a six-man tent ten yards from the jungle and a sign that said "Danger, Japs, Keep Out." He ignored the sign and explored nearby caves formerly used by Japanese soldiers. After a stint on Iwo Jima, he returned to Saipan and he and eight others shared more elegant quarters: a beachfront villa.

The nature of his letters changed during this period as he became more philosophical. In a November 6, 1945, letter, he praised his father "for the way in which you allowed—nay encouraged—we children to pick out our own vocations and destinies. I think some of the world's unhappiest misfits are those who permitted well-meaning but domineering parents to shape their fortune." He then outlined a "credo" he previously had written to Stewart:

> (1) Despite a positive desire for the contrary my best speculation and thot on the fundamental nature of the universe and man is to agree with Spinoza who said in effect that to him it appeared that nature has succeeded in concealing rather ably from man its secrets, and that the only honest philosophy was a healthy agnosticism—distinguished from atheist—the belief that one cannot know absolutely and finally the nature of God and the universe. That an organized universe of God's hand exists may well be; at my present stage of development I simply and candidly say: "I don't know." I am a *Christian*—in the literal sense that I believe firmly in the philosophy that Christ taught—we do not live by our own law—and we are our brother's keeper. Were all the world believers

and exponents and living the LDS religion I feel sure we would have a world somewhere near that of which Christ taught—but I have seen too much unhappiness (unnecessary unhappiness among mankind in general) resulting from denominationalism as we have it today. I would like to see one worldwide denomination of Christian (or call it what you will) people living together in trust and brotherhood.

(2) With this rather uncertain basis for a starter on what foundation, I'm sure you will ask, can I base my morals, my ethics. I can answer that by saying that I believe firmly in the equality of mankind in general—black, white, yellow, or red—and believe in treating each of them by the golden rule because that is the soundest basis of an enduring general happiness.

(3) I believe in having in life every possible enjoyment—since I don't know the purpose of life I think it best to assume that life was intended to be a happy state. And by happiness I mean not the vulgar and transitory sensual pleasures particularly, but the permanent and thorough happiness of a well adjusted and balanced man living in a suitable environment. I can best be happy by being a friend to others, by trying to help everyone with whom I am in contact. I suppose a prerequisite of all of this pursuit of happiness would be achieving for myself a reasonable degree of economic security.

(4) The last motivating factor, or intent or what have you, in my current existence is to use whatever initiative and intellect I have in attaining the most responsible and demanding position in my chosen profession of which I am capable, and to use whatever influence I may possess in the betterment of the social, economic, and intellectual status of all those who may be influenced by me.[4]

Udall found time to consider his future as a lawyer, and wrote J. Byron McCormick, dean of the University of Arizona College of Law, to ask indirectly whether he might speed up graduation by receiving credit at the law college for his military courtroom efforts. McCormick rejected the idea, but did point out that Udall could finish law school in two years, and that he was eligible to enter the school without further prerequisites.

At Christmas, he told his parents: "I feel so much older than when this thing started 4 long, long years ago. For perhaps the first time I have the frustrated feeling that there is so much to do, and that time is flying too hastily by. I'm sure of only about two things: (1) that today is an entirely different world from that of 1941 and (2) that I'm an entirely different person."[5]

On March 15, 1946, Morris, who had been promoted to captain on December 27, 1944, took on the status quo when he urged that the army be desegregated. He was ahead of his time and ahead of the world. The proposal was contained in a letter to the American Veterans Committee, a national organization that was considered far more liberal than the American Legion, the Veterans of Foreign Wars, and other similar organizations[6]:

> I think the time for equal treatment of our Negro soldiers is long overdue. We have had in the various units of the army with which I have served Americans of every conceivable antecedent (save one): Indian, Chinese, Nisei, Arab, Russian, Mexican, Hawaiian, etc, etc; men who were assigned to these organizations on one basis: their aptitudes and skills. I have been happy to have had the opportunity of working, living, eating, relaxing with these fellow citizens.
>
> And I propose that the army, at least, now cease treating the Negro as a social leper ("problem") requiring separate quarters, messes, exchanges, chapels, and amusements, and treat him as they treat any other racial minority.
>
> Such an urgently needed reform need not arouse the hysteria and extremes of emotion usually evoked by any move interpreted as giving the Negro "social equality." I think it patently clear that we cannot establish social equality by fiat— it must always remain a status of mutual acceptance. In off-duty hours, one's present right to select friends and associates will stand unassailed, though I think the tendency to choose friends of similar interest and background will, of course, remain. And if any of the white soldiers in such a project desire to play golf, or drink a beer during leisure hours with their colored comrades, they should have that right, too (though today the mass of the army's unproclaimed restrictions forbid).[7]

Udall also undertook to understand management-labor relations, and wrote his father a five-page, single-spaced letter advocating national legislation that would prohibit both lockouts and strikes and establish "judicial machinery for the compulsory settlement of economic disputes." He said, "We must by law protect the employee from exploitation by unscrupulous or avaricious management, and we must protect society at large from the wastage of labor's prolonged strikes. And as a third, and equally important safeguard, we must protect the employer from the depredations of irresponsible labor organizations."[8]

Captain Udall also inserted his opinion in a family disagreement over whether seventeen-year-old brother Burr should enlist following his 1946 graduation from high school. In a letter to Burr, he said, "The principal arguments against service as I get it are (1) the 'unwholesome' atmosphere conducive to a degeneration of character, and (2) the waste of a year's time. The fear of contamination, and the resultant effort to isolate themselves from the rest of society, are the standard devices of the weak and effete members of the group in their escape from unpleasant reality. Hell, if you haven't got the strength of character to associate with any element and still keep your own goals and ideals, then your isolation is just a camouflage for an existent weakness."[9]

Shortly after graduation, Burr and two friends boarded a bus for Phoenix where they enlisted in the army. Burr served eighteen months, most of it in the Philippines.

Morris Udall was discharged on June 26, 1946, eleven days after his twenty-fourth birthday. He purchased a car with poker winnings from the boat trip home, then headed for St. Johns.[10]

One of the veteran's first goals was to accomplish what he had been refused by the military: to learn to fly. He did so at the St. Johns airport, using the GI Bill to cover the expense. "My mother—it says something about her courage with a one-eyed pilot in an old single-engine—wanted to be my first passenger," he recalled.[11]

Flying became a hobby and over the years he owned three small planes in partnership with Marvin Borodkin, who spent thirty years as an air force pilot, then practiced law in Tucson and often piloted Udall on Arizona campaign trips.

Borodkin visited St. Johns that summer, and Udall persuaded him to go for a flight. It was a two-seat aircraft, and Udall decided to land on the highway to impress Borodkin, who was in the back seat unable to see over his much taller friend. The craft touched down, bounced along, then hopped a ditch before the one-eyed pilot could bring it to a stop.[12]

It was flying that first brought Udall into contact with Barry Goldwater, the longtime Arizona senator and unsuccessful 1964 Republican presidential nominee. "The first time I ever saw Barry was when he flew in with [Republican governor of Arizona] Howard Pyle. St. Johns International Airport was a dirt strip. We had never seen an airplane up there until he flew in," he said facetiously.[13]

The relationship between conservative Republican and liberal Democrat ultimately became quite close, and Udall's failed run for the Democratic nomination in 1976 gave birth to one of the jokes favored—and wrongfully claimed—by both men. Writer Larry L. King, a close friend of Udall's for many years, was one of the speakers at a 1977 Saints and Sinners roast of the two Arizonans. When King stood up at the Shoreham podium in Washington, D.C., he pointed to the two losing candidates and noted that "Arizona is the only state in the union where mothers can't tell their sons they can grow up to be president."[14]

Udall loved the line, and used it often. It received new attention in 1988 when former Arizona governor Bruce E. Babbitt failed in his bid for the Democratic presidential nomination. Then, Republican senator John S. McCain played with the joke when he unsuccessfully sought the 2000 Republican nomination. McCain, however, had moved to Arizona in 1981 after retiring from the navy.

THE TUCSON YEARS

*T*he University of Arizona was changing when Morris Udall returned in the fall of 1946. Like campuses all over the United States, its classrooms were bulging as the nation's young returned from the military.

The boys who had gone off to war had returned as men, and their Congress encouraged a college education by providing the GI Bill of Rights to pay at least part of the cost. The federal aid made it easier for those who had interrupted their higher education, and it also opened the classrooms to many others who otherwise would have lacked the finances.

When Udall departed the University of Arizona at the end of the 1941–42 school year, enrollment was 2,789. When he returned at the start of 1946–47, the student body had jumped to 5,062. Law dean Byron McCormick had previously rejected Udall's appeal for special credit for his military legal work. However, the dean noted that Morris, like everyone else with two years of undergraduate work and a minimum C average, was eligible for admission. Udall returned to his old room-and-board job in the infirmary basement and set about acquiring a formal law education to complement his military trial work.

Bob Pickrell returned the same year and credited his friend with helping him through law school. He and several others would go to Udall's infirmary room before a test, Pickrell recalled, and "Mo would write an outline on a piece of paper and give a lecture. He had one of the most beautiful minds of anyone I've ever known."[1]

The College of Law was situated in a three-story, red-brick building just inside the western edge of the campus. It was across from the university library and was fronted by palm trees and an expanse of grass. Charles E. Ares, later a Udall law partner and subsequently University of Arizona law school dean, said Udall would spend the first half or third of an exam period thinking and note-making under a palm tree, then go inside and type nonstop.[2]

It was an all-star class. Pickrell, a Republican, became a superior court judge and the state's attorney general; Raul H. Castro, a Democrat who later succeeded Udall as county attorney, went on to become a superior court judge, governor of Arizona, and U.S. ambassador to El Salvador, Bolivia, and Argentina; Samuel P. Goddard Jr., a Democrat, spent one term as governor of Arizona; Robert O. Lesher became a state supreme court justice; and Estes D. McBryde served as a superior court judge. Lesher and Udall placed first and second, respectively, in the forty-five-member class of 1949.

Udall concentrated on law and basketball during his first year back. He and brother Stewart sat next to each other on the bench when the 1946–47 basketball season opened against West Texas State College, now West Texas A&M University. Stewart, twenty-six, had been a second-team All Border Conference guard in 1939–40 but did not play during the war and did not play in that contest. He quit the team afterward, deciding that he was out of shape and lacked the skills he once had possessed.[3] Morris, twenty-four, was a reserve forward and got into the game in the final five minutes with the score tied 38–38.

"My getting in the game at all was simply a fluke," Morris recalled. "The regular center, benched for lack of hustle, was resentful. When his tiring replacement obviously needed to be taken out, the star angered the coach by taking too much time to get off his jacket. Coach [Fred] Enke, never one to be done a favor by a temperamental star, looked down the bench and his eyes fell on me. 'If he is not ready, Mo, you get in there.'" Udall responded by scoring 11 points in a 54–43 victory.[4] No question, he was a first-stringer thereafter.

It was the second spectacular season in a row for the Wildcats. The preceding year had been the first full season following the war, and the coach's son, Fred W., later a seven-year National Football League quarterback with Detroit, Philadelphia, and Baltimore, had returned to school along with a host of other veterans. That club posted a 25–5 record with young Enke, Tim Ballantyne, and Linc Richmond named to the All Border Conference first team, and Marvin Borodkin and George Genung selected on the second team. The year Morris joined the team, Richmond and Enke won All Border Conference honors with Junior Crum and Borodkin on the second team. The club compiled an 18–3 record.

The five-foot-eleven Borodkin and the six-foot-five Udall were roommates on the basketball trips and occasionally had to share a double bed. Morris slept diagonally; otherwise, his feet would hang over the edge. Borodkin filled in where he could. On the road, Borodkin said, "Most of us were not studious, but Mo read and remembered. He could scan and remember. Studying for Mo was not what it was for others."[5]

Udall posted a 10-point scoring average his first year. It jumped to 13.3 in his final year as the Wildcats remained Border Conference champions but were a less impressive 17–10 overall. Udall and Enke were first-team all-conference with guard Billy Mann on the second team.

The final season game against the New Mexico Lobos gave birth to one of the most oft-told eye stories: "The Albuquerque papers had featured a long story about the Wildcat . . . who was . . . captain of the team and its leading scorer, doing all of these things with a right eye made of glass," Udall said. "I had one of those nights athletes dream about when everything I threw in the air went into the basket. With two minutes to play, a 20-point lead and 24 points to my credit, the coach took me out to a friendly ovation. Our bench was directly under the press table and an Albuquerque sports writer leaned over and said, 'You are a liar. No one plays like that with a glass eye.' I took the thing out of its socket and handed it to him with the put-down, 'Mister, I haven't been able to see much out of this, maybe you can use it better.' "[6]

Teammate Enke said Udall's eye was dislodged in one game, and action was stopped while everyone searched the floor, much as they do today for a wayward contact lens.[7]

With basketball out of the way in the spring of 1947, Udall turned his attention to a run for the student body presidency. It was an example of what brother Stewart later would describe as Morris's penchant for political audacity. He ran against "the entrenched fraternity-sorority system, and he did it as an independent," Stewart said.[8] Subsequent Udall challenges of the university administration, in the Congress, and for the Democratic presidential nomination would be mounted with the same willingness to question the status quo.

Udall won and immediately began what was to become a pattern: He made friends with his opponents. James F. McNulty Jr. had managed the campaign of the losing presidential candidate; nonetheless, Udall named McNulty as chair of what became a rather controversial Assembly Committee. McNulty himself ran for student body president the following year, but lost to the Udall-supported candidate, Merrill Windsor. "I never made that mistake [running against Udall] again," said McNulty, now a Tucson attorney. The two men became close political allies, and McNulty, also a Democrat, served one term in the U.S. House with his friend.[9]

Before his term was over, students had taken control of the committee that selected visiting performers; reduced prices and increased rebates in the bookstore; established nonprofit operation of the soda fountain; loaned $2,500 in student funds to establish a cooperative grocery in a veterans' housing area; and won a voice in choosing a new football coach.[10]

The list of accomplishments also included desegregation of the "Coop," the school's only dining facility. That action occurred one day in the fall of 1947 when Morris and Stewart, who was nearing the end of his law school education, went to get a quick bite to eat. As they approached Old Main—the Coop was located in its basement—they noticed the usual group of blacks gathered outside by the fountain. The two dozen blacks enrolled in the university were allowed to purchase items inside but were required to consume them outside. The brothers decided to change the policy.

Morgan Maxwell Jr., son of the principal of the city's all-black Dunbar School (grades 1–8), was a freshman then. Morris and Stewart walked up to the group and asked whether anyone would volunteer to eat inside. Maxwell stepped forward and remembered Morris saying: "This policy is going to change." They entered, sat down, and were served without a ruckus because of the general respect for the Udall brothers. "Stew and Mo made it very clear I was a student and I could eat there," Maxwell said. Thereafter, blacks and whites ate inside.[11]

Morris was still studying law when the 1947–48 school year concluded. Six units and he would be ready for the January 1949 state bar examination. The future looked simple, but then Denver Nuggets owner Hal Davis came calling, asking Udall to play for his fledgling entry in the two-year-old National Basketball League (NBL). The league members were Syracuse, New York; Anderson and Hammond, Indiana; Oshkosh and Sheboygan, Wisconsin; Waterloo, Iowa; Dayton, Ohio; and the Tri-Cities team representing Moline and Rock Island, Illinois, and Davenport, Iowa. Udall quickly arranged to complete his legal education with help from the University of Denver College of Law.

The Nuggets were to pay Udall $6,000, but it is unlikely that he received much more than a few hundred dollars for the 62-game schedule. In a letter to his parents, he wrote: "If this deal pays off (and it looks pretty good now) it won't be until next spring, and I can see that I'm going to have to about finance myself until then."[12]

The NBL life was not plush. "We traveled in a reliable, though sensitive, DC-3," Udall wrote. "We stayed in small hotels and ate when and where we could. Laundry facilities being scarce, the presence of the team was quite noticeable as we packed our game uniforms and shoes along with us wherever we went. I was probably the most conspicuous as I also carried approximately 10 pounds of law books along with me." Udall completed his coursework and went home briefly to take the Arizona bar exam in January 1949, finishing first among twenty-five. Classmate Robert Lesher took the exam in July and placed first among sixty.

As the season neared its end, the team lost its airplane and had to travel in private cars, Udall's Nash Rambler and those of two other players. "We were going to make those last five or six games," he said. "We had to swing around the Midwest."[13]

The Nuggets finished 18–44, losing 15 consecutive contests to set a league record. The club also fared poorly at the box office, and Udall received $3,000 of his salary in what probably were worthless franchise stock certificates.[14]

Whatever his financial difficulties at the time, it is probable that Udall remembered his military experience and fattened his wallet by playing poker. "Mo was a poker player deluxe," said teammate Jim Darden. "We were grounded by a blizzard for three days in Waterloo and we played poker for three days."[15]

Udall enjoyed his year with the Nuggets, once writing home: "Sure wish they had pro-ball in Arizona as I could combine it and law during the next few years. Our boss, Hal Davis, likes my leadership and has offered me the job of coaching the team next year, which I'm afraid I'll have to turn down."[16] The season after Udall left, 1949–50, the NBL merged with the stronger Basketball Association of America, giving birth to the National Basketball Association.

Profit or no, he never regretted his time in Denver. "No, I never got a dime of it," he said, then added: "I milked that one year of pro ball for more publicity and more good laughs than anything you can think of."[17] Thirty-two years later, Udall's professional career was honored when the Basketball Hall of Fame in Springfield, Massachusetts, hung his portrait in a special section devoted to leaders of government and business.[18]

The Nuggets experience also brought him into contact with Patricia Jeannette Emery, a twenty-two-year-old airline ticket agent. She had attended a game with her brother, Walter Emery, and his wife, and they walked past Udall as they were departing. "I really admire you," she told Morris. "He asked me my name and he called me and there was no one else." Patricia usually worked the midnight shift. She would watch the game, and Mo would walk her to work. Later in the day, they would meet for a snack and conversation.

She was raised an Episcopalian, but was inactive. He was an inactive Mormon. Both opposed the Latter-day Saints dogma on race, which banned blacks from entering Mormon temples and prohibited them from becoming lay priests or church officials. They drank coffee and tea, contrary to Mormon policy. They talked of marriage.

She was intimidated by the idea that Mo's father Levi was a judge and would want to perform the marriage ceremony.[19] They eloped, and were married in a civil ceremony on June 15, 1949, in Lordsburg, New Mexico. It was his twenty-seventh birthday; she was twenty-three.

The season with the Nuggets concluded Udall's time in organized athletics, but the high school, university, military, and professional sporting life had taught him much. As brother Stewart noted years later: "In sports, you win and you lose and you go on. The practice and determination infuse confidence in you."[20] Morris would go on to win and to lose, but, unlike many politicians, the grace and humor with which he accepted defeat only seemed to increase the respect in which he was held. A loss always was followed by a step forward.

Basketball behind him, Morris drove south to Tucson where he joined brother Stewart in the practice of law. The young attorneys took whatever cases came their way.

They represented Tucson-area service station operators in an effort to shut off the city's first self-service gas station, arguing that drunken drivers would be unable to pump their own gas and that employees might fail to look for smokers in incoming cars. The Pima County Board of Supervisors soon made the situation moot by legalizing self-service stations.[21]

They won $16,000 for a Winkelman, Arizona, miner who lost an eye to a tear-gas pellet when a Gila County deputy broke up a fight among World War II veterans. The miner originally had been turned away by a major Phoenix firm. "You get hopeless cases when you're a young lawyer," Stewart said, "and we had time to do this." The thrust of the defense was to cast doubt on whether the deputy had exercised "the proper use of force" to quell the "breach of the public peace." But the defense attorney opened the door to defeat when he questioned whether the plaintiff's attorneys knew the value of an eye. To avoid their own disputes, the brothers had adopted a policy that whoever won a coin flip would deliver the closing argument. Morris had won this coin toss. He removed his glass eye to show the jury that he did, indeed, understand the worth of an eye.[22]

They won a price-fixing case against the State Board of Barber Examiners, which had tried to shut down the one-chair shop operated by a one-legged Osage Indian, Charlie Love, who had been working without a state license and who charged fifty cents rather than the board-mandated one dollar. Love, fifty-two, was illiterate and unable even to take the state test. He had been a barber since the age of sixteen and had been cutting hair in Tucson for thirteen years. He supported a wife and two children on the income.[23] A sweet victory of sorts for onetime barber Morris Udall, who had cut the family hair and had operated a below-scale university barber shop of his own. The Udalls had undertaken the case at the request of an anonymous benefactor. It was not until 1983 that Morris Udall identified the individual as William R. Mathews, editor of the *Arizona Daily Star,* and disclosed that Mathews had paid them $500.[24]

While the Udalls were handling civil cases, Pima County attorney Robert D. Morrison was investigating prostitution and gambling. At the end of 1950, Morrison appointed Morris Udall to a part-time job as his chief deputy, primarily to conduct the trials of former county attorney Bryce H. Wilson, former sheriff Jerome P. Martin, and former under-sheriff Maurice T. Guiney. In those days, lawyers could serve in the county attorney's office and continue a private practice.

Udall twice ended up with hung juries in his attempt to prove that Wilson had accepted a $50 bribe from the earnings of a prostitute. He won a conviction against Martin for receiving a $200 bribe to protect a prostitute from prosecution. Three gambling conspiracy charges against Guiney were dropped after he entered a no contest plea to income tax evasion.

Morrison, an ambitious politician, decided to seek election as the state's attorney general, and Udall promptly announced that he would try to succeed his boss. Udall won the election without great difficulty.

As county attorney, Udall sought to create a top-notch staff and then give each member the freedom to act. His deputies included Charles Ares, who had been a clerk for U.S. Supreme Court Justice William O. Douglas; Alfredo C. Marquez, who later was named a U.S. district court judge; plus Morrison holdovers Raul Castro and Mary Anne Reimann Richey, who later served as a superior court judge and a U.S. district court judge. "His philosophy was to hire good people and essentially leave them alone and let them do their work," Ares said.[25] Udall carried his own caseload and continued to practice part time with his brother.

Udall had always won friends for his good nature and quick wit. He learned of their courtroom value early in his term as a prosecutor. "One of the first cases I prosecuted involved a man accused of drunk driving," he said. "The defendant surprised me by hauling in five of his drinking buddies to attest to his sobriety on the night in question. In my summation, I told the jury that the defense's argument reminded me of the bartender who shoved the last five patrons out the door at closing time.

When the group reached the car, the leader turned to one of the men and said, 'Simpson, you drive, you're too drunk to sing.' " He won the case, won praise from the judge for his humor, and "from that moment on, I began to collect funny stories and use them regularly in opening and closing arguments."[26]

He also established a reputation for fairness and openness. "Morris' attitude, characteristically, was that he and his staff were as good as anyone they faced, that they could work harder, and that it didn't make too much difference what tricks the other side could pull," Ares wrote. "A young deputy assisting Morris in a capital case was astonished when he was directed to set aside an office where the two defense lawyers could examine the complete prosecution file in privacy before the beginning of the trial."[27] Udall and his attorneys adopted the practice long before the state established pretrial discovery rules.

Udall's term in office was only nine months along when the unexpected occurred: Representative Harold A. "Porque" Patten, a Tucson insurance agent, announced he would not seek a fourth term in the House. It was the job that brother Stewart ultimately would win, and the job Morris apparently wanted but decided against after consultation with his wife. The congressional opening triggered one of the few ugly moments in their brotherly relationship.

The decision by Democrat Patten was revealed on September 24, 1953. Less than two months later, the *Arizona Daily Star* carried a two-paragraph brief that said: "County Atty. Morris K. Udall, often mentioned as a possible candidate for Congress from Arizona's second district, apparently is not running for that office. 'I have no ambition to be president or to run for Congress,' he said in preliminary remarks yesterday to a speech on enforcement of gambling laws."[28]

In his 1988 book *Too Funny to Be President* Udall wrote: "In 1954, Arizona's Second Congressional seat appeared ripe for the taking, and I considered running for the House of Representatives, but for reasons of seniority and familial solidarity, I deferred to Stew."[29]

He said it in stronger terms a year later: "I had wanted to go to Congress all those years and here's my older brother who wasn't the political figure that I was. If any Udall was going to run it should have been me, I felt. I had been elected county attorney and so on. But he had been on the Amphi School Board and active in some of the desegregation cases and was a good lawyer and had his following. So I stood aside." The matter was discussed with their parents, he said. "They loved us both and hated to be put in a position of having to choose. And they didn't choose. I made the choice. It was a tough one."[30]

But in a mid-1970s interview with historian/journalist Abraham S. Chanin, Udall had said: "I wanted to run but my wife thought I was too young, and she was terribly opposed to going to Washington. I let her talk me out of it; I always regretted it."[31] Patricia Udall could not remember the details, but said the Chanin interview carried the ring of truth.[32]

The possibility of either brother seeking the job was indeed subject to family guidance. Don Udall, a superior court judge in Navajo County, was considering the race, and father Levi decreed that Uncle Don had first rights. Throughout the fall and winter, Stewart contemplated a campaign and even wrote his uncle about his plans should the opportunity present itself.[33] At the same time, Morris "was telling everybody all winter that he wanted to run for judge," Stewart said.[34]

Uncle Don revealed his noncandidacy during the 1954 state bar convention, April 22–24 in Tucson. Morris declared his candidacy for the superior court judgeship on May 1.[35] Stewart announced for Congress on June 16.[36]

The brotherly argument began after their uncle withdrew. Stewart said that Morris had not sought the congressional seat, but he feared that his judicial candidacy would suffer because there would be too many Udalls on the ballot. "Mo went through the roof," Stewart said. "He told me off. He said he had prior rights because he was in public life."[37]

Both actually had been in "public life." Morris, of course, was the elected county attorney. Stewart had been a vice chairman of the Pima County Democratic Party, had twice managed county gubernatorial campaigns for the Democratic nominees, and had been elected to the northside Amphitheater School Board.

Years later during research for this book, Stewart Udall was shown his brother's statement about the influence of Patricia on the 1954 decision. He called it eye-opening, saying: "I didn't know that he was even giving it a thought all winter long. I can see why he could be resentful. I now think he made that up about too many Udalls on the ballot. It was a mixture of his wife talked him out of it and he was resentful because he had run for county attorney. He probably thought: 'The door opens and that's the golden opportunity—that's politics.' "[38]

They did a good job keeping their rift between themselves, for few, if any, friends saw outward signs of the dispute.

Morris embarked on an energetic judicial campaign, flying his own Piper Tri-Pacer to such Pima County voting sites as Lukeville, Ajo, and the Tohono O'odham (then called Papago) Indian villages of Santa Rosa and Sil Nakya.[39]

Nonetheless, Morris did indeed lose his quest for the Democratic nomination for judge, a victim not of too many Udalls on the ballot but rather of his place in the alphabet. Opponents Irving Kipnis and Joe Reilly were listed ahead of him, and his name was located on the voting machines where even friends complained that they could not find it.[40] He subsequently led a successful drive to eliminate the alphabetical order and replace it with rotation of names.

The loss left Udall feeling empty, and he and Patricia gathered up the leftover campaign literature—enough to last through the general election—and went looking for a trash bin. They found an empty one and dropped the packages in one by one, each causing an echo when it hit bottom.[41]

The defeated candidate figured his political life had been terminated, and he set out in new directions. He signed up to teach a class in labor law at the University of Arizona College of Law, and he returned to private practice. "I got to where I was getting recognition as one of the good personal injury people in the Southwest," he said. "I broke the record three times with the highest verdict in a personal injury case." He cited judgments of $148,000 and $125,000, sizable sums for the 1950s.[42]

Morris used his airplane as a tool for his personal injury practice, hiring photographer Tunney Wong to snap aerial photos. On at least one occasion, an aerial photo backfired. Thomas Chandler, his friend and frequent courtroom opponent, recounted how a Udall client sought damages for a broken hip, claiming she was unable to see a poorly marked hotel step. Udall presented the aerial photo to the jury, and the supposedly invisible step was quite clear from 800 feet up, Chandler said.[43]

Attorney J. Daniel O'Neill, who headed Udall's Tucson office for ten years starting in 1981, said Udall would use any excuse to go flying, "and he got to thinking, 'God, there are lawyers all over downtown who've got clients that write wills and want their ashes spread over the Catalinas or Pusch Ridge or wherever. I could charge enough to spread ashes to pay for the gas in the plane.' So they got the first client's ashes and they put them in a paper bag and they went out to the foothills and put the bag outside to empty the ashes and all the ashes came flying back into the airplane. Practically suffocated poor Tunney. So he went back to the drawing board, and figured out it would work if he had a rock in the bag and held it and shook the rock on a string."[44]

Udall also represented some criminal defendants, including Sheriff's Sergeant Norman C. Simmers, fifty-nine, accused of first-degree murder in the gunshot slaying of his forty-one-year-old girlfriend. Simmers claimed she was shot five times as he struggled to take the gun from her and prevent a suicide.

Marvin Cohen, who would become a longtime friend, was fresh out of law school when the summer 1957 slaying occurred. Udall called him to the shooting site and directed Cohen to stand on the roof of the woman's trailer home and try to determine the trajectory of the gunshots. The point was to show that the shots came from all different directions while the two struggled.

The case went to trial in September, and it was a classic confrontation: Morris K. Udall, former county attorney, against Raul Castro, one of his former deputies and the man elected as his successor, although Udall had supported another Democrat, Gordon G. Aldrich, in the primary.

The final witness was a surprise, testifying that he had heard a man yell "I'll kill you, I'll kill you." Udall dispatched Cohen to the trailer court to interrogate neighbors, and one individual said he had been watching a movie on television in which the "I'll kill you, I'll kill you" lines were recited at about the time of the killing. Udall and Cohen determined the movie to be *Roadhouse* with Ida Lupino, Cornel Wilde, Richard Widmark, and Celeste Holm. The discovery occurred too late to be used, but Udall still brought back a hung jury (ten to two for acquittal). Simmers was unhappy about a retrial, so he fired Udall, and the ensuing attorney used the movie as evidence. It did not work. Simmers was convicted of manslaughter, which Cohen called "the difference between Morris Udall and anybody else trying the case."[45]

Attorneys who watched him practice called Udall a master.

"He was an extraordinary trial lawyer," Cohen said.

Stanley G. Feldman, who became chief justice of the Arizona Supreme Court, said, "I learned to practice law in a way by watching Morris."[46]

"Morris was born to it," former dean Charles Ares said. "He taught me a lot, but he couldn't teach self-confidence. He was instinctive. He was a wonderful trial lawyer. He had an ability to talk sense to juries. He had an ability to make things understandable to juries and to make connections with them."[47]

Said Chandler: "Morris would seek a maximum dollar in settlement of cases; we'd go to trial and the judgment would be higher. The jury trial is a theatrical production and from beginning to end, Morris played them to the hilt. He walked in right on time—not early—raring to go." He was "a master at deciding the order of witnesses, was never petty, small, sarcastic; he was open and straightforward. He was charitable, tolerant of everybody and their ideas."[48]

Stewart Udall used many of the same words and phrases in describing his brother's performance years later in the U.S. Congress: "When he took a bill to the Hill, it was theater," Stewart said. "He rarely lost if he took it to the floor. He mastered it. His presentation was so cogent."[49]

Tucson was still a small city in the 1950s, starting the decade with a population of about 50,000 and concluding it with about 235,000 in the metropolitan area. Almost all lawyers maintained downtown offices within walking distance of the courthouse. A special collegiality existed among the attorneys, and Feldman recalled sitting with others in the Udall office, 222 North Court Avenue, celebrating a victory by Morris. The office window provided a clear view of the street. "Morris got the whiskey bottle out . . . then he saw the old man arriving" and quickly started clearing away the glasses, cigarettes, and ashtrays. The cleanup was complete by the time father Levi Udall, a justice of the state supreme court and former Mormon stake president, arrived to visit his son.[50]

His political career seemingly a thing of the past, Udall nonetheless continued the workaholic ways he said had made him happiest when in the military. He decided to write a definitive work on evidence, so he rented space in a building across the street from his primary office. He would arrive about 7 A.M. and remain until midmorning. "Morris never did just the job given or that he undertook," Ares said.[51] The effort resulted in *Arizona Law of Evidence,* a book that still bears his name and that of a coauthor, the most recent University of Arizona law professor to update the work.

He headed the Arizona volunteers for Democratic presidential nominee Adlai E. Stevenson in 1956 and was a delegate to the Democratic National Convention. He chaired the successful 1960 modern courts initiative that gave the Arizona Supreme Court power over the state system, and instituted other administrative changes.

In 1958, Udall helped establish a locally owned bank, the Bank of Tucson, serving as its vice president and treasurer. In 1960, he was one of the founders of the Catalina Savings and Loan Association, later serving as board chairman. He was a director of the Metropolitan YMCA, a member of the board of the Arizona-Sonora Desert Museum, and director and legal counsel for the Better Business Bureau.

Chandler said Udall "never wasted a minute. He used his time better than anyone I ever knew. If he stopped to talk to you on the street, it was about something specific. Chitchat was not his style."[52]

Udall had grown to accept his judicial defeat and the fact that his brother was in Congress, apparently planning to make it his life's work. He turned his eyes back toward the bench after his father decided to retire early so Morris could be appointed to his supreme court seat. Then his father died of a stroke on Memorial Day in 1960, and Republican governor Paul J. Fannin appointed Mo's uncle Jesse Udall, a Republican.

Jesse Udall's appointment was symbolic of the changing political scene in Arizona, a state that had been staunchly Democratic up until the end of World War II. During Arizona's first thirty-eight years, from 1912 to 1950, only four Republicans were ever elected to statewide office. It had been a conservative state, to be sure, but many registered as Democrats solely to be eligible for governmental patronage. This group, labeled "Pinto Democrats" for its tendency to vote Republican in the general election, was reinforced after the war when a host of young men who had been stationed in the state returned to seek their fortunes. Arizona also was moving from an economy based on the three C's—cattle, copper, and climate—to one relying more on tourism and expanding to include electronics and manufacturing.

The GOP began to break through in 1950 with the surprise election of J. Howard Pyle as governor. He had capitalized on his statewide prominence as a radio war correspondent and radio personality plus the state's reluctance to elect a woman, Democrat A. C. "Ana" Frohmiller.

The switch to a two-party state was solidified two years later when Pyle won reelection and, of more significance, Barry Goldwater ousted Democrat Ernest W. McFarland, the Senate majority leader (Lyndon Johnson was his whip), and John J. Rhodes defeated Democrat John R. Murdock, chairman of the House Interior Committee, despite the fact that Democrats outnumbered Republicans three to one. What ultimately was to become a Republican takeover of the state was well under way, and Mo Udall would later become a lonely Democratic voice in Arizona's delegation.

"So here I was," Udall said. "Couldn't go to Congress, my brother's blocking the way; couldn't be a judge, my uncle's blocking the way. It looked like I was through. So I accepted it, a rather bitter pill."[53]

One year later, Morris K. Udall would be a member of the U.S. House of Representatives, filling the seat vacated by Stewart after he was appointed secretary of the interior by President John F. Kennedy.

Stewart easily had won a fourth term in the fall of 1960. Republican Mac C. Matheson had not expected to win, but he did want to establish himself for 1962 in case Stewart ran for the U.S. Senate. "The best thing is a familiar name," said Matheson, then a Tucson radio man and now retired in the Phoenix area. His name and his voice were known from his work at radio station KTUC and an earlier unsuccessful run for a Tucson City Council seat. He lost again, as he expected. The margin was significant: Stewart Udall, 81,597; Matheson, 66,143.

In the special election, Matheson received a free ride in the Republican primary, whereas Morris faced five opponents in the Democratic primary. He received 21,075 votes, more than all five combined.

The match against Matheson on May 2, 1961, was different. Matheson came on strong, running against "big brother Stew," federal aid to education, scholarship aid for college students, medical assistance for the aged, minimum wage legislation, and the welfare state. Udall took the opposite view on each of the issues. At one debate, Matheson, also a

Mormon, said the nation's capital resembled a Hershey candy bar, "half chocolate and half nuts."[54]

Republicans backed Matheson strongly. The state party supplied money, trained campaign workers, and provided a twin-engine aircraft and pilot. State chairman Stephen C. Shadegg later regretted the support, saying: "I was embarrassed by Matheson's crude sense of humor, his insensitive racial jokes, his undeviating devotion to the extreme principles of the John Birch Society. The voters were smarter than I—they picked Mo Udall."[55]

Turnout in the special election was light, primarily because it included only the one contest and therefore lacked the voter interest common to a regular election where a multiplicity of state and county offices are at stake. Udall finished with 51,304 votes to 49,197 for Matheson—a margin of 2,107. It was the closest contest of his congressional career.

The Morris Udalls were Washington bound.

THE OUT-OF-TOWNERS

Thirty-eight-year-old Morris K. Udall arrived in Washington, D.C., on May 16, 1961. It was a city he had visited only once during a brief troop-train stopover in 1944.[1] He was enthusiastic about plunging into representing Arizona's Second Congressional District, but his wife, Pat, was less than excited about moving from the Southwest.

Udall over the years told the story of one of his children saying a bedtime prayer when leaving for Washington:

Now I lay me down to sleep
I pray the Lord my soul to keep
God bless Mommy, Daddy, Grandma
And sister, and now goodbye God
We're going to Washington.

It may have been one of Mo's attempts at humor, but like most jests it had a ring of truth to it.

It did promise to be an exciting time with the handsome, young, and articulate John Kennedy in the White House and brother Stewart in the cabinet. "I came with high hopes and a pragmatic political philosophy that was largely Roosevelt-Truman-Stevenson in origin," he said.[2] He also knew he had to overcome being known as Stewart's little brother and that he had to make his own mark.

The venerable Democratic senator Carl T. Hayden and his Republican counterpart Barry M. Goldwater came to Udall's office—brother Stewart's former office—to welcome Mo, as he was more often being called away from home. "I was quite impressed that both of them would make the pilgrimage across the Mall to see me, although I guess that's tradition," Udall said.[3] He was sworn in by House Speaker Sam Rayburn, the last time the aging Democrat would perform such a ceremony. In November, Rayburn returned to his Bonham, Texas, home to die, ending an era of "to get along, go along" leadership style.[4] They were words that Udall would often ignore. In fact, he and other young congressmen were insulted by such counsel.[5]

Udall was easy to spot as he tried to find his way around the Capitol. At a lean six-foot-five and sporting a crew cut, bow tie, and wide leather belt studded with turquoise stones and garnished with a silver buckle crafted by a Navajo, he was a sight to behold. He was from the Southwest and wife Pat liked him to dress that way. She, too, adorned herself in western wear, often wearing squaw dresses in the button-down world of Washington, D.C. Writer Larry L. King described Udall as a "disconcerting combination of painful country-boy shyness and a bawdy cowlot humor."[6] Years later, Udall noted that Indian jewelry was a rage fifteen years after he wore that buckle. "In short, I wasn't the rube Larry depicted—although I certainly did have a lot to learn."[7]

Brother Stewart lacked the time to help Udall get adjusted because he was busy learning what it would take to be secretary of the interior. Stewart referred his brother to King, a former newspaper reporter from west Texas, who was the administrative aide to Representative J. T. "Slick" Rutherford, an El Paso Democrat. Mo approached King and said, "My big brother told me that you would show me how to operate." King and Mo hit it off immediately and went on to be longtime friends. At one time King was perhaps Mo's closest friend away from the halls of Congress. Said King: "I took to him. He brought his own people with him and that's probably why Stew steered him to me."[8] King showed him how to organize his office. One of Udall's strengths turned out to be his hiring of staff members. Just as he had in the county attorney's office, Udall hired a young, bright, and hardworking staff.

The first two staff people were Roger K. Lewis, a quiet, low-key man who was administrative assistant, and Richard C. Olson, legislative assistant, executive secretary, and owner of a boisterous laugh. Lewis was a Phi

Beta Kappa, 1952 graduate of the University of Arizona who had been a newspaper reporter in Phoenix and a copy editor in Tucson. He stayed with Udall until the end of 1978, when he took an early retirement.

"Mo and I had a close relationship, but separate relations," Lewis recalled. "In other words, I kind of did my thing and he did his thing, but my thing, of course, was in his name and a lot of things he delegated and trusted me to do and . . . he always kept his finger on what was going on. . . . There was a lot of stuff I didn't bother him with . . . he trusted my judgment. A congressman can't possibly do all the stuff that's expected of him."[9]

Olson, a University of Arizona philosophy graduate, had reported for the *Tucson Daily Citizen* from 1950 to 1955 and then opened a public relations agency. He worked for Stewart Udall during his congressional campaigns and handled media relations for Mo's congressional race in 1961 and three months after Mo was sworn in joined him in his Washington office. Olson remained with Udall for ten years until he took a job as director of information for the Wilderness Society and editor of its magazine, *The Living Wilderness*.[10]

Lewis's responsibility was running the office and meeting district needs while Olson worked on legislation and helped Udall with speech writing. They worked closely and harmoniously.

Terry Bracy, a congressional intern in 1965, joined the staff full-time in 1967. Bracy, an intense, self-confident former TV reporter, became Udall's legislative assistant. Udall was an avid reader, consuming books, newspapers, position papers, whatever helped him reach a position. His staff corresponded with him through memos. "Mo reacted far better to paper than to spoken ideas," Bracy said.[11]

His staff appreciated Udall for his handling of personnel matters. He rarely became involved in their personal affairs, delegated authority with ease, was never condescending, and rarely rebuked staff members.[12] Bonnie C. Kell, a legislative assistant, remembered: "It is not verbalized, but there are certain standards he requires and you know instinctively if you are doing it right or not without any reprimands from him." She said rather than reprimand, he taught how to do it better. Neither did he force his workaholic habits on them, although most worked extremely hard during long hours. Said Bracy: "He cares nothing about staff hours as long as the work is done and the phone is answered. . . . He picks people who are talented and has confidence in letting them do things in their way. He lets the staff organize itself."[13]

John B. Gabusi, who had operated a Tucson-based survey research firm, joined the staff in 1967 and stayed until after the 1976 presidential election. He said Udall ran an unstructured office. "Mo was never that organized," he said. "Everybody knew what he had to do. Once he accepted you as having the talent he expected, then he let you go."[14]

After Udall established his staff, he began learning the names of each of the other 434 House members.[15] He apparently learned that trick from the House doorkeeper, William M. "Fishbait" Miller, who clipped pictures from magazines so he could greet new congressmen properly.[16]

"I carried a little book of names and pictures, and kept it by my bedside," Udall said. "You go up to a guy who's been here a year and call him by name and say, 'I understand you represent Schenectady,' or whatever, and I'd point out something interesting about each person. It pays off. If there's a vote going on and he comes in here and it's my bill, and otherwise the forces are equidistant, pushing him either way, he'd give you the benefit of the doubt because he knows you."[17]

Udall also was trying to find his away around Capitol Hill. He had ventured into the maze of tunnels that connect the Capitol with the House and Senate buildings and had become hopelessly lost. To avoid embarrassment, he asked a Capitol policeman if he could tell him where Congressman Udall's office was. "Sure, Congressman," came the reply. "Your office is down the subway, one turn to the right, and up to the seventh floor." Udall slunk away humiliated. He said he studied a detailed map of the Capitol for six hours before venturing out again.[18]

Speaker Rayburn spotted Udall on his second day on the House floor and invited him to preside briefly during a routine quorum call. Udall was thrilled. Also during his first week, he was invited to the White House with thirty-five other congressmen to get acquainted with President Kennedy.[19] "I remember having stars in my eyes," he said. "I was at the White House . . . and here I am sipping drinks on the portico of the White House with John Kennedy."[20]

Not long after that he wrote Rayburn a detailed letter—Larry L. King called it one of "impossible length and complexity to . . . a man congenitally offended by a single word when grunts or smoke signals might do"[21]—proposing a mechanism for balancing the budget and a review of the seniority system. He closed the letter offering to meet with Rayburn at any time.

Udall said Rayburn "must have found this earnest entreaty both presumptuous and laughable."[22] He never heard from Rayburn. (The authors could find no copies of the letter, even in Rayburn's papers, giving rise to the thought the letter had been trashed.) King said that Udall suffered from the assumption "that he mattered more to Washington than the realities . . . a common freshman malady."[23]

From his first days in Congress, Udall said he was confronted by some of the oldest and most basic questions of representative democracy: "For whom does a legislator vote? Which do I put first, Arizona or the nation? Do I vote my strongly held convictions or those of a majority of my constituents at that point in time?"[24] Answers to those questions would haunt Udall several times during his thirty-year House career, giving rise to incongruities that opponents tried to exploit.

Udall became active in the Democratic Study Group (DSG), taking over for his brother, who was one of the founders, along with Representatives Eugene McCarthy of Minnesota, Lee Metcalf of Montana, Henry S. Reuss of Wisconsin, and Frank Thompson Jr. of New Jersey. The DSG was a loose affiliation of about eighty liberal to moderate congressmen who operated independently of the House leadership.

Two years later, Mo helped to expand the bipartisan seminars for freshmen that his brother and others had started in the 1950s. His purpose was twofold: He wanted to avoid having the freshmen go through a trial-and-error learning process as he had, and he used the seminars to recruit them in his efforts toward House reform. Udall also made it a point to meet newcomers almost as soon as they walked through the door. "Udall was always available to help me, no matter what my problem or what time," said Representative Jonathan B. Bingham of New York.[25] It paid off in political IOUs.

He further made himself visible to incoming representatives when he co-wrote *Job of a Congressman,* a 446-page book published in 1966 on how to set up, staff, and operate a congressional office. It was widely used, perhaps only behind the *Congressional Record* and the House rules, as a guide to surviving those first few months in office.

The respect and goodwill he gained from these new congressmen often translated into crucial votes from Republicans as well as Democrats.

Udall's first two assignments were on the Post Office and Civil

Service Committee and the Interior and Insular Affairs Committee. It would seem logical that Udall would seek a seat on the Judiciary Committee because he was a lawyer. Judiciary was headed by Democrat Howard W. Smith of Virginia, perhaps the most ruthless chairman of all. What could Udall accomplish there? Besides, there were no vacancies.[26] He took the seat on the Post Office Committee because that was all that was available to the congressman with the least seniority in the House. Udall said one of his colleagues told him, "Hell, boy, you'll be able to put a new post office in every village and hamlet in your district."

"And I did," Udall said.[27] Udall's 1964 Republican opponent for the congressional seat remembered how that had helped Mo. William E. Kimble, a Tucson lawyer, was campaigning when he visited the Wellton-Mohawk Republican Women's Club in western Arizona near Yuma. It was at the end of a hot, tiring day and Kimble was in a bad mood. He walked into the meeting to find four women awaiting him. They told Kimble: "We really like Mr. Udall. He's a nice man and he got us a nice, new post office." Kimble was livid. "You're talking about a goddamn post office and I'm talking about the future of the country," he told the women.[28]

Udall took a seat on the Interior Committee because he thought he might be helpful to Arizona's chances to get the long-sought Central Arizona Project, an ambitious plan to deliver Colorado River water to the rapidly growing desert cities of Phoenix and Tucson. One of Udall's strengths was to turn a bad situation to an advantage. He used his position on both committees to help reform the seniority system and to advance projects he supported, namely bringing water to the Arizona desert and to restructure the postal system.

Udall chafed under the seniority system that had ruled the House since 1911, when it was adopted to remove power from tyrannical House leaders. When Udall arrived in Washington, no serious challenge to the system had been undertaken in twenty years. "Most congressmen, it appeared to me, seemed content to tolerate a process that rewarded longevity, not merit—and thus ensured mediocrity," he wrote.[29] That would change and Udall would be at the forefront through efforts of the Democratic Study Group.

Three weeks after he was sworn in, Udall sat down and wrote a letter home, a newsletter that he felt was an important means of communicating with his constituents, who were spread throughout Arizona. In

1960, Arizona had two congressional districts. The other one was represented by Republican John Rhodes, and it encompassed Maricopa County, where half of the state's population resided. Udall's district surrounded Rhodes's district much like a doughnut surrounds a hole. It included all of Arizona's thirteen other counties.

Udall called his first newsletter "my first groping experience." The chatty, personal newsletter reached a relatively small audience of Arizona newspapers and several hundred friends and campaign workers.[30] It briefly described his struggles with learning the system and some of the memorable events he had participated in.

The newsletters evolved almost through trial and error. Looking back, Udall said in 1972 that while he was on target on a number of them, sometimes they showed that "my foresight was something less than perfect—it ranged, in fact, from superb to atrocious."[31]

In 1962, Udall was offered a newly created federal judgeship in Arizona. The offer was tempting because Mo's wife, Pat, was unhappy with Washington—she disliked politics—and wanted her husband to stay in the West. What more could he want? He earlier had wanted to be a judge and it would make his family happy. So when Senator Hayden, his colleague from Arizona, called to see if he was interested, he could not very well ignore him.

"I was kind of stunned because we had just moved to Washington and I was starting a congressional career and it was all quite exciting and here was the prospect of a lifetime federal appointment," Udall said.[32] He thought to himself that if he had been offered the judgeship anytime in the previous ten years he would have jumped at it.

He said he talked with his wife and brother Stewart before deciding against taking the judgeship. Pat Udall was enthusiastic about it, Olson said. He wrote several memos to Udall and Pat, arguing that Mo Udall should wait for a seat on the U.S. Supreme Court.[33]

Udall said his "feeling was that a congressional career offered some interesting prospects—the Senate maybe—no one knew what was going to happen in '64." He said he told Hayden his decision and as he walked away from Hayden's office he shook his head, thinking, "You damn fool, someday you're really going to regret this." He returned to his office, poured himself a drink, and asked himself how many of his lawyer friends would even have a chance to turn down a federal judgeship.[34]

In 1963, talk indeed turned to the Senate seat held by Barry Goldwater, who was pursuing the 1964 Republican nomination for president. If Goldwater won the nomination, his seat would be vacant. He had said he would not seek the presidency and run for the Senate at the same time, as Lyndon Johnson did when he sought the vice presidency and his Senate seat in 1960. Udall's wife, Pat, opposed his running. "She felt I needed more seasoning in the House and this wasn't the time to go," he said. "It was tougher and tougher for Democrats to win elections in statewide races."[35] Nonetheless, Udall made fairly frequent appearances in Phoenix, which was outside his congressional district.

Udall also had his sights set on a leadership role in the House. He was building a following among the young liberals and believed if he stayed put he could eventually work his way up to Speaker. "There was a serious question whether I should gamble what I felt was a very good career and a lot of good things going in the House on what, at best, was a long shot for the Senate."[36] Udall also noted that Hayden aide Roy Elson badly wanted Goldwater's seat—with Hayden's blessings—and that he, Udall, feared a bloody party primary. Even if Udall won the primary, he probably would have had to face Republican Paul Fannin, the state's popular governor. Udall believed he could have beaten Fannin, "but [that's] something I'll never know."[37]

There was no guarantee Goldwater would win the nomination. If he came up short, he would return to Arizona to seek reelection to the Senate. Mo felt there were four reasons for not running against Goldwater: He loved the House of Representatives; his wife was against it; the conservative Phoenix newspapers would tear him up; and, "besides, I've taken a poll, and Barry Goldwater beats the hell out of me."[38] But the polls also showed that Morris and Stewart were the favorites among Democratic candidates to take on Goldwater, who the polls said could beat any opponent.

Udall won another term in the House, worked hard, and began to shine. As friend Larry L. King noted, "He slowly earned laurels as a serious legislator and witty speaker who knew the parliamentary backwaters. If perhaps a shade bright or a touch more ambitious than the average junior, he was not yet atypical; he paid deference to his elders and kept his institutional nose clean."[39] Not for long.

A RISING STAR

o Udall got his first break in a leadership role during the 88th Congress. It was on an issue important to him: the Civil Rights Act of 1964. Because southern lawmakers opposed the legislation and Representative Hale Boggs of Louisiana was the party whip, the Democratic Study Group managed the bill. Udall, a rising star, was chosen as the whip for northern and western members.

Civil rights legislation was a major plank in the Democrats' platform, and on June 19, 1963, President Kennedy had asked Congress to pass the most far-reaching and comprehensive civil rights bill in the nation's history. In a July 29 newsletter to constituents, Udall told them he favored the general objectives on voting rights, public accommodations, school desegregation, use of federal funds, and job opportunities. Kennedy was assassinated on November 22, but Lyndon Johnson carried forth the legislation as part of his Great Society.

Udall said that although Arizona had made some strides to end racial discrimination, they were too few. The real problem, he said, was not the exclusion of blacks from restaurants and hotels, but job discrimination. He pointed out that federal legislation was needed because states had "failed to meet their responsibilities." Noting that only 3 percent of Arizona's population was black, Mo said, "One might say there is no political mileage in the civil rights issue in our state."[1] Udall was doing it because he believed it was right, not because it gave him any political advantage.

During the next two races for reelection he had to answer to charges that he spoke one way in Tucson but voted another way in Washington, D.C. The issue was brought up during the 1962 race by his Republican opponent, Richard K. Burke, a University of Arizona political science professor, who accused him of being a "captive of the [Kennedy administration's] New Frontier."[2]

In a letter to William A. Small Jr., publisher of the *Tucson Daily Citizen,* Udall wrote: "I don't like hypocrites. If this charge is true, I am one." But, he said, Republican opponents had never been able to provide any proof where he had voted contrary to his public statements. He said that during his first two years he and Arizona's other representative, conservative John Rhodes, had voted the same way 55 percent of the time. "Either he is a fifty-five percent socialist, welfare-state spender, or I am a fifty-five percent real genuine conservative."[3] Udall went on to defeat Burke 64,510 votes to 46,219.

Two years later, the charges were brought up again, this time by Republican William Kimble, the Tucson lawyer and a former Cochise County superior court judge. Kimble's campaign ran ads that asked: "Will the real Mo Udall stand up?" He suggested that Udall "talked conservative and voted liberal."

Election night Kimble and Udall went to the *Arizona Daily Star* office for interviews. Kimble, who was certain that he had lost the race, wore one of Udall's "MO" buttons turned upside down to say "OW." It was a gesture that Udall himself would use at least twice in his career after a painful loss. Udall outpolled Kimble 86,499 to 60,782. Kimble got the message. He dropped out of elective politics himself but returned in 1982 as chairman of Udall's reelection campaign.[4]

For Mo Udall, 1965 was a breakout year. He was deeply involved in promoting the Central Arizona Project, the mammoth project to divert Colorado River water to central and southern Arizona.

He also was good at bringing federal dollars to Arizona. Udall's district was the recipient of millions of dollars in defense spending because of military bases at Fort Huachuca Army Base and Davis-Monthan Air Force Base and an army proving grounds in Yuma. In 1971, for example, the total federal defense expenditure in the Second District was $348.9 million, or about $625 a person as compared to the national average of $285 a person. The total federal outlay for the district was

$731.5 million, or about $1,310 a person as compared to the national average of $1,010.[5]

House members were beginning to recognize that Udall had the traits necessary for good legislative work. His law training allowed him to pay attention to detail, he was patient enough to listen to varying points of view and reach a compromise, and he was a hard worker.

Mo Udall had it in for the Marlboro man almost from the day he stepped onto the House floor. He was against smoking but rarely was he in his office when he was without an unlit cigar clamped between his teeth. He would chomp on it while thinking or during office discussions. He kept a spittoon next to his desk. "It was truly gross," said former aide John Gabusi.[6] He avoided being seen in public with the cigar, an act that might have been seen as flouting the Mormon church, which prohibits the use of tobacco, alcohol, and coffee.

He and seven other congressmen urged President Johnson to veto a bill that required a warning label on cigarette packages that smoking can be a health hazard. They said the bill was too weak. The Senate had passed the bill 72–5 and the House approved it 286–103. Others who joined Udall in the July 16, 1965, letter to the president were Senators Robert F. Kennedy of New York and Gaylord Nelson of Wisconsin and Representatives Richard Bolling of Missouri and John E. Moss of California. The letter said the warning label, "instead of protecting the health of the American people, protects only the cigarette industry." They pointed out that the cigarette industry itself admitted that the labeling requirement would have little or no effect on cigarette use. Nonetheless, the president signed the bill without comment.[7]

Udall went so far as to send out a questionnaire in which he asked constituents what they thought of limiting beer, wine, and tobacco advertising on television until children were in bed. Udall said he received a letter from a West Coast advertising man that suggested children needed protection all right—from congressmen like Udall.[8]

In 1965, Udall was named to the Public Land Law Review Commission, an appointment that took him around the country for hearings about how public land was being used and how it should be used. It provided Udall with an invaluable insight when in subsequent years he sought legislation to protect millions of acres of wilderness, set aside scenic Alaska lands, create strip-mining laws, and unsuccessfully seek a change in the Mining Act of 1872. Through his service on the commission, he also saw the value of compromising to achieve environmental goals.

The nineteen-member commission, chaired by Representative Wayne N. Aspinall of Colorado, spent five years and $7 million compiling a report that made 130 recommendations for ways to use 770 million acres of federal land. At the commission's urging, legislation was introduced in Congress in early 1972 that was designed to give the federal government more control over use of private lands and a comprehensive charter for managing public land. Udall played an active role in bringing about compromises that would appease the Nixon administration and environmentalists. The environmentalists sought to lock up the land from development while the administration wanted fewer controls over private land and greater use of public land. Both initially were taking an all-or-nothing approach, which, without compromise, could lead to no law at all.

The bill passed but only after Udall told environmentalists: "You have to weigh what you're going to lose if this bill is defeated. You're going to lose the good things in the bill, particularly the land-use section. I think we have to go with what we can get now and work for changes later on." He urged environmentalists not to fight the bill. "They really haven't taken an objective viewpoint."[9] It was classic Udall: Giving a little was better than getting nothing at all. It was a strategy he would use later to win passage of the Alaska Lands Act, which set aside more than 100 million acres of Alaska wilderness.

Also in mid-1965 Udall joined a long list of members of Congress who sponsored bills on population control, saying the world was confronted with a "population revolution, diluting the effects of economic progress, creating new problems of housing, food, welfare, education, and employment."[10] Udall's bill would have created the federal Offices of Population Problems and authorized a White House Conference on Population in 1967. It was one of those incongruities. Here was Udall, who had five brothers and sisters and six children of his own, urging birth control on others. But as he saw it, "The time is rapidly approaching when a large family, whatever its comforts to the home or ego, may be a disaster to the community, the nation and the world."[11] He said every family with two or more children should make a voluntary decision to have no more.

One of the sponsors of the population control legislation was Democratic senator Ernest Gruening of Alaska, who Udall said talked him into being a co-sponsor. Udall wrote to Gruening that he would do so despite having a large Catholic constituency. "I introduced your bill today," Udall wrote to Gruening. "I hope you find me a job when I lose this one." Gruening returned the letter with a handwritten note on the bottom that said, "Dear Mo: Leaders are often alone."[12]

Representative Jerome R. Waldie of California called Udall "the bravest man in Washington" when he introduced him to his aide Robert A. Neuman in a Washington, D.C., airport. "He has sponsored a population control bill and has six children," Waldie said.[13]

In early 1965, Udall was selected as secretary of the Democratic Study Group, whose 165 members made up a majority of the Democratic members of the House. It was the first time since it was organized in 1959 that the group included a majority of the Democrats. It also chose Udall as its whip. He would again be asked to marshal the vote. None was more important to the DSG than the Voting Rights Act of 1965. Again the responsibility fell on northern and western lawmakers to muster support for what was the most comprehensive voting rights legislation in ninety-five years. The bipartisan bill proposed putting an end to literacy tests in order to vote. Again southerners opposed the bill.

The bill proved a little stickier for Udall than the civil rights legislation because his home county, Apache County, was singled out by Attorney General Nicholas deB. Katzenbach as one of the few areas outside the South that required a literacy test to vote. Along with Apache County, seven southern states, Alaska, and one county in Idaho required the test. Udall strongly supported the bill, surely remembering his father's court decision that gave Indians the right to vote. The bill brought opposition from Apache County officials, including boyhood friend Dick Greer, then the county attorney. Greer noted that the county had a population of 36,000, of which 25,000 were Navajos and Apaches. If they voted regardless of whether they could read or write, they would outnumber others by a 2½ to 1 margin, Greer said. The bill was signed into law by President Johnson on August 6.

In early 1964, Pat Udall, suffering from rheumatoid arthritis, moved back to Arizona, telling her husband that she did not know whether she would return to Washington. Udall visited Tucson during congressional breaks. When he arrived in September 1965, Pat told him she wanted a divorce. "It was quite a blow," he said, "but I had seen that it was bad on the kids and bad on me. It was a strain for both of us, so I didn't argue with her very much."[14]

The divorce became final in January 1966, and Udall remained single until December 1968 when he married Ella Royston Ward, a secretary of the postal subcommittee that Udall chaired. It was Ella who helped change Mo's appearance from western hick to suave Washington insider. He exchanged the bow tie and Indian jewelry for business suits and long ties. He let his buzz cut grow out to a stylish swept-back look. He now looked more like what people thought a congressman should look like.

In 1967, Udall was complaining about the high cost of being a congressman—from running for reelection to operating his office. "The name of the game is money and the ability to raise it," he said.[15] Money, he said, was corrupting people in public life and giving unnecessary influence and power to special-interest groups and lobbies. That power, he said, was a serious threat to the American political institution.

He deplored the rising costs of conducting campaigns and the influence of public relations and advertising people, who put forth a packaged candidate sold like "a new laxative or detergent." He complained about campaigns that poll voters to find out what voters want rather than what they need. It was like "polling high school students," he said, "to learn which courses are easiest and most fun, then drafting the curriculum accordingly."[16]

Name recognition was the name of the game, he said, with individuals like Olympic decathlon winner Bob Mathias and Hollywood actor George Murphy, both Republicans, winning public office, not so much because of their stands, but because people knew their names. Udall complained about the costs that he said he had to pay from his salary for trips home, district office expenses, public information, and the like. He had been the sponsor of a bill to raise congressional salaries from $22,000 to $30,000, which, of course, endeared him to his colleagues. Low salaries, he said, forced lawmakers to seek outside income. "We need to end the practice of law by members [of Congress] and involvement in outside businesses to the highest extent possible," he said.[17]

Even though Udall was getting along okay on his new congressional salary, congressmen were not the fat cats the press said they were, he said. Udall introduced legislation that would limit campaign costs, provide federal funds for campaigns, require public disclosure of expenditures and contributions, require free radio and television time for candidates, establish a short general election campaign, write a congressional code of ethics, and require members to file income statements. Adopting his legislation, he said, "could breathe new life into American politics and recapture our political system from the moneychangers."[18]

Many members of Congress were outraged over his proposal to divulge personal finances, he said. He noted that he and six other congressmen had voluntarily made those disclosures in January 1964. "Yet most members continue to vote on legislation vitally affecting personal business interests the public doesn't know they have."[19] Three years later, on January 10, 1967, the number of public disclosures had increased to twenty-seven.

Udall revealed that 80 percent of his income came from his congressional salary. The remainder, he said, came from honorariums, dividends, other investment income, royalties from sales of his law book, and payment of one or two old legal fees only then collected. He also said he owned a 1965 Mustang automobile and a 1966 Piper Cherokee airplane, on which he owed $10,000, and had cash, notes collectible, and other assets worth $15,000. "It's not particularly pleasant to lay your personal affairs before the public," he said, "but I feel better having done it—first-class in fact."[20]

He said he divulged his holdings because "I believe that the people I represent are entitled to know of any conflicts of interest which may exist with respect to matters coming before me as their congressman. And I believe they have a right to know if my personal fortunes somehow advance while I am holding public office."[21] Indeed, twenty years later, in 1987, Udall disclosed that he had $1.2 million in personal assets including stocks, real estate holdings, and savings accounts. He reported an income of $182,871, including his $89,500 congressional salary.

In a 1967 *Playboy* article, Udall attacked the Corrupt Practices Act of 1925 as a farce. He said loopholes left little accountability for expenditures, particularly on printing, postage, telephone, and travel. "That is like telling your wife that her use of the department-store charge account is limited to $100 per month except for hats, dresses, fur coats, and shoes—on which there is no limit."[22]

It took four years for Congress to pass campaign finance reform. Udall helped draft the Federal Elections Campaign Act of 1971, the first major revision of campaign finance laws since 1925. Candidates were required to report on the money they raised and spent, and they were restricted in the amount that could be used for political advertising. The law was credited with helping to expose the Watergate scandal in 1973.[23]

After the scandal broke, Udall and others, including Representative John B. Anderson of Illinois, who chaired the Republican Conference, agreed that the 1971 law did not go far enough. They drafted the Clean Elections Act of 1974. It provided that the government would finance congressional and presidential campaign costs. "Surely today," Udall said, "the American people are ready to put up a dollar or two a year to have a clean, decent, brand-new system of House and Senate [publicly funded] elections in this country." The proposal for congressional funding failed, but one authorizing matching funds for presidential candidates passed. Udall would take advantage of that when he sought the Democratic nomination for president the next year.[24]

One of Udall's House votes in 1965 would cause him no end of trouble, particularly during his bid for House leadership roles and his 1976 presidential bid.

He voted against repealing Section 14(b) of the Taft-Hartley Act, which permitted states to enact right-to-work laws that banned compulsory union membership as a requirement for employment in industries where unions were represented. His vote came despite enormous pressure from the White House and organized labor. It was a difficult decision philosophically for the liberal Democrat, but politically he had little choice. Three times—the last in 1950—Arizona voters by large margins had turned away efforts to eliminate right-to-work laws. He said that although he never supported right-to-work laws, his constituents voted overwhelmingly for them. It would have been political suicide to vote to repeal Section 14(b). Fellow Arizona Democrat George F. "Duke" Senner voted for repeal and was turned out of office at the next election. Udall's vote against labor cost him dearly later on.

One of Udall's House colleagues, Democrat Henry Reuss of Wisconsin, remarked years later, "If it kept him in office, I'll forgive him."[25] Said Evelyn Dubrow, then a lobbyist for the International Ladies' Garment Workers Union: "We all understood why" Udall voted against repeal, "but if we were to keep everybody else's feet to the fire, we couldn't let Mo go. The labor movement was intransigent on the right to work . . . anyone who voted for it would be in trouble. That was the only time labor was annoyed with Mo."[26] It was a long-standing annoyance among some unions, despite the fact he voted with labor 80 percent of the time.[27]

On July 28, 1965, the House voted 221–203 for repeal, but the bill died in the Senate. Arizona today remains a right-to-work state. Nonetheless, the Committee on Political Education, the political arm of the AFL-CIO, gave his campaign $1,000 and endorsed Udall's reelection in 1966 over the Republican candidate, businessman G. Alfred McGinnis. Udall beat McGinnis 66,813 to 45,326 and two years later defeated him again 102,301 to 43,235.

Udall also became an active participant in Members of Congress for Peace through Law (MCPL), a low-profile organization designed "to coordinate Congressional concern for world peace into specific action."[28] The group was formally organized in 1966, growing out of a small cast of senators and representatives who met informally in a luncheon group dating to 1959. Early members included Republican senator Jacob K. Javits of New York and Democratic representative Robert W. Kastenmeier of Wisconsin. By 1970, the group had 116 members, 29 senators and 87 representatives. Udall said the organization offered "a place where Members of Congress don't feel they'll be chopped up by partisanship" when speaking.[29]

Given its liberal foreign policy orientation, the Members of Congress for Peace through Law provided a natural meeting ground for congressional critics of U.S. policy in Southeast Asia. Its main function was to provide an information clearinghouse for members of Congress and citizens' groups working to end the Vietnam War.[30] As Udall's opposition to the war began to grow in 1965 and 1966, he would draw more and more on the organization to help him formulate his views.

Some of Udall's closest colleagues were those Democrats who were ardent members of MCPL and the Democratic Study Group—people like

Phillip Burton of California, Thomas S. Foley of Washington, Lloyd Meeds of Washington, Abner J. Mikva of Illinois, George E. Brown Jr. of California, and Kastenmeier. They became part of a poker group that met regularly for about ten years, usually at the home of either Kastenmeier or Burton.

Foley described Udall as a "steadier, more cautious, more careful, more traditional, good poker player." Burton, who was known as a "bomb thrower" in his congressional policies, was more of the "swashbuckling" poker player. He was an "outrageous bluffer," Foley said. Once, Foley said, the betting got out of hand, with about $2,000 in the pot. He said they came to their senses when they realized that someone could get hurt financially or that others might have some heavy explaining to do to their wives. They also worried about creating ill feelings among themselves. After that, the group put limits on bets.[31]

In late 1970, Udall endeared himself to a great many of his colleagues by steering through the House a $9,000-a-year congressional pay raise. It allowed members the option of using the funds to hire more staff, instead of fattening their paychecks.[32] Udall often carried unpopular causes. "He was always the point guy on these chickenshit ideas that other House members ran away from," said aide John Gabusi. "He created mechanisms on little things that were getting the members in trouble at home. He knew they'd owe him. It was part of the dynamics."[33]

While there may have been calculated efforts to line up IOUs, Udall had no trouble supporting legislation that might turn some congressmen against him if he believed the legislation was the right thing to do. The Postal Reorganization Act of 1971 was a case in point. He aligned himself with the Nixon administration, which asked Udall to sponsor the legislation because it was wary of other members of the postal committee who had heavy union and party support. The administration wanted to take patronage out of the post office. Udall agreed because he believed that the postal system was in danger of collapse under the weight of congressional patronage.[34] "There was an undercurrent of resentment on both sides of the aisle against taking jurisdiction away from Congress," said Representative Edward J. Derwinski, a Republican from Illinois.[35]

In addition, the legislation brought labor's ire because it threatened job security and the right to negotiate union shops within a new independent postal corporation and its 750,000 union members. In the end, the unions won a 5.4 percent pay raise, a compression from twenty-one years to eight years of the time required to reach full seniority pay, and collective bargaining, but with no power to strike.[36]

Gabusi, who was the principal staff person for the legislation in the House, said Udall made no friends among the unions "because he minimized [their] point of view. At the end of the day, Mo was not their champion. He didn't think what they sought was good public policy."[37] Again, his stand would cost him down the road.

The new postal service turned out to be anything but a success. By the fall of 1975, it had lost $2.9 billion over the preceding three years. A movement began in Congress to revoke its financial independence and require yearly appropriations requests. Udall blamed the Nixon administration for the problems, but agreed the postal service needed another restructuring. Despite the early troubling problems, the changes led to today's independent postal system.

Udall managed to find time to poke a little humor at the postal service as well. When asked how he would control inflation, he remarked, "Maybe we ought to turn it over to the post office. They may not stop it, but they'll damn well slow it down."[38]

The 1960s and early 1970s found Udall in a situation that seemed to contradict a philosophy that generally argued against monopolies and bigness. Again, it centered on constituent interest, this time that of the two family-owned daily newspapers in Tucson. He co-sponsored legislation that would allow the morning *Arizona Daily Star* and the afternoon *Tucson Daily Citizen* to continue in an agreement that fixed prices, pooled profits, and created a monopoly in the market.

The *Star,* considered a Democratic newspaper, and the *Citizen,* which was strongly Republican, had entered into an agreement in 1940 in which they maintained independent news and editorial functions but jointly operated the advertising, circulation, general business, and production departments. Without the agreement, competition might have driven one of the papers out of business, they contended.

The Justice Department had been investigating the Tucson agreement and twenty-one other such arrangements for possible antitrust violations. Justice Department attorneys decided to make Tucson the test case when the *Citizen* owners purchased the *Star* in 1965. Almost immediately, Senator Carl Hayden, the Arizona Democrat who chaired the Appropriations Committee, introduced the Failing Newspaper Act, which was designed to legalize their illegal acts. The bill went nowhere. Then U.S. district court judge James A. Walsh ruled that the agreements were indeed violations of the Sherman and Clayton antitrust acts. Udall and 107 others revived Hayden's bill, this time calling it the Newspaper Preservation Act. It authorized joint operations if one newspaper was in "probable danger of financial failure," and used a grandfather clause to legalize the previously illegal arrangements.

"The most compelling reason I support this bill," Udall said, "is that I fear a single editorial voice in a city the size of Tucson more than I fear the disadvantages that arise from merging the commercial operations of two newspapers but maintaining separate editorial voices." He said modern newspaper economics ruled out heavy competition and noted that the trend in larger cities was toward a single newspaper. "I believe that runs against the very basis of a free society," he said, and "therefore, I support, as a compromise, the arrangement that maintains separate, private editorial voices."[39] He also might have had a more practical reason. As he was to say years later, "Nobody likes to take on your friendly editor in a business where an endorsement can make a difference."[40]

The bill languished until March 10, 1969, when the U.S. Supreme Court upheld the lower court finding against the Tucson newspaper agreement. Immediately, the newspaper publishers of America saw a common interest and flexed their muscles. In September, Richard Berlin, president of the Hearst Corporation, went to see Richard Nixon, who had continued the Johnson administration's war against mini-monopolies. A couple of days later, the Commerce Department gave a surprise endorsement to the bill. With White House opposition removed, the Newspaper Preservation Act sailed through Congress, and Nixon signed it into law on July 8, 1970.

The *Star* and *Citizen*'s joint operating agreement was grandfathered in under the new law. Was the *Citizen* grateful? The newspaper, which had supported Udall, decided that he was no longer fit for office and endorsed his Republican opponent, dentist Eugene Savoie, during the 1972 election.

Meanwhile, the *Star* had been sold to the Pulitzer family of St. Louis in 1971, and six years later the *Citizen* was purchased by Gannett Newspapers, the nation's largest chain. Interestingly, the two papers maintained almost equal circulation figures—about 43,000 each—at the time of the Pulitzer purchase, but at the start of the year 2000, the *Star's* circulation was more than double that of the *Citizen,* 113,000 to 44,000.

In 1978, Gannett purchased Combined Communications Corporation, which owned two major dailies, seven television stations, thirteen radio stations, and outdoor advertising. Udall called the merger "a case of a whale swallowing a whale."[41]

Udall maintained an interest in family-owned newspapers and in 1977 introduced the Independent Local Newspaper Act, which he said would help newspapers stay out of the hands of chains. It would have authorized weekly or daily newspapers not owned by chains to establish trusts that would finance future estate tax liabilities from current newspaper profits. He was unable to gather sufficient support and abandoned the effort in 1986.

Udall worried about media concentration, especially with newspapers, throughout his time in Congress. Even though he gave up on his plan to save independent ownership, he spoke out repeatedly against the dangers of centralized ownership and the emphasis on the bottom line. "A newspaper is not just another grubby way to make a buck," he once said. "You lose something when you go the conglomerate route."[42]

On another occasion, Udall remarked: "Today, what the titans of the chains want is profits—not power—just money. I fear that the quest for profits and higher dividends for their growing list of stockholders will transcend their responsibility to maintain an independent and dedicated influence in the community. As the diversity of the American newspaper is lost—so is the diversity of America."[43]

In 1972, Udall published a new book, *Education of a Congressman: The Newsletters of Morris K. Udall,* edited by Robert L. Peabody. It was 384 pages and included twenty-three newsletters, a reprint of a *Harper's* magazine article about his run for majority leader of the House, and a look back at his years in Congress.

He took an occasion in 1971 in a lengthy interview with James E. Cook of *Arizona* magazine to reflect on how he operated during his ten years in office:

> Every man has his own philosophy of office. Some of the fellows here, their goal is simply to get re-elected. . . . I'm here

because I believe in some things and because I want to leave a mark and depart with the feeling that I have changed policy, shaped the directions of the nation. A congressman can be a teacher as well as simply a weathervane holding up a finger every week to see which way the wind is blowing and then voting accordingly.

I think most people's philosophy is, "Look, we can't be in Congress every day, we can't study public policy. Let's pick someone who's intelligent, who has good judgment, and let's send him to study the questions. Let him tell us what he thinks is right, then let's have a discussion about it and see if he can't convince us." The people of Arizona have let me be independent. Occasionally I'm wrong, but I think most of the time when I've been out ahead I've been right and history and public opinion have confirmed me.[44]

Udall concluded the interview by stating that he had every reason to believe that Senator Edmund S. Muskie of Maine would win the presidency and he might be appointed to his administration. "I've found that you just play the cards fate deals you, and I don't know where I go from here. I'm going to finish up this term and probably run for another term and see what happens."[45]

What happened was that the Democrats lost the presidency and Udall served those two more terms and then set his sights on the big prize: the presidency in 1976.

CAUGHT ON A TREADMILL

In the late 1960s, Mo Udall took two courageous steps concerning the Vietnam War, one that brought him considerable attention, the other in which he shunned the spotlight. The first was his break with the Johnson administration over the war; the second was to help reveal the massacre of at least 100 civilians by U.S. soldiers at My Lai.

In 1967, the nation was beginning to be torn apart by the Vietnam War. For Udall, who long had harbored doubts whether the United States should be involved in Southeast Asia, the time had come. No longer could he stand idly by and watch more and more American soldiers being killed.

He had long been torn between his loyalty to a Democratic administration and his doubts. His public stance since the time he had been elected to Congress was to support the administration's efforts to contain Communism in Southeast Asia. Personally he was uncertain of that U.S. role. His staff, particularly administrative assistant Roger Lewis, was becoming more adamant that the war was wrong.

Udall had supported the U.S. efforts in Vietnam from the day he first ran for Congress, but his position began to change as the war escalated. A congressional hearing in Tucson on October 10, 1966, changed his mind on the war. Udall and Congressman Edward R. Roybal, a California Democrat, scheduled an informal congressional hearing at the Pioneer Hotel in downtown Tucson. "I don't intend for it to be a political event. I hope to provoke a discussion. . . . It is kind of an experimental thing . . . I am pioneering a little bit."[1]

That hearing, Udall would say later, turned him against the war and toward a break with President Johnson. "I will say that this day of hearings had a profound effect upon me," Udall said in a preface to the more than 200 pages of testimony released June 1, 1967. "It is one thing to read the newspapers and the mail from your constituents; it is another to talk to people face to face and probe their thinking."[2] Udall sent a copy of the testimony to the White House. About 150 people attended the hearing. Thirty people spoke, including thirteen University of Arizona professors who opposed the war. Udall said he was disappointed that more people did not show up to support the administration's moves in Vietnam.[3]

In March 1967, Udall wavered even more. He voted for a supplemental Vietnam appropriation before the House, but said, "I am not very happy about it. I am unhappy because we are involved in this war at all. As far as I am concerned, it is the wrong war in the wrong place at the wrong time." The nation, he said, was caught on a treadmill "and sometimes I think we have no interest in getting off." Despite his unhappiness, he said: "I see no alternative to hanging on until a decent peace can be arranged."[4]

At the same time, Udall was worried about undercutting or embarrassing his brother Stewart, who was in President Johnson's cabinet as secretary of the interior. He also wondered whether he would be committing "political suicide" by coming out against the war because of the hawkish mood in Arizona. Every time he came close to opposing the war, briefings by Johnson, Secretary of State Dean Rusk, and Secretary of Defense Robert S. McNamara "would temporarily quiet my doubts."[5]

Udall also was beginning to rebel against President Johnson's policy of trying to maintain guns and butter, that is, fight a war overseas while trying to combat poverty and social ills at home. "This is nonsense," Udall said. "In the past two years, I have seen the great promise of the war on poverty shrivel and nearly die. . . . The conduct of this war disturbs me greatly. In casting my vote to keep it going—a vote I find necessary if our nation is not to be greatly imperiled—I simply want it understood I am not lending my unequivocal support to the policies requiring that expenditure."[6]

In mid-1967, Udall made up his mind. He knew he could no longer maintain his silence. He began the first draft of a speech that would call for the deescalation of U.S. involvement in Vietnam. He worked on the speech for three months with the help of legislative assistant Richard Olson. Udall wrote out thirty pages and Olson helped edit it. The final version was twelve pages.

When interviewed in late September by the *Christian Science Monitor*—one of 205 congressmen polled—Udall let it be known he no longer supported the manner in which the war was being conducted. He urged a halt to the bombing, enclaves for U.S. forces, and efforts to negotiate an end to the war.

Udall said that when he first went to Congress he made commitments to himself to make the tough, unpleasant decisions as they came, to speak out when being silent might be easier, to admit his mistakes, and to advocate new policies when old ones had failed. "These are noble sentiments, easier to espouse than to follow," he said. In this case, he was true to his commitment.[7]

Udall and his brother Stewart had been talking for some time about the war, so it was no surprise to Stewart when Mo told him he was going to give a speech withdrawing his support of the Vietnam War. Udall was to speak on October 22 at the Sunday Evening Forum, a popular event in Tucson held at the University of Arizona auditorium. "We had discussed the issue several times and I shared many of his conclusions," Stewart Udall said. Stewart was concerned that if Johnson learned about the speech too far ahead of time, the president would demand that he try to dissuade his brother. So Stewart suggested that Morris withhold publicity until after he delivered the speech.[8]

Although Udall heeded his brother's advice, four days before the speech he had a copy delivered to the White House. Udall enclosed a letter to Johnson, telling him he was a loyal Democrat who admired the president's "exceptional leadership" and accomplishments. He told Johnson it was painful for him to write the letter "containing a message I am sorry to have to send. After many months of careful and responsible deliberation, I have reluctantly but firmly concluded that our Vietnam policies are unwise and should be substantially modified." He told the president he would express his views that Sunday.[9] He also put it into the mail to his constituents two days later so that it would arrive not long after the speech. That assured there would be no turning back should he get cold feet.

President Johnson's staff wasted no time analyzing the speech. In a memo to Johnson the day before the speech, aide Walter W. Rostow called it "the most politically effective statement I have yet seen for a policy of unilateral de-escalation plus enclave, because he makes it personal and apparently—perhaps truly—sincere." But, Rostow said, Udall's speech was based on "factually false assumptions and arguments."[10] He said that Udall was wrong in saying that casualties were mounting. He said that during May 1967 there were 1,233 U.S. soldiers killed but in September the number killed had dropped to 775. What effect the memo had or what action Johnson might have taken is unknown. Of the 500,000 U.S. troops in Vietnam, 9,353 had died during 1967 as the war escalated. By war's end, 47,369 had been killed in battle.

After the speech arrived at the White House, Udall received offers of a personal briefing by Rusk and calls from presidential aide McGeorge Bundy while he was still in Washington. He turned them down. The next day he caught a plane to Tucson.

As he was getting dressed to go to the auditorium on Sunday night, he received a long-distance telephone call from Undersecretary of State Nicholas Katzenbach with a final administration appeal.[11] Katzenbach told him the president had read the speech and wondered whether Udall could deliver some other speech. "Gosh, Nick, I'd like to honor the president's request, but unfortunately it's already in the mail," Udall replied.[12]

Udall called it "one of the most difficult speeches of my career. . . . This was my home turf. . . . As I walked to the podium, however, my mood was more somber than blithe . . . and I knew that my audience . . . was bound to include large numbers of prominent citizens, many of whom would not be pleased by the thrust of my remarks."[13] About 1,700 people were in the auditorium. University of Arizona law school dean Charles Ares, his onetime law partner and friend, introduced Udall. Ares had known the contents of the speech for a week. "I knew he was struggling with it. It was the right thing to do. For him, it was an important thing to do."[14]

Generally, the climate in the country supported the war. Only a handful of representatives and a few senators—Democrats Mike Mans-field of Montana and Frank F. Church III of Idaho, and Republican Charles Percy of Illinois, for example—had expressed doubts about the country's role in Vietnam, but no one had spoken as eloquently as Udall. Most of the country supported the hold-the-line position in the war and rejected the Goldwater policy of winning the war. Udall was going to urge complete withdrawal. "Now I was preparing to join the loonies and peaceniks with a speech that argued that the Vietnam policy embraced by my country, my president, and my party was tragically flawed."[15] He gave the speech on a weekend of anti-Vietnam demonstrations at the Pentagon, which Udall specifically condemned.

He knew that speaking out against the war would alienate him from the president and perhaps hurt his chances to move up in the House leadership. In the back of his mind, he even thought his position could cost him his seat in the moderate-to-conservative district he represented.

He had a copy of the speech before him, but, as he did routinely, he ignored the text and spoke extemporaneously. He knew what he wanted to say. "No way he could deliver it word for word," Olson said. "It was too long. He always spoke from memory . . . he never read speeches or testimony."[16]

The speech's title—"The United States and Vietnam: What Lies Ahead?"—offered no hint that Udall's position had changed. But he wasted little time once he began his speech:

> Tonight I want to talk about war and peace, about presidents, dominoes, commitments, and mistakes. . . . Two years ago, when this country had fewer than fifty thousand men in Viet-nam, I wrote a newsletter defending the president's Vietnam policy and pleading patience and understanding for what he was trying to do. I have thought about that newsletter many times with increasing dismay and doubt as the limited in-volvement I supported has grown into a very large Asian land war with a half-million American troops scattered in jungles and hamlets, fighting an enemy who is everywhere and no-where, seeking to save a country which apparently doesn't want to be saved, with casualties mounting and no end in sight. . . .

Many of the wise old heads in Congress say privately that the best politics in this situation is to remain silent, to fuzz your views . . . to await developments. . . . But I have come here tonight to say as plainly and simply as I can that I was wrong two years ago, and I firmly believe President Johnson's advisers are wrong today. I have listened to all the arguments of the administration and read all the reports available to me, attended all the briefings, heard all the predictions of an eventual end to hostilities, and I still conclude that we're on a mistaken and dangerous road.[17]

Stewart Udall said that of all of his brother's many talents, two of them that he displayed regarding his position on the Vietnam War were his "uncommon ability" to analyze the pros and cons of public issues and the courage to disagree and give the reasons for his dissent.[18] "He was a very good trial lawyer. He could take a weak case and make it into a strong case," Udall said. "He was brilliant in making an argument. When he went home and made that speech, he took all the arguments that President Johnson, Dean Rusk, Robert McNamara, and others were making to justify the Vietnam War policy, went through them one by one, and demolished them. Mo was not daunted by the circumstance that he was a lowly member of the House who lacked access to the national security secrets that supposedly dictated the Vietnam War policy," Stewart said. "He based his analysis on common sense and on his own beliefs about his country's ideals and the appropriate use of U.S. power."[19]

Clearly, it was difficult for Udall to break with the president, although he denied that was his intent, but he made his case eloquently and forcefully. At the end of the speech, he had won them over with his conviction, character, candor, and courage. The audience gave him a standing ovation.

In announcing his position, Udall said: "Waiting for things to happen is not leadership, and steering a safe political course is not the highest order of public service. This speech is not an easy or pleasant task for me." He noted that as late as February of that year he had defended the president in a visit to Cambridge University in England when questioners were highly critical of the U.S. role in Vietnam.

"And let me make clear there is another thing I am not doing," he said. "I am not breaking with President Johnson, either as chief executive or as leader of my party. Nor am I joining that group of anarchists who are marching on Washington, attempting to block the entrance of the Pentagon, counseling defiance of Selective Service, or sending money to the Vietcong."

He urged Johnson to deescalate in Vietnam. "People will vilify you, or accuse you of appeasement," Udall told Johnson. "Countless armchair generals will tell you victory was just around the corner. But in the end I believe the American people will rally behind you when they realize that this decision will strengthen our country and advance its interests." He warned the president that if he ignored the path Udall proposed that the Republicans might seize the White House by doing so. "But I don't think they will give us that kind of option," he said. "I expect their candidate to be a Nixon or a Reagan who promises us even more bombing and more escalation and more likelihood of blundering into World War III."[20]

After the speech, Udall fielded written questions from the audience that Ares selected from those that fit the situation. Ares said he and Udall agreed to plant one question: "Have you talked to your brother about this and does he agree with you?" Mo answered, "No, I have not talked to him and I have no idea whether he agrees with me and I don't think he does."[21] That, of course, was false. The next day, the *Arizona Daily Star* quoted Udall as saying that his brother had tried to talk him out of giving the speech. That, too, was false, Stewart Udall said. "In matters of politics, I am not my brother's keeper, nor is he mine," Mo Udall said.[22]

The speech was reported by virtually every newspaper in the nation. A headline in the *New York Times* said, "Rep. Udall Splits with Administration over War."[23] A week after the speech, Udall's office had received 500 to 600 letters, with those agreeing with his stand running 12 to 1.[24] He said that he received many more than he expected from academics, clergymen, and liberals, all of whom praised him for his courage. He also said he received dozens of letters from conservatives and Republicans who noted they had never voted for Udall but that he was right in his stand on Vietnam.[25]

Udall was proud of the speech and wrote that he hoped to be remembered for it, despite the troubles it caused him. Strong indications exist that it did cost him dearly as he tried to move up in the House leadership, although his stand earned him a solid following among some of the House's younger members.[26]

At the same time, Udall said he did not want to overstate the importance of the speech. "In the great chorus of oratory so characteristic of that time, mine was just another voice," he wrote. "Plainly a number of senators and several of my House colleagues were ahead of me in seeing our error, and in being willing to face the tough decision to speak out."[27]

Udall said that at a White House function the following week, Johnson was cordial and as he often did while trying to make a point, grabbed Udall by the lapels to say he was sorry that he had given the speech, but that he had read "every word" of it. "And I honestly thought he held no animosity and had accepted my break as an act of conscience," Udall wrote. But Johnson did hold grudges and he would retaliate when Udall sought a House leadership post.

Stewart Udall said he never heard from Johnson or other administration officials on the speech, suggesting that the tide was turning against the president, that he knew it, and that he saw no reason to magnify the situation.[28] A few months later, Johnson announced he would not seek reelection.

Udall's worst fears were realized in 1968 when Republican Richard M. Nixon defeated Democrat Hubert H. Humphrey for the presidency and began to escalate the war. In one particularly harsh statement on May 4, 1970, Udall recalled that five years earlier he had acquiesced in the escalation of the Vietnam War. "I assumed the president knew what he was doing. I shall not make that mistake again." He vigorously attacked President Nixon on the floor of Congress for his decision to send troops into Cambodia, calling it "likely to do more to destroy the fabric of our society than any other act of recent years."[29]

In mid-October 1969, Udall was among forty-seven House members who signed a letter supporting antiwar demonstrations across the nation, a contrast to the 1967 speech when he deplored similar protests.

Early one April morning in 1969, administrative assistant Roger Lewis opened the mail in Udall's office to find a photocopy of a three-page letter. It was a particularly well-written letter addressed to "The Congress of the United States" by twenty-three-year-old Ronald L. Ridenhour of

Phoenix, Arizona. What Ridenhour wrote would touch off one of the saddest, most horrific periods of the Vietnam War. Apparently, he sent twenty-four letters to members of Congress and government officials, including the White House. Few, if any, other than Udall, followed up on the letter.

The letter asked for an investigation of the mass slaughter of men, women, and children in the Vietnam village of My Lai, called "Pinkville" by U.S. military forces. Ridenhour said he had heard about Pinkville a year earlier and that he was skeptical, but that he began to hear similar massacre stories from others. He was serving in the army in April 1968 in Vietnam when he heard the first report. He was told that a young second lieutenant by the name of "Kally" machine-gunned dozens of the village people.

"Exactly what did, in fact, occur in the village of 'Pinkville' in March, 1968 I do not know for certain," Ridenhour wrote, "but I am convinced that it was something very black indeed. . . . I hope that you will launch an investigation immediately and keep me informed of your progress. If you cannot, then I don't know what other course of action to take."[30] In more routine cases, letters like Ridenhour's would be sent to the congressman from the district in which he lived. But the letter had such a ring of authenticity to it that Lewis knew it could not be ignored. "It was such a convincing letter that I thought, well, this is something we should look into. It shouldn't just die."[31] He gave it to legislative aide Olson to take home and read overnight. The next day Olson told Lewis, "Roger, we have got to demand an investigation," and they took the letter to Udall.[32]

"The first three paragraphs caught me," Udall said. "I wanted to know more about it."[33] Udall told Lewis to find Ridenhour. Lewis ran him down at Pomona Men's College in California and he appeared satisfied that the college student knew what he was talking about. What Udall learned about Ridenhour was that he was no radical, no peacenik, that he was someone who deeply cared about his country. Ridenhour would say later, "I was in a moral dilemma. I had to decide which was the greatest betrayal—the betrayal of my buddies who told me about it and trusted me, or the betrayal of what America is supposed to stand for. If this country stands for what it says it stands for, there wasn't any choice."[34]

On April 4, Udall sent letters to Secretary of Defense Melvin R. Laird and Representative L. Mendel Rivers, chairman of the House Armed Services Committee, urging that the charges be looked into. Laird also had received Ridenhour's letter and claimed eight months later that he started an investigation ten days before any congressman had asked him to. In fact, he said, it was his action, and no one else's, that led to the probe.[35] Ten days after receiving Udall's letter, Rivers, an outspoken backer of the Vietnam War, advised Udall that he had asked the army for an investigation. The next day, Colonel Raymond T. Reid, chief legislative liaison for the Department of the Army, told Udall that the army was looking into the allegations. Nine days later, Udall received a letter from the army promising a thorough probe.[36]

Unlike Laird, Udall sought little credit for his role; in fact, he and his staff were somewhat dubious about how his role might play with his constituents. He avoided seeking headlines, he said, and he wanted the investigation to run its course with due process. If anything, Udall credited Rivers with bringing the case into public view. "If the letter to the secretary of defense had just come from me, they would have routed it to some public affairs officer in Vietnam and I might never have heard anything," Udall said. "But when Rivers wrote, it made a difference."[37] Udall noted that fellow Arizonans Senator Barry Goldwater and Representative John Rhodes also had passed along their copies to army authorities.[38]

Army officials said they feared that publicity would hamper the gathering of testimony and assembling of evidence. On August 11, Major General William A. Becker asked to meet with Udall, saying he had some confidential information. Lewis was worried that the army "may try to somehow give you confidential information to keep you from saying anything."[39] Olson said army officials met several times with Udall, but he and Lewis never learned what had been said.[40]

Meanwhile, Ridenhour was growing restless. He said at one point he felt like "a guy who is screaming his guts out in the middle of a crowd and everybody is walking by, just walking by."[41] On August 29, Ridenhour called Udall's office and talked with Olson. Olson wrote a memo to Udall that said Ridenhour was "expressing great impatience at the lack of progress. . . . He sounded very much as though he was about to go to the papers with it. I told him he was certainly free to do whatever he thought best. But I said we had reason to believe some progress was being made in the investigation and felt obliged to wait until it was completed before assessing its merits." Olson told Ridenhour that Udall and his staff also were concerned "about the possibility of a whitewash."[42]

About this same time, Seymour M. Hersh, a freelance writer, was pursuing the story, one for which he would win a Pulitzer Prize. A handwritten note, probably by Lewis, in the Pinkville file said about Hersh's effort: "book to be xplosive; few heroes" and "Mo told him he could of grandstanded but did not want publicity, only wanted to get to the bottom of it."[43] On November 13, Hersh broke the first story. The next day, Hersh called Ridenhour and they talked for five hours about what Ridenhour knew.[44]

According to a chronology of Pinkville prepared by Udall's staff, the next significant information the office heard was an Associated Press report out of Fort Benning, Georgia, dated September 6, 1969, that Lieutenant William L. Calley had been charged with the murder of an unspecified number of Vietnamese civilians in 1968. Four days later, Udall received a letter from Colonel Reid saying that charges had been filed September 5 against Calley. The massacre now was public knowledge.[45]

The word also was out that Udall had played a role in the outcome. Olson wrote in an undated memo probably in mid-November that "someone, probably Ridenhour, is giving Mo undue credit for Pinkville. As I said earlier, this is an extremely dangerous issue and one in which we ought not to play any more role than did other members of the Arizona delegation or other Members of Congress." Olson did not explain what he meant by "extremely dangerous," although he probably was referring to a political sense. Olson noted that Udall's role was minor. "We had nothing to do with breaking the story—in fact we, as well as other recipients of his March letter, scrupulously avoided any publicity, even after the original accusation against Calley was announced in early September in Fort Benning."[46]

On April 28, 1970, Udall wrote a proposed magazine article that urged constituents to write letters to their congressmen. In it, he noted that citizens were wrong if they believed that the letters would have no impact. He referred to Ridenhour's letter as one that did. Udall said it would have been an even greater tragedy than My Lai if the government had failed to investigate the charges. "I am absolutely convinced that this greater tragedy would have occurred if it had not been for my young friend Ronald L. Ridenhour and the letter he wrote me. . . . One citizen, one young American whose friends urged him not to 'get involved,' one letter saved our country from the guilt of a monstrous cover-up of the whole, shameful My Lai affair."[47]

THE REFORMER

$\mathcal{S}$ enator Everett M. Dirksen, the Illinois Republican who was minority leader from 1959 to 1969, once was asked about the chances of
adopting congressional reform. He replied: "Ha, ha, ha, and I might add
ho, ho, ho."[1] Mo Udall was not laughing.

Udall believed the strict seniority system was at the root of Congress's inability to solve some of the country's problems. It was a system
that allowed dictatorial committee chairmen, who had arrived at their
stations only because of longevity, to determine the fate of legislation.
"Old-timers always comfort us with the crack that, 'The seniority system
is bad, but the longer you're here the better you'll like it,'" Udall said.[2]
He noted that the committee member who had served twenty years was
not just 5 percent more powerful than the member who had served
nineteen years. "If the former is chairman of a committee he is 1,000
percent more powerful."[3] Udall was impatient and ambitious, both for
himself and for the country. So were dozens of other young members of
Congress.

Once he got his feet on the ground after his election, he picked up
where brother Stewart had left off, although Mo had more audacity than
Stewart. While Stewart worked quietly and effectively through the committee structure to bring about reform, Mo took a bolder stand, one that
would heap attention on him for years to come. Not all of it worked to
his advantage.

In addition to working with the Democratic Study Group and lining up support through improved freshmen orientations, Udall was striving to transform the House—that is, to take power out of the hands of a few and ensure a more democratic process. To say that Mo Udall was a prime mover would do discredit to the dozens of other House members bent on the same goal, people like Phil Burton of California, Eugene McCarthy of Minnesota, Lee Metcalf of Montana, and Richard Bolling of Missouri. Taken together, their efforts led to a reconstituted body by 1975.

When Rayburn died in November 1961, the speakership fell to his longtime ally, the colorless, sixty-nine-year-old John W. McCormack of Massachusetts. McCormack's elevation was without opposition, but with less than universal support.[4] He was satisfied with the way Congress operated, yet he was far less skillful in running the House than Rayburn. By 1969, he faced a rebellion among the young members and by the end of his term in 1971, he had retired.

Morris Udall joined the Democratic Study Group soon after being sworn in and became one of its more active members. In addition to getting settled at the House, he also was consumed with efforts to build the ambitious Central Arizona Project.

He saw the seniority system at work on the Interior Committee, which was chaired by the autocratic Wayne N. Aspinall of Colorado, who was wary of efforts to divert Colorado River water to Arizona. While some committee members, particularly the fiery Burton of California, were adamant about removing Aspinall, Udall was more cautious. But he carefully watched the former peach farmer.

Udall made his first major public complaint about how Congress operated in a February 7, 1964, newsletter. He wrote the first of a two-part series to constituents entitled, "Is Congress Sick?—1: Creeping Paralysis on Capitol Hill." In a tactful and politic manner, Udall said the basic problem with Congress was not its members, but "the machinery they operated."

Udall praised the strong leadership of Rayburn and Lyndon Johnson, who had been Senate majority leader, for getting several important pieces of legislation through during the 1950s by the sheer power of their personalities. With Rayburn's death and with Johnson as vice president, new leadership had taken over. He called the new leaders, McCormack and the Senate's Mike Mansfield, "able men trying against overwhelming odds to operate a ship which is all anchor and no sail." Continuing the analogy, Udall said, "The ship of Congress has a competent crew but its engine is badly designed and its rudder won't steer."

Congressional reform might have been a difficult concept to sell back home or to the American people as a whole. The issue dealt with process rather than substance, but the process was at the heart of being able to pass substantive legislation, particularly regarding civil rights and labor issues.

Udall complained that despite staying in session for the full year in 1963, little legislation of importance had passed. "The creaking congressional machinery isn't anti-liberal or anti-Kennedy or anti-Johnson. It's pro status quo. It is against change—good change or bad change. In Congress it's just as hard to repeal bad old laws as it is to pass good new ones."[5]

In his second newsletter two weeks later, Udall again attacked the "machinery" that he said "gives every advantage to those who say 'no' over those who say 'yes'; to those who want deadlock over those who want issues resolved; to those who want delay over those who want action now."[6]

He criticized the seniority system again, saying, "To get the 20 years of seniority it takes to become a major chairman a congressman . . . must represent a 'safe' one-party district that would ensure his re-election."[7] Years later, when Udall was chairman of the Interior Committee, such a safe district allowed him to advance environmental goals for the rest of the nation that might have been less acceptable in Arizona.

Udall also was frustrated because the House rarely legislated on Mondays or Fridays. For someone whose consuming passion was politics to the point of workaholism, that was unacceptable. It was a practice in Congress by some eastern and southern congressmen to leave on Thursday night and return on Tuesday morning from their hometowns, where they had law practices or other business interests. Important votes were scheduled for the middle of the week. "This not only drags the sessions into late fall, but throws an unduly heavy load of committee work on Western, Midwestern, and more distant Southern members who cannot afford to commute," Udall wrote in his newsletter.[8]

Udall said Congress "worships old procedures and uses worn out machinery in an unsuccessful attempt to attend the business of a huge, jet-age nation." He called on his constituents to "get interested and aroused" about House reform, because Congress would never reform itself through internal pressures alone.[9]

In 1965, the Democratic Study Group reached its highest membership at 180. The increased membership gave extra clout to convincing McCormack to institute a series of reforms, including the formation of a Joint Committee on the Organization of Congress. On May 12, Udall essentially repeated the proposals he had made in his newsletters before this committee. After ten months, the committee unanimously brought forth sixty-six reform proposals. The most important provision called for a "committee bill of rights," which, among other things, would prevent chairs from exercising arbitrary power.[10]

The Senate passed the reform package and when it went to the House, McCormack, who found it too radical, referred it to the Rules Committee. McCormack wanted the package watered down. One Rules Committee member said McCormack "put the bill in the refrigerator," where it languished for more than three years.[11]

Such arbitrary decisions failed to endear McCormack to the Democratic Study Group. Nor did they draw Morris Udall and McCormack closer. That and other decisions led Udall to challenge McCormack for the speakership in 1969.

While Udall was observing Aspinall's high-handed tactics on the Interior Committee, he also was getting a firsthand look at the power of committee chairmen from Tom Murray, a Tennessean who ran the Post Office and Civil Service Committee, on which Udall sat. Murray was so authoritarian he refused to adopt rules or even call the committee into session. That infuriated Udall, who was trying to revamp the postal system, which was wallowing in political patronage. Udall was able in 1965 to ramrod a series of rule changes through the committee that established eight subcommittee chairmen, thereby setting the stage for an end to postal patronage in 1970.[12]

One of Udall's interns, Terry Bracy, watched Udall operate on the committee. Bracy was a graduate student in political science at the University of Arizona when he joined Udall's staff. He later worked full-time with Udall through his presidential bid, serving as one of his closest aides.

Bracy called Udall's effort to end-run Murray one of the most significant steps to break down the seniority system. "They could go around committee chairmen who were uncooperative and they did. They set rules and improved rules. They put subcommittees in charge of many things."

Udall was adept at taking a position, good or bad, and making significant improvements. Instead of being stuck on the postal committee, Udall "made something of it," Bracy said. "He used this little committee, which was a nothing committee, to impose congressional reform on the system and ultimately he went on and used that committee to take the post office out of patronage." Udall knew that in order to pass significant legislation he had to crack the procedures first. "Mo was a great thinker with broad creative ideas," Bracy said, "but he was also an enormously able legal mechanic, and he understood how the law was used and how procedures were used."[13]

In 1965, Udall called for shorter sessions of Congress accomplished through better scheduling of legislation. He also urged a modification of the seniority system to allow each party by secret ballot in caucus to choose its top-ranking member on each committee from its three senior committee members, an idea whose time was yet to come.[14]

Another small step toward House reform occurred in 1965 when the Democratic Study Group persuaded Speaker McCormack to strip committee seniority from two southern congressmen, Representatives Albert W. Watson of South Carolina and John Bell Williams of Mississippi, who had supported Republican presidential nominee Barry Goldwater (they eventually switched parties and became Republicans). Southerners chaired two-thirds of the House committees, including Appropriations, Armed Services, Commerce, Rules, and Ways and Means. Only three key committee members were even born in the twentieth century. Armed Services was particularly a target of the DSG, because its chairman was Vietnam hawk L. Mendel Rivers of South Carolina.

Then in 1966 the antics of the Reverend Adam Clayton Powell Jr., the charismatic black preacher who was elected to Congress from Harlem, brought great public visibility to abuse by committee chairmen. Mo Udall played a major role, one in which he had nothing to gain and everything to lose.

Through the seniority system, Powell, the "King of Harlem" as he was often called, had risen to be chairman of the Education and Labor Committee. First elected in 1944, he remained in office for a colorful and controversial twenty-four years, proving himself to be a pain to his colleagues. The married Powell liked attractive women, fancy dress, and frequent junkets to exotic places at taxpayer expense. He flaunted his lifestyle as well. "I don't care what anybody says. I'll do exactly what I want to do. If it's illegal, immoral, or fattening, Adam Powell is going to do it. I intend to live my life."[15] His constituents loved him and returned him to office term after term, despite his excesses. Once, as a campaign opponent began berating Powell's infidelities, he was interrupted by one of Powell's supporters, who said, "Aw quit it, man. The cat's livin'."[16]

The House became fed up with Powell in 1966 and launched an investigation. Among other things it found he kept his estranged wife on his payroll at $20,000 a year although she did no work.[17] Powell fired back, as he always did when he was under attack, that his colleagues were singling him out because of his race.

When Udall was running for reelection in 1966, he was surprised to hear so many questions from constituents about Powell. He decided the time had come for him to do his part to "rein him in." He made the decision despite liking Powell, whose office was two doors from his; aide Bonnie Kell said Udall, Powell, and Frank Thompson Jr. of New Jersey occasionally shared an after-work drink. Udall viewed the Powell action as a thankless but necessary task.

Udall found it distasteful to take on the only black committee chairman in Congress, but he also saw that he could use it to his advantage. Perhaps he could win over the seniority-entrenched southerners. Udall also would attend House prayer breakfasts. "He wasn't religious," Bracy said, "but he made every prayer breakfast. That was the way he kind of tied himself with the southerners. He worked every angle."[18]

Arkansas Democrat Wilbur D. Mills, one of the new breed of House southerners, asked Udall to make the motion to remove Powell. "Mo really liked Adam Clayton Powell," Bracy said. "It's just that he couldn't defend him anymore."[19] After long soul-searching, Udall decided to propose stripping Powell of his chairmanship but allow him to remain in office.

McCormack was livid when he heard what Udall proposed. "He barged into a meeting of the Democratic Study Group to chide me for having the effrontery to announce my intentions without consulting him. Our relationship would never improve after this," Udall said.[20] McCormack opposed any censure of Powell.

Udall had little to worry about from his constituents. His district contained few blacks, and he would be safe from reprisals. Even so, few could find fault with Udall's civil rights record. "I have attempted to live my life and construct my philosophy of life so that I could look straight at any person and speak my mind without worrying about the possible racial or ethnic overtones," he said.[21]

Powell was confident he could win any skirmish, primarily because of, as Udall put it, "slavish deference to seniority, his symbolic standing with the black community, and the binding traditions of the House."[22] The traditions were changing, as Powell would soon discover.

When the closed-door caucus of 248 Democrats convened on January 9, 1967, Powell was in attendance, something rare for him. A vote to temporarily suspend Powell's chairmanship failed, 88–122, and then Udall's motion was considered. Udall said Powell should lose his chairmanship because of mismanagement of his committee's staff and travel funds. He told the caucus that Powell should keep his seniority and that if he rehabilitated himself he should return to the chairmanship. He told Powell that he was his friend and that perhaps the caucus's action might head off efforts to deny him his seat. At the end of his statement, Udall looked at Powell and said, "You are a gifted man; I envy the intellect, eloquence, and the personality you have been given. Indeed, I have always believed that had your gifts been used in other ways you would have been one of the great men of our time."[23]

In a voice vote, the caucus overwhelmingly elected Carl D. Perkins of Kentucky as the new chairman. Udall called the move "unprecedented in modern times. My view was simply this: a chairmanship is not a right; it is a privilege. . . . Mr. Powell's abuse of that chairmanship had brought discredit upon his party, and his unfitness to hold it had been demonstrated to my complete satisfaction."[24]

After the vote, Udall said, "This story is done. The public has won. He is no longer chairman of this committee and probably never will be again. He is no longer in control of the staff. Are we going to kick a man when he is down? . . . Race is not involved but the cold fact is that 20 million fellow citizens [the approximate number of black Americans in the country] will think it is if we act in haste."[25]

In his newsletter to constituents, Udall praised Powell for being the equal of Martin Luther King Jr. in magnetism and intellect. "But King has something Powell has not: exemplary character and moral force. . . . His lack of King's character threw this magnificent potential away."[26]

Powell immediately left the caucus and told reporters that his removal was "a lynching—Northern style."[27] Then he went on national television where he called Udall a "Mormon racist," a charge that would be cast again about him when he ran for president, although nothing could be further from the truth.

Apparently seeing that it was the will of Congress to depose Powell, McCormack asked Udall to make a motion to "temporarily and conditionally" seat Powell, pending an investigation by a select House committee of seven members. That would give Powell the due process he was entitled to, Udall noted. "This, we thought, would dramatize the distinction we were trying to make: the voters have an absolute right to send a representative—be he or she genius, idiot, nincompoop, or miscreant—to Congress, but they don't have the right to dictate who shall chair congressional committees," Udall said.[28] "Powell is not my idea of an ideal congressman. . . . I doubt that he could be elected in California, Illinois, or Connecticut—or perhaps anywhere but Harlem." He noted that 74 percent of the electorate had voted for him at the last election despite his activities.[29]

The morning of the vote on whether to seat Powell, he and Udall met at the rail on the House floor. Powell looked worried and his usual jaunty manner had faded some. "I want my seat, baby," he said.[30] He then asked Udall if he thought it would help if he spoke on his own behalf. Udall replied that his argument for seating Powell would be based on due process, that he had not been given a hearing. He told Powell that if he appealed to fair play and stayed away from taunting House members that it might be helpful.

Powell agreed and wrote out a speech on two pages of a yellow pad. It began: "My dear colleagues, I have been among you for twenty-four years. No one can say that I have not run my committee in a fair and responsive manner. Today all I ask is a chance to be heard before drastic and unprecedented action is taken." Udall was impressed with the plea and agreed to give Powell five minutes.

When Powell's time came, he marched to the podium and discarded the speech for a tirade against the House. "He who is without sin should cast the first stone. There is no one here who does not have a skeleton in his closet. I know, and I know them by name. . . . Gentlemen, my conscience is clean. My case is in God's hands. All I hope is that you have a good sleep tonight."[31]

Because it was his motion to seat Powell, Udall closed the debate by saying, "I must have had four hundred letters, complaining 'You have got to do something to punish Adam Powell.' But I have not had a single letter that says, 'You have got to punish Adam Powell's constituents' . . . if we do not let him be seated as we have always done under the precedents of the House, we are going to punish not him but his constituents . . . we will do great damage to the great American tradition of due process of law if we follow this course."[32]

He said to deny Powell his seat would be overkill after the vote stripping him of his committee chairmanship. "Let me make it clear that the mighty has fallen, the ax has come down, the story of Adam Powell, free-wheeling chairman, is ended; that house has tumbled down and nothing we do will change it. The public has won. . . . The House is vindicated all because of what the Democratic Party did yesterday."[33]

But Udall's motion was rejected by a vote of 126–305, with no Republicans voting for it. A Republican motion by minority leader Gerald R. Ford of Michigan to deny Powell his seat, pending a five-week investigation of his fitness to serve, was approved by a 363–65 vote with every Republican voting for it. Udall voted against the motion.[34] It was the first time since 1807 that a member had been denied a seat after being duly elected.[35]

The reason Powell changed his speech became clear after the vote. Busloads of supporters from Harlem had come to the Capitol to protest Powell's treatment. He was playing his race card, standing defiant to his white colleagues. He retreated to the Capitol steps to address his faithful followers, hoping to play the role of martyr.

The day after the vote, Udall said he "didn't expect instant and universal acclaim" for his actions, but he was "somewhat surprised" by the fact that he was damned by civil rights groups. He also felt a white backlash and a strain in relations with the House Democratic leadership.[36]

Powell was eventually ousted and then went on to win a special election ordered by the Supreme Court to fill the seat. Even though he remained at his home in Bimini, he won 86 percent of the vote. But the

House again excluded him, forcing him to file a lawsuit challenging the constitutionality of the House's actions. He won that suit and returned to Congress for the 1969 session, but in the 1970 primary he lost to Charles B. Rangel. Two years later, he died of cancer.

Udall, the reformer, went to work again. He said the Powell fiasco required that the House set up a committee on standards and conduct, that the House should have a system of public disclosure of outside business and financial interests, and that the seniority system needed revision. He said Powell's abuses were possible because the seniority system guarantees a chairman almost unlimited power with virtually no supervision or control. "If committee chairmen were selected by any democratic method," he wrote, "chairmen would be compelled to act responsibly and honorably—or face removal. In my judgment, the Powell case would never have occurred if he had not been protected all these years by the shield of rigid seniority rule."[37]

Udall called the Powell episode a watershed for both the press and the Congress. He said the press began to keep a closer watch on the private behavior of public men and women. As for the seniority system, Udall said the chairmen were alerted that previously accepted behavior patterns would no longer be tolerated. He said Powell's lasting gift was that it gave an impetus to reform.[38]

That reform was still a long way off.

CHALLENGING THE
LEADERSHIP

o Udall had been in Congress almost eight years. He was impatient with the pace of House reform. He could not abide Sam Rayburn's motto "to get along, go along." Rayburn was long gone but little had changed under his replacement, John McCormack.

The House seniority system was under assault in a number of quarters by young congressmen. They knew they had to challenge the old ways no matter what the expense if they were going to enact social legislation. Only Mo Udall would have the courage—indeed the audacity—to go right for the throat. His challenge of McCormack helped Udall break away from the pack, and he could now depend on a following among young House liberals. Udall launched bold, but unsuccessful, forays at House leadership posts in 1969 and 1971. Not surprisingly, he conferred with brother Stewart along the way.

In the 91st Congress, which convened in January 1969, Democrats held a 243 to 191 margin—with one vacancy—over the Republicans, despite Richard M. Nixon's election. Most telling was that the average age of House Democrats was fifty-seven and a half; Udall was forty-six. In addition, 24 percent of the House Democrats were older than sixty, with three members older than eighty, and therefore higher on the rung of the seniority ladder. Udall's appeal lay with those under fifty—40.7 percent of them.[1]

Not since 1891 had the House elected a Speaker with as little as eight years of experience—Udall had seven and a half years—and the average years of service for Speakers since 1899 was twenty-six years.

McCormack made it clear in his direct, abrasive style after the November elections of 1968 that he wanted to return as Speaker for at least one more term. His support came from older liberals, urban Democrats, and southerners. Perhaps as many as a hundred older liberals were in the House, and they embodied the thinking that dated back to Franklin Roosevelt's New Deal. On the other side were as many as fifty Democrats more interested in civil liberties and social equality. As one young Democrat who wanted to remain anonymous told the *New York Times:* "The trouble with John McCormack is that he is completely out of touch with modern American politics."[2]

In addition, Nixon's election would put McCormack at a disadvantage in dealing with a Republican White House. He would be only a leader of the congressional opposition rather than the lieutenant he had been in the Democratic Johnson administration. Worries about his age— he was seventy-seven—also arose, including whether he had the intellectual drive or the proper public image to serve as the Democratic spokesman.[3]

Udall shared these concerns. No one was willing to stick out his neck because of McCormack's power—except Udall. It was typical of Mo, the risk-taker. He also knew that his challenge might alienate the senior House members and kill his future chances to be included in the leadership. Plus, it was unheard of for a modern Speaker to undergo a challenge. Udall faced insurmountable odds, but he had lost before and bounced back.

Said David R. Obey, the Wisconsin Democrat: "[Udall] understood that political death is not when you lose an election; political death is when you have the power to do something and don't do it."[4] Udall believed that for reform to occur it had to begin at the top. As early as April 1968, he began exploring the unthinkable—challenging McCormack as House Speaker when Congress resumed in January 1969. In doing that, he would be attempting to step past Carl B. Albert of Oklahoma and Hale Boggs of Louisiana, who were next in line.

On November 22, McCormack sent a letter to House Democrats requesting that he be returned as Speaker. Five days later, Udall responded that in all likelihood he would support McCormack for another term. He told McCormack that, despite gossip, there was no organized or serious effort to advance a candidate against him. He said he admired McCormack's contributions to his country. At the same time, he said the Speaker would be performing a higher service to his party if he would step down but remain in the House "as long as you wish." Udall apologized if he sounded presumptuous, but he said others felt the same way. "It is a fact in politics that too many people tell us what they think we want to hear and not what they actually feel," Udall wrote in the letter to McCormack. "You will make a serious mistake if you conclude that the talk of new leadership in the House comes only from Dick Bolling and a few others of his point of view." He said other members from all levels of seniority, sections of the country, and different political philosophies agreed.[5]

It took McCormack until December 10 to respond. The Speaker said he had a high regard for Udall and he did not consider the letter presumptuous. "But in all frankness, I must say that if such a suggestion came from almost anyone else, I would consider it 'presumptuous,'" he sniffed. Like a stern father, McCormack then began to lecture Udall: "I know you will respect my frankness in the following observation that on a number of occasions quite a few Members have criticized you in my presence, but I have always defended you." He then thanked Udall for his support.[6]

Even as late as December 6, the young Democrats, including Udall, were searching for someone to challenge McCormack. Udall had hoped someone else would step forward—perhaps Wilbur Mills, the chairman of the Ways and Means Committee. As chairman, Mills had exploited the leadership weaknesses of McCormack and majority leader Carl Albert. He was a power behind the scenes and few challenged him, but Mills declined to run.[7]

Albert also was approached about running against McCormack, but he, too, would have none of it. "I was McCormack's friend," Albert wrote. "As majority leader, I was also his chief lieutenant. The difficulties he faced placed me in an odd position." He said the press was predicting that younger members were ready to turn the speakership over to Albert and that in fact some of McCormack's "younger and brasher critics" had approached him. "If Carl Albert was the only person in Congress who could unseat him," Albert wrote, "McCormack was going to stay right where he was."[8]

Soon thereafter, Udall began circulating a six-page draft among close supporters for their feedback. In a December 20 memo, Udall wrote that Jerome Waldie of California felt that Udall would decide against running so he pledged his support to McCormack. But, Udall noted, "[Waldie] will be with us on secret ballot." Benjamin S. Rosenthal of New York, Brock Adams of Washington, and others were working for Udall converts and reported "a great deal of enthusiasm and few rejections."[9] They set up a January 1 reception at the home of Patsy T. Mink of Hawaii to give freshmen members a pep talk about the need to back Udall.

Rosenthal told Udall that Lester L. Wolff of New York wanted a change but thought Udall would lose and that it would be a mistake to try. Otis G. Pike of New York signed on, but John J. McFall of California noted he had been in a tough reelection race and could not afford to be for change. Rosenthal also told Udall that New York's freshmen were generally favorable, but they were worried they would receive less than desirable committee assignments if Udall lost.

On Christmas Eve, Udall telephoned McCormack at his home in South Boston. After McCormack wished him a happy holiday, Udall drew a deep breath and told him he would be challenging him for the speakership. McCormack replied that he "hardly expected that from you." Udall said McCormack "didn't keep me on the line long."[10]

The day after Christmas, Udall sent out a letter saying that he would put his name before the caucus as a candidate. He wrote that a number of his colleagues could do a respectable job, including Albert, but that none had stepped forward. He brushed off suggestions that the challenge would weaken the party, saying: "The House, if properly organized and led, can restore its influence and can again become the independent, constructive force it once was; we need not simply react to the plans and programs of the executive. The House can and should be a source of innovative programs to meet national problems." He closed the letter by seeking suggestions, advice, criticisms, or expressions of thought. "It's lonely out here in orbit; say something."[11]

Just before the January 2 vote, Udall wrote Albert asking that the process be carried out with dignity, without arousing any lasting wounds or ill feelings. To achieve this, he suggested that speeches be temperate, restrained, and impersonal. He also urged a secret written ballot.[12]

Udall was confident that he had eighty-one supporters, about a third of the possible votes, if everyone who said they would vote for him did. He drew up a thirty-two-page worksheet showing how he thought each Democrat would vote. He sent a three-page memo to brother Stewart outlining problems and procedures. Most were routine and parliamentary, but Udall did promise to reopen the vote to all comers if he won, hoping that he would still emerge as Speaker. "Spread word to my supporters, still going for broke," he wrote.[13]

When the vote came, Udall was soundly beaten—178 for McCormack, 58 for Udall, 4 for Mills, and 1 blank. Some of his "commitments" drifted away at the last moment. As one House member put it, "Udall was very gracious. Of course, when you're standing there in a pool of blood, I guess gracious is the thing to be."[14] According to Udall's friend Larry L. King, the vote "did not prevent maybe a hundred statesmen from later seeking out Udall to whisper that they had stubbornly stayed hitched."[15] Udall said he thought he would do better based on private assurances. "But on a secret ballot a man can vote his conscience with or against you. I think it's a tradition worth preserving."[16]

The vote was transmitted that very day to the White House, where President Johnson was spending his final days in office. Johnson took delight in Udall's defeat, a payback of sorts for Udall's speech opposing the Vietnam War fifteen months earlier. Udall said that Johnson "reportedly relished my comeuppance."[17]

Perhaps with a push from Udall's unsuccessful bid to replace him, McCormack announced he would not seek another term. At least Udall would have liked to think that. The *New York Times* did. In an editorial the day after the vote, the *Times* said, "Thanks to [Udall], a change in the Speakership two years from now has moved from the probable to the virtually inevitable."[18]

The day after his defeat, Udall dissected the Speaker contest with "some postmortem thoughts," eleven pages of why he lost and where he would go from that point. In it, he virtually tracked every vote, state by state, as to who did or did not vote for him. The move to throw open the nomination if he beat McCormack backfired, Udall said. Mills, Albert, and other ambitious congressmen apparently figured that if Udall won and then threw the speakership open, as planned, Udall would still be a favorite to ultimately win the speakership, thereby leaping over them. Udall said he underrated the extent to which members would consider themselves morally bound by letters of support sent to McCormack before Udall announced he was running.

He also found President Johnson's fine hand in the process. "I am thoroughly convinced that LBJ sent word, especially to the Texas delegation, to shoot me down because of my stand on Vietnam," he said. In addition, he suspected that AFL-CIO president George Meany had lined up support against Udall because of his vote on right-to-work in 1965. "If labor was opposing me because I was too conservative, one would think that I would therefore be more appealing to the southerners, but, to many of them, I had to be opposed because I was too liberal and a member of the [Democratic Study Group], etc.," Udall wrote.[19] He believed that McCormack had told House members that he would step down in two years and that he received many votes based on that decision and their loyalty to him.

Udall could see a bright side. In two pages attached to his "postmortem thoughts" entitled "Some thoughts on how to win while losing," Udall said he doubted he would face reprisals from McCormack, who "isn't that kind of guy." He said he was going to work with the Speaker "to do everything I can to make [the House] responsive to the real needs of this country." He also thought that the experience would enhance efforts to bring greater House reform. He suspected that McCormack would react to the uprising and that when the Speaker stepped down, Albert, who would probably seek to succeed him, would have to respond to the cry for reform. In fact, McCormack agreed to hold monthly caucus meetings, something the House liberals had sought for some time because they helped serve as a check on the arbitrariness of the leadership and some committee chairmen.[20]

"I'm really excited about the response I received," Udall said. "It has great significance for the future—not necessarily for Mo Udall personally but for revitalization of the House of Representatives and the Democratic party."[21] At the beginning of the 1970s, Udall said he believed that of all the many policy and institutional changes of the past decade, those of most lasting significance to the nation may well prove to be the much-needed reforms within the House of Representatives.[22]

Udall said he would support majority leader Albert for the speaker-ship when McCormack retired. "He's a man with a lot of drive, a lot of ideas, and considerable ability," he said. He did not write it down, but his thoughts also were on succeeding Albert as majority leader.[23]

Thomas P. "Tip" O'Neill Jr. of Massachusetts, who became Speaker in 1977, called Udall's decision to challenge McCormack "the biggest mistake Mo ever made." He said that McCormack never forgave him, a fact that came back to haunt him two years later.[24] It is unlikely that Udall classified his effort as a mistake.

Udall had a chance meeting with McCormack outside the House chamber several days after the vote. Writer Larry L. King described the meeting:

> [Udall] was confronted by the Speaker. "Maurice," the old man said—he always South-Bostonized Udall's name to Maurice U-dahl—"I want to shake your hand." Udall inquired as to the honor's purpose. The old man was sadly reproving; "Well, Maurice, I received a clipping quoting you that I won't shake your hand." No, Udall said, he had referred only to certain of his supporters. "Why, Maurice, who said that?" Udall mumbled, scuffed the marble floor, and wished a quick deliverance. "Maurice," Old John ultimately offered, "let by-gones be bygones." Udall himself could not have suggested a better deal. They traded reassurances of mutual high regard, the Speaker disavowing any wish to extract reprisals. Mo Udall remembers a giddy euphoria. Outside of official receiving lines, that was the last time John McCormack offered to shake his hand.[25]

If Mo Udall had learned anything in life it was that defeat was a temporary setback and that he should continue to pursue his goals. As early as January 10, 1970, he was contemplating another try at the leadership.

House members were growing increasingly dissatisfied with Mc-Cormack's stewardship, and the rumblings of resentment and rebellion were precipitated by a federal grand jury indictment handed down against his chief of staff for influence peddling.[26] The charges may have encouraged McCormack to seek another term in his desire to vindicate himself. In addition, he had obtained 167 pledges of support for another term as Speaker a full year ahead of time.[27]

Nevertheless, on May 20, 1970, McCormack decided to retire at the end of the session and urged House Democrats to replace him with Albert. McCormack said only that he was living up to his 1968 promise to retire and that his wife, to whom he was devoted, was seriously ill.[28]

Udall was one of the first to line up behind Albert, and he was the first to announce he would run for majority leader, announcing on the day that McCormack made his announcement. If elected majority leader, Udall would be next in line for the speakership, probably within the next ten years. He was only forty-eight years old. He could be patient.

Some of his supporters wanted him to oppose Albert, but he refused. "No," he said, "Carl's in line, he's respected, and I think he'll do a good job." Udall was hoping to get Albert's endorsement, but the Oklahoman known as the "Little Giant"—he was five feet, four inches tall—adopted a hands-off policy. "We didn't expect Carl to shout Udall's praises from the Washington Monument," a Udall adviser said, "but we did hope he might wink at somebody."[29] Udall remarked that Albert's silence on majority whip Hale Boggs "speaks volumes. After all, they've been in the leadership together for ten years."[30]

Udall knew he had to counter the roadblocks that hurt him in the speakership race: He was leapfrogging others in the line of command; some members were angry at his vote on the right-to-work legislation; and they feared he was too radical in his approach to House reform. In addition, he had to hurdle resentment built up among the old guard for his challenge of McCormack.

If it came down to Boggs and Udall, the Arizona Democrat thought he could pull it off. Udall had proved popular with House members for two reasons: He was a true liberal in the days when liberals were widely represented in the Democratic Party, and he had secured passage of legislation to give automatic pay raises in Congress. "This endeared him to members," Tip O'Neill said, "because if there's one thing that congressmen really love, it's a pay raise. But if there's one thing they really hate, it's having to vote for a pay raise. Under Udall's plan, they would receive pay raises automatically—without having to cast a vote that would be unpopular at home."[31] Other federal pay legislation Udall pushed through raised congressional pensions. That gave incentive for members to retire earlier, a subtle way to attack the seniority system.

Three other candidates announced they were running for majority leader. All threatened to siphon support from Udall. They were James G. O'Hara, an even more serious liberal from Michigan; westerner B. F. Sisk of California; and Wayne Hays of Ohio.

O'Hara decided to run with the promise of labor support. Backers urged Sisk to run because he was entrenched in House tradition. And Hays? Perhaps Hays said it best: "Well, last summer when Hale Boggs was drinking and making a horse's ass of himself, he asked me to talk him up. I drew a blank. People didn't want him. They didn't want Udall and his bunch of clowns. I figured what the hell, it was wide open."[32]

Udall may have had an early lead and Boggs was clearly worried, so much so that he had a colleague approach Udall to offer him the appointed post of majority whip, third in line for the speakership, if he and his backers would support Boggs.[33] Udall declined, but he may have wished he had not. Boggs began mending fences, telling his colleagues that he was next in line on the leadership ladder; that if he lost the race, he could get thrown out by voters at home; and that the South had to stick together against the liberals like Udall.[34]

Udall had his own problems. Labor was against him, not only for his vote against repealing the right-to-work provision in the Taft-Hartley Act, but because American Federation of Labor leader George Meany disliked Udall's dovish posture. The Congress of Industrial Organizations' Andrew D. Biemiller, a former congressman turned lobbyist, was backing O'Hara.

He was not surprised to learn, either, that "Old Jawn" was rounding up his troops to support Boggs, not necessarily because he felt the Louisianan was the best candidate, but because he opposed Udall.

A key for Udall was to land a big hitter like Edward P. Boland of Massachusetts, who could bring the Northeast contingent with him. Boland was a respected liberal and he agreed to nominate Udall. "Those people who serve the cause well will be the first I consult and counsel with as leader," he told Boland and others. When Boland signed on, Udall predicted victory.

Udall arrived home after midnight on the day of the vote, sat down with a drink in front of the fireplace, and mused about his chances. He concluded that he was deluding himself and that too much of his support was soft. He went to bed about an hour later thinking that this bid—like his run for the speakership—also would fall short.[35]

The morning of January 19, 1971, the 254 House Democrats began drifting into the caucus room, maneuvering between the dozens of reporters, lobbyists, staff, and spectators. The first order of business was to elect a caucus chairman, a post Daniel D. Rostenkowski of Illinois had held for two terms. Olin E. Teague, a Texas conservative, upset Rostenkowski. In a long-standing tradition, no caucus chairman had served more than two terms and it apparently was time for Rostenkowski to be pushed out. The change gave a boost to Udall, who thought that perhaps the House was ridding itself of its past leadership, although he felt certain that Albert would win the speakership, which he did, hands down, in the next caucus vote.

In midafternoon, the next step took place: voting for majority leader, the crucial balloting of the day. The winner needed 125 votes of the 248 who would cast ballots, and voting would continue until someone reached that total. The nominating speeches began with Boland putting forth Udall's name, which was seconded by Thaddeus J. Dulski of New York, William J. Green of Pennsylvania, Tom Foley of Washington, and Graham Purcell of Texas. Such speeches are unlikely to change votes; if any did, it was the seconding speech of Boggs by Wilbur Mills, who no doubt solidified the southern vote and those of uncertain freshmen.

When the first totals came in, Boggs had 95 votes, 30 short of the needed total, but ahead of Udall's 69, Sisk's 31, Hays's 28, and O'Hara's 25. It was far from over. Udall needed to secure 56 votes from those who had voted for the bottom three.

No sooner had the results been announced than Hays and O'Hara dropped out. Hays threw his 28 votes to Boggs, and then O'Hara surprised most observers by turning against his old friend Udall and endorsing Boggs. Sisk thought about quitting but decided to stay in for one more ballot. On the next ballot, Udall picked up 19 votes for a total of 88. Boggs pulled down 140, more than enough to secure the post.

O'Hara, who had labor's backing, may have endorsed Boggs because of Udall's vote against repealing the right-to-work provision in the Taft-Hartley Act. McCormack's presence was felt, too. "He forgets very hard," said a Massachusetts Democrat.[36]

Other factors, Udall believed, were that Boggs swayed freshmen Democrats to his side "in the belief that he could give them committee assignments" and that Hays consulted with Boggs and agreed to act as a "shill" to take votes from Udall, "knowing that he couldn't hold them forever."[37] Plus, Udall's support of abortion and his divorce may have hurt him among Catholics.

After the vote, Udall took the floor to compliment Boggs for being a "national Democrat," one who could speak for all Democrats, and moved that his election be unanimous.

When he returned to his House office to his disconsolate staff, Udall turned his "MO" button upside down to say "OW," reminiscent of the action of unsuccessful Republican opponent William Kimble when he lost the 1964 race to Udall. He then asked his staff if they knew the difference between a cactus and a caucus. "Well," he said, "a cactus has all its pricks on the outside."[38] It was one of the few times that Udall expressed anger when events failed to go his way. Years later, he advised James C. Wright Jr., who was seeking the speakership, that unless someone promised him his vote "in front of witnesses," he should not count on it.[39]

Ella Udall told her husband she was glad he did not win. Reminiscent of another Udall—Mo's mother's remark to her husband, Levi—she said, "We can take vacations, Mo." Udall was more interested in talking about "what ifs."[40]

The *New York Times* lamented Udall's loss in a January 20 editorial and said that Udall would have been "a more innovative and constructive choice." Udall typed across the bottom of the editorial torn from the paper, "Where were they when we needed them?"[41]

If it was Udall's desire to reform House procedures by challenging the leadership, he at least had some success, for on January 20, the Democrats approved changes that gave added responsibility to junior members and more authority to the caucus.[42]

Udall had one last hope if he were ever to become a formal leader in the House. He could seek the post of majority whip, but only if the post was made elective, rather than appointive. Albert supported the move to make the whip elected. He liked Udall and thought that perhaps with Udall in the leadership ranks dissident liberals would be appeased. And with Albert's support, Udall could likely win the post.

Boggs would have none of that. He wanted someone loyal to him and he sought someone from the Midwest or Northeast to help bring geographical balance. Udall's opponents talked Albert out of his position. Loyalty was important, they said. When Wilbur Mills joined the chorus, any hope of making the position elective was gone. The caucus tabled action, and Udall's last-gasp chance at the institutional leadership went with it. Albert and Boggs chose Tip O'Neill, a friend of former Speaker McCormack's.

Had Udall been selected, he might have been Speaker in six years. Albert stepped down in 1977 and Boggs died on October 16, 1972, in an Alaskan airplane crash. Tip O'Neill got the job.

When he failed to land the whip job, Udall swallowed his pride and campaigned for a seat on the Ethics Committee. That did not happen, either. "I got the message," Udall said. "There's nothing here for ole Mo. I'm catching on." Udall was even questioning whether he had any future in the House. "This decision . . . shows me my future here: I can become chairman of the Post Office Committee, with luck, when I'm sixty."[43] He wondered what was next—a run for the Senate, perhaps teaching, or a law practice. He had his sights set on lofty goals—much higher.

A week after the leadership vote one of his young aides, John Gabusi, prepared a five-page memo for Udall that listed two options: He could "resolve to be the best damn congressman from Arizona," or he could continue as a national spokesman concerning the nation's problems. Then, without elaboration, at the end of the memo Gabusi wrote: "A corollary to this approach for the next two years would be your involvement in presidential politics. I have no judgment yet as to the necessity, or reasons why you might be interested. However, it is there and won't go away and we ought to discuss it."[44]

Gabusi did not define what he meant by "presidential politics," but it would be clear soon enough. With Udall's leadership hopes all but dashed by the precocious runs against McCormack and Boggs, perhaps he could try to leapfrog again—this time all the way to the White House.

He would enter the next stage of his career knowing that he had done his best to loosen the rigid seniority system in the House. "I was saying two and three years ago that every institution in society had changed drastically in 20 years. The business corporation is much more socially aware and different in its outlook. The family, the home, schools, universities are nothing like they were. The one institution that didn't change was Congress. I used to say that you could exhume a congressman from 1920 and he'd never know he'd been gone. You can't say that anymore."[45]

In 1975, the chairmanships of four committees changed hands; the former chairmen had a total of 100 years of seniority. And in 1985, Representative Les Aspin of Wisconsin leaped over seven more senior members to gain the chairmanship of the House Armed Services Committee.[46]

THE CENTRAL ARIZONA
PROJECT

*I*f Mo Udall regretted any action he advocated in Congress, it might have been the Central Arizona Project (CAP) and the two Colorado River dams that it originally included.

In each case, potential damage might have outweighed the need to provide water for agricultural and municipal use to the desert stretching from Phoenix to Tucson. Seventy-five percent of Arizona's residents in the mid-1960s lived there; 90 percent of the industry and 60 percent of the irrigated land lay within the corridor. Arizonans in the early 1960s were using 4.3 million acre-feet of water a year, 3 million of which was pumped out of the ground. Only 700,000 acre-feet was being replaced through rainfall and snowmelt percolating into the ground, a process called recharge.

Tucson was the largest city in the nation without surface water. In 1963, the population of the Tucson metropolitan area was about 275,000. Udall said the city could not "safely grow" beyond 400,000 without additional water. With the CAP, he said, Tucson could plan on enough water to support 800,000 people. Parenthetically he added: "And, for my part, that just might be a good place to stop."[1] At the turn of the twenty-first century, the Tucson-area population was about 825,000 and still not drinking CAP water.

Udall had little political choice but to support the CAP and the dams.

The CAP was a motherhood, American flag, and apple pie issue in Arizona. Udall surely would have been voted out of office had he opposed the project. Every member of the Arizona congressional delegation backed it. Brother Stewart, who was secretary of the interior in the Kennedy and Johnson administrations, said the "political hair was short" on the CAP. "No water, and you're dead politically."[2]

The dream of building aqueducts from the Colorado River to central and southern Arizona had consumed the congressional delegation since statehood in 1912. Udall remembered his grandfather David King Udall talking about bringing water to the desert when Mo was a boy.

When Udall was elected, he stepped into the effort. He remarked several times that he gave more attention to the CAP, particularly between 1963 and 1968, than any other legislative project. "My days and nights (and many Sundays and holidays) for the past five years—the busiest and most satisfying time of my life—have been filled with the problems of the big, muddy, Colorado River," he said.[3] Even though the project was signed into law in 1968, Udall and others in the Arizona congressional delegation had to fight up through the mid-1980s for its funding.

Seven states—Arizona, California, Nevada, New Mexico, Wyoming, Colorado, and Utah—had struggled over use of the 1,450-mile-long Colorado River since the early 1900s. The river produced anywhere from 5.6 million acre-feet of water a year to 24 million, depending on snow and rainfall. One acre-foot of water equals 325,851 gallons, the amount used by a family of four in one year.[4]

In 1922, representatives of the seven states created the Colorado River Compact, which divided the states into lower and upper basins. Each basin was to receive 7.5 million acre-feet of water annually. Arizona, California, Utah, Colorado, and Nevada were in the lower basin. Arizona was to receive 2.8 million acre-feet a year, California 4.4 million, and Nevada 300,000.

Plans to transport water to central Arizona got a boost in 1944 when the Arizona legislature appropriated $200,000, with matching federal funds, to develop a plan for diverting 1 million acre-feet of the Colorado River. In 1947, Democratic senators Carl Hayden and Ernest McFarland introduced a bill to put the plan into action. The $700-million project called for building a hydroelectric dam—referred to as a "cash register dam"—on the river in Bridge Canyon between Grand Canyon National

Park and Hoover Dam. The electricity would be used to lift river water 985 feet over the mountains into an aqueduct near Parker, Arizona, and to generate revenue to help repay the construction costs. The water would then flow through a 330-mile aqueduct that would end in Tucson.

The project ran into opposition, mainly from California lawmakers who feared they would lose water needed to meet growth in southern California. California was drawing 5.3 million acre-feet of river water, 900,000 more than its allotment. Twice the Senate approved CAP legislation, but it was defeated each time in the House.

California's argument was that the cost of shipping water to central Arizona far outweighed the benefits. With no CAP, California could continue to draw needed water. Republican senator William F. Knowland of California expressed his opposition this way in a February 5, 1950, letter to McFarland: "The proposed Central Arizona Project would use water of doubtful ownership, lift it nearly twice as high as the Washington Monument, convey it farther than from Washington to New York, require federal appropriations of more than a billion dollars to irrigate 200,000 acres of privately owned, war boom desert land that could not, and would not be required to pay any of the construction costs, and would raise crops that are now surplus and subsidized by the U.S. government."[5]

The House finally directed California and Arizona to settle their argument by either reaching a negotiated agreement or submitting the question to the U.S. Supreme Court. Arizona chose the latter and filed suit on January 19, 1953. The case took eleven years to settle. The Supreme Court appointed a special master, Simon H. Rifkind, a former federal judge, to make a recommendation. Rifkind held protracted pretrial conferences that covered 28 months, required 132 days of hearings, and involved 35 attorneys. He heard from 340 witnesses that resulted in 25,000 pages of testimony bound in 43 two-inch-thick volumes, and reviewed 4,000 exhibits.[6]

On June 3, 1963, Rifkind recommended that Arizona be allotted 2.8 million acre-feet of Colorado River water. The next day, Arizona's two senators, Barry Goldwater and Hayden, introduced CAP legislation in the Senate and Representatives John Rhodes, Duke Senner, and Mo Udall introduced a similar bill in the House. Both bills would authorize the CAP construction, the projected cost of which then had soared beyond

$1.1 billion. The Supreme Court upheld Rifkind's recommendation on March 9, 1964.

The fight had just begun. Arizona still had to secure passage. Udall noted that one of the uncertainties was that other House members would like to return to their districts to tell voters how they killed a $1-billion project. And, he pointed out, California had the political power of thirty-eight House members while Arizona had three.[7]

Mo Udall's brother Stewart had his own plans for securing the CAP through his cabinet position. As interior secretary, Stewart Udall believed he had to propose a regional water plan in the lower basin, one that would appease five states, not just one. He believed he would have a better chance of winning approval of that plan than one that would serve just Arizona. He wrote to Hayden on June 12, 1963, that he was secretary of the interior of the United States, not the interior secretary for Arizona.[8] In fact, he said, the president should fire him if he represented just Arizona.

For his part, Mo Udall publicly agreed to "get behind any strategy which will win."[9] He appeared to be walking the line between keeping the Arizona delegation happy and his brother happy when he said, "We ought at least to understand and explore this strategy." Arizona's only goal, he said, "is water for Arizona at the earliest possible date." In a newsletter sent to constituents on July 12, Udall laid out five reasons to support a separate CAP and ten to proceed with his brother's plan. But his conclusions were noncommittal. Instead, he called for Arizona's leaders to work together to achieve a solution quickly. "Partisanship and politics have no place in these discussions," he wrote.[10]

In mid-August, Stewart Udall laid out the massive Pacific Southwest Water Plan, designed to appease five states—Arizona, Nevada, New Mexico, California, and Utah. The two-stage, $4-billion plan to provide water to the five states would take thirty years to complete.[11] It would be paid for with revenues from the sale of power generated by two new Colorado River dams, one at each end of the Grand Canyon. Apart and aside from the plan, the dams would prove a firestorm for Stewart and his brother.

Stewart Udall had been warned that conservationists would oppose the dams but insisted that he had to put "people above scenery" in times of water shortages.[12] The Pacific Southwest Water Plan almost caused a rebellion in the Arizona congressional delegation and did touch off a rift between Stewart Udall and Hayden, who felt Arizona would be short-changed by the ambitious plan. Keith S. Brown, chairman of the Arizona Republican Party, referred to Stewart as "a former native citizen and now a hatchet man for the new frontier. . . . [He] is doing everything in his power to block Arizona from obtaining its long fought-for goal." He suggested that Stewart might be trying to trade Arizona's five electoral votes for California's forty in the next presidential election.[13]

By late January 1965, Stewart Udall had reached a compromise with the governors and senators of Arizona and California that would guarantee California its water even in a drought year; Stewart promised to come up with a plan to import an additional 2.5 million acre-feet of water into the Colorado.[14] That was later increased to 6.5 million acre-feet, with the hope that water from the Northwest's Columbia River could be imported by the upper and lower Colorado River basins.

The compromise led to the introduction of a bill authorizing construction of the Lower Colorado River Basin Project to provide water for Arizona, Utah, New Mexico, Nevada, and California. Dams at Bridge Canyon and Marble Canyon were a key component.

Before that plan could gain momentum, conservationists launched an all-out assault, and the nation's budding environmental movement received an enormous boost when the dams were eliminated. Mo Udall found himself in the middle of the controversy. "In retrospect, it is clear that the battle of the Grand Canyon dams was a central, symbolic event which played a major role in awakening environmental awareness in America," Udall said.[15] "At the time," he said, "the environmental movement consisted of a ragtag band of bird-watchers and backpackers and a handful of well-intentioned, relatively impoverished organizations whose grasp of lobbying and public relations skills was unremarkable and whose political clout was, with rare exceptions, negligible."[16]

Environmentalists, particularly the Wilderness Society and the Sierra Club, had won one victory in their effort to block a proposed Green River dam at Echo Park in Dinosaur National Monument in the late 1950s. To halt that dam, they had to compromise by accepting a dam at Glen Canyon just south of the Utah border with Arizona.

Glen Canyon was one of the most remote, inaccessible locales in the United States. Writer Marc Reisner described the canyon as "a stretch of quiet water drifting sinuously between smooth, rainbow-colored cliffs. Labyrinthine and cool, some of the canyons were as lush as a tropical forest, utterly incongruous in the desert."[17] When the dam was completed it formed Lake Powell, which flooded the canyon for 200 miles north across the Arizona border into southern Utah. Years later, Stewart Udall said damming Glen Canyon was a mistake. "It should have been a national park," he said.[18] Goldwater said that if he had any vote that he could change, it would be his vote on the Glen Canyon Dam.[19]

The Sierra Club's David Brower had almost single-handedly stopped the Echo Park dam but at the cost of sacrificing Glen Canyon. Brower said that he was "partly responsible for its needless death" in 1963.[20] He vowed never again to compromise on a dam. That set the stage for the battle over the dams proposed at each end of the Grand Canyon. "If we can't save the Grand Canyon, what the hell can we save?" Brower asked.[21] His campaign became a major national cause célèbre.

Bridge Canyon is 80 miles downstream from Grand Canyon National Park and a dam would back up water 93 miles, 13 miles into the western edge of the park. At its deepest, it would have been 90 feet in a 2,500-foot-deep canyon. The only people able to see it would have been river rats and hardy outdoorsmen. Mo Udall predicted that the lake behind Bridge Canyon would turn the national monument into "one of the great visitors' attractions in the West." He said the views would be spectacular from boats. He also called it conservation to save hydro-electric power going to waste on the Colorado River.[22] The Marble Canyon dam was to be situated 60 miles below the Glen Canyon Dam.

The dams could provide benefits to 30 million people in the seven basin states, mostly through generated power and augmented water supplies, Mo Udall said. Neither the Marble Canyon nor the Bridge Canyon dam could be seen from any road or trail overlook in Grand Canyon National Park with the exception of Toroweap Overlook, which "hardy types" could reach from a circuitous route around the park to the north. And then all they would see was a beautiful, narrow strip of water extending up toward the edge of the park, he said. On the stretches of the canyon where the dam was to go few would see it, Stewart Udall said. "Scenery is a rather ephemeral thing if no one ever sees it."[23]

Mo Udall later called his decision to support the two dams "one of the most wrenching decisions I've faced . . . in Congress."[24] He was torn between preserving the environment and his commitment to the CAP, which was supported by ninety percent of his constituents. As he did with his labor vote in 1965, Udall sided with his constituents. In hindsight, he regretted his support of the dams, but in fact threw his political energy into trying to win their approval.[25]

As CAP hearings began in Congress, the environmentalists unleashed their most powerful attack to date. On June 9, 1966, the Sierra Club published two full-page ads in the *New York Times, Washington Post, San Francisco Chronicle,* and *Los Angeles Times.* One said: "Now only you can save Grand Canyon from being flooded—for profit." The other said: "Should we also flood the Sistine Chapel so tourists can get nearer the ceiling?" The second ad referred to the U.S. Bureau of Reclamation's argument that tourists could better appreciate the Grand Canyon from motorboats.

The $15,000 ads caused a stir, but nothing like the one the next day when the Internal Revenue Service went after the 40,000-member Sierra Club, threatening to take away its tax-exempt status if it continued to lobby against the dams. Dozens of newspapers accused the IRS of trying to stifle the Sierra Club. In addition, thousands of letters poured into the Bureau of Reclamation, which would have jurisdiction over the dams.

"I never saw anything like it," said the bureau's Dan Dreyfus. "Letters were arriving in dump trucks. Ninety-five percent of them said we'd better keep our mitts off the Grand Canyon and a lot of them quoted the Sierra Club ads."[26] Members of Congress received thousands of letters from an outraged public.

Although Mo Udall never confirmed it, Brower was convinced that Mo was behind the IRS action. Brower insisted that Udall had confided to him in Udall's office that he had indeed sicced the IRS on the Sierra Club but refused to admit it publicly because of the public reaction that followed.[27] Udall later denied he played any role in the IRS action. Even Floyd E. Dominy, the head of the Bureau of Reclamation, said Udall called in the IRS. Dominy added that he wished he had thought of it himself.[28] Udall did write a letter to Sheldon Cohen, assistant commissioner of the IRS, the day after the ads appeared, asking whether contributions to the Sierra Club elicited by the ads were tax deductible. The letter, however, did not ask for an investigation into the Sierra Club.[29]

Brower later said: "People who didn't know whether or not they loved the Grand Canyon knew whether or not they loved the IRS."[30] Nonetheless, the club's tax-exempt status was lifted and Brower, who ran the ads without the club's approval, later was fired. He then formed Friends of the Earth, a rival environmental group. The wide publicity of the IRS investigation stirred the wrath of the American public even more. California's Republican senator Thomas H. Kuchel said it was "one of the largest letter-writing campaigns I have ever seen." Stewart Udall said he received 20,000 letters addressed directly to him. Mo Udall said he was deluged with mail.[31]

The same day the ads appeared, Udall took the House floor to denounce the "inflammatory attacks" on the dams, commenting, "I must say that I have seldom, if ever seen a more distorted or flagrant hatchet job than this." He said the Grand Canyon between the two dams would be untouched for 104 miles, including all of the park's interior.[32]

Mo Udall accused Brower of leaving the impression that the Grand Canyon would be filled with water from rim to rim when he used the word *flooded.* "I don't think there can be any doubt of Mr. Brower's intention of selecting these words. Clearly he wanted the American people to believe that the Grand Canyon they know—the national park—would become a lake if these dams were built."[33] Udall called deceptive one of Brower's tactics to refer to the Grand Canyon as the entire stretch from Lee's Ferry to Lake Mead. Geologically that was true, but, Udall said, he was talking only about the section of the canyon within the national park boundaries.[34]

Twenty-two years later, in *Too Funny to Be President,* Udall wrote: "In hindsight, what amazes me most about the dams we nearly built on the Grand Canyon (and the one we did build at Glen Canyon) was how cavalier the process was. Here were congressmen nonchalantly contemplating the drowning of hundreds of miles of free-flowing rivers—rivers that most of us had never seen, except perhaps from a plane. The Bureau of Reclamation's engineers wasted little time studying the environmental impact of Glen Canyon Dam. They just built it. That seems incredible to me today."[35] And at the turn of the twenty-first century, fluctuating water levels released from Glen Canyon Dam were eroding beaches and harming wildlife in the Grand Canyon.[36]

Mo Udall also defended construction of the Glen Canyon Dam, which created Lake Powell. He called it an "incredibly beautiful lake" that provided thousands of Americans "with sights never before imagined." He said that while he did not argue in favor of the dam, "new beauty has been created, and now for the first time people can get there to see it."[37]

Udall said that instead of attacking the legislation as ruining the Grand Canyon, the Sierra Club ought to praise the people who drafted it "because it gives such great respect" for the canyon. "Far from ruining the canyon, these dams will insure that no serious and damaging incursions will occur in the future," Udall said. "The job will be done, and it will be done right."[38]

Despite the brouhaha over the dams and the IRS, legislation authorizing the Lower Colorado River Basin Project was working its way through the House. For the first time since 1950, the House Interior Committee was going to hold hearings. Carl Hayden felt the Senate Interior Committee also would move the bill as soon as the House approved it.[39]

But Wayne Aspinall, the chairman of the House Interior Committee, proved to be another problem. Aspinall, a Colorado Democrat, was quick to point out that the upper basin was entitled to half of the annual 15 million acre-feet of river water, but had no projects proposed to use its share. He worried that if Arizona got its project, it would have little motivation to help the upper basin. He also questioned whether the river might be overallocated. Udall tried to argue that was not the case, and at any rate, there was always the possibility that Columbia River water could be imported.[40]

For his part, Stewart Udall was concerned that unless some compromise was reached President Johnson would be taking "unwise and unnecessary political risks," including a "violent political reaction from Congress." Stewart was ready to give up one dam and seek water from the Pacific Northwest.[41] Both Udalls underestimated the opposition to importation of Columbia River water, despite the fact that 185 million acre-feet was being wasted when it was discharged into the Pacific Ocean each year. Aspinall secured assurances that he would get five projects for Colorado before he would open CAP hearings. One Bureau of the Budget official called Aspinall's proposal blackmail, but Aspinall got what he wanted.[42] The Interior Committee released the bill, which had now reached a construction cost of $1.7 billion thanks to the Aspinall "goodies." Aspinall won his five reclamation projects, but in 1969 he was defeated by an environmentalist and his projects still have not been built.[43]

In the meantime, Mo Udall was doing some vote counting, a practice he would learn was risky at best. He figured he had the votes to get the bill out of the House Rules Committee, the last stop on the way to a floor vote. On the floor, he believed he had 260 votes for CAP, 42 more than were needed to send the bill to the Senate.[44]

But two members of the Rules Committee from California balked at the bill, claiming that an effort would be made on the House floor to delete provisions for California's water guarantee and for water importation plans. Mo Udall and his Arizona colleagues were furious. Talk even turned to Arizona building the CAP by itself. The CAP legislation remained bottled up in the committee and died when Congress adjourned in 1966.

Udall and Rhodes said opposition from the Pacific Northwest to Columbia River water importation and the "distorted and misleading national campaign to 'Save the Grand Canyon'" were two prime reasons the bill was killed. They said they would be back in 1967 with three alternative ways to build the CAP—a bare-bones bill "with or without one of the dams"; a modified Colorado River regional bill; or a go-it-alone project by Arizona without federal assistance.[45]

It would be none of those. Interior Secretary Udall came up with a new plan, one that would eventually be approved, but not without a flurry of opposition, even from his own state.

Stewart Udall, however, knew the political realities. He knew he had to have the support of the Johnson administration, conservationists, and Congress. Johnson had yet to announce he would not run for another term and it would have been politically unpopular to approve any plan calling for the Grand Canyon dams. So Udall dropped both dams and proposed expansion of the Grand Canyon National Park, a massive thermal generating plant fueled by coal strip-mined from the Hopi and Navajo reservations to replace dam electricity revenues, and the CAP. He also agreed to drop any designs on Columbia River water, an attempt to win over Democrat Henry M. "Scoop" Jackson of Washington, chairman of the Senate Interior Committee.[46] He also proposed assuring

California that it would get its 4.4 million acre-feet of water before Arizona drew out its 2.8 million acre-feet in the case of a drought. None of the Arizona delegation supported Udall's proposal to expand the national park. Representative Rhodes said it would burden the project with a nongermane issue.[47]

Mo Udall eventually got behind his brother's $832-million plan despite introducing his own bill that called for the dam at Bridge Canyon. He could see the bill inspired by his brother's plan was going nowhere but urged the Arizona delegation to support it in the interest of gaining the CAP. He also called on the delegation to be willing to compromise. He said "there will be no House bill passed this year without Arizona, California, and Colorado working together."[48]

Udall had hoped the bill would sail through Congress this time, but Aspinall held power yet unwielded. The chairman disliked the plan, worried about what Colorado might lose from it, and considered it giving in to the conservationists. He adjourned his committee and went home to Colorado before Congress had finished its business in late 1967. Hayden forced his hand when he sought Senate approval for the project as a rider to the whole public works appropriations bill. Aspinall knew that Hayden could force a floor vote and agreed to move the bill, but only after again extracting authorization for the five Colorado projects.[49]

To Stewart Udall, his plan was the only one ever likely to get through Congress and it had to be done before the end of the 90th Congress in 1968. He was ready to step down as interior secretary after the presidential election and he knew Arizona would lose the power of Carl Hayden's forty-two years in the Senate when he retired in 1968 at the age of ninety-one.

While his brother was pushing his latest plan, Mo Udall was addressing water groups in Las Vegas, Cheyenne, Denver, Albuquerque, San Diego, and a particularly hostile crowd at a town hall meeting in Los Angeles. He told the groups Arizona would win the CAP "either with your help or over your dead bodies."[50]

In 1967, two University of Arizona agricultural economists, Robert Young and William Martin, said the high cost of CAP water under the approved plan would drive Arizona irrigators out of business and reduce the growth of cities and industry. Farms would be more profitable if they used groundwater, they said, and therefore they would not buy CAP water. CAP backers angrily dismissed their study.[51] Environmentalists leaped to their side.

Despite the warning, the bill made its way slowly but smoothly through Congress when it reconvened in January 1968. When the bill came up for a vote in the House, Mo Udall and John Rhodes put into operation a whip system involving the offices of 31 representatives from the basin states that could reach 170 members within ten minutes. Stewart Udall used his own personal influence to round up votes.[52]

House-Senate conferees—including Senators Jackson, Clinton P. Anderson of New Mexico, Frank Church of Idaho, Hayden (all Democrats), the Republican Tom Kuchel of California, and Democratic representatives Harold T. "Bizz" Johnson of California, Aspinall, and Udall—met for eight days behind locked doors. The conferees agreed to Jackson's request for a ten-year ban on studying the use of Columbia River water. A compromise also was reached on the California drought allotment. Anderson was able to extract the Hooker Dam for New Mexico. Mo Udall said that by compromising, "In effect, we gave away much of our 'paper victory' in the court to get our aqueduct built."[53] That was the important outcome.

On September 30, 1968, President Johnson signed the bill into law, with Hayden and Stewart Udall standing alongside and Mo Udall towering over the rest of the delegation between John Rhodes and Hayden aide Roy L. Elson. Johnson expressed pleasure at seeing "California and Arizona sitting there arm in arm smiling at each other."[54] After the signing, Hayden remarked with a touch of irony and perhaps a pun, "Today is the high water mark in my career as a U.S. senator."[55]

Mo Udall bragged about all the good that would come from the CAP, including providing a sound economic base, a $465-million construction payroll, and no dams. "Personally," he said, "I'm happy that Arizona can 'have its cake and eat it too'—build CAP and have the Grand Canyon left as it is."[56]

Among those in the East Room of the White House, David Brower sat watching the end to his bitter fight over the dams. He must have been especially pleased when in 1975 Congress passed a bill co-sponsored by Mo Udall and Barry Goldwater that added Bridge and Marble Canyons to Grand Canyon National Park.[57]

FINISHING THE JOB

*T*he Central Arizona Project was authorized, but it had no funding. That was the big battle until it was completed in 1991. CAP construction began in 1970, and by early 1977, $390 million had been spent on the power plant at Page and about 95 miles of the 190-mile aqueduct from Parker Dam to Phoenix was completed or under construction. In total, 20 percent of the CAP was completed.[1] Still left to be constructed were the Granite Reef Aqueduct, the Orme Dam, the Salt-Gila Aqueduct, and the Buttes Dam.

The project ran into a potentially damaging problem when the Arizona Bureau of Mines discovered a pair of geologic fault lines where the CAP plan called for the Orme Dam, a $240-million structure that would stand 195 feet high at the confluence of the Salt and Verde Rivers thirty miles north of Phoenix. The Yavapai Indian tribe worried that the dam's reservoir might flood most of its reservation. Environmentalists claimed the dam would destroy bald eagle habitats and threaten 2,000-year-old archaeological ruins.[2]

Then, on February 14, 1977, Udall joined seventy-two other members of Congress and urged new president Jimmy Carter to stop "construction of unnecessary and environmentally destructive dams" and "trim off the waste of tax dollars on unnecessary projects."[3] Five days later, Carter took the advice and called for the end of funding for nineteen major water projects, including the CAP, for a savings of $7.6 billion.

Carter said the CAP and four other projects "would have worsened the water shortages and salinity concentrations in the Colorado River . . . jeopardizing our water agreements with Mexico."[4] Congress labeled the proposal Carter's "hit list." Few people apparently had been listening when Carter had said several times after his election that "the federal government's dam building era is coming to an end. Most beneficial projects have been built."[5]

What Udall had meant in the letter to Carter was that he wanted to stop other projects, not the CAP. At almost $1.8 billion, it had become the most expensive water project in U.S. history.[6] Udall was shocked and angered by the inclusion of the CAP. He did not rebut Carter's economic arguments but pleaded eloquently, "Water is life in the desert. We have not always used our water wisely, but we are moving to correct our mistakes."[7] He told his southern Arizona constituents, "The CAP is not a land dealers' hustle. It is the key to orderly development of our state's resources and its future."[8]

The hit list eventually failed because of enormous political pressure. Udall called it "a Washington Day ambush." The press labeled it Jimmy Carter's "War on the West."[9]

Udall defended the Arizona project before a review team appointed by the Carter administration, telling the board: "I am convinced that the net impact of this project on man's environment will be one of enhancement." Udall and the Arizona congressional delegation were willing to give up the Orme Dam to save the CAP. After seven hours of testimony, Udall told the review board: "If the sentiment heard here today persists, Orme Dam is dead. You can forget about it."[10] Instead, a new dam—the Cliff Dam—would be proposed on the Verde River, but that, too, would be eliminated.

Udall held one key to keeping the CAP alive. Now chairman of the House Interior Committee, he could play an important role in Carter's energy policy and in dealing with future water projects. Carter finally backed down on the CAP, but only after Orme Dam was eliminated and other modifications were made.[11] The CAP had slipped through the noose again.[12]

If Udall thought he had problems with the Democratic Carter administration, they would seem inconsequential compared to the upcoming skirmishes with the Republican Reagan administration, particularly James G. Watt, its interior secretary. When Watt was nominated, Udall said that was like putting Dracula in charge of the blood bank. When Watt objected, Udall changed it to putting Colonel Sanders in charge of the chicken coop. Udall feared that the controversial Watt would be "up at 8 in the morning undoing things that took Congress years and years to put in place."[13] The CAP was one of those "things."

In June 1981, Watt told Udall that he might hold the CAP's Tucson aqueduct hostage if the Arizona Democrat refused to go along with the Reagan administration's budget and tax proposals. "If we don't get the votes out of Arizona and the Western states," Watt said, "we won't be able to carry the president's program, and it's got to happen. . . . If we can't get the liberals of Arizona to vote for tax cuts and budget cuts, there isn't much economic activity that's going to demand a lot of new water. America is stagnant, and it's just critical."[14] Udall countered that adequate money was available in both the Republican and Democratic budget proposals. "There's no reason why the project cannot be funded and continue on schedule."[15]

The conflict extended for months with each attacking the other over slights, disagreements, and even Watt's fundamentalist Christian beliefs. On August 18, Watt gave an interview to the *Washington Post*'s David Broder that angered Udall. Watt said that unless Udall stopped hostile questioning of Reagan administration officials in his committee, "I can't do anything" to advance the Tucson aqueduct. Watt said of Udall: "He understands I'm not against the Tucson aqueduct. And he understands I'm pretty much in control of the decision on when and how it gets built. There are parts of this job I enjoy."[16] He admitted that one of his pleasures was "twitting the liberals."[17]

Udall accused Watt of trying to punish him by holding the Tucson aqueduct hostage. He said he had tried to cooperate with Watt. "I have always prided myself as a man of reason—an individual who does not unnecessarily pick political fights or create controversies." He said that during his efforts to see the CAP through to completion he had worked with many secretaries of the interior. "Never have I seen a more blatant example of petty party politics than I am seeing now," he said. "I am shocked that he believes he can use something as critical as the CAP for his own personal political motives."[18] Two can play that game, Udall said, adding that it would "be illogical to suggest I am going to go out of my way to help this man."[19]

Watt eventually approved the project, but not without a declaration that he had been committed to the aqueduct since 1969. "That was six years before the citizens of Tucson made a public commitment in June 1975," he said.[20]

When Watt stepped down in October 1983, Udall said: "I can't say I'm sorry to see James Watt leave, but I can't say I expect much of anything to change. . . . [The Reagan administration] has enjoyed billing itself as warring with environmental extremists."[21]

The CAP received its funding allocation in 1981 in part because of a political trade-off Udall made with eleven House members from North Carolina, according to former aide Henry C. Kenski Jr. Udall's staff recommended that he vote for an amendment to a bill that would abolish tobacco subsidies, which certainly would have been in keeping with his past action against tobacco interests, but Udall voted against the amendment and told Kenski: "I did something you're not going to like." Udall voted against the amendment to secure the North Carolina votes for the CAP, Kenski said.[22]

By the time of the CAP dedication on November 15, 1985, Watt was gone and Donald Hodel had taken over the Department of the Interior. Hodel was on hand the day the button was pushed to move Colorado River water to Phoenix. Mo Udall told the Phoenix crowd that it seemed his life had been measured by milestones in CAP's history, dating back to the Colorado River Compact, signed the year he was born.

In taking pride in the CAP, Udall also noted that the "era of big projects and even bigger dreams . . . is drawing to a close." He said he and Barry Goldwater agreed that the CAP could not be approved in the new atmosphere. He stopped short of saying perhaps it should not have been. That would come later.

There were lessons to learn from the CAP, Udall said. One was that there were "limits to things: to water, to land, to federal money." Another, he said, "is that we can't run roughshod over Indians or environmentalists or the city people or anyone else."[23]

In 1987, the Arizona delegation gave up the $385-million Cliff Dam to appease environmentalists so they could get an agreement for the remaining CAP funding. Arizona received $237 million more to carry on. The total cost had now reached $3.8 billion.

On October 1, 1993, the Bureau of Reclamation declared the CAP complete, and water users became obligated to pay off federal loans used to finance the CAP, which had now reached $4.4 billion.[24]

So was all the effort worth it? Mo and Stewart Udall began to have their doubts. As early as July 1975, Mo Udall was questioning the validity of the mammoth project. "By the time we finally got it passed," he said, "the environmental movement had arrived. Now what I thought would be the centerpiece of my career looks very dubious—to me and a lot of other people."[25]

In 1982, Udall told a reporter for *Sierra,* the Sierra Club magazine, that if he could turn the clock back to 1910, it would have been wiser to build ten cities like Yuma along the river instead of losing water to evaporation in aqueducts from Parker Dam to Tucson. "But we've passed the point of no return on that, and the project was sacred to the people of Arizona."[26]

Mo Udall said in 1987 that although he had supported the CAP, he probably should not have because its water will serve Phoenix and Tucson urban centers instead of outlying farming areas. "Now we have cotton farms selling out and taking their money to enjoy in La Jolla [California]—and cities building lakes so people will have lakefront homes in the desert. . . . If I had to do it over, I think I'd say, 'Leave the water in the river,'" Udall said.[27]

Two years later, he admitted he should have opposed the dams. "I was on the wrong side," he said. "I can only thank God that the growing environmental movement outgunned those of us . . . who favored the dams."[28]

Stewart Udall called the CAP "an example of bad planning, an example of bad economics. . . . I naturally have a lot of regrets," having spent "fourteen years of my life" working on it.[29] He said he doubted that money would have been allocated for the CAP if Congress had known the water was going to municipal rather than agricultural use. "If you had told me . . . in the 1960s, 'Well the reason we need this water is for urban growth,' I don't know if we could have sold it to Congress."[30]

Environmentalists won their dam battle, but it produced a coal-fired plant that polluted the air over the Grand Canyon.[31] An argument could be made that perhaps the dams would have been better for the environment. Little doubt exists that in terms of the environment, perhaps the state would have been better off without the dams or the plant.

The dam fight turned David Brower into "one of the giants of conservation history."[32] And after Brower left, the Sierra Club became a militant champion of environmental causes, one with which Mo Udall would work closely.

The CAP cost almost $3.5 billion more than anticipated, and its victory left an ambiguous legacy. According to author Robert Dean, the Page plant resulted in huge strip mines that scarred the Hopi and Navajo reservations. Emissions from the plant created air pollution in the pristine Four Corners area that added to the buildup of greenhouse gasses in the atmosphere. The plant transformed the reservations into an energy colony for the benefit of whites while the Native Americans received a fraction of the market value for their coal and, in exchange for the plant, waived their claim to 50,000 acre-feet of water that had been apportioned to them in 1948.

Completion of the project in 1993 left the agricultural and municipal beneficiaries in a state of crisis and disarray, fulfilling the 1967 predictions of University of Arizona economists Robert Young and William Martin, Dean said. Farmers were not using CAP water and the payback was being left to the cities.

The CAP spigot was turned on in Tucson in 1992. It delivered CAP water to 85,000 homes, but the tap was turned off in September 1994 because of outcries that the water was so full of minerals it corroded water pipes and poured out bad-tasting, foul-smelling, murky water. The city began pumping groundwater again. At the start of the twenty-first century, the city was still looking for a way to use CAP water. Without it, city officials said, the water table would continue to drop, sinkholes would develop, and the quality of water would diminish.

As Dean, a Tucson resident, said: "The longer-term consequences will not become apparent for years."[33]

THE HUMOROUS MO

*H*umor was Mo Udall's stock in trade. One of the reasons people liked him was that he was funny. Someone once said that it is difficult to dislike a person who makes you laugh.

Udall used humor to set people at ease, to make a point, to entertain, to break a tense moment. "Humor can disarm an enemy," he would say. "It's possible to use humor in a new way, to tell a foe that it's possible to laugh together and do better. I had a rival, a lawyer, who was on the opposite side of every issue I believed in. We had a silent feud for two years. Then we were assigned to the same case and we won it together. So I wrote him a note: 'Dear Jim, (formerly "you lousy bastard.") It was a pleasure to work with you.' "[1]

Humor also was Udall's shield; he used it to keep people from getting too close to him. It was almost an oxymoron—humor attracted people to Udall and it set up a wall around him to prevent intimacy. He also used it to overcome uncomfortable social situations. He was poor at small talk or cocktail party talk and would resort to humor. Udall also may have used humor to cover up his own pain. Said former aide R. Kent Burton: "He was at once one of the kindest, most intelligent, and in some ways, most puzzling men I have ever known. He had his share of pain and disappointment in life. But he always kept it inside and covered it with a lot of humor. Admirable in one way, but probably unhealthy in another."[2]

Udall's humor was almost always kind, generally self-effacing, and always topical; that is, it fit the moment. He believed biting or sarcastic humor not only devastates the opposition but leaves a sense of bitterness.[3] That's not to say he never made an insensitive remark or cracked an off-the-cuff comment that proved less than funny. Sometimes his mouth moved at a pace faster than his brain. He would put his foot in his mouth on occasion and wish later that he could retract his statement. For the most part he meant no harm and was subject to the gaffes anyone might make. He certainly never intended to show disrespect to anyone.

One such faux pas may have cost him the presidential support of writer Nora Ephron, now a movie producer. Friend Larry L. King played host to a gathering of writers in New York City to introduce them to Udall. Others attending were William Styron, Nat Hentoff, Jules Feiffer, Tom Wicker, Russell Baker, David Halberstam, and Roger Wilkins. During the gathering, Ephron asked him about his stand on women. Part of his response was a joke he borrowed from his father. It went: An Indian was riding his pony and his wife was walking alongside him on the way to a village. He was asked why his squaw was walking and he answered, "She no got pony." King said Ephron was offended and declined to support Udall.[4]

Once during a political gathering of women in Washington, D.C., Udall told a joke that could not help but offend the audience. "Eleanor Roosevelt took an overnight Pullman train to Chicago and got the lower berth," he said. "The man in the top berth snored. At intervals, she'd bang on the bottom of the top berth. He'd stop snoring for a while and start again. Finally, she banged hard. The man said: 'It ain't gonna do you no good lady. I saw you when you got on.'" Udall later attributed the story to former presidential candidate Adlai Stevenson when he repeated it in a newspaper article during which he acknowledged that "women's rights enthusiasts might find (it) unacceptable."[5]

One of his former aides, Anne Scott, said Udall was never sexist when dealing with staff, constituents, or lobbyists, but "he did sometimes fail to grasp the sensitivity of different audiences. . . . I honestly think Mo just thought [the Roosevelt joke] was a funny joke."[6]

At the same time, he could help his audience laugh at themselves. On one such occasion, he was addressing a fund-raising event in Spokane, Washington, for House colleague Tom Foley. An Episcopal bishop and his wife were in the audience. Foley began to worry when the jokes got down to barnyard humor. Udall told the story about the minister who told a parishioner that he had prayed for her the night before. "You didn't have to do that," she responded. "If you'd just phoned me, I'd have come right over." The bishop's wife dissolved in laughter. Udall stole that joke from Stevenson as well.

He knew the value of humor when tensions were high. "Humor can be a powerful weapon in politics," he said. "You can warm up people in an audience and get them to identify with you. You can make a point through humor better than any other way. Humor can diffuse anger, break tension, or lighten a tough moment. It may even move an opponent a little closer to your side."[7] Whether Udall was a master of psychology by purpose or by accident, his use of humor served him well. Humor allowed individuals to at least be momentarily distracted from the issue. It also gave people time to think, to head off negative emotions, to transmit a sense of trust, to readjust the focus. He learned that self-deprecating humor helped keep the confidence of disagreeing sides. Timing also was integral to success, he discovered.

When he sought the Democratic nomination for president in 1976 he was often asked if he was tough enough to be president. Some thought he might be too soft. Writer James J. Kilpatrick once wrote that Udall was "too funny to be president,"[8] hence the name of Udall's semi-autobiography, which he wrote with son Randy and aide Bob Neuman in 1988. The 249-page book sold about 15,000 copies.[9]

Representative John B. Anderson, a Republican from Illinois, said Udall was "probably a little bit too good-natured and too good-humored . . . there was an innate kindness about him that made it hard at times for him to really step on people that needed to be stepped on."[10]

He had such a warehouse of jokes that he could draw on one at a moment's notice. Much of his humor was planned; he had four notebooks filled with jokes and he would often reread them to keep them in his mind.

His sense of humor was real; he was generally a funny man, with a quick wit. "I am often accused of having a sense of humor," he would say. "It's better to have a sense of humor than no sense at all."[11]

He began collecting legal and political jokes, yarns, and saws early in his career. He drew on jokes his grandfather David King Udall had used in frontier Arizona in the late 1800s. "I've got jokes that Ben Franklin used in the late 1700s. I've got jokes about bureaucrats, voters, Yasir Arafat, Jesus Christ, Calvin Coolidge, Republicans, Democrats, Indians, animals, Mormons, Jews, blacks, whites, politicians, polygamists, and polygamist politicians . . . thousands of them," Udall said.[12]

When Arizonan Sandra Day O'Connor was nominated to the Supreme Court, the evangelist Jerry Falwell called on Christians to write in protest because she had voted to uphold abortion and had been president of a Planned Parenthood chapter. Senator Barry Goldwater responded that Christians should line up to kick Falwell in the ass. Udall tore the newspaper article out and wrote the following and sent it to Goldwater: "That's a good idea, but it wouldn't accomplish anything because Falwell is a good Christian and he would simply turn the other cheek."[13]

Goldwater was a friend. They were poles apart in their political philosophies but were drawn together by their gentle, gracious senses of humor, and they would spar unmercifully, with Mo often getting the upper hand. For example, during the congressional debate over whether the United States should relinquish the Panama Canal, Mo said about Goldwater: "Barry does not hear very well, and I told him that I had seen the dentist and that I didn't quite know what to do about my root canal. Barry replied, 'Well, all I can say is that we bought it, we paid for it, it is ours and we are going to keep it.'" Mo called Barry the ultimate conservative, "someone who didn't see anything happen for the first time."[14]

During the Johnson administration, Udall was the pitcher/manager of the Democratic congressional baseball team, which played the Republicans once a year. Mo said he had two pitches: the Great Society gopher ball and his newly developed credibility sinker, which has so little stuff you really can't believe it.

Udall was in great demand as a speaker because of his political acumen and humor. He often would begin with the line, "I'm reminded of a story." Groans and chuckles would rise from the audience as they knew they were in for a treat. Off he would go telling one story after another. Some people had heard the jokes before but could not help but laugh.

Some of his jokes became outdated. Nonetheless, as one wag put it: "He treats jokes the way he treats his friends; he loves the old ones as much as he loves the new ones."[15]

Once while telling a joke at a homecoming breakfast of University of Arizona athletic lettermen, former football player Virgil Marsh interrupted him, saying, "Hey, Udall, we heard that one before." Udall looked at him and said, "Dammit, Marsh, if I was playing Beethoven's Ninth Symphony, would you tell me don't play that because you've heard it before?"[16]

Udall was a master of delivery. "Telling a joke is a lot like dancing a waltz," he said. "You have to feel the tempo. If you lose the punchline, you lose the joke. Being humorous is a skill. It involves phrasing, body language, timing, and inflection. You should never read a joke. You have to deliver a striking shaft of truth naturally. The minute you strain, you lose the spontaneity."

He made no secret that he stole jokes. He often quoted humorist Art Buchwald, who said you should credit the original joke teller the first two times "then the hell with them. They probably stole it from someone else anyway." He always tried to volunteer to speak first at a luncheon or dinner, he said, particularly in Washington, where he could use a stolen joke before someone else did. By 1985, he had compiled 1,200 jokes. "I steal," Udall said, "from everyone from Lincoln to Reagan."[17]

At Mo's memorial service on March 4, 1999, in Washington, D.C., Energy Secretary Bill Richardson said Mo showed him how to steal a good joke. "And if what I heard today is any indication," Richardson said, "many of Mo's friends have taken this sentiment to heart. There is outright robbery going on here—and you know what? I think Mo would have loved it."[18]

Udall told the politician's prayer so many times, people thought he wrote it, but Marvin Mandel, when he was the Democratic governor of Maryland from 1970 to 1977, had it mounted on the wall over his desk. It said: "Oh Lord, teach us to utter words that are gentle and tender, because tomorrow we may have to eat them."[19]

Udall would have speeches prepared for him, but he preferred to speak extemporaneously, which prompted him to make a joke about it. He said his advisers told him once that he deviated from his speeches too much. He then promised them he would read every word of their speeches from then on because he did not want to be known as a textual deviate.[20]

The political satirist Mark Russell remembered when Udall arrived in Washington in the early 1960s as a gangly freshman congressman with a crew cut. "At first, few of us in the Capitol bothered to remember his name. That changed the night of his debut as a dinner speaker, an evening which could be likened to the unknown understudy in a Broadway show becoming a star overnight."

Udall was the last speaker of the evening, following a half-dozen well-known orators who had been well received, all tough acts to follow, Russell remembered. "Udall shuffled to the microphone and in his unexpected resonant twang, his mischievous delivery signaled a parody of a phony politician's folksiness: 'My fellow Americans—my heart is as heavy as a bucket of hog liver tonight!' He continued his high-pitched irony throughout a monologue covering all the issues of the moment with great levity. From that point on, no evening of speech making in Washington would be complete without Mo Udall."[21]

Udall also liked a practical joke now and then. Russell took the brunt of one for his unmerciful jokes about Udall's dwindling chances of attaining the 1976 Democratic presidential nomination. Not long after Jimmy Carter was nominated, Russell and Udall attended a dinner in Tucson. When Russell left to get into his rental car, a police officer was standing next to it. The officer told Russell that the car had improper tags and was illegally parked.

"Matters were not helped when I discovered I had left my wallet with driver's license in my hotel room on the other side of town," Russell said. "As he started to escort me into the squad car, I insisted that if we went back inside, my good friend Congressman Udall could straighten the whole thing out."

Reluctantly, the officer agreed and they went inside to find Udall surrounded by a group of people. Russell walked up to him and said, "Mo, could you vouch for me to the officer here—there's a little mix-up." At that point, Udall turned to the cop and said, "I'm sorry, I don't know the man. He's an impostor. Kindly take this man out." After some guffaws, the officer let Russell go.[22]

In 1978, he told an audience that he was planning to run for president in 1980 on the one-eyed ticket. "I call on one-eyed people to arise. We have nothing to lose. Throw these two-eyed people out. They have screwed up our country. It is time to give one-eyed government a chance."[23] During his presidential campaign he was asked while playing golf whether he had a handicap. "Handicap? I'm a one-eyed Mormon Democrat from conservative Arizona . . . you can't find a higher handicap than that."[24]

Members of Udall's family are uncertain where he got his sense of humor. His father, Levi, was proper, even stuffy. Morris said that his father was "never a superb spinner of yarns [but] he did have an appreciation for the role of humor in human affairs. His courtroom stories and tales of early St. Johns fascinated me and inspired me to follow in his footsteps." Because of his role as a community leader, Levi often began his talks with a joke. He even kept a collection of them in a musty, yellow file. After Levi died, his son Burr went through the file and found entries for "Funerals (stock)" and "Funerals (special)." "That says something about my father's organizational abilities and dry sense of humor," Morris said.[25]

Mo Udall may have gotten the gift of humor from his mother, Louise, family members say. But truth be told, he probably got it from both parents. Brother Burr, a Tucson attorney, is the only family member whose humor approaches Mo's. While not a jokester, he is a wonderful storyteller.

Udall usually tended to be cautious about ethnic and religious jokes, because they could backfire. The closest he got to religious humor was when he remarked that Palestine leader Yasir Arafat would die on a Jewish holiday. Someone asked him how he knew that. Mo replied, "Anytime Arafat dies will be a Jewish holiday."[26]

"The best jokes are those that succeed in making all of us laugh together—not at someone or some group or someone's religious beliefs," he said. "Done well, a good joke can always make us feel a little better—and done in poor taste, nothing can make us hurt worse. Good political humor is never cruel, ridiculing, or belittling," he said. "It must be gentle, nudging at a weakness rather than exploiting a glaring personal characteristic. And I might add, off-color jokes are not worth the risk, and if you rely on them, you'll likely acquire a reputation you hadn't bargained for."[27] But, he warned, when telling an off-color story, be sure to "know your audience."[28] That was for public consumption, for Mo Udall liked an off-color joke as much as the next person, and he did not mind telling one when women were present, something that was far less acceptable in his day than today.

Udall saw humor as a way of reflecting humility, a way of self-deflating his own ego. He knew that he could not get caught up in his own importance if he was to be effective.

Udall could even poke a little fun at his death. He said he wanted to be buried in Chicago so he could stay active in politics.

MO'S AUDACITY

The day had gone poorly. Mo Udall was up at 5 A.M. and he was hungry, thirsty, and tired when he flew into Sacramento for the California Democratic Convention later that day. When he landed, it was at the wrong airport, "and there aren't that many airports in Sacramento," he said. No crowd greeted him, nor was there any press on hand. When he checked into his hotel, he was assigned to the Gerald R. Ford suite.[1] He wanted to talk with California governor Edmund G. "Jerry" Brown Jr. before the convention began. Brown, himself thought to be a presidential candidate in 1976, told him he had little time available, "especially [for] unknown presidential candidates," as Udall put it. They agreed to meet after 11 that night.

As he waited outside Brown's office he had a good idea what the session would be like. It would be, he said, "an awkward, formal exchange of courtesies, both of us acutely aware that we would very likely wind up competing for the same job. . . . And I remember wondering if anyone else could be ambitious or foolhardy enough to stay up so late for such a silly pointless ritual." He found out soon enough. As he was summoned to Brown's office, another not-so-well-known political candidate was leaving.[2] He told himself: "Udall, you may be a long shot . . . but that is one fellow who is going to be out of it quickly."[3] His name was Jimmy Carter.

Udall called that night a harbinger of things to come on the long, lonely road for the Democratic presidential nomination in 1976. In the popular vote, Carter finished first, Brown second, George Wallace third, and Udall fourth. Carter received 6.2 million votes; Brown, 2.4 million; Wallace, almost 2 million; and Udall, 1.6 million. But Udall would come in second to Carter in delegate votes at the Democratic National Convention in New York City eighteen months later, with 329½ votes to Carter's 2,238½.

The Sacramento convention was one of the first major events in the Udall campaign for the Democratic nomination for president, a move so brazen that brother Stewart called it audacious. Mo could have resigned himself to being happy in the House by gaining some power at a ripe old age, even though he thought the best he could hope for was becoming chairman of the less than prestigious Post Office Committee in 1982 at the age of sixty. He might even have taken a shot at the Senate seat held by former Republican governor Paul Fannin. Instead, he set his sights on the White House.

Longtime friend Charles Ares said Udall would have been unhappy just making the best of it. "The worst thing Morris could contemplate was a static situation, where nothing was moving, where we weren't trying to do better, doing new things. And I mean that's what pushed Morris to do this."[4]

It was virtually unheard of for anyone from the House to seek the presidency. Udall aspired to be the first one since James A. Garfield in 1880. "And he got himself shot," said Udall ruefully.[5] One pundit called the House "the bleachers of Washington power politics."[6] Interestingly, after Udall's futile but admirable attempt, a House member has sought the presidential nomination every election since. Undoubtedly, though, Udall was the longest of long shots.

Udall's ambition was given impetus at the end of 1973 when two of his ardent House backers, David Obey and Henry Reuss, both of Wisconsin, approached him about running. Udall had no false modesty and took to the idea from the beginning, Reuss said. "He didn't give us a lot of argument," he said.[7] Udall told Obey he had been thinking about running and that he would if enough House members wanted him to.[8] Aide Terry Bracy said he had approached Obey and Reuss about urging Udall to run. "There are no real drafts in American politics," Bracy said. "There are only strategies and Mo was part of that strategy."[9]

Obey and Reuss began passing a petition among House members in early 1974 urging Udall to explore running for the Democratic nomination. The word "explore" was key because some members might decline to sign if it were an all-out endorsement. "In our judgment, Representative Morris K. Udall of Arizona is not only one of the most effective legislators and engaging personalities in the House, but a man whose record and leadership ability could have widespread national appeal," the petition said.[10] Among the signers were Patricia S. Schroeder of Colorado, Bob Kastenmeier of Wisconsin, Otis Pike of New York, Claude Pepper of Florida, Fortney "Pete" Stark of California, John Seiberling of Ohio, Andrew Young of Georgia, and the Reverend Robert F. Drinan of Massachusetts. Udall would say later that the petition "was an essential tool in getting me in the race and getting that early attention you have to have."[11]

Obey was a great admirer of Udall's. "When you buy a president," he said, "you buy his psyche. That's why I like Udall. He's fresh, he's sensible, he's smart, and he lacks all traces of pomposity. He has just the personal characteristics that could catch on."[12]

The petition gave Udall credibility, and the fact that the stature of the House was on the rise because of the Nixon impeachment inquiries by the House Judiciary Committee helped as well. Still, Udall wondered whether anyone would pay attention to a relatively obscure House member. He knew he had to overcome that obstacle.[13] Udall would indeed make people pay notice before the race was over.

Udall began thinking about running in 1973, especially when it looked as if Senator Ted Kennedy was going to skip the race. What gave Udall hope was that the presidential nominating process had been taken away from the political brokers and put to a popular vote in the primaries. Presidential primaries were an opportunity for the little-known candidates to meet the people. A victory here and there even in the smallest of states could bring much media attention, which was essential for a successful effort.

Udall said people often called him "Senator," assuming that if he was running for president he must be a senator. "I never quite figured it out," he said, "but House members don't have the mystique. There's an aura when a senator or a governor arrives. But a House member is just good old so-and-so."[14]

Aide Bracy recognized that Udall would have to be a more aggressive candidate than the conciliatory legislator he had become. "In the House, you are taught to express disagreements in the most harmonious way, to accommodate legitimate complaints," Bracy said. "In a presidential race, the premium is on those who can best explain how they are different."[15]

Udall had to campaign hard if he was going to make an impact in the New Hampshire primary on February 24, 1976. He knew the state was a place where front-runners had failed and dark horses had become serious contenders.

While he was gearing up for New Hampshire, he also was traveling throughout the country in an attempt to become better known. He spent many a lonely day meeting people and speaking to groups from dawn till midnight. He grabbed food when he could and occasionally slept in supporters' spare rooms in beds too short for his frame. "The trick I found to finally getting to sleep [in a strange bed] is to admit that you can't go to sleep and you'll just close your eyes and rest," he said.[16]

When he arrived at airports he often wondered whether anyone would pick him up, and sometimes no one did. At a news conference at the Salt Lake City airport, he told a gathering: "It's great to be in North Panguitch again and see all you people. That's where I am, isn't it?"[17] Udall found himself playing the name identification game; he often was mistaken for his better-known brother Stewart.

Questions about the Mormon church dogged him. He told audiences he had been an inactive member of the church since before World War II, saying: "For more than 25 years I have held and expressed a deep-seated and conscientious disagreement with the church doctrine on the role of blacks. . . . I continue to hope that in its own way in good time the Mormon church will find a way out of the dilemma which distresses me and many other Americans both in and out of the church."[18] Mormon doctrine prohibited blacks from taking leadership roles in the church, a rule that was abolished in 1978. He told audiences that he had "not found a need for organized religion in my adult life."[19]

Fund-raising was a big problem. He was strapped for money right up to the Democratic Convention. At least his opponents were unable to call on big donors to pour millions into their campaigns, thanks to the new campaign reform he had helped write. The law, he said, was one of the reasons he could be in the race. With those restrictions he hoped to create an equal footing with his opponents. Even so, his aides were telling him he needed to raise $10 million.[20] He would fall far short.

Udall was not a wealthy man and so could not contribute his own money, and he promised his wife, Ella, that he would avoid going into debt to finance his ambition. He put brother Stewart, his campaign manager, and Stanley Kurz, the campaign treasurer and an old army air corps buddy, in charge of making sure he did not. "What I want to emphasize is that I have no intention of spending future years working to get out of hock," he wrote in a February 11, 1975, memo to his staff.[21]

To Mo Udall, his brother was the perfect choice for campaign manager. They became known as "Stewdall and Modall."[22] Stewart drew from the strength of the Kennedy campaigns in which family members put their own egos aside to help one another. "So Stew agreed to step in, at least in these early stages, and knock some heads together and put together a basic organization which would emphasize loyalty to me and my interests," Mo said.[23]

Udall's other campaign staff members were bright, young, and nationally inexperienced workers who admired Mo. In fact, some Washington cynics were saying that Udall's campaign was top-heavy with loyalists and lacked the experience of the aides of Alabama governor George C. Wallace and Scoop Jackson.

After Stewart Udall, second in charge was John Gabusi, thirty-four, coordinator of the fifteen western states. He had been Udall's reelection campaign manager from 1968 to 1974. Terry Bracy, thirty-two, was his congressional legislative assistant and joined his staff full-time in 1968. Press secretary Bob Neuman, thirty-five, was a former California newspaperman. Issues coordinator Jessica Tuchman, twenty-eight, held a doctorate from the California Institute of Technology and was the daughter of historian Barbara Tuchman. Others were scheduling director Ronald J. Pettine, thirty; fund-raising coordinator Marcie Kripke, twenty-three; and regional coordinators Paul Tully, thirty, Edward F. Coyle, twenty-seven, and Susan Marshall, thirty.

Four of his six children joined him on the campaign trail, as did his stepson Vince Fabrizio: Mark, twenty-four, a Williams College graduate; Judith ("Dodie"), twenty-three, a University of Arizona graduate; Anne, known as Bambi, twenty, a Vassar junior; and Brad, eighteen, who was delaying entering Stanford for a year. Udall reflected later about the "special traumas of family members torn by distaste for the whole political process." Udall said Mark had done well campaigning in New Hampshire in the fall of 1975 but did not go back the next year. Udall did not explain why but noted, "He was widely loved and people wanted to see more of him."[24] Mark had a bit of the politician in him, no doubt about that. In 1998, he was elected in his own right to Congress as a Democrat representing the Boulder, Colorado, area.

Dodie dropped out when she became disillusioned with the political sleaze-slinging, she told the *Tucson Citizen*. "In '76, nobody would ever talk about issues with me," she said. "I think it was because I was a woman. . . . I couldn't handle the staff people, the Secret Service. I was feeling more private. . . . What scared me most was that you were always, always, always in the public eye. . . . I got lonely and scared."[25]

Anne spent almost the entire final ten months on the campaign. She said the campaigning "gave me confidence about relating and interacting with people." And she got to know her father beyond holidays and vacations: "My father had just been somebody I read about in the paper."[26]

Brad worked for five months in Massachusetts, New Hampshire, and Iowa and enjoyed being with his father, for he, too, had spent little time with him.

Udall's brother Stewart made major sacrifices. He lost time and money, and Mo said Stewart "was put down by some of the press on the basis of off-the-record comments by people at my headquarters." Mo defended Stewart, saying he was "extremely good on a lot of things, including direct mail, money; he protected me, looking out for my interests at all times."[27] Stewart often stood in for Mo when he was unable to attend an event, particularly before environmental groups. "If you can't send the candidate himself," Mo said, "the best possible substitute is the candidate's brother, who is also managing the campaign and someone in his own right, not a Billy Carter."[28] The latter reference was to Jimmy Carter's brother, who was seen as a beer-guzzling buffoon.

Gabusi said Stewart had an "intellectual arrogance" and that he was above it all. He said Stewart would lecture his brother, causing Mo to chomp down on his cigar. It may have appeared that Mo was being deferential to his brother, but that was just his way of handling him, Gabusi said, adding, "Over time, Stewart's opinion came to be devalued."[29]

Mo Udall's staff was pushing him to test his endurance. "One of the things we are doing in this phase of the campaign," said Bracy, "is to find out how much Morris Udall wants the presidency."[30] Udall agreed. "One of the reasons I am out here is to find out how much I can take. And getting used to four or five hours' sleep."[31] On another occasion, he remarked: "This business of running for president is pretty rough. It tests your stamina, your digestion, your marriage, and your sense of humor."[32] But he was getting to like it. He said it was like swimming in a mountain lake. "At first it's an awful shock, but then it starts to feel good. You feel invigorated, strong, and pretty soon you're telling yourself, 'I can stay in here forever if I like.' "[33]

Others indicated they might run, particularly because President Gerald Ford appeared vulnerable. Among them were Minnesota senator Walter Mondale, Massachusetts senator Ted Kennedy, former Georgia governor Jimmy Carter, Oklahoma senator Fred R. Harris, Indiana senator Birch Bayh Jr., former North Carolina governor Terry Sanford, Texan Lloyd Bentsen, Jackson, and Wallace.

Udall believed that, with the field divided among so many choices, six or seven of them, himself included, would come to the Democratic Convention with too few delegates to win on the first ballot. "The 1976 convention will be the first brokered convention in the history of reform," Udall joked. "I say let's get the presidential nominating decision out of the convention and into the smoke-filled backrooms where it belongs." He might have a chance that way, he suggested.[34]

Udall indicated in May 1974 he might seek the nomination and began gaining the media attention he so desperately needed. *Washington Star-News* columnist Milton Viorst called him "a powerful speaker, radiating a rough-hewn Western magnetism. He may be the answer to a party which, for a decade, has searched futilely for charisma."[35] He formally announced he was running on November 24, 1974.

Asked why, Udall said: "You have a sick apple tree. The extreme liberal sees that tree and says, 'Let's cut it down and plant a new one.' The conservative yells, 'Leave that fine old tree alone.' I guess the Udall position is, 'Let's prune away some of the dead branches because the tree is basically still strong and with help will grow.' "[36]

Udall received his first real national exposure at a mini-convention of the Democratic Party in mid-December 1974 in Kansas City. Up to that point, said press secretary Neuman, the media had been dismissing his campaign as far-fetched. He gave a rousing speech and held a reception afterward. "It was the first real test we had. And I thought he did well. He displayed his humor and self-deprecation and told stories that wowed the delegates." Neuman said it also was the first inkling that the national press "was very fond of him." Another candidate was also thought to be far-fetched at that time—Jimmy Carter. Neuman said the Carter-Udall relationship was never good. "I think that Carter always envied Mo's easy relationship and the affection that the national press had for him that they did not have for Carter."[37]

Udall's wife, Ella, was somewhat reluctant about the campaign. "She found out he was running when he made the announcement on television, and she was pissed off about that from day one," said Iris Jacobson Burnett, an aide who traveled with Ella.[38]

In the early stages, Ella rarely traveled. "She was not . . . fully committed to this whole exercise," Neuman said.[39] She was cooperative, but showed little enthusiasm for campaigning. Some of Udall's aides were concerned that she might be a negative factor. The staff's anxiety over Ella stemmed from her volatile temper and, at times, heavy drinking.

Burnett became close to Ella after Udall asked her to travel with them. "He wanted someone to provide companionship, help, and because she couldn't be trusted to be alone," Burnett said. Ella was fun-loving on trips, but often her drinking would make her nasty, particularly to staff. The staff grew to dislike her. She loved to go to the hotel bars in the late evenings, where she would charm the press. "And the press loved her," Burnett said. Her job, she said, was to make sure that Ella did not get ugly with staff. "You couldn't be sure she wasn't going to get ugly with them if she was drunk." Ella ultimately fired Burnett when she stood up for a young volunteer, Burnett said.

She often cajoled Mo into joining her for late-night carousing, much to his physical detriment, Burnett said. "She would drag him to the bar. And then we would try to entertain her so that he could go back and go to sleep because he really needed not to be up until three o'clock in the morning with her."[40]

Ella felt more comfortable in less pretentious settings. At a cocktail party in Columbus, Ohio, aide Coyle said Ella "was a disaster. She didn't fit in at all." She hated the formality of such parties, he said. The campaign then moved to Cleveland where they attended a gathering of "blue collar/ethnic types" at a beer hall. "She was just terrific, doing the polka. She was wonderful." Coyle said Ella was good at small talk and she liked people, and Mo "was better when she was with him."[41]

Ella would chastise Mo, but rarely in public, with most of the scenes occurring in the hallway or in their room. Mo would never be confrontational with her, Burnett said. "And I think he was right not to take her on because you know she'd get really ugly. She wasn't the kind of person you could deal with rationally."[42]

Udall's early campaign concentrated on what he called "the three E's," economics, energy, and the environment. Critics questioned how much he knew about foreign affairs, as well as health, education, and urban issues.[43]

He spent the last five months of 1974 visiting twenty-five states, lining up support and seeking exposure. His effort was beginning to pay off—he started getting the attention of the political writers across the nation. George S. McGovern's successful 1972 pursuit of the Democratic nomination made it clear that no candidate could be ignored. Udall also knew he had to entertain the press with a mix of issues and wit, a talent he pulled off well the entire campaign.[44] The press came to adore him.

As 1974 drew to a close, he could look back on events that boosted his long-shot chance at the White House. Perhaps nothing helped him more than the news that neither of the two leading liberals, Mondale and Kennedy, would seek the nomination. "Viewed in hindsight," Bracy said, "I now doubt if the Udall candidacy could have gotten very far . . . had not Kennedy bowed out." He said Mondale's withdrawal left the liberal wing looking for a candidate. "By attrition," Bracy said, "their spotlight falls on MKU."[45]

Kennedy, in fact, told a Phoenix dinner gathering that Udall was "one of the finest congressmen the House has ever had." He called Udall "a big man with big ideas who stands tall over other congressmen."[46]

Bracy said the media turned their attention to Udall with Mondale and Kennedy out of the race. "They like MKU, and, what the hell, why not give him a shot?" Bracy was encouraged by the public relations that Udall had achieved during 1974 based on "the absence of competing talent, a boost by [Udall's] peers, a friendly press corps, and [Udall's] reputation as a serious legislator and articulate spokesman for change."

Bracy urged Udall to capitalize on the fact that voters "can't quite believe he is a politician. Mo's great genius is that he, and he alone of the crop of candidates, projects honesty with an intensity that absolutely confounds voters." He said 1975 was an important year because political reporters had no election to cover and would be looking closely at the candidates, and Udall's constituency during 1975 should be the press, opinion leaders the press influences, and the public. Effort needed to be spent lining up television and radio and giving speeches that would provide maximum visibility.

Direct contact with the public would be downplayed until 1976, Bracy said, because it was not the best use of his time. Bracy also offered a peek into Udall's personality in keeping the personal contact to a minimum: "[Udall] is not well suited for a coffee-and-handshake campaign even though the conventional wisdom growing out of 1972 rates this technique highly. It frankly bores MKU and tires him. . . . Those who don't appreciate what is involved ought to accompany MKU on one of those murderous, mind-numbing, coffee-guzzling, 72-hour treks to New Hampshire."[47]

On one trip, Udall ran into a situation in New Hampshire that might well be the most-quoted vignette of the entire campaign, brought up years afterward as a sign of his self-deprecating humor. Not long after Udall announced his candidacy he walked into a local barbershop and began introducing himself. "Hi, I'm Mo Udall and I'm running for president," he said. "Yeah, we know," the barber replied. "We were laughing about that this morning."[48]

On January 19, 1975, Stewart Udall sent his brother a three-and-a-half-page memo that he called the " 'basic document' of the campaign right now." In handwriting across the top to a friend he wrote, "Glory be, we have a candidate who will let himself be managed."

Stewart told Mo the only way he could win the Democratic nomination would be to achieve victory on the first or second ballot. "With some breaks you should have a better chance than McGovern to go all the way." Stewart noted that McGovern's campaign was misdirected because McGovern thought that by winning the nomination he was a shoo-in for the presidency.[49] Mo's campaign aides also were advising him to avoid taking positions that would get him nominated but would hamper his ability to win the general election, as they did McGovern.[50]

Stewart urged Mo to get House members involved. "The House is a potential source of real strength." He also advised his brother to "demand time for reflection—and don't let us exhaust you or over-schedule you." He said Mo should let Ella dictate his schedule. "She will know better than anyone when you are over-extending yourself and need a weekend break. . . . I'll back her up anytime she has strong opinions about the schedule."

Stewart said the New Hampshire and Wisconsin primaries should be Mo's priorities, calling them crucial. He told Mo to make time every day for personal calls on labor leaders, officials of important national organizations, and people like former ambassador W. Averell Harriman, Senator J. William Fulbright of Arkansas, and presidential adviser Clark Clifford. He also said Mo had to master the main issues and to react incisively to the events of the day. "The education of Mo Udall must be given a very high priority in 1975—never forget that."

What made the Kennedy brothers remarkable, Stewart said, was their capacity to grow. "Do your homework, learn to listen, and sharpen your sensitivity to the hopes and dreams of other Americans. . . . Finally be yourself. Much of JFK's appeal came from the fact that he obviously enjoyed being himself. One way honesty manifests itself is by an absence of pretense or posturing. The adventure is not worth the effort unless you have the tranquillity to know that you can take the worst—an ignominious defeat—and come out a better person."[51]

Nineteen seventy-five would be a time for educating Morris Udall, but also a time for Mo Udall to be educating the country about who he was, telling voters about the candidates: "You ought to look at who he is and not what he says."[52]

Udall's humor helped him enormously, but some worried that perhaps he would not be taken seriously. Once, a *Wall Street Journal* reporter asked him: "Are you prick enough to be president?" He was shocked by the question. It apparently had not occurred to him. Bracy was concerned about it as well. He told Udall that the national press corps found him "an irresistibly interesting, bright, and witty fellow who would make a hell of a good president, but can't possibly get there. Why? Because you are too nice, too humble, too much of an idealist to arrive at the brutal decisions and compromises which by observation they have learned are necessary to achieve the objective. . . . They see you not as a winner but as a tragic loser—an Adlai Stevenson who was too good to be president."[53]

Washington Post political writer David Broder said Udall "lacked a certain ruthlessness that might be necessary to reach the very top."[54]

Udall said with a touch of bitterness about his critics: "They are waiting for someone named Franklin Delano John Fitzgerald Jones."[55]

By mid-April, after Udall had spent several weeks campaigning in New Hampshire, his efforts seemed to be paying off. A poll by the *New Hampshire Times* put him on top with a voter preference of 25 percent—8 percentage points ahead of President Ford and leading Harris, Carter, Jackson, and Bentsen by margins of 9 percent to 21 percent.[56] But he had a long way to go. Udall's staff could not understand Carter's success. "We just saw him as some obscure governor from an obscure state, not to be taken very seriously," Burnett said.[57]

Udall already was experiencing financial difficulties. Money spent on direct-mail solicitation of funds was coming out of the administrative budget, and the money was not coming in fast enough to replace it. "I think it is important serious consideration be given to the fact that . . . unless we begin working on it, that we may be out of cash," Gabusi wrote in a March 31, 1975, memo to Stanley Kurz and Stewart Udall.[58]

On June 24, 1975, Udall got some good news. As brother Stewart put it, "the wilderness survival" phase had been concluded. The campaign could expect $1 million in contributions by the end of the year and Mo was eligible for $1 million in matching federal funds, Stewart said. It would come in January, just in time for the primary season.[59] He raised the money in small donations in twenty different states. Overall, Mo had raised about $350,000, far below Wallace's $3.7 million and Jackson's $2.3 million.[60]

Udall was in Phoenix to attend a fund-raising event to begin his presidential campaign in Arizona. He told Bracy that he was feeling ill and that his cousin Cal said he should see a doctor, but he had declined. At 3 A.M. the morning of July 26, after the fund-raising event, he and Bracy were sharing a room at the Adams Hotel when Udall began moaning, "Oh, my God. Oh." Bracy thought he was having a heart attack. Udall refused to let Bracy call an ambulance, but they went downstairs and obtained a taxi. He was diagnosed with pneumonia. "Mo was never physically the same after that event," Bracy said. "He tired easily. . . . Looking back now I have no doubt that was the event that brought Parkinson's on."[61] Udall had met with Dr. Jerome H. Targovnik and asked that he check him over. Targovnik said it took three chest X rays before it was discovered Udall had pneumonia. It was treated with antibiotics.

Robert A. Reveles, a special assistant to Udall from 1967 to 1969, had gathered a group of Latinos at the hotel and went to see Udall in his room. He found him lying on the floor stretching his back. Later, Udall made a brief appearance before the group, Reveles said, and then excused himself because of his discomfort. "It was the first inkling that Mo's health was a challenge," Reveles said.[62]

Udall lay on the floor, Targovnik said, to ease the pain caused by the pneumonia, which had settled at the base of his lungs and his diaphragm.[63] Targovnik vigorously denied that the incident was a precursor to his Parkinson's disease, which was diagnosed in 1979. Udall and Targovnik became friends, and as Udall's Parkinson's worsened in later years, Targovnik often traveled with him on lengthy trips.[64]

After being treated for his pneumonia, Udall wanted to get back to work sooner than his condition warranted. It was his first major illness since meningitis when he was a youngster.[65] "Clearly, . . . the incident was the beginning of his physical decline," Bracy said. "He required afternoon naps just to get through the day." Bracy was assigned to enforce discipline on his schedule. "I quickly became a hated figure in the scheduling office, and with the political organizers, as a result. But I never said anything to them about his illness."[66]

On August 10, Udall left for a weeklong fact-finding trip to Israel with issues coordinator Jessica Tuchman. He returned extremely tired.[67] "It may have contributed to my health problems by getting me out of bed too quickly after the episode in Phoenix," Udall said.[68]

His status as a divorced man also was getting attention. No president had been a divorcé. Udall noted that former vice president Nelson Rockefeller, Kansas senator Robert J. Dole, President Gerald Ford, and former California governor Ronald Reagan had divorces in their families. "In the future, I suspect that divorce might be a factor depending on the circumstances, but it never again will be an automatic disqualification," Udall said.[69]

Udall was flying in and out of airports on a daily basis. He had visited forty-five states by the summer of 1975. It was difficult for this basically shy man to meet thousands of people, shaking hands at coffee klatches, standing outside plants to greet workers on their way through the doors. He was happier in a room full of people where he could crack jokes and give his stand on the issues. If it was uncomfortable for him, most people did not notice. They saw a relaxed, easygoing style.

Some people, however, saw him as too distant, too remote, too unable to make personal connections, Coyle said. He said the "rap" the staff heard during the campaign was that he was "kind of hiding some-thing" with his humor. "I'm not sure quite what it was, but he was personally just not able to connect very well with people," Coyle said.[70]

Meanwhile, the campaign focused on the first real primary in New Hampshire after Gabusi decided to minimize the Iowa caucuses. Then, in late September, Gabusi pulled out to handle a personal problem. He recommended the young Jack Quinn as his replacement and second in command to Stewart Udall.

Quinn believed that Udall had to win two out of the three races in Iowa, New Hampshire, and Massachusetts "or the press will write us off before Wisconsin." Iowa and New Hampshire were wide open, but Jackson was thought to have a big lead in Massachusetts. Quinn and other campaign workers believed that voters were looking for the candi-date who had positive feelings for people and affirmed their belief in "the goodness of America," so they sought to stress Udall's character and that he was "big" enough for the job.[71]

Udall had established three offices in Iowa, which would select delegates to the national convention during a January 19, 1976, caucus. Although he was optimistic about Iowa, he had fared poorly in a straw poll on October 27 when Carter came in first with 23 percent of the vote, and Udall finished a distant fifth. He referred to it as that "silly poll," but he recognized that Carter had received an "incredible flow of press" from it. The *New York Times* headlined the story: "Carter Appears to Hold a Solid Lead in Iowa as the Campaign's First Test Approaches."[72]

The Udall campaign was beginning to take notice of the former Georgia governor. Carter and Bayh, the Indiana senator, were the only ones Udall had to worry about, Quinn said. Also lurking in the back-ground was Hubert Humphrey, the former vice president, who was hoping to steal the nomination in a deadlocked convention. Quinn told Udall: "You, to date, are genuinely recognized as the candidate with no enemies. Humphrey, though, is the 'candidate' with many friends. We must go to the convention . . . with more delegates than anyone else to head Humphrey off at that point."[73]

The campaign's optimism was not shared by one Udall activist, Curtis B. Gans, an organizer for Eugene McCarthy's campaign in 1968. He told Udall the campaign was in dire trouble. He said Udall's troubles could be blamed on an "inadequate and often incompetent staff" and "a gross lack of strategic judgment." Gans told Udall he was the most qualified candidate but that "in the opinion of every journalist and politician I have talked to in the country, [the campaign] is the worst campaign of all those running with the conceivable exception of [President] Gerald Ford, who has even a little more going for him." He called on Udall to take more control of his campaign or "there won't be one within two months."[74]

Bracy said the campaign was running smoothly until Gabusi left. "Then the chaos began, then all the sharks got in the water." Bracy said he never had confidence in other staff members after Gabusi departed, and nasty infighting began. "Could Mo have settled it? Probably. Was he ready to settle it? Almost never. . . . Mo always said that when liberals form a firing squad they form a circle."

Bracy said that although Udall was intent on winning the 1976 nomination, "Mo was convinced that he'd have to run at least twice to have a chance to win." He did not push himself as hard as he could, and resentment built up in the staff because Udall did not work around the clock, Bracy said. The staff failed to realize that Udall was not well and that he was looking toward future campaigns: "Mo always had enormous ambition, but there was a governor on it."[75]

Udall noted that Carter had no job and could campaign full-time. "At the same time I was trying to get a strip-mine bill through the Congress, trying to get a land-use bill, trying to protect my voting record, trying to get home to Arizona once in a while. And Carter had nothing else to do except keep this rigid, tight little schedule he had fixed."[76]

Bracy said the fundamental flaw was that Udall was cast as a liberal, when his real strength was as a reformer. Carter usurped that position by describing himself as a Washington outsider and with his statement "I will never lie to you." Said Bracy: "Mo gave up his position as the reform candidate to Carter and in the end that position was going to win."[77]

Udall got a clean bill of health from his physician, Jerome Targovnik, on November 20, 1975. "Anyone who can campaign 18 hours per day, seven days per week must be in good health to survive this," Targovnik said. "There are no medical contraindications for his running for the office of president."[78]

Udall was finding the campaign road grueling. He wished he could cut it back to 70 percent of what he was doing because he was always tired; there were too many meetings and too much pressure to succeed. On one stop he was handed a speech that was too long. With an hour, he said, he could have made it better, but he had to boil it down as he went along. He often ran behind schedule and was forced to catch a nap on a plane and give himself a cold-water shave before heading to another meeting. He ate poorly, grabbing meals when he could. "People who have been around campaigns follow a rule that when food is available, eat it, because one never knows when that might happen again," Udall said.[79]

He flew in a beat-up old DC-3, nicknamed Tiger. Bracy called the aircraft "a pathetic, and I thought, dangerous two-engine job."[80] One pundit said the plane looked like the one that took Ingrid Bergman away from Humphrey Bogart in *Casablanca*. Once, Udall saw the irony of his shoestring campaign when his plane, also called the Basler Bomber after the charter company, was parked next to Carter's United 727 charter at a Wisconsin airport. Udall's plane cost $16,000 a month to lease. Udall gave up flying his own plane until after the election because of the rigors of the campaign. "Then either it's back to a Piper Cub or it's going to be Air Force One," he said.[81]

In mid-December, Stewart wrote Mo a memo he said he never gave to him. He warned that the campaign was "sucking up money like a tapeworm." The staff, he said, was "faction-ridden with nearly everyone more concerned about internal power struggles than what is being accomplished by the campaign as a whole."[82]

Mo Udall's goal during the campaign was to carve out a constituency from "the progressive center." He preferred to call himself a progressive rather than a liberal. Asked to explain the difference, Udall said it's like the law professor who asked a student, "What's the difference between fornication and adultery?" The student replied, "Well, I've tried them both, and I can't tell the difference."[83] He said on NBC's *Meet the Press* that the word *liberal* "is kind of a barrier to communication with people. . . . I didn't change anything I had advocated. I simply said: 'This is a barrier to communication. Let's not use this word.'"[84]

By the end of 1975 Udall had traveled more than 300,000 miles and visited nearly 150 cities in 43 states.[85] He still had a long road ahead. The February 24 New Hampshire primary was seven weeks away.

SECOND-PLACE MO

*A*s 1976 began, Mo Udall was trying to squelch speculation that he might drop out of the presidential campaign and run for senator in Arizona after Republican Paul Fannin announced he would not seek reelection. He accused supporters of other Democratic candidates of advancing the rumors. "This unfounded idea has spread widely enough that much to my regret I feel it necessary to state emphatically what I thought by now had become abundantly clear: That I am a candidate for president and for president alone," he said. "Any contender who thinks otherwise is engaging in wishful thinking."[1]

He admitted that he had briefly considered the Senate race but decided to continue the presidential quest. "It is sad that in life you can't always choose the way you might wish to," he said.[2] That sounded like an echo of 1954 when he wanted to run for Congress but deferred to his wife Pat.

He knew he could keep his options open because the filing date to seek reelection to the House came after the Democratic National Convention. As it turned out, Udall probably could have won the Senate seat. Two Republicans split the party during a nasty primary battle, and the winner, Representative Sam Steiger, was soundly beaten by former Pima County attorney Dennis W. DeConcini. Udall also may have realized that by returning to the House he might move up to chairman of the

Interior Committee because two or three people ahead of him in seniority were uncertain about seeking reelection.[3]

While Carter had been working Iowa for a year, Udall got in late. After Gabusi's departure and Quinn's decision to push harder in Iowa, Udall did put some effort into the campaign. It was too little, too late. He had two events set up on consecutive days but no TV cameras showed up.[4] While campaigning, he asked rural farm audiences whether they knew the difference between a pigeon and an Iowa farmer. "A pigeon," he said, "can still make a deposit on a tractor."[5]

Udall spent eight days before the Iowa caucus hunting for Iowa delegates, a move that left him open to second-guessing. One aide based in New Hampshire, Joanne Symons, called the strategy "stupid," adding, "We were all screaming, 'What's he doing in Iowa? Get him back here because we can win here.' . . . If he'd won here, if he'd beaten Jimmy Carter, I think Carter would have been dead."[6]

Udall aide Jessica Tuchman said the indecision over whether to hit Iowa hard hurt. "I don't think we ever got it straight in our heads. We didn't think that New Hampshire was going to be absolutely crucial, but we didn't decide until too late whether Iowa was going to be important or not."[7]

Udall finished fifth in the January 19 Iowa caucus with 5 percent of the vote, trailing Carter's 27 percent. "The Iowa caucus was a low point. . . . I thought 'What the hell, this is all going to be over pretty soon.' "[8]

Although only 14,000 people had voted for Carter, he jumped to the front in the media's eyes. *Time* and *Newsweek* printed 726 lines about Carter; Udall received 30.[9] But perhaps the loss might work in Udall's favor. If he were able to beat Carter in New Hampshire, it might be perceived as a big upset.[10]

Udall estimated he visited a hundred living rooms across New Hampshire, talking to groups of twenty to seventy people. He worked at campaigning but "I never felt myself totally immersed in campaigning. Physically, I couldn't drive myself to campaign full blast from dawn past midnight." He had a difficult time with glad-handing, but he knew it was necessary. "I found it hard to persuade myself that a handshake and a half-second of eye contact really affects a citizen's decision on who should occupy our highest office," he said.[11] During a tour of a paper mill in Groveton, Udall asked: "Why do I have the right to stop these people from their work?"[12] Symons attributed Udall's reluctance to greet people to shyness. "Unfortunately, people got the impression he was cool and distant."[13]

With all the liberals in the race, Carter had the right wing of the Democratic Party to himself. Had just one liberal, such as Fred Harris or Birch Bayh, dropped out, Udall might have finished first. Or if someone to the right of Carter, like Scoop Jackson or Lloyd Bentsen, had entered the race, Udall might have won. The "ifs" and second-guessing came easily after the fact.

Jimmy Carter received 23,373 votes to Udall's 18,710 in the February 24 primary. Carter earned 28.4 percent of the vote followed by Udall with 22.7 percent, Bayh with 15.2 percent, and Harris with 10.8 percent. The three liberal candidates received almost 50 percent of the vote. Carter beat Udall by just over 4,600 votes, but the media coverage failed to reflect that margin. Carter's picture was plastered on the covers of *Time* and *Newsweek* with in-depth coverage inside. Carter received 2,630 lines of coverage, and Udall 96.[14] The free publicity and goodwill were enormous. Udall thought the story was that he was "clearing out the left," but the news media focused on Carter's success.[15] A *Time* magazine reporter later told Gabusi that the magazine had two covers ready, one of Carter and one of Udall.[16] Udall estimated it would cost $250,000 a week to generate the kind of publicity that the New Hampshire victory produced for Carter.[17]

Carter's victory kept alive a record that no one who ever won the presidency had lost the primary in New Hampshire.[18] "I should have taken those eight days in Iowa and gone into New Hampshire," Udall said. He figured he was gaining on Carter by 1,000 votes a day and with eight more days in New Hampshire, he could have pulled off a victory.[19]

Udall sat out the March 9 Florida primary, a decision he later regretted. He said that he would have pulled enough votes from Carter to give Wallace the victory, perhaps slowing down Carter's juggernaut. But Udall detested Wallace's policies, so when Carter's people convinced him that it was essential to beat Wallace, he agreed to stay out. "It not only made good sense to me," Udall said, "avoiding the swamp that is Florida, the immense amount of money and time you would have to pour into it, but I didn't think that the party was really going to nominate Jimmy Carter."[20]

There is no question that Udall was tired from all the campaigning, but he kept plodding ahead, going from one gathering to the next. Between appearances in Massachusetts he sighed: "It would be the greatest relief in the world to me to know now it's no use. You find yourself almost wishing someone would tell you for sure—that it's no use—so you could quit. You start just looking forward to it ending, even if it's losing, just for it all to be over with."[21]

Udall's campaign in Massachusetts received a boost when former Watergate prosecutor Archibald Cox agreed to support him. For all the criticism Stewart Udall was being handed, it was he who wooed Cox to the effort.[22]

Carter irritated Udall. Mo could not see him as president and was baffled about why he did so well in Iowa and New Hampshire. Everywhere he looked there was Carter. Udall did not have to worry about the Arizona caucus, did he? Carter was there, too, working hard as always. "Incredible," Udall said. "He's even out there in Arizona, running around. The sonuvabitch is as ubiquitous as the sunshine."[23]

Jackson won the March 2 Massachusetts primary, but with only 22.3 percent of the votes. Udall ended up second with 17.7 percent, Wallace was third with 16.7 percent, and Carter received just 13.9 percent.[24]

Udall was buoyed by his second-place finishes in New Hampshire and Massachusetts, saying he had gained "mo-mentum." Birch Bayh dropped out, and while he failed to endorse Udall, Mo did pick up some of Bayh's supporters for the April 6 New York primary. Udall felt he had grabbed the liberal banner and now was "the only horse to ride."[25] While some observers felt Udall would find it easier to attract financial help, he was having a difficult time lining up support from labor and blacks. They said he had not been closely associated with those groups in the past. They also were saying that the liberal wing of the party was less dominant than in 1972 when it had the Vietnam War to oppose. Sure, Udall had the environmentalists, but their fervor failed to match the Vietnam War rallying cry. And Hubert Humphrey was still waiting in the wings.[26]

After back-to-back second-place finishes in New Hampshire and Massachusetts, Wisconsin became the key state. "We have got to win Wisconsin or our campaign is in trouble," he said.[27]

Wisconsin was Udall's kind of state, a mix of progressive thought, farm vote, and ethnic blue-collar big-city vote.[28] But three weeks before the April 6 election, Udall's polls showed that he trailed Carter 17 percent to 34 percent. Stewart recalled: "We both agreed that, well, he's going to lose—but at least let's go down with class. Don't whine. We were just so sure that we were going to lose, and lose badly, in Wisconsin. You just can't come back from a 2-to-1 deficit in three weeks."[29] He almost did.

Ten days later, Udall's pollster told him he had closed the gap to 4 percentage points, trailing Carter's 34 percent. It was time for a big push. Udall had hoped to spend $350,000 in Wisconsin but by then had raised only $100,000, and Stewart doubted whether any more would come in. A week before the primary, Udall's media advisers urged spending $25,000 on TV ads, but Stewart vetoed the expense. When the advisers appealed to Mo, he overruled Stewart, but the time slots were no longer available. Stewart was trying to keep Mo from going broke, "but every time Mo smelled a little victory, he changed the mandate a little. But he kept telling me, 'You've got to protect me.' "[30] While Udall was getting no air time, Carter's ads were everywhere. Udall also canceled a mailing to 100,000 rural households because of a lack of funds.[31]

Jack Quinn defended Stewart's action in cutting off funds. "A week ahead, no one knew it would be that close. You couldn't say [more television] would change the tide. It was not an irrational judgment at the time." He said he believed that "it was not unfair or unreasonable" for Stewart to conclude that the expenditure would be wasted.[32]

Fred Harris was feeling pressure to throw his support to Udall. Harris said he stayed in the race because his labor supporters in Wisconsin were candidates for delegates to the national convention. If Harris withdrew, they felt they would not be elected. Harris also said that if he withdrew he could have been unable to receive matching campaign funds from the Federal Elections Commission. Undoubtedly, Harris's backing of Udall would have turned the tide. Harris received 8,185 votes, of which Udall could have expected to get 90 percent.[33]

Udall's vote on right-to-work probably hurt him in Wisconsin as well. Harris said labor was Udall's "Achilles' heel. . . . A lot of labor was hostile toward him. 14b [the right-to-work provision in the Taft-Hartley Act] was the litmus test for labor, and it was the final chink in his armor. In those days, labor did not choose the candidates, but it did have kind of a veto. Some people in labor had kind of a hard time warming up to him."[34]

Despite the uneven planning and budgeting, Udall took the lead during the early returns. NBC and ABC predicted a Udall victory, although CBS held off. Supporters were euphoric. Even the *Milwaukee Sentinel* printed in its early edition: "Carter Upset by Udall." At 10:30 P.M., Udall walked into his hotel's ballroom to cheers of "Go-go-go-go" and a band playing "On Wisconsin." When they quieted down, Udall told them: "Oh, how sweet it is!"[35] David Obey warned Udall not to declare himself a winner. "I'm not convinced you've won," he told Udall.[36] Obey and Henry Reuss cautioned that the rural vote had not come in yet and that those precincts might be attracted by Carter's religious fundamentalism.[37]

By 2 A.M. the vote had started to swing toward Carter. When it was clear he had won, Carter lifted the *Sentinel* over his head à la Harry Truman with the *Chicago Tribune*'s 1948 headline "Dewey Beats Truman." The pictures of Carter raising the newspaper dominated the news coverage the next day, obscuring Carter's dismal finish in New York: Henry Jackson of Washington got 38 percent of the delegates; Udall, 25.5 percent; Carter, 12.8 percent; and 23.7 percent were uncommitted delegate votes.[38] Carter won in Wisconsin by fewer than 5,000 votes out of more than 670,000 cast. Two liberals, Harris and Bayh (who already had withdrawn from the race), pulled down more than 13,000 votes, most of which could have gone to Udall. Udall collected 95 delegates between New York and Wisconsin while Carter received 61, but Carter got far more news coverage.[39]

"I have changed my statement of last night," Udall told reporters after the Wisconsin primary. "Everywhere I said the word 'win,' strike that and make it 'lose.' "[40]

On reflection, Ruess wrote: "Obey and I still believe that had Udall won, he could have restored to the nation the elan of the 1948–1968 years and thus would have changed for the better the history of the twentieth century's last quarter."[41]

Soon after the Wisconsin primary, aide Jessica Tuchman wrote a blistering two-and-a-half-page memo to Udall saying that his campaign "was crumbling at a terrifying rate. Here in the headquarters, and everywhere else around the country, everything has stopped. Morale is destroyed." She blamed it on the lack of leadership. "Stewart and Stan Kurz have consistently terrified you with predictions of giant debt that were unfounded." She said the campaign was in trouble because of amateur and incompetent decision-making.[42]

Mo Udall was aware of the chaos in his campaign, but he was not one to interfere. He was too busy campaigning to deal with internal struggles. Besides, he always walked away from staff disputes. Later, in an outline for a proposed book about the campaign, Udall acknowledged the "problems of staff/SLU [Stewart L. Udall] misunderstandings leading to progressively worse division." He said it was a legitimate question that if he could not run a campaign organization, how could he run the country?[43]

Quinn was frustrated as well. "We were routinely involved in squabbles over decision-making," he said. "I look at the Carter campaign and I see it was run by a submarine commander who didn't tolerate that sort of crap."[44] "[Udall] was more of a courtroom lawyer who wanted to hear from all sides, and let all the evidence come in, and arbitrate different views—which at times was awkward and time-consuming," Quinn said. Tuchman said that Udall would delegate "enormous authority . . . that was a problem."[45] Udall's trait of delegating authority dated back to his days as county attorney, and he again defended his brother: "Part of the problem was that Stew wasn't at headquarters every day and was a good figure to dump blame on when they didn't want to blame me."[46]

Months later, Udall reflected on how the lack of money had hurt him. "I'd already gone into debt. . . . My wife was concerned. I'd seen candidates going on the lecture circuit [to bail themselves out of heavy debt]. . . . Maybe putting up my home for mortgage. . . . [But] I promised my wife I wouldn't. She loves her home. . . . We had hit all our friends. We were over our heads. All of the scrounging, the borrowing hadn't done it. . . . [But] one more turn of the wheel would have done it."[47]

While Udall was trying to buy media, Carter was getting it free: 43 percent of all network news on the Democratic race was devoted to Carter, along with 46 percent of the newspaper coverage and 59 percent of the magazine attention. It seemed as if the media had conceded the race to Carter.[48]

Udall's second-place finishes in Wisconsin and New York made just a good enough showing, one party liberal said, to keep his candidacy alive "with a respirator."[49]

In his home state, Udall was unable to sew up all of the 25 delegates, with Carter getting 5 and Wallace 1. Cousin Calvin Udall, a Phoenix lawyer, was his Arizona campaign manager.

Udall pollster Peter Hart wrote to Udall that if he were to have any chance to win the April 27 Pennsylvania primary he would have to undertake "massive spending" on the media and stress the economy and jobs, integrity, Udall's character, and that Udall was "ahead of the times on major issues." At the bottom of the memo, Stewart Udall wrote: "Great! Now what do we do? Go rob?"[50]

Hart's poll showed Carter ahead with 34 percent of the vote, Jackson with 25 percent, and Udall with 15 percent. "We kept telling ourselves, 'If we can just get the liberals,'" Mo recalled. "We thought the liberals might coalesce in Pennsylvania—that the liberals were going to rally there."[51]

Udall again put Obey on the hot seat. He asked Obey if he would go to a black Baptist church in Pittsburgh "to explain what Mo Udall was all about. I had never been in a black Baptist church in my life. . . . I discovered at that point that the task was a little bit tougher than the one I thought . . . because Jimmy Carter . . . had been in that very church the Sunday before."[52] Obey called it "a symbol of the incompetence of the campaign." He said because Carter had visited the church earlier "not a vote was to be had for Mo."[53]

Obey blamed some of Udall's campaign problems on inexperience. He said that when a House member runs for president, "it is a simple fact that they are inexperienced. It was amazing that he did as well as he did. It was a testament to his own personal excellence."[54] Mark Shields, who ran Udall's Ohio campaign, said one of Udall's problems was that he had never run a campaign larger than a congressional district.[55]

Talk invariably turned to Udall perhaps dropping out and accepting the second spot on the Democratic ticket. Udall replied, "I'm against vice in every form, including the vice presidency."[56]

During the Pennsylvania campaigning, Carter made a gaffe that Udall saw as an opening, but he was unable to capitalize on it. Carter remarked that he would not actively tamper with the "ethnic purity" of American neighborhoods. One of Carter's most ardent supporters, Representative Andrew Young of Georgia, called "ethnic purity" a "Hitlerian" term and urged Carter to recant. Udall, who saw a chance to gain a foothold with the black constituency, said: "We should have no place for thinly veiled hints at the politics of racial division." Later he said Carter's statement would "sentence our minorities to their ghettos for life." At another stop, he criticized Carter "for preaching ethnic purity and voluntary busing on the white side of town and [playing] soul brother on the black side of town."[57]

Apparently, the racial statement failed to hurt Carter. He won 37.2 percent of the vote, Jackson received 24.7 percent, and Udall garnered 18.8 percent.

Michigan was the next primary, on May 18, and the predictions were poor. Hart told Udall that he was trailing Carter 19 percent to 52 percent. Said Stewart: "We just assumed we were going to lose and lose badly. . . . But we also thought we just might be able to hang on to the end—because if we did, and if the convention was truly an open convention, we thought Mo just might be able to end up as vice president."[58] If Mo thought that was possible, he may have blown it when he began negative advertising, an almost desperate act. Pollster Hart said the ads were "the only way left."[59] They attacked Carter for his fuzziness on the issues. Udall was dismayed that Carter had the ability to be on two sides of an issue at the same time. It was difficult for his opponents to pin him down as a conservative or a liberal.[60] This complaint echoed the charges that Republican William Kimble and the *Tucson Daily Citizen* leveled against Udall in the 1964 congressional election.

According to author Martin Schram, Carter retaliated. Three days before the Michigan primary, Detroit's black mayor, Coleman Young, accused Udall of supporting the racist policies of the Mormon church. Young made the accusation while speaking on Carter's behalf before a gathering of black Baptist ministers. Young said that while Carter had tried to open the front doors of his church to blacks, Udall's church "won't even let you in the back door."[61] Udall supporters argued that Udall had left the church over its policies toward blacks but that Carter still was attending the church in Plains, Georgia, that continued to bar them. Udall expressed some belief that, in fact, Young's charges may have helped him by creating a white backlash in Michigan's suburbs and rural areas.[62]

Udall responded by saying that he must have been making inroads with black voters for Young to make such a statement. He said he had split with the Mormon church over its policies toward blacks thirty years earlier. Young then called him a "crybaby and whiner." Udall called for Young to apologize and for Carter to repudiate the accusation. Neither did. Carter aides called Udall's negative advertising unfair. "Let Udall stew—he deserves it," said one.[63]

Young later apologized, but it came on August 5, long after Carter had won the Democratic nomination. With his typical grace and civility, Udall told Young he accepted the apology. "I was hurt and puzzled by the entire episode but it is all over and buried now."[64] Privately, Udall never got over his anger at Young.

In Michigan, Udall made up a deficit of 33 percentage points and ran his closest race yet, losing by 2,245 votes out of 659,000 cast. Between them, the liberals Sargent Shriver and Harris had received about 10,400 votes. It was Udall's fifth runner-up finish, with Carter receiving 44 percent of the vote to Udall's 43 percent.

Obey blamed Udall's loss in Michigan on Young's "no-good, thuggish thing. . . . Mo was hurt, angry . . . he said, 'That son of a bitch, he knows it's not true.' Anyone who knew Stewart or Mo knew they were absolutely color blind, and I mean with passion."[65]

Udall's close finish slowed the Carter march to the nomination somewhat, along with Carter's weak showing against two latecomers, California governor Jerry Brown and Idaho senator Frank Church. Church beat Carter in Nebraska and Brown defeated him in Maryland. "There is not going to be any stampede [toward Carter]," Udall said. "There is not going to be any rush to judgment."[66]

Next on tap was South Dakota and its June 1 primary. Udall and Church worked out an understanding that Udall would work at beating Carter in South Dakota and stay out of Rhode Island. In exchange, Church would stay off the ballot in South Dakota. Carter's polls showed him leading Udall by 12 to 13 percentage points.[67]

Udall campaigned hard in South Dakota. He took a five-hour automobile trip to Mount Rushmore for a twenty-minute speech. He quoted the four men whose faces graced the mountain—Abe Lincoln, Thomas Jefferson, Teddy Roosevelt, and George Washington—about the qualities needed to be president. The backdrop made the trip worth it, Udall said.

Udall desperately needed the support of South Dakota's George McGovern. But it was not forthcoming. In fact, McGovern publicly fired two of his aides for joining a stop-Carter movement only hours before the primary. Udall believed that action was an oblique endorsement of Carter and cost Udall a victory.

Udall may have lost McGovern several weeks before. McGovern had endorsed Udall in Massachusetts, the only state McGovern carried against Nixon in 1972. But a Udall campaign aide ridiculed the endorsement, saying, "That's good old 1,000 percent George," a reference to McGovern standing 1,000 percent behind Senator Thomas F. Eagleton of Missouri for the vice presidential nomination in 1972 after it was revealed Eagleton had undergone shock therapy for depression. Eagleton finally withdrew and was replaced by former Peace Corps head Sargent Shriver.

"I did not need that kind of hassle," McGovern wrote in his 1977 autobiography, "so I abandoned the intended national effort for Udall and decided to stay on the sidelines."[68] Carter beat Udall 24,573 to 20,055, another second-place finish from the persistent and consistent Arizonan. More than that, it gave encouragement to Church to enter Ohio. Church's thought was that if Udall could not beat Carter, maybe he could.

Udall's last, best hope was going one-on-one with Carter in Ohio. He could run second no longer; he had to have a first-place finish if he were to remain a credible candidate. But Church jumped into the race, stealing votes from Udall and assuring Carter of another victory. "If we fragment again, Carter wins," Udall said.[69] He said he stayed out of Church's way in Oregon; Church should have stayed out of Ohio. Udall had some nagging thoughts that maybe, just maybe, Church entered the June 10 Ohio primary to draw votes from Udall. Just maybe it was a deal with Carter that might lead to the vice presidency.[70]

For his part, Church wanted Udall out of the race as well, because, he said, Udall was no longer a viable candidate. Udall responded: "I know it's a long shot. I can recognize a long shot as well as anyone else. I look at one every morning when I shave."[71] Carter won Ohio with 52.2 percent of the vote, while Udall received 21 percent and Church 13.9 percent.

Two days after the Ohio primary, Udall reflected on his losing race against Carter in a lengthy interview with Ben Cole of the *Arizona Republic*'s Washington bureau. He said he made a tactical error by assuming that the convention might turn to him when delegates could not agree on a nominee. He also said it was unlikely that Carter would pick him as the vice presidential nominee. "His pattern is not to be very forgiving," he said. "It's not likely he would choose me, even though some of my friends are pushing me." Udall also bristled at the suggestion that he was the "liberal" figure in the race. He said he was put in the liberal pigeonhole by the media.[72]

Despite the coverage, Udall believed the media had treated him fairly.[73] He liked members of the media who traveled with him and they liked him, and Udall enjoyed their high jinks. Once they gave him a set of toy teeth that would clatter when wound up to poke a little fun at Jimmy Carter. Another time, they threw a rubber chicken at him. He and Ella got back at them when they took to the aisles of the reporters' bus and doused them with water pistols. The press best liked to travel with Udall and Ronald Reagan, who was running for the Republican nomination against Ford. Reagan talked about Hollywood and Udall talked about sports.[74]

On the night before the Ohio primary, the press and his staff staged a surprise party complete with songs and skits about the campaign, including the ditty "Second-Place Mo," sung to the tune of "Second Hand Rose." They gave him a canvas straitjacket emblazoned with the "Udall for President" logo. Udall was moved by the party and when he went to the podium to express his thanks, his wife remarked, "Look at Mo. He's got a tear in his good eye."[75]

Udall was hoping to go to the convention with about 450 committed delegates. He wound up with 329½. That would give him some leverage in the unlikely possibility that there was a deadlock. If nothing else, he might be able to have a stronger voice in the party platform.

Traveling in cramped airplanes and cars was taking a toll on the lanky Udall. He had severe pain just below his left knee. He once said, "I'm going to die of cancer of the kneecap." He thought he might have phlebitis "or some damn thing." A doctor told him it was from lack of use and that he needed to exercise more. He started running up stairs whenever he could.[76]

By this point, even Udall was referring to himself as "ol' second-place Mo." Not everybody could come in first, he told reporters. "Even George Washington, the father of our country, married a widow."[77] He had spent almost two years stumping for president, and only 5 percent of the people interviewed for a Gallup poll in early 1976 indicated they would vote for Udall for president.[78]

Udall continued to have financial problems. The campaign was chronically short of funds. "What we get in the morning goes out in the afternoon," said aide Edward Coyle. Udall was forced to give up his chartered plane and to take commercial airlines and he was staying in second-rate hotels. At one point, the campaign was paying its bills hour-by-hour as money arrived from direct-mail contributors.[79] Stewart was sending out requests every two weeks from a direct-mail list of 80,000 supporters that would bring in $100,000 each time.[80]

The last blow was when American Express filed suit against Udall for $112,000. "We are most hopeful that our fund-raising efforts in the coming weeks, coupled with matching funds from the Federal Elections Commission, will allow us to satisfy all our creditors in the very near future," he said.[81]

The fact was that despite his almost two-year effort he had had little success in switching Democratic voters over to his side. While Carter had moved up from 4 percent in a Gallup poll at the beginning of the year to 53 percent by mid-June, Udall had climbed from 2 percent to only 5 percent.[82] Not only that, but Carter had raised $11.6 million to Udall's $4.6 million.[83]

At a rally of about 1,000 cheering and tearful supporters at the Roosevelt Hotel in New York City the day before the convention, Udall reminded them that he had entered twenty-two primaries and lost every one, finishing second seven times. "The people have spoken—the bastards." They laughed at the joke, an old one at that.[84]

Udall met with Carter before the session when the candidates would be nominated. He told Carter that he would release his delegates after he was nominated so that the Democratic Party would be unified.[85]

Udall was nominated by former Watergate prosecutor Cox, who told the cheering delegates that Udall "proved that a public figure, even in political contests, can exemplify the best spirit of liberty; that honor need not surrender to ambition; that open-mindedness is consistent with conviction; that civility can accompany tenacity; and that humility should go hand-in-hand with power." He said Udall had "dissipated the despair and raised the spirits of millions of young men and women wishing to enter politics as an honorable profession."[86]

The speech lasted one minute and fifty-six seconds. The conventiongoers roared so loud and so long—longer than Cox's speech—that Udall told them, "If this goes on much longer, I just might accept the nomination."[87]

Despite the bitterness that had broken out late in the campaign between Udall and Carter, Udall was magnanimous at the end in making a graceful exit from the race. He told delegates that in Tombstone, Arizona, a grave marker reads simply: "Johnson . . . done his damndest." And, Udall said, "I guess that was the story of the Udall campaign." Then he released his 329½ delegates to vote as they chose. "When Jimmy Carter says he'll beat you, he'll beat you, and he beat us fair and square. . . . As I leave the convention hall tonight, I'm going to have one of those green buttons that dogged me all over America. Tomorrow I'm enlisting as a soldier in the Carter campaign and I'm going to do everything I can. . . . Jimmy Carter is a good man who will make a strong president."[88]

"It takes a lot to get up and do that," said Carter aide Landon Butler, watching on television.[89]

Udall also was quietly decrying Mondale's good fortune. Udall noted that Mondale had pulled out of the race early on because he didn't have the "fire in the belly" to do what it took to seek the nomination. Then at the end, he was chosen as Carter's running mate. Udall noted that it "could just as easily have been the other way around."[90]

Mo Udall personally got out of the race debt free as he had promised his wife, but his campaign was $200,000 in debt. Udall said he accrued the debt "by little bits and pieces of running up personal loans, running up hotel bills at places where they were foolish enough to give us credit, not paying salaries, etc."[91] At one point early in the campaign, Maria Carrier, a key New Hampshire aide, threatened to quit unless she received two months of back pay at $300 a week.[92] When Udall arrived at the convention he poked a little fun at himself for the debts he had run up. "I came here," he said, "to avoid my creditors and to get a little bit of that money that may be left over from the last Carter party."[93]

The situation got so bad after he had withdrawn that when he tried to charge a room service meal, the waiter demanded cash. He paid the waiter and was left with $2. He got campaign treasurer Kurz to give him $300 and he put up a personal check. "Is this any good?" Kurz asked. "About as good as those checks you've been writing on my campaign fund," Udall chuckled. "Well, then," Kurz said, "I think I'll drop it on the floor and see how high it will bounce."[94]

The final insult came after Carter delivered his acceptance speech. Mo and Ella went back to the Roosevelt Hotel about midnight, just the time when the Secret Service detail was to end. He and Ella were asked to attend a party with the Arizona delegation. He was so used to telling the Secret Service where he was going that he stuck his head into their command post. "Is it OK if I go to the Arizona party down on the fifth floor? Do you care?" A man in the post said, "I don't care at all. I'm the telephone man," as he ripped out the phone lines. "My limousine and everything turned into a pumpkin," Udall said to himself.[95]

The next day he and Ella flew to Washington, D.C. They carried their own bags and there were no cameras or cheers. When they reached their home in McLean, Virginia, Udall was told that a U.S. marshal had been there twice to serve him with papers over the American Express suit.[96]

Hubert Humphrey told Udall after the campaign that in his lifetime most people who ran for president and lost had been diminished in the public's eye. He told Udall, however, that his career reputation had been enhanced by the campaign.[97]

Udall went out on the road again, this time to sell America on Jimmy Carter. It was on those trips that he realized that two things made his two-year effort worthwhile: One was the thundering reception he had received at the nominating convention; the other, the receptions he was accorded while campaigning for Carter in places where Udall had done well during the primaries. "It suddenly dumped on me like a ton that I had built an intensely loyal national following, that I was somebody to the people. I was the symbol of their ideals and the progressive things they had fought for and believed in, that I stood for these things." He said that 3,000 people turned out at the University of Michigan to greet him. "It was a very sobering, yet rewarding thing to think that all out there over the country there's an army of people who believe in you and that you stand for something," he said.[98]

After the election, Udall returned home to Virginia to catch up on the maintenance of his house. While cleaning rain gutters, he fell from a ladder and broke bones in both arms. Carter called Udall on November 17 to commiserate and to ask for advice on appointments to the cabinet and other major positions. Udall detailed the conversation in a memo two days later. On the bottom he wrote, "I suspect this was more or less going through the motions, but who can say?" He called Carter back later on the 17th and chatted for ten minutes. He offered the name of Idaho governor Cecil D. Andrus as secretary of the interior, whom Carter later appointed. He also recommended New Mexico governor Jerry Apodoca because he was qualified and a Chicano had never served in the cabinet. He also suggested Brock Adams of Washington for a cabinet post. Carter later appointed Adams secretary of transportation. He rejected Udall's recommendation that Andrew Young of Georgia be named secretary for Housing and Urban Development, or for Health, Education and Welfare.[99]

Ella Udall refused to go with her husband to Carter's inauguration. "There wasn't an ounce of malice in it," she said. "It was purely a personal thing, an emotional thing. I thought I could put it all behind me. But the notion of standing there on the platform, beside Mo, watching Rosalynn and all . . . "[100]

KEEPING THE HOPES
ALIVE

*D*espite his loss of the Democratic nomination for president, Mo Udall was not a beaten man. He had lost before and always bounced back. He learned from his defeats and he remained optimistic. He retained his dream of one day moving into the White House, although his chances were less than good. Opportunities to seek the highest office in the land would present themselves twice more, in 1980 and 1984. Neither went far.

Two years after his unsuccessful 1976 presidential bid, Udall still failed to excite voters. A 1978 Gallup poll showed him with a 3 percent popularity rating for the 1980 presidential race. Senator Ted Kennedy was favored by 53 percent and Carter, the incumbent president, by 40 percent.[1]

Udall knew he had no chance if Kennedy ran. In mid-December of 1979, he endorsed Kennedy, a move he said was pro-Kennedy, not anti-Carter. He was fairly certain that Carter would lose to whomever the Republicans nominated, probably former California governor Ronald Reagan. Udall called Kennedy "a gifted, tested leader."[2]

When Kennedy lost nine of the first ten primaries—he won only in his home state of Massachusetts—a coalition of liberal leaders reassessed its position. They included Douglas Fraser, president of the United Auto Workers; Joseph Rauh, a Washington labor and civil rights attorney; and Jerry Wurf, president of the American Federation of State, County, and

Municipal Employees. The leaders asked Udall if he would be willing to take on Carter. Udall said he would, but only if Kennedy agreed to it.[3]

The plan was never carried out. Just before the New York primary the United States supported a U.N. Security Council resolution condemning Israel for building settlements in Arab territories on the West Bank. That infuriated Jews. Carter said the vote had been a mistake because of a breakdown in communications. Still, it raised questions about his competency.[4]

Jewish voters constituted a third of New York's Democratic electorate and Kennedy trounced Carter 59 percent to 41 percent. He also won the Connecticut primary that day, 46.8 percent to 41.3 percent. With Kennedy on the rebound, the talk of drafting Udall ended.

In mid-July 1980, independent presidential candidate John Anderson, Udall's colleague from campaign finance reform days, sought Udall for his running mate, although he doubted Udall would accept. "There's no way I could consider that," Udall said emphatically, even though he and Anderson had good rapport. "If I had decided to retire [from Congress] maybe," he said.[5] Udall suggested that former transportation secretary Brock Adams might be a good choice for the second spot. Anderson considered Udall's brother Stewart, who had endorsed Anderson.[6]

Carter won enough delegates for the nomination going into the Democratic National Convention in New York City in August, although Kennedy vowed to fight to the end. Right up to the vote, talk turned to drafting Udall as a compromise candidate because so many delegates were dissatisfied with Carter. At that point, Udall had already accepted Carter's request to give the keynote address. Udall said no. "If nominated, I would run—for the Mexican border," he said. "If elected, I would fight extradition."[7]

As the keynote speaker, Udall said he saw himself as a healer. The convention was expected to turn into a bloody brawl with Kennedy's backers trying to change the rules to allow delegates to vote for whomever they wished. Carter had a lock on the first-ballot nomination otherwise. "Until Senator Kennedy gives up, it's a very difficult assignment," Udall said. "Anything good I say about one side may be booed by the other."[8]

Udall pledged to give a unity speech, saying: "I'll come down hard on Republicans and say favorable things about Democrats."[9] Carter held off the Kennedy forces and won renomination. Udall delivered his unity speech. Not once did he mention Jimmy Carter's name, choosing instead to attack Republican nominee Reagan.

Udall drew on history. He looked at the address of Alben W. Barkley of Kentucky during the bitter 1948 convention fight when it appeared Harry S. Truman's presidency was in trouble. Barkley, then a senator, avoided talking about Truman, instead attacking Truman's opponent, Thomas E. Dewey.[10] Barkley ended up as Truman's vice presidential nominee.

To no one's surprise, Udall's keynote address was packed with humor, including the story he stole from Barkley about the Kentucky moonshiner who, at gunpoint, forced an accomplice to try his white lightning, then handed the gun over so he could be forced to take a swig, too. What the analogy referred to, Udall said, was that "we Democrats have got to hold the gun on each other for the next 100 days, or we'll have this Reagan disaster upon us."[11]

Reagan defeated Carter in November and seemingly advanced the opportunities of Democrats to challenge him in 1984. Udall would be among those considering a run.

By mid-July 1982, Udall was hinting about running again but was being coy about actually jumping into the race. He had built up a $1-million war chest through his Independent Action political action committee (PAC), headed by former aide Edward Coyle. It was the tenth-wealthiest PAC, according to the Federal Election Commission.[12]

In late 1982, Udall proclaimed himself medically fit and announced he might go after the Democratic presidential nomination if he could recover from his "terminal indecision." His statement came after Kennedy had announced on December 1 that he would not run. "I don't want to be a spoiler," Udall said. "But if I can be the one to put it together, I want to be there and give it a shot."[13] Udall said he began to get calls from friends and colleagues urging him to run again.[14]

Mark J. Brand, a political consultant who had helped in Udall's 1976 campaign, put together a series of trips during which Udall was warmly welcomed. Brand wondered how much of the emotion Udall encountered "could be transformed into political power."[15]

After Kennedy's announcement, Mo and Ella met at his McLean, Virginia, home with friends Marvin Cohen, the former chairman of the

Civil Aeronautics Board; Jim McNulty, the newly elected congressman from Arizona; actor Cliff Robertson; former aides Terry Bracy, then a lobbyist, Brand, and Coyle; and friend S. Rosemary Cribben. All agreed that 1984 might be Udall's last chance but that his Parkinson's was a big barrier. Robertson and Cribben urged him to run. McNulty told Udall: "Mo, you blow the bugle and I'll march."[16]

Finally, Bracy spoke up and said, "Mo, goddamn it, you're ill, you've got no business running for president." Bracy told Udall that if he felt Udall's health would allow it, he would be the first in line to support him. "Mo, you're an ill man," Bracy said. "You can't possibly take this on."[17]

Five days later an article in the *New York Times* about the state of Udall's health distressed administrative aide Bruce A. Wright, who called it "bad news." Wright said that until doctors gave Udall a clean bill of health, "we ought to avoid stories and comments on Parkinson's disease." The article quoted an unnamed Udall political strategist as saying that Udall was best during the day but by evening was fatigued and was in bed by 10 P.M.[18]

In early January, he was waffling about running. "Yesterday I was probably leaning toward it, today maybe against it," he said. He was flattered by the attention, saying, "It's nice to know there's that sort of residual support lying around six years after I ran." He was getting little encouragement from his family, however. He said his six children and brother Stewart opposed his candidacy and wife Ella had "limited enthusiasm."[19] They worried about him tarnishing his political image.

Ella still fretted about finances as the 1976 campaign was just paying off lingering debts. "I told him if he ran he had to find a campaign manager old enough to shave, and he had to find the means to pay for the campaign," she said. Ella and Mo went to Bethany Beach, Delaware, over the Christmas holiday, where he asked her if she would be willing to go through another brutal campaign. "That's the word he used—brutal. We walked the beach. I said, 'If that's what's in the future, count me in now.'" That may have been said for public consumption; indications were that she did not want him to run again.

Udall looked ruefully at his chances. "I wish I'd been younger, or come to Congress and gotten involved a few years earlier than I did. But it's gone, and this is the last go-around. I don't want to make a mistake."[20]

His friend Barry Goldwater was urging him to run. "I encourage you to put your hat in the ring," he said. "I think you have a real good chance of winning the nomination."[21]

Then he attended the California Democratic Party convention in Sacramento in mid-January. It was on that tiring trip that he realized, while flying home with Cohen, that he was physically unable to meet the rigors of a presidential campaign.[22]

On the way home, Udall stopped in Phoenix, where he met with friends and supporters. In sessions at the Hyatt Hotel in downtown Phoenix, Udall met with groups of no more than ten prominent backers to make the meetings seem more select. He held five or six of the sessions. Some were held on different floors. Udall would move from floor to floor seeking advice. He received mixed messages. Most said he should run; others thought it was best to let it pass. John P. Frank, a Phoenix lawyer who helped arrange the meetings, said there was "no instant enthusiasm or optimism. . . . This fund-raising thing is inter-related with the Parkinson's disease question," he said. "People will want to know: Is this the last lance of a wobbling Don Quixote, or is it a real run for the roses? There is a concern over whether the contributors will feel they are contributing to a live one or not."[23]

Afterward, according to aide Perry G. Baker, Mo and his staff discussed the meetings. Mo remarked: "Nobody has the balls to look me in the eye and say, 'Don't run.' "[24]

A couple of days before he made his decision, Udall and his wife were sitting in their home when she asked: "Mo, do you want to be president?" He looked up and said: "I really do."[25] It was not to be.

Finally, the decision had been made. His staff set up an announcement on February 9—his wife's birthday—at the National Press Club. He called friends and supporters the night before telling them his decision. He concluded he probably could not raise enough money, his Parkinson's was a political handicap, and he would be getting in the race too late.[26]

At the Press Club gathering, he told the throng of reporters and supporters with his usual wit and grace. He said his Parkinson's was not the reason; it was time and money. He received a standing ovation, even from supposedly dispassionate reporters. After the speech, Udall was asked by reporters whether he would accept the vice presidential nomination. "The obvious answer is sure," he said. "It beats the hell out of serving on the Interior or Post Office Committees."[27]

Newspapers around the country bemoaned Udall's decision. Said syndicated columnist Sandy Grady: "Damn. Now we're stuck with all these intense, somber candidates who'll talk endlessly about the infrastructure." The *Washington Post* said that even though Udall would not be running he "wound up a winner in the eyes of his audience and his supporters."[28]

Udall could not quite let go. He was still going to hang in there by running as Arizona's favorite son, one last-ditch hope that perhaps the convention would turn to him in a deadlock, a convention that was unconcerned about his Parkinson's. It would not cost him much money to take that stance.

On July 4, Udall formally announced he would be a favorite son, hoping to use his delegates as a bargaining tool in case of a second, third, or fourth ballot. "This is a chance for us to get together and honor a man who has done a lot for this state," said Alan Stephens, a veteran state legislator. "And who knows, lightning might strike."[29]

Udall set up a budget of $70,420 to operate campaign headquarters in Tucson and Phoenix, hire staff, prepare literature, and travel.

The favorite-son campaign seemed to be moving along well when on January 24, 1984, Ohio senator John Glenn announced that he was putting his name on the Arizona ballot. Udall now had competition for Arizona's forty delegates. Then six other candidates jumped in. "This opens the door to expensive and perhaps bitter campaign battles between the candidates and prevents us from perhaps having a unified delegation at the convention," aide Bruce Wright said.

On February 2, Udall withdrew "with the best interests of my party at heart." He said he would work for the party and the eventual nominee.[30]

The presidential aspirations of Morris K. Udall had ended.

At the end of October 1985, about 300 Mozos, as Udall's 1976 campaign workers called themselves, gathered at a Washington reunion at the Holiday Inn to relive their effort to put Udall in the White House. It was called a "Udall for President Survivors" party. "All you losers, welcome tonight," Udall told them. He said any group that could celebrate a loss ten years later "is perhaps a group I should not be affiliated with."[31]

SAVING THE ENVIRONMENT

*N*ineteen seventy-six had been a year of defeat for Mo Udall. He had lost primaries and a presidential nomination. The strip-mining bill he had been pushing had been buried by the Rules Committee after two vetoes by President Ford. Adding injury to insult, he had broken both arms when he fell from a ladder while cleaning the rain gutters at his home.

Nineteen seventy-seven had to be better. For one thing, a Democratic president was in office, even if he was the man who conquered Mo for the nomination. For another, some shuffling was ahead for House committee chairmanships.

James A. Haley of Florida, who had succeeded Wayne Aspinall, had retired, thus opening up the Interior Committee chairmanship. Bizz Johnson of California was the ranking Democrat ahead of Mo and the likely selection. At the same time, the Democrats chose James C. Wright of Texas as the new majority leader. That made available the chairmanship of the Public Works and Transportation Committee, where Johnson also was the ranking member.

Poker-playing friends Udall and Phil Burton of California, next in line behind Mo on Interior, hatched a plot. They told Johnson they would not oppose him if he sought the chairmanship, but they would make life difficult for him thereafter. Johnson, whose philosophy generally ran to dam building and opposing environmentalist causes, chose

Public Works.[1] Udall took over Interior and named Burton head of the National Parks Subcommittee and himself chair of the Energy and Environment Subcommittee. He also created a new subcommittee on Alaska lands and selected John Seiberling of Ohio as its leader.

Udall's morale was up, but his broken bones were still healing, and Roy S. Jones Jr., the committee counsel and associate staff director, recalled that one of the new chairman's first comments to the staff was: "The first person who tries to shake hands with me, I'm going to fire you."[2]

The infighting behind him, Udall faced an agenda that most immediately included revival of the strip-mining bill, revision of the Mining Act of 1872, examination of the state of nuclear energy, and preservation of Alaska lands. It was a full calendar.

The strip-mining bill had a long history, and solutions had been sought for nearly two decades. President Kennedy had created the Appalachian Regional Commission, headed by the thirteen affected governors, to seek solutions to the poverty that had appalled him so during his 1960 campaign. Interior Secretary Stewart Udall had begun work specifically on strip mining.

Surface miners simply scraped off ground and vegetation to remove the coal, destroying animal habitats, scarring the landscape, polluting water with acid, and causing landslides. Strip mining created erosion so serious that the silt poured into streambeds, altering their courses and rates of flow and causing flooding. Environmentalists pushed for action. One Sierra Club publication told about "Old Muskie," a $25-million earth-moving machine used in Muskingum County in southeastern Ohio. It used a 310-foot boom and a 22-cubic-yard bucket to tear out 22 million cubic yards of dirt and rock in less than two years.[3]

The Appalachian Regional Commission did not focus on strip mining at first, deciding instead that the infrastructure needed shoring up to attract the industry to provide employment. To encourage such activity, the federal government offered to finance 80 percent of any improvement. The states or local governments would be responsible for the remainder.

The commission was in for a surprise.

Donald A. Crane, a key commission staffer who later moved on to a similar spot with Mo Udall, said the railroad owners asked for a private meeting, explaining that they made most of their money hauling coal and thus could not go public with their comments. "They said, 'Every place we haul coal out of is such an environmental disaster with waste piles, silted-up streams, dirty communities,'" Crane recalled. "'It doesn't matter how much money you put in, no one will come.'" Industry would like the geography, the access, the labor, but it would run away fast from the environment, Crane said.

The railroads urged an environmental cleanup before all else.[4] While the commission and Interior Department had been studying, the state of Pennsylvania had been doing it: It converted strip-mined land into parks, demonstrating clearly that reclamation was possible. Interior and the commission also determined that individuals could mine, reclaim, and make money at the same time, a concept that would be challenged consistently by Presidents Nixon and Ford.

Democrat Ken Hechler of West Virginia sponsored the first bill in 1971. The House Interior Committee remained under Wayne Aspinall, and the old guard still ran things. Democrats Wayne Hays of Ohio and Burton pushed for a ban on all strip mining. The measures never made it out of committee.[5] Haley succeeded Aspinall in 1973, the first year in which subcommittee chairs received real power with the ability to handle their own budgets and hire their own employees. At the same time, Udall took over the subcommittee on the environment. Mo worried about applying the same law to all types of mining. His home state was a major copper producer, and hard-rock mineral mining also created environmental damage. It, too, ravaged the land, and the list of abuses included subsidence, fire potential, waste, groundwater pollution, and air pollution. Still, different variables were at play.

Ultimately, Crane said, it was decided that one law could not cover all mining, and the focus remained on coal and surface mining, a temporary use, as opposed to underground mining, considered a permanent use. The bill would ban coal strip mining wherever the disturbed land could not be productively reclaimed.

As the measure progressed, Crane said, Udall developed another major principle: Individuals and companies should not be held accountable for previous environmental damage, if what they did was legal at the time. Damaged land, however, should be reclaimed and appropriate employment could be provided through a 35-cent-a-ton fee. The idea was that those miners who lost their jobs could be employed to restore the land.

The legislation made it to the House floor for the first time in late 1974 and passed on a voice vote, although an earlier procedural vote of 198–129 made it clear that the measure lacked enough support to override a promised veto by President Ford.[6] The Senate also approved the bill by voice vote.

Ford found himself in the middle of an administration dispute when he exercised his power with a pocket veto, allowing the measure to die without signature while Congress was in recess. The president and Frank G. Zarb, head of the Federal Energy Administration, argued that the bill would reduce significantly the nation's annual coal production and increase unemployment, something the Appalachian Regional Commission wanted to reduce. Rogers C. B. Morton, Ford's interior secretary, and Russell Train, the Environmental Protection Agency administrator, took an opposing view and urged the president to sign the bill.[7]

As a new session began, Udall pushed the bill back through the House and in May won a 293–115 vote for passage. The Senate provided voice-vote approval.[8] The bill was essentially the same as the one Ford had allowed to die, and the president again exercised a veto.

The House scheduled an override vote on June 10, and Udall took the floor for a final argument. The administration, he said, asserted that the bill would throw 36,000 people out of work, but countered: "The Mineworkers and the AFL-CIO say they will support the bill and the bill will not cost jobs, when we are told by people who are not notable in their support for workers that it will cost jobs." Interior Secretary Morton contended, too, that jobs would be added, not lost, Udall emphasized.

He appealed to the members to follow the advice of Mark Twain, who said, "Do what is right, and you will please some people and astonish the rest."[9] Udall failed by three votes to win the necessary two-thirds vote for an override. For a second time, the measure was dead.

The Interior Committee cleared the bill again in 1976, a presidential election year, but this time it perished when the House Rules Committee voted 9 to 6 against allowing floor debate.[10]

With the new year and the new title of chairman, Udall pushed the measure again, and the final version put together by a conference committee won 325–68 approval in the House and an 85–8 victory in the Senate. New president Jimmy Carter happily signed the bill.

The law regulated private property, and it was far from perfect. Staffer Loretta Neumann recalled that it was the first time coal mines had come under federal regulation, and said she had never seen such viciousness over legislation.[11]

Udall was unhappy with provisions that exempted parcels of two acres for personal or commercial use. Crane said, "It was a way for the small Appalachian strip mine operators to continue doing their business. . . . Coal operators in eastern Kentucky, southwest Virginia and Tennessee set up operations, using contract miners on two-acre plots that were exempt."[12]

Udall kept the loophole in mind and ten years later saw a parliamentary way to close it.

Udall learned in April 1987 that two Senate mining industry supporters, Wyoming Republicans Alan K. Simpson and Malcolm Wallop, had introduced a minor amendment to the surface-mining law. Udall promptly traded his support of their amendment for their support of his legislation to abolish the two-acre exemption, and quietly moved the bill through the House. "Mo was terrific on the two-acre exemption," an environmental lobbyist said. "That was the old Mo in action."[13]

How effective was the Surface Mining Control and Reclamation Act? Ten years later, reporter Ben A. Franklin wrote that "hundreds of thousands of acres have been returned to productive use while many other tracts have been left ravaged." Franklin quoted Interior Department official Jed Christensen as saying that nearly 1.5 million acres of strip-mined coal land—or 2,343 square miles, "larger than the state of Delaware"—had been reclaimed. He wrote, however, that environmental groups complained that more than 6,000 strip mines had been abandoned without reclamation or penalty assessments.[14]

Even before he took charge of the Interior Committee, Udall had begun work on reform of the Mining Law of 1872. The changes, discussed as early as 1971, would affect only federal land, but they covered the hard-rock mining—copper, gold, silver, uranium, iron, aluminum, nickel, lead, and others—so important to the western states. In fact, mines in his own state of Arizona produced 57 percent of the nation's copper, and the mineral often was referred to as "King Copper." The federal law was written when the nation was trying to open up the West and to encourage resource discovery, often by the stereotypical lone prospector with a pick and shovel. The law decreed that the mineral belonged to the one who discovered it. It required a minimum of paperwork and a small fee to establish ownership of both the ore and the land. No royalties were required. It left the land and the ore and the profit in the hands of the one who had found it. A 1920 law removed the so-called energy minerals, such as oil, gas, and coal, from the law and instituted a system in which the finder would lease the federal land and pay royalties.[15]

Udall sought to apply the same requirements to hard-rock minerals and in an early statement said the proposed legislation would be essentially the same as that enacted by Arizona for mining on its own state property.[16]

He introduced his legislation on March 30, 1977, and immediately came under heavy criticism from the mining industry. Udall argued that the federal land belonged to all of the people, and should remain that way with environmental controls placed on anyone who received permission to mine. Opponents argued that the costs would be too high and predicted an end to mining exploration.

In a statement on his bill, Udall contended that change was needed to assure the nation and its citizens "a fair return for the extraction of their irreplaceable mineral resources," and to protect environmental values. "In an age where one man with a bulldozer can devastate a hillside in a single afternoon," he said, "the government needs to have some idea of what activity is taking place on the public lands."

Prospectors would be required to obtain a free license, to file a notice describing the area, and to provide assurance that they would not cause "significant disturbance of the environment." If they proceeded to actual mining, they would pay to lease the land, provide the government with royalty payments, and take reasonable reclamation steps.[17]

Udall worried about economic concentration, writing his legislation to bar "horizontally or vertically integrated oil companies from receiving leases. . . . I believe it is absolutely imperative that we halt the trend toward control of our national resources—and hence of our national destiny—by a handful of multinational corporate giants. Each step we take toward this across-the-board domination," he said, "is a step away from the old-fashioned ideal of competition that is the basis of our economic policies. This kind of massive economic combine, beyond any conceivable efficiencies of scale, makes it more difficult for us to respond to shifts in economic or technological circumstances."[18]

He dismissed the argument that the size of the energy conglomerates was needed to assure economic strength, saying: "It is no more valid today than it was when the antitrust laws were first enacted. I am not convinced that the way to meet the capital needs of mineral development is to turn over yet another critical industry to Exxon and its sisters; our real need is for a vigorous, competitive, independent mining industry."[19]

The campaign in mining states against his proposal was intense. Small miners jumped in big in his own Pima County, where more than one-third of the state's copper was produced. Mo had criticized unsightly and unproductive exploration scars near Tucson, and the pick-and-shovel Arizona Small Mine Operators Association announced a recall drive, an act of questionable legality.

Udall agreed to speak to the group, and staffer Ken Burton recalled that he was peppered with baiting questions afterward. When someone asked if his mining reform ideas amounted to socialism, Burton said Mo responded "something like, 'If you believe that the American people deserving a fair price for their land is socialism, if you believe that reform of these prices set in the 18th century is socialism, if you believe that the fair market pricing of land is socialism . . . then, yes, I'm a socialist.' The group was videotaping all of this. The quote 'I'm a socialist' was later edited out of context and given to Mo's opponent. I think it aired once or twice."[20]

The group needed 45,532 signatures by January 11, 1978, but it failed to submit even one. The organization president, Glynn Burkhardt, refused to disclose or display any signatures acquired, although at one point he claimed 58,000. In pulling out, Burkhardt said only: "After much thought and discussion we have concluded that this is not the time or the issue to push the recall." Udall declared: "These 60,000 signatures were not filed because they couldn't be. They just don't exist."[21]

While the small miners failed to convince Udall to drop the bill, it is probable that the big companies did. An article by C. J. Hansen, associate general counsel for the Anaconda Company and onetime president of the Arizona Mining Association, told this story:

With Tom Chandler, the Tucson lawyer who was a longtime friend of the congressman, Charlie Stott, then with Anamax, and myself, then with Anaconda, we spent several hours with Mo Udall one evening. We told him all of the troubles then being encountered by the mining industry, water litigation, the high costs of environmental compliance, steep state taxes, weak copper prices, and unfair foreign competition.

Finally, he said, "Okay, you guys have convinced me that the Arizona mining industry has more than enough problems right now. I'll drop my sponsorship of the leasing bill." He made the announcement the next morning, drawing a lot of harsh criticism from the environmentalists and anti-mining groups.[22]

Stewart Udall described the switch as "the only time Mo ran from a fight. He picked the fight and then abandoned the field."[23] Burton called it a case of Mo becoming disgusted and deciding "to chuck it. He realized the battle had been defined by the opposition and he had lost the high ground in the noise."[24] Committee aide C. Stanley Sloss said, "It was too hot an issue. The chairman's priorities were strip mining and Alaska. He couldn't do both. There are only so many days, so much energy, and so much political horsepower."[25]

In addition, Udall's attention was turning to nuclear energy. He had chaired the House Nuclear Oversight Subcommittee and had become concerned about safety and secrecy. In an April 1976 statement he cautioned "that we have made an enormous commitment to a technology prior to having a good understanding of its adverse impacts," and he suggested that too much reliance was being placed on "experts" whose answers did not wholly satisfy him. He said further that "the operations of the NRC [Nuclear Regulatory Commission] must be opened to public view."[26]

With his elevation to committee chairman, Udall found himself in a position to do more. A year earlier, Congress had become fed up with its own Joint Committee on Atomic Energy, which, over the years, had been more of an industry booster than it was a watchdog.

In the 1950s and 1960s, the joint committee presided over visions of a controlled nuclear sea-level canal through Nicaragua and a six-mile runway in Idaho for a souped-up, presidential Air Force One. Popular slogans included "Pounding Swords into Plowshares" and "Producing Electricity That's Too Cheap to Meter."

By the mid-1970s, industry leaders were projecting more than 1,000 reactors by the year 2000, recalled Henry R. Myers, Udall's top nuclear energy aide.[27] As the millennium approached, the total was about one-tenth of the earlier prediction, and Paul Parshley, another key staffer, said, "It is unlikely there will ever be another nuclear plant."[28]

Such was not the expectation when Congress disbanded the Joint Committee on Atomic Energy, transferring financial authority to the House Appropriations Committee and legislative jurisdiction to the Interior Committee. The industry was exploding with optimism, regardless of who the congressional overseers might be. The Udall committee was less excited.

Parshley said one of the first actions Udall took was to force the NRC files open, thus allowing opponents of nuclear projects to intervene "in a meaningful way. There was a high level of public scrutiny. He made the commission more forthcoming."[29]

"Mo had a reasonable, sensible quality about him and that had an effect," recalled Victor Gilinsky, who served two terms as an NRC member. "No one ever thought Mo was grandstanding; they respected him. He was not after headlines as some other congressmen were. He had a Lincolnesque quality. He was sensible." Udall's impact came from the way he handled himself, Gilinsky said. "He would ask a series of questions, and once the questions were asked, you were forced to confront it [the status quo]. He wasn't one for threatening. He was a force for sense and reason." As with any committee, Gilinsky said, the ultimate impact depended on staff people, and "Mo had good staff people who stuck their teeth into the ankle of the commission and held on and Mo backed them up."

Udall challenged a Nuclear Regulatory Commission report that said there was more risk of being injured by a meteor than damaged by a nuclear accident. The agency decided it was loosely worded and did not stand up. After that, Gilinsky said, "We didn't try to defend the impossible."[30]

The NRC took its new position just before the March 1979 accident in Pennsylvania at the Metropolitan Edison Company's nuclear plant in the Susquehanna River on a sandbar known as Three Mile Island. The plant was about ten miles downstream from the state capital of Harrisburg, center of a population of 650,000 people. A valve leaked, causing the core of the Unit 2 reactor to melt. By the time President Carter visited, four days after the March 28 incident, an estimated 140,000 people had evacuated in fear of their lives. The crisis ended, and it took three years to determine how serious the accident had been: Half of the ten-foot-long core had melted; five more feet would have meant disaster.

Activists had been protesting nuclear plants for years, but the Three Mile Island drama aroused a whole new army of opponents. Nonetheless, Myers, Parshley, and Gilinsky agreed the decline in nuclear power already had started. "There was too much jumping in without construction experience," Myers said, "and a failure to anticipate how tough the NRC regulations were." He said contractors falsified records, but the NRC caught many of them. He and Parshley said environmental ramifications and sheer economics—what they called "a premature commitment to an unproven technology"—caused the decline, although Parshley said Three Mile Island "put the nail in the coffin."[31]

Gilinsky recalled that *Business Week* magazine had written in December 1978 that "the lights are going out on nuclear power." Utilities, as regulated monopolies, were used to doing what they wanted and passing the cost on to ratepayers, he said, calling it an undisciplined environment with no serious cost control, but with nuclear power, the costs were passed on and it seemed like government was guaranteeing safety.[32]

In an interview in the same issue of *Business Week,* Udall described the industry as "on the threshold of proving that it is a fairly safe technology. If it falters, it is going to falter on economics and waste disposal. The great dream of nuclear that we all had in the 1950s was that it would be so cheap that you wouldn't have to meter it. We're finding . . . that if you factor in all the true costs of nuclear, coal is now competitive. We're finding, 'Well, my God, if it isn't even cheaper, why run all those risks of proliferation and so on?' "[33]

The reference to waste disposal was a sign of action to come: an attempt to establish locations for high-level nuclear waste, primarily radioactive water and spent uranium fuel rods, which were being stored at the individual nuclear plants in deep water pools. Low-level wastes were created in every state by the radioactive contamination of items used by the nuclear plants, hospitals, and industry. Three states contained dumps for the low-level garbage.

Andrea Dravo spent much of her time as a Udall aide working on high-level nuclear waste disposal. She recalled that the Department of Energy was moving ahead with plans to drill an exploratory shaft in Hanford, Washington, a plan the Joint Committee on Atomic Energy had supported. Dravo said the department also was searching for sites elsewhere, and once published a map that showed shaded areas where dumps could be constructed. "It covered over half the country," she said, "and everyone was opposed."[34]

Udall took over as chairman of the Interior Committee in the middle of the dispute. Progress was slow as no state wanted a high-level nuclear waste dump. One step forward occurred in the closing hours of the 1980 Congress when agreement was reached giving the states responsibility for burying the low-level waste.

Two years later, again as Congress was nearing adjournment, Udall led negotiators to an accord on the Nuclear Waste Management Policy Act. It required the Department of Energy to conduct environmental assessments and recommend two repositories—one in the West, one in the East.

In 1986, however, the Reagan administration suspended the search for an eastern site and identified Hanford, Washington; Deaf Smith County, Texas; and Yucca Mountain, Nevada, as the western candidates.[35] By mid-1987, Udall was fed up, and he accused the Department of Energy of betraying the public's confidence by politicizing what was supposed to be a scientific selection. "We wanted this [act] to be fair," he said, "but that went down the drain."[36]

Udall called for a scientific commission to review the selection process and direct a negotiator to seek a volunteer site. At the same time, Senator J. Bennett Johnston Jr., a Louisiana Democrat, pushed for selection of one of the three western sites and payment to the host state of $100 million annually. Johnston's approach won out, although Congress lowered the amount to $20 million.

"In 1987, Mo was fading," Dravo said, "and Senator Johnston said Nevada should be chosen because it was the smallest and had the least political clout. Mo just sat back and that was that," she added, saying Parkinson's disease had slowed the chairman down.[37]

Construction is under way at Yucca Mountain, and it is scheduled to open in 2010, twelve years after the government-promised opening of 1998.

ALASKA'S CROWN
JEWELS

*M*o Udall had never even visited Alaska when he became a leader in the largest conservation success in the nation's history, the preservation of 104.3 million acres of what became known as Alaska's "crown jewels." He did not stand alone. Democratic representative John Seiberling of Ohio, the environmentalist Alaska Coalition, President Jimmy Carter, Republican representative John P. Saylor of Pennsylvania, and brother Stewart all played indispensable roles. Throughout the effort, however, Mo Udall remained the point man.

Once, during the 1977 hearings in Alaska, he and Seiberling were hanged in effigy in Sitka.[1] Another time, the junior chamber of commerce booth at the 1979 Fairbanks County Fair charged $1 to throw a long-necked beer bottle through a hole beneath pictures of Udall, Carter, and the Ayatollah Khomeini of Iran. Carter was a target because of a gasoline shortage and his failure to win release of hostages held by the Ayatollah. "By the time the fair ended," Udall wrote, "the heap of broken shards beneath my face [was] higher than that below the Ayatollah or J.C. . . . The fact that this was the first time I had bested Carter in any political contest (to say nothing of the Ayatollah) was small consolation."[2]

Approval of the bill, H.R. 39, to preserve the federally owned land in Alaska as wilderness, national parks, wildlife refuges, and national forests came after nine years and a lot of hard words between conservationists and Alaska development interests.

For environmentalists, it was little short of glorious. The action helped preserve for everyone seven major mountain ranges, ice fields, glaciers, fjords, wild rivers, volcanoes, vast forests, and even an area of sand dunes. It created ten new national parks and expanded three others. The law provided space for bears, wolves, moose, mountain goats, Dall sheep, bison, elk, and giant herds of caribou; fur-bearing animals such as the otter, beaver, mink, fox, lynx, wolverine, and muskrat; and 400 species of birds, including golden and bald eagles, falcons, hawks, owls, and swans.

Opposition was heavy from oil and gas, mining, and timber interests. Inside the state, the political establishment predicted a gloomy economic future if development was limited, while the rugged individualists who sought to escape societal structures feared a greater intrusion by government and other outsiders.

Both sides knew some sort of legislation was a certainty. The argument generally keyed on how much and where. Carter's interior secretary, Cecil Andrus, proposed 92 million acres, while Udall and Seiberling called for 146 million acres when they put forth H.R. 39,[3] a designation that remained throughout the conflict. The Kennecott Copper Company suggested protection for only 15 million acres. The Republican governor of Alaska, Jay S. Hammond, argued that 25 million acres would be sufficient,[4] questioning whether Alaska could be "both oil barrel to a nation and national park to the world."[5]

The dispute had its genesis in the 1958 act that made Alaska a state. The federal government already owned most of Alaska, and Congress authorized the new state to select 104 million acres as state land, and to do so over twenty-five years. By the mid-1960s, the state had chosen only about one-fourth of its acreage. Interior Secretary Udall became concerned about the rights of Eskimos, Aleuts, and Indians, most of whom lived off the land and some of whom were nomadic. In 1967, he imposed a two-year ban on the transfer of federal lands used by natives. A year later, the Atlantic Richfield Company and the Humble Oil and Refining Company discovered oil on state land at Prudhoe Bay, and an 800-mile pipeline was approved to carry the oil south to Valdez. Native groups worried even more about their rights, and Stewart Udall extended the prohibition for two more years as he departed office in January 1969.[6]

Seeking to resolve native claims at Prudhoe Bay and to speed up the pipeline access, Congress in 1971 moved to approve the Alaska Native Land Claims Settlement Act, which authorized $942 million and 44 million acres to be given to about 60,000 Eskimos, Aleuts, and Indians.

Enter Morris Udall and Saylor, the leading Republican environmentalist of his day. They proposed an amendment to the claims bill that Udall said would "allow the American people a shot at some prime acres before they are all gone."[7] Congress approved the 130-word statement as Section 17(d)(2) of the native claims act. It authorized the secretary of the interior to identify 80 million acres suitable for national parks, wildlife refuges, and national forests and for Congress to protect the land no later than December 18, 1978. Only after this protection could more land be signed over to the state and the natives. The designation "D-2" became an anathema to opponents of the subsequent, bitterly contested Alaska National Interest Lands Conservation Act. Even today, Republican representative Don Young of Alaska refuses to depart through an airport gate labeled D-2.[8]

Seiberling joined the Interior Committee in 1972, and three years later, after reading a *National Geographic* article on Alaska, decided he should see for himself. The National Park Service organized a two-week trip for Seiberling and several other congressmen. He took "800 pictures" and subsequently developed a slide show for other committee members.[9]

A little less than two years remained to fulfill the requirements of D-2 when Udall became chairman of the Interior Committee in 1977. He talked committee members into creating the Subcommittee on General Oversight and Alaska Lands, then chose Seiberling as chairman because he was the ranking Democrat who had been to Alaska. Thus was created the team that would carry D-2 to its 1980 conclusion. H.R. 39 was introduced on January 4, 1977.

The strategy, Seiberling recalled, was to make the Alaska conservation effort a national issue. The Alaska Coalition was formed, and it ultimately included more than fifty environmental groups such as the Sierra Club, the Wilderness Society, the National Audubon Society, the League of Conservation Voters, and the National Wildlife Federation. The state of Alaska, meanwhile, hired five lobbyists, and the oil, timber, and mineral companies created Citizens for Management of Alaska Lands.[10]

Hearings first were conducted in the lower forty-eight states, with 1,000 witnesses heard in Washington, Chicago, Atlanta, Denver, and Seattle. "A consensus developed in the country that we have to protect our heritage," Seiberling said.[11] In July, the subcommittee moved to Alaska, listening to another thousand witnesses in the bigger cities of Sitka, Juneau, Ketchikan, Anchorage, and Fairbanks, and then moving on to eleven towns. Seiberling took his subcommittee into the bush, too. The group later conducted seven more days of Washington hearings. Seiberling chaired almost all the sessions, sometimes sitting for twelve to fourteen straight hours. Young, Alaska's only representative, called Seiberling "Iron Pants."[12]

The 1977 trip to Alaska was the first for Udall. At one point, National Guard helicopters landed on a plateau amid snow-covered peaks in the Wrangell Mountains. Mo climbed out and gazed at the Nizina and Chitina Canyons, then exclaimed, "I want it all!" committee staffers Loretta Neumann and C. Stanley Sloss recalled, emphasizing that the comment was delivered in joking fashion, and everyone laughed.[13]

Early on, Democrat Lloyd Meeds, a poker- and golf-playing companion of Udall, suggested that he and Udall obtain temporary licenses so they could go fishing while in Alaska. According to Meeds, Udall declined at first, but Meeds persisted, and Udall acquired a permit. Later, the traveling party camped at Selby Lake north of the Arctic Circle, and Mo had free time. Sloss said game and fish wardens landed their plane on the lake, set up a tent on the shore, then paddled a boat across to check for licenses. They departed without citing anyone. Meeds theorized later that someone in the congressional traveling party must have alerted the wardens to try to embarrass Udall.

The Alaska hearings triggered a variety of responses. Neumann and Sloss said Sitka and Ketchikan were more hostile than friendly, Anchorage and Fairbanks were about fifty-fifty, and the villages generally were friendly.[14]

During the hearing at Togiak on the Bering Sea, Seiberling said that several elderly people spoke in their native language, and one man declared: "We native people depend on the land for everything . . . if you allow the land to be destroyed, God will forgive you because he is merciful, but our children will not."[15]

By the time the measure cleared the Interior Committee at the end of March 1978, the number of acres totaled 95 million. The Merchant Marine Committee, which had jurisdiction only over the wildlife refuges, reported its version on May 4. The two committees ultimately produced a consensus, but a Meeds amendment converted it into a pro-development, substitute bill. Udall aide Roy Jones and other staff members suggested Udall then amend the Meeds measure, but Mo hesitated in the interest of fair play and friendship. Six minutes later, Jones said, Udall did offer his own amendment after first clearing it with friend Meeds, who may or may not have understood the import of the action. The original Udall-Seiberling bill, protecting about 120 million acres, thus became the Meeds bill, which became again the original Udall-Seiberling bill. The House approved the amended version on May 19 in a 277–31 vote.[16]

Said Udall: "I am confident that Alaska lands legislation can be enacted into law this year so that you and I, and your children and grandchildren, and my children and grandchildren, will be able to know that a part of our great natural heritage located in the state of Alaska will be protected and preserved for the enjoyment and edification of all people for all time."[17]

He was dead wrong about it being enacted that year.

Young had battled the measure in the House. Alaska's senators, Democrat Mike Gravel and Republican Ted Stevens, would do the same, and ultimately the unilateral action of Gravel would prevent enactment in 1978. Neither Alaskan belonged to the Senate Energy Committee, but Stevens joined the discussion sessions. Gravel stood at a distance. He preferred "guerrilla tactics" compared to Stevens's "walk down a primrose path."[18] When the bill finally emerged from the Senate committee still carrying the Udall-Seiberling label, Stevens expressed unhappiness, saying: "No one at home will understand you've made any changes at all."[19]

As Congress neared adjournment, Interior Secretary Andrus joined House and Senate negotiators in working out a consensus that covered 96 million acres. Stevens assumed some measure would pass, and he sought the best possible terms for his state. At the last moment, Gravel jumped in hard, making new demands, and the compromise was broken. Gravel and Stevens had been at odds before, but this action destroyed any sense of compatibility. "You've got yourself a big battle now, buddy," Stevens shouted. He said more delays would be encountered in the transfer of federal land to the state, and "you carry the burden."[20]

Indeed, the congressional deadline for passage of a bill was December 18, 1978, and President Carter already had promised action. With a stroke of his pen on December 1, the president invoked the Antiquities Act of 1906 to create seventeen new national monuments covering 56 million acres, a decision that only Congress could revoke. In this fashion, Carter protected some of the land.

A new Congress arrived in January 1979, and it was time to start again. Another surprise awaited as the makeup of the Interior Committee changed slightly. The committee debated several approaches, and in the end a bill pushed by Louisiana Democrat Jerry Huckaby cleared the committee by one vote. It was development oriented and backed by Alaska's Young.

Reporter Dennis Farney of the *Wall Street Journal* wrote that Udall lost because of the young Turk movement he had helped spearhead years earlier. Committee chairmen had been deprived of their autocratic power, and Udall was learning the hard way what he and others had wrought. "The older I get, the wiser I get," he said, referring to "Udall's Fourth Law," which is: "Every reform always carries consequences you don't like."[21]

Looking ahead to a floor vote, Udall acquired Republican John Anderson of Illinois as a co-sponsor after Seiberling agreed to step aside to allow a display of bipartisan support.[22] Pennsylvania's Saylor, who would have been the logical GOP partner, had died in 1973.

The chairman now turned to a familiar parliamentary option: the amendment process that he had used so effectively a year earlier. The Merchant Marine Committee sought to substitute its "oil and gas patch-driven bill," which carried the name of another Louisiana Democrat, John B. Breaux, and Udall came in with the 127.5-million-acre, Udall-Anderson substitute. Aide Jones remembered that all three measures were debated at the same time, and the Breaux forces decided to sweeten their version to lure voters from Huckaby. This amendment to their own substitute brought everyone to the floor, and Udall quickly decided the time was right. He and his lieutenants stationed themselves at the doors, telling everyone to vote for the Breaux changes.[23]

"It was vintage Mo," Jones said. "He skewed the vote," and the Breaux forces could not determine whom to lobby. Then Udall told his troops to remain on the floor, saying: "We're going to start the jury speeches." The 127.5-million-acre, Udall-Anderson substitute won decisively, thus replacing the Breaux bill and then the Huckaby bill. It passed by a vote of 268–157.[24]

Unfortunately for Udall, it was another parliamentary success that led only a short distance. Gravel and Stevens still awaited, their positions little changed. Gravel threatened a filibuster but relented when Governor Hammond and a fifteen-member, home-state committee endorsed the Senate Energy Committee bill. Stevens wanted passage, asserting that the uncertainty had frightened investors and increased unemployment and bankruptcy filings. At the same time, Democrat Paul E. Tsongas of Massachusetts had moved to the Senate. Tsongas had served on the House Interior Committee, and Udall aide Jones moved over to advise him. Tsongas crafted a substitute that would set aside 125 million acres, as opposed to the committee's 102 million. This time it was Stevens who stopped the action. He feared the Tsongas measure would pass.[25]

Another year, another effort.

In 1980, the bill easily cleared the House, 360–65, with its 127.5 million acres intact. Interior Secretary Andrus applied additional heat to the Senate by withdrawing 40 million more acres from development and noting that it could return only when Congress approved the lands bill. Gravel and Stevens won approval for a delayed vote—after July 4—when Gravel promised not to filibuster. It was a promise he would break.[26]

Senate floor debate began on July 21 but was halted by majority leader Robert C. Byrd, a West Virginia Democrat, after it disintegrated into a shouting match, including one between Stevens and Colorado Democrat Gary Hart. Debate resumed in early August, but Gravel instituted a series of parliamentary delays. One day he used quorum calls and other maneuvers to force senators to return for more than eight hours.[27] That did it for Arizona Republican Barry Goldwater, who called Gravel's actions "horseplay." After a recess for the Democratic National Convention, the Senate shut down Gravel with cloture, voting to close debate on the bill, which cleared the way for real action. Within days, Gravel was defeated in his primary bid for reelection. On August 19, the Senate voted 78 to 14 for a slightly reduced, 104.3-million-acre bill.[28]

Udall and the environmentalists wanted the House version and were in no mood to compromise, but, Udall said, "we have worked too long and too hard on this fight for the spirit of tough but reasonable compromise to desert us now. There is no reason not to play the ninth inning just because the first eight have been so hard."[29]

Then the political atmosphere changed. Ronald Reagan was elected president, and Republicans achieved a majority in the Senate. Nonetheless, the environmental community put intense pressure on Udall to reject the Senate bill, aide Mark F. Trautwein said, adding that when he told Udall of the pressure, "Mo cut me off. 'No way, doesn't anyone understand that Ronald Reagan is about to become president?' It was a no-brainer to Mo."[30]

"I don't like the present version," Udall said. "I think it has many weaknesses, but I would say the Senate-passed version has 85 to 90 percent of the basic things that I wanted to see in an Alaska lands bill. I don't claim that this is a great victory [for environmentalists], but on balance, it's the thing to do."[31] In a later interview, Udall was less formal, saying: "There's an old country-western song that says, 'There's a time to hold 'em and a time to fold 'em.' I decided the time had come to fold 'em. And I was right."[32]

Udall cautioned that further efforts to strengthen the bill could mean no bill at all, and he added: "By more than doubling the size of the national park system and the national wildlife refuge system, and by nearly tripling the size of the national wilderness preservation system, the bill provides essential protection to much of America's greatest frontier, and it does so while making key resource areas available for development."[33]

While conservationists ultimately accepted the Senate bill somewhat grudgingly, Alaska lobbyists were even less happy, said Langhorne A. "Tony" Motley of Citizens for Management of Alaska Lands. "In the House, we were beat by the blue-jeaned backpackers," Motley said. "In the Senate we were done in by the silver spoon crowd—those born with silver spoons in their mouths."[34]

The House accepted the Senate version of H.R. 39 on November 12. "The passage of the balanced Alaska lands has been my highest environmental priority since the beginning of my administration," Carter said, "and the bill approved today resembles the proposals I sent to Congress more than three years ago."[35] Carter, hailed by some as the environmental president, signed it into law on December 2.

Udall heaped praise on the Alaska Coalition, saying its network of activists applied pressure quickly when needed. "We could find out in an instant that some senator was about to join up with somebody on a bum amendment, and we'd have five people from his home state who had credentials as supporters of his who would show up or would get on the telephone," Udall recounted. "We did the ultimate kind of civics and lobbying jobs that you read about in the textbooks." He also lauded Seiberling, saying, "I was very proud to help quarterback that whole effort with John Seiberling and a lot of other good people. . . . He [Seiberling] was the unsung hero in a lot of this, and had a lot more to do with some of these things than I did."[36]

The years have softened some of Alaska's hard attitudes toward the congressional decision to conserve its lands. In his 1994 autobiography, former governor Hammond wrote that "perhaps the most ironic aspect of this incredibly divisive battle between conservationists and developers is the possibility, once oil and the minerals are depleted," that the Alaska National Interest Land Claims Act may prevent the state "from returning to the traditional 'boom-bust' cycle that has plagued its economy since the days of Russian exploitation." Hammond said visitors spend more than $1 billion annually, "maintaining almost 14,000 Alaska jobs and generating millions in revenue to state and local governments. More than 52,000 Alaska jobs are now directly affected by non-resident spending— thousands more indirectly."[37]

Alaska natives remained supporters as the years went by. President Julie E. Kitka spoke for the 110,000-member Alaska Federation of Natives at a 1999 Washington memorial service for Udall. "I would not be exaggerating when I say the foothold we now have for building our future as indigenous peoples in the United States is built on the strong foundation Chairman Udall put in place," she said. Kitka cited "strong legal protections in federal law which protect our subsistence way of life," calling them "the sole legal protections we have and we treasure them and hold them tight." She went on, "Chairman Udall recognized that many of our communities are in deep distress. He had an appreciation for the many positive aspects of our communities and helped us build on them. It is not an overstatement to say our people have longer lives, better health care, better housing, better education, greater economic opportunities because of his interest and help."[38]

Despite the bitterness of the legislative battle, Udall retained his sense of humor throughout. A few years after passage of the bill, he returned to Alaska and remarked: "Times have changed for my coming up here. I think I'm doing better now. When people wave at me, they use all five fingers."[39]

In his 1988 book, Udall noted: "In Alaska, where conservationists are the only endangered species, 'Udall' became a slur, an epithet. I have it on good authority that of the thousands of babies born in Alaska during the past two decades not one has been named Stew or Mo."[40]

A FRIEND TO THE
INDIAN

*M*o Udall went to Washington hoping to establish his own political path, but the realities of the time dictated that he abandon his desire for a seat on the Judiciary Committee and instead join the Interior Committee. His brother Stewart had been there before him, and Arizona's interests, particularly the Central Arizona Project, required his presence. In typical fashion, Mo's attitude turned a previously undesirable situation into a positive one.

Along the way, Mo began traveling down unanticipated side roads. He was to become the champion of the American Indian, for whom the Interior Committee bore House responsibility. Before he resigned after thirty years in Congress, Mo would play the major House role in improving the lives of Indians in the United States. Stewart called him the "best friend the Indians ever had."[1]

From his position as chairman of the Interior Committee, Mo guided 184 bills through the Congress, many of them individual efforts to help just one of the more than 500 tribes. For example, in 1983, he crafted a measure that awarded federal recognition to the 400 members of the Texas Band of Kickapoo and provided them with a 100-acre reservation near Eagle Pass, Texas.

When Udall retired, Senator John McCain, an Arizona Republican, noted: "Even before he attained the powerful chairmanship, Mo labored in an often fruitless vineyard of Indian issues. . . . He did not work so long and so hard for personal glory or political gain. He did so because he cared for the dignified people in Indian tribes across the land and for the sanctity of the federal commitment memorialized in over 350 treaties with Indian tribes."[2]

Udall's interest in Indians was nothing new. He had been influenced by his parents, Levi and Louise, and his first wife, Patricia. In 1948, Levi had written the state supreme court opinion that gave Arizona Indians the right to vote. In 1951, Louise had begun a quarter century of Indian service and friendship that included writing the biography of a Hopi friend, Helen Sekaquaptewa. As a child, Pat had traveled the reservations with her father, Roe Emery, a dealer in Indian artifacts. "The tie to the reservations, the Indians, Arizona, and New Mexico also was a tremendous bond between MKU and myself," she said. "We often took our youngsters to the ceremonies at Hopi."[3]

Mo Udall served notice of his knowledge of Indian affairs in a 1965 talk in which he said, "The Indians have far too long occupied a no-man's land with regard to their rights as Americans." He warned against "assuming that all Indian tribes are alike." He also endorsed a "second bill of rights" that included a good education; a useful and remunerative job; adequate food, clothing, and recreation; a decent home; adequate medical care and the opportunity to achieve and enjoy good health; and adequate protection from the economic fears of old age, sickness, accident, and unemployment. "I believe," he said, "that, through economic assistance and educational opportunity, the Indian people will attain their rightful status in American society."[4]

Udall's most active period in dealing with Indian matters came after he took over as chairman of the Interior Committee. Representative Lloyd Meeds of Washington had been running the Subcommittee on Indian Affairs, but he opted out after a close reelection campaign. Udall selected Teno Roncalio of Wyoming as his replacement. Roncalio withdrew two years later.

No senior member was willing to handle the post, said longtime aide Franklin D. Ducheneaux. "There were too many political headaches and no gains for the senior members, so Mo did it. It was a liability to westerners and of no benefit to eastern members."[5] Nonetheless, Ducheneaux said Udall "was not an accidental advocate. He had a lot of sympathy for Indian problems. He was supportive of tribal government and sovereignty."

Ducheneaux, a member of the Cheyenne River Sioux tribe, was an attorney who had worked for the Office of Economic Opportunity and the Bureau of Indian Affairs before serving briefly as executive director of the National Congress of American Indians. He then was hired by Meeds and remained as the Interior Committee staff counsel on Indian affairs until 1988, when he quit to become a lobbyist for individual tribes.

"Mo's influence went way beyond the bills introduced," Ducheneaux said. "He was the major influence from 1977 to 1990, even in his weakness [from Parkinson's disease]."

Ducheneaux also praised Udall for preventing legislation harmful to Indian interests, saying: "Bills to strike at the heart of Indian treaty and other rights never saw the light of day during Mo's chairmanship. Mo sat on those anti-Indian bills, often in the face of heavy pressure from some of his colleagues to move on them."[6]

One of the most significant actions occurred in 1978 when the Indian Child Welfare Act was written into law. It was designed to put an end to unethical adoptions that ignored tribal rights, culture, heritage, or family feelings. During debate, Udall had declared: "Indian tribes and Indian people are being drained of their children, and as a result, their future as a tribe and a people is being placed in jeopardy."[7]

That same year, Udall steered through Congress the American Indian Religious Freedom Act, which was designed to protect the right to believe, express, and exercise the traditional religions of the American Indian, Eskimo, Aleut, and native Hawaiians.

The Indian Gaming Act most certainly caused a moral dilemma for Udall. He opposed government-backed gambling. Still, he believed in Indian sovereignty, and "felt if the states could do it, the tribes should have the same right," Ducheneaux said.[8]

Until the mid-1980s, tribes had limited themselves to occasional bingo halls. At the same time, Reagan administration funding cuts began having a severe impact on state and tribal revenues. Some states turned to lotteries for help, and the tribes sought similar salvation. Decisions by two U.S. circuit courts upheld tribal rights to sponsor gambling if the state did so, but one also held that a tribe could not sue the state to win permission. "Now," Ducheneaux said, "the tribes were crawling on their hands and knees." The gaming bill "was very intrusive on tribal rights" because it required a compact between the state and the tribe, he said, but it allowed the tribe to sue if the state refused to negotiate in good faith.[9] Udall steered the measure through, winning approval on October 17, 1988.

Udall was not always successful. In the mid-1980s, he found himself in a tight spot in the century-old land dispute between the Navajo Nation and the neighboring Hopi tribe. The 8,000-member Hopi tribe never engaged in hostilities with the United States but had been given 2.5 million acres under an 1882 executive order by President Chester A. Arthur. The 200,000-member Navajo tribe had received 15 million acres under a series of treaties and executive orders.

Over the years, Navajos settled on Hopi land, and in 1958, a federal court gave the Hopis exclusive right to only 650,000 acres and directed that the remaining 1.85 million acres be declared a joint-use area. The joint-use concept failed, and in 1973 Congress approved the relocation of 10,000 Navajos. Udall voted against the plan. By 1986, an estimated 300 Navajo families remained on Hopi land, had not applied for relocation benefits, and had indicated no intention of moving.[10] To most, the land was sacred or their traditional home or both.

To try to resolve the issue, Udall and McCain, then a member of the House, introduced legislation to create a land swap, to require a Navajo payment of $300 million in mineral resource royalties from coal on two pieces of Navajo land, and to require the Hopis to provide sixteen acres to each of sixty-two Navajo families if they wished to remain in Hopi territory. The bill was supported by the Navajos, but Hopi tribal chairman Ivan Sidney called it "another effort to reward the Navajo tribe for their disobedience to law, contempt of court, and threats of violent conduct."[11] Udall and McCain withdrew the measure when the Hopis, Senator Barry Goldwater, and the Reagan administration refused to support it.[12] Ultimately, a federal court oversaw a negotiated settlement that allowed the Navajos to remain if they signed a 75-year lease with the Hopis. Somewhere between 300 and 1,000 Navajos were believed to live on Hopi land as the twenty-first century began.[13]

Udall also put together the 1989 Native American Graves Protection and Repatriation Act, bringing together the Society of American Archaeology and major Indian organizations. He won approval of legislation that aided economic development. In 1986, he worked to improve health care, and he co-sponsored a bill designed to prevent Indian youth alcoholism and substance abuse.

In a home-state matter, he and McCain helped forge the $125.4-million settlement of an 83-year-old legal battle over water rights between the Salt River–Pima–Maricopa Indian community and the cities of Phoenix, Tempe, Mesa, Chandler, Gilbert, and Glendale. Udall called the 1988 agreement "a testament to the art of political compromise."[14]

Udall used his understanding of human nature and process to advance the Indian cause. In one instance, former aide Deborah Sliz recalled, President Reagan had vetoed the Southern Arizona Water Rights Settlement Act, which resolved a dispute between the Papago (now called Tohono O'odham), neighboring mines and irrigators, and the city of Tucson. Udall slipped it into an administration-backed bill authorizing projects in Wyoming and Missouri. When it came to the floor, Udall told staff members to leave his side, saying: "I want to just stand up and drone on and have people think this is an inconsequential bill." Said Sliz, "We went to the back of the room, and he got it done."[15]

Mo also was sensitive to the feelings of individuals. Artist Seth Eastman had been commissioned by Congress for paintings depicting Indians of the West, and his re-creation of an Indian scalping a white man hung on the Interior hearing room wall. It was titled *Death Whoop*. Committee member Ben Nighthorse Campbell, a Northern Cheyenne who was then a Democratic representative and now is a Republican senator from Colorado, objected. Udall ordered the painting removed and called a news conference. "My esteemed colleague here," he said, "objects to the surgical operation this Indian gentleman is performing on this white gentleman. And if he's offended, then I'm offended."[16]

Udall's leadership was recognized in 1985 when he was awarded the first lifetime achievement award by the Americans for Indian Opportunity, a Native American issues think tank supported by more than sixty tribes. "On almost every piece of Indian legislation since he arrived in Congress, Mo Udall has taken the lead," president LaDonna Harris told about 2,000 people. Instead of a plaque, the organization presented Udall with a gold-tipped eagle feather encased in crystal.

"For too long," Udall said, "we've tried to make over Indians in our own image—tried to get them driving a convertible down the freeway in a three-piece suit. Some Indians want this, but most don't. They want the same kind of rights other Americans have to determine their own lives. But we've never given them the tools to run their future. Our sins are many. Indian health care is a disaster. The housing situation is outrageous. And there are many bright young Indians who would like to go to school, but can't get the scholarships."[17]

Eleven years later, the name of Morris K. Udall played a new part in Indian education when the nonprofit foundation that Congress established in his name created a summer congressional internship program for Native Americans.

THE CONSENSUS
BUILDER

*A*fter taking over the Interior Committee, Mo Udall sought to take the environmental middle. That often riled environmentalists, who tended to see matters as an all-or-nothing solution. Critics said Udall compromised too quickly, rather than holding out for more substantial gains. "We are having some hideous fights with Mo on issues like nuclear regulation, reclamation law, the coal-supply pipeline," an environmental lobbyist said.[1]

Udall began to institute practices that he had urged when he was seeking House reform a few years before, such as scheduling of bills and openness in proceedings.

Representative Robert Lagomarsino, a California Republican, called him the fairest chairman he had known.[2] "Disregarding our differences on the issues, he is always fair, competent, and able. On some issues he's not as strident and he is perhaps more willing than others to compromise, trying to persuade them to come to the middle."[3]

Some members complained that Udall was too "soft." Committee members, especially Democrats, were not worried about retribution if they crossed Udall.[4] At least one lobbyist did not see it that way. Rob Smith, the Sierra Club's Southwest representative, said Udall rejected the accepted practice of taking an extreme position and then bargaining some of it away. Instead, he said, Udall "seeks to make the compromise before he introduces the bill. You may end up in the same place, only everyone isn't as angry."[5] Said Charles M. Clusen of the Alaska Coalition: "He's not someone who gets someone in the corner and puts the squeeze on. He argues his case on the merits and lets it sit."[6]

Udall believed in compromise. "The way you move ahead is to keep everybody happy and not leave bloody bodies behind," said former aide Matt James. Udall liked to see both sides win. "He didn't slam things down your throat," James said. "He always took the long view that he would have to work with these guys. It was a process of compromise. He had a good heart for people."[7]

His evenhanded manner was noted when he was named legislator of the year by both the nuclear energy industry and the Sierra Club in 1987.[8]

Udall also got along with the female members of the House, despite the fact it was a male-dominated institution. When Pat Schroeder of Colorado arrived in 1972 she was one of thirteen or fourteen female members. She said she recognized that Udall came from a Mormon and sports background but he always treated her well. She noted that when she arrived, there were no female police, parliamentarians, pages, or doorkeepers. "It was a men's club. I saw the rest of the bunch and Mo looked good."[9]

Former aide Anne Scott said, "Mo was not a sexist. He did favor and feel comfortable with a certain kind of personality . . . someone who could tell a joke, who was very smart, who could get the job done." She said Udall avoided shy people because then there would be too much silence since he also was shy.[10]

In 1978, Udall was to face his toughest election since he first was elected to Congress in 1961. He began campaigning not long after his appendix burst and he contracted peritonitis. He underwent emergency surgery on April 5 in Washington, D.C., and came through it in good condition. After a short recovery period, he returned to Congress and to the campaign. His opponent was Thomas B. Richey, a so-called gentleman rancher from Sierra Vista and a former state legislator. Richey had been promised as much as $250,000 from Texas oil interests and Alaska "boom-or-bust" developers but was to take in nowhere near that much.

District voters had some lingering negative feelings from the presidential campaign, feelings that Udall was a national politician now, not one who represented only them. Longevity in office "is a good reason to get rid of you," Udall said. "Being an incumbent's not all it's cracked up to be."[11]

In addition, he was making fewer trips home because of his full schedule, first as a presidential candidate and then as Interior Committee chairman. He also was the only Democrat in the Arizona congressional delegation, and conservative voter registration continued to gain in his district. Said an aide: "Every time there's a blizzard in Buffalo or Detroit, we get 5,000 more conservative retirees in the district."[12]

Udall appealed for funding by noting that "a determined militant, right-wing clique in Phoenix . . . is determined to run me out of office." Udall defended his record and responded to Richey's attacks that he had forgotten his constituency. "I've been to the top of the mountain politically but I've never forgotten my heritage and my roots," he said. "I know who I am and where I'm from."[13]

The cost of winning reelection was skyrocketing. Udall had spent $45,791 in 1976 to beat former Vietnam prisoner of war Laird Guttersen, who spent $31,008. In 1978, he was forced to spend $295,268 to outpoll Richey, who laid out $139,431.

Udall told voters they would be foolish to vote out a powerful committee chairman in favor of a freshman.[14] At one point when he seemed to tire of defending his record, he turned to a Tucson reporter and said with mock gravity: "They have discovered I am a liberal. The well-kept secret is out."[15]

Although it was his closest race since 1961, Udall still won handily, with an almost 10,000-vote margin over Richey out of about 103,000 votes cast.

Udall also was getting back in Carter's good graces. Udall had been persona non grata at the White House for refusing to quit the primaries in 1976. Udall did not help himself by fighting Carter's effort to end water projects such as the Central Arizona Project. Still, Carter needed Udall if he were to get congressional approval of civil service reform, a pet project and a campaign promise. Carter also realized that Congress was no longer a body that just provided advice and consent; it was now wielding greater power because the Watergate scandal had damaged the presidency. Carter was perceived as a weak president, and reform had given more power to the House.[16]

The president asked Udall to usher the civil service reform through the House Post Office and Civil Service Committee, on which he sat. The committee chairman, Democrat Robert Nix of Pennsylvania, turned the reform hearings over to Udall, who got the changes through the committee, despite opposition from federal employees and congressmen who represented districts with great numbers of federal workers.[17] The bill was designed to create incentives for good work and to ease the way for managers to terminate incompetent workers.[18]

In a survey of members of Congress in 1980, Udall was rated as the second most respected House member behind majority leader Jim Wright of Texas and the most effective committee chairman in getting legislation through Congress. He ranked third as the most persuasive debater in the House behind Wright and John Anderson, the Illinois Republican. "Mo Udall is one of the few members who commands instant attention when he speaks," said Representative Richard L. Ottinger, a New York Democrat.[19] *Washingtonian* magazine said he was the most respected legislator in either the House or the Senate.[20]

Udall's last serious challenge came in 1980 against Republican Richard Huff, a millionaire real estate developer who sought his seat. Huff, fifty-three, a fervent conservative and born-again Christian, undertook an aggressive campaign he had learned at a right-wing candidates' school sponsored by Representative Guy Vander Jagt of Michigan.[21] Huff spent almost $550,000 to unseat Udall, while Udall spent $860,395.[22]

To his credit, Huff made no issue of Udall's Parkinson's disease, but attacked his record. "If our problems today are not caused by congressional leaders, then who is to blame?" Huff asked. Huff derisively called Udall "a friend of the butterfly" for his environmental stands.[23] His TV ads declared that Udall had ties to eastern liberals and that he was too liberal for the changing district.[24]

Udall kept his sense of humor despite the attacks. Once during the campaign, he said: "I've decided from [Huff's] ads that if you have falling hair, dandruff, loose dentures, low-back pain, or a lousy sex life, Mo Udall caused it, he meant to cause it, and he enjoys seeing you suffer."[25]

Udall's pollster, Henry C. Kenski, discovered that a fifth of the voters had lived in Udall's district for five years or less, which could cut into his support base. Udall resorted to negative campaigning against Huff, although it made him uncomfortable. One of the reasons he had avoided it was that although Udall was a master communicator, he lacked media savvy. "He really was from a prior age," said Kenski, now associate professor of communication at the University of Arizona and southern Arizona regional director for Republican U.S. senator Jon Kyl. "He was not a strong media politician. He couldn't find the camera. . . . He didn't have the killer instinct for doing the negative."

Kenski noted that Udall had little knowledge of mass culture. His passions were politics and sports, particularly the National Football League's Washington Redskins. Kenski and Bruce Wright said Udall had been approached to become commissioner of Major League Baseball and the National Basketball Association, but no offers were ever made.[26] Once he was scheduled to meet with actor Ed Asner of the popular *Mary Tyler Moore* TV show, but Udall was unfamiliar with him. "I don't think he saw a lot of movies or television," Kenski said. "Work was his religion; it was the consuming passion of his life."[27]

Udall attacked Huff as a "packaged candidate" financed by out-of-state interests and said Huff refused to debate and that district voters deserved better.[28] He complained about the influence of "Big Oil" on the race. "Some big oil companies, not content to have a hammerlock on your wallet, have decided that they should be entitled to buy a congressman from the Second District of Arizona," he said.[29] One reporter said they campaigned "like two tarantulas in a bottle."[30]

Senator Barry Goldwater threw his support to Huff, calling Udall "a nice, decent man," but "very, very liberal. . . . I think that Huff has a chance of retiring Mo."[31] It was not to be. Udall defeated Huff by 28,000 votes out of 119,000 ballots cast.

Arizona's population was growing, and the state was about to get a fifth congressional seat. In 1981, the state legislature created two districts out of Udall's district. One covered the east side of Tucson and southeastern Arizona; it was considered relatively conservative despite a 51.1 percent Democratic registration. The other took in west Tucson and stretched to Yuma on the California border and then north into Phoenix; it had a 64 percent Democratic registration and a 35 percent Hispanic population.[32]

Arizona governor Bruce Babbitt, a Democrat, accused the Republicans of jeopardizing Udall's seat "by playing politics" with district lines. Udall was confident he could win in either district, but noted: "I've been a Tucson congressman all my life. This would make me a Phoenix congressman."[33]

State senate president Leo Corbet, a Republican, defended the new districts. He noted that no Republican congressman had that kind of edge and that Mo could win in either one.

Udall aide Bruce Wright said "our hearts say to run in the east, but our heads tell us to run in the west." Residents in both new districts wanted Udall for their congressman, but he chose the one that took in parts of Phoenix and Tucson. He joked that he opted for the district with the best chimichangas (a deep-fried burrito).[34] He compared the district's shape to that of a "pregnant octopus." Nonetheless, it made him a certain bet for reelection. The choice also prevented an ugly primary fight among several Hispanic politicians who eyed the seat.[35]

Longtime friend Jim McNulty won election in the eastside district but held the job for only two years before losing to Republican James T. Kolbe.

Udall seldom encountered truly angry constituents in Pima County, but immigration reform efforts that began in the early 1980s put him in just such a situation: Young Hispanics, who had worked for and supported Mo on almost every issue, yelled out against his stand on the Simpson-Mazzoli bill.

The measure carried the names of Republican senator Alan Simpson of Wyoming and Democratic representative Romano Mazzoli of Kentucky. The two most contentious provisions were sanctions against employers who knowingly hired illegal immigrants and temporary resident status to individuals who had entered the country illegally before 1982.

The southern Arizona dispute focused on employer sanctions, which some Hispanics said would give employers an excuse to adopt a whites-only hiring policy. Udall supported the provision, saying current law covered only undocumented workers, but should also include exploitative employers. McNulty shared the view.

A march and protest at Udall's Tucson office occurred on June 22, 1984. Leading the effort was a group of young activists, including attorney Isabel G. Garcia, now the Pima County legal defender; school board member Raul M. Grijalva, now a Pima County supervisor; state senator Jaime P. Gutierrez, now a University of Arizona assistant vice president; and Salomon R. Baldenegro, now a University of Arizona research analyst.[36]

A crowd estimated at 300 to 500 protesters walked to Udall's office and tried to enter en masse to sign the guest register. The group was temporarily stopped at the door by Daniel O'Neill, Udall's district representative. "I told them, 'We can't have the entire mob in here,' " O'Neill recalled. The use of the word "mob" ignited a brief argument, and ultimately, O'Neill cleared the doorway and the protesters pushed their way inside. O'Neill said that was the only time he could remember Udall reprimanding him. "He thought I had incited a riot . . . he called me and said, 'Don't ever let that happen again.' "[37]

Udall was not in Arizona but arrived later. He scheduled a July 2 meeting with a different group of Hispanics and agreed to appear at a July 11 community meeting at El Rio Neighborhood Center.

Hispanics invited to the July 2 meeting included businessman John L. Huerta, now a University of Arizona fund-raiser; Arnold Elias, whose appointment as Tucson postmaster Udall had arranged, and his wife, Martha; *Tucson Citizen* columnist Richard Salvatierra, a retired State Department officer who had served extensively in Latin America; South Tucson mayor Daniel W. Eckstrom, now a Pima County supervisor; and attorney Richard J. Gonzales, the only representative of a younger generation.[38] It was a closed meeting, but Bruce Wright reported afterward that some participants had urged Udall to vote against the Simpson-Mazzoli bill because of the section on employer sanctions. Huerta said he remained unhappy with employer sanctions, but "I think Mo did the best he could in a bad situation . . . [but] the bill is not palatable to most of the Hispanic community.[39]

About 250 people turned out for the nearly two-hour El Rio meeting. Afterward, Udall said, "I've been amazed a little bit, surprised, and disappointed at the pessimism of my Hispanic friends. I'm more optimistic our country can find ways to do this" without encouraging discrimination.[40]

Fifteen years later, Isabel Garcia called the session "sort of disappointing. Mo was angry. We were great admirers of Mo. Make no mistake about that. It was just that one issue, employer sanctions. He lashed out at us for the process, almost like we were ungrateful. Mo was our friend and we continued to support him. We knew what reality was." Some in the crowd shouted "No more Mo in '84" and later demonstrated outside McNulty's headquarters. Garcia regretted the outbursts and the McNulty protest, saying she and other organizers were unable to control some of the dissidents. Udall, of course, won his election; McNulty was defeated by Republican Kolbe. Garcia suggested that employer sanctions laid the foundation for an anti-immigrant sentiment that now has spread throughout the United States.[41]

In 1986, the Senate approved the Simpson-Mazzoli bill by a 60–30 vote. The House cleared it by a 230–166 vote. Udall voted with the majority despite the argument of legislative assistant Anne Scott, who contended that employer sanctions would set the stage for discrimination against people of color.[42]

Explained Udall: "I am torn by concern that employer sanctions will lead to discrimination in employment against certain Americans—particularly Hispanics and Asians. And yet, without some form of compelling provisions in the law, what is there to stop greedy and exploitative elements of our society from continuing the shocking abuses of the past?" He praised the bill's citizenship opportunity provision, saying it will bring "people out of the shadows and offer them the opportunity of freedom and citizenship. Those who have established themselves and their families in this country in the legitimate search for economic opportunity have a right to the dignity and humaneness of legalization." Udall said all congressional decisions were reached through a balancing of interests. "I voted for the bill and I am convinced that it is more good than bad," he said. "The tradeoffs are there. We have wrestled with this issue for more than a decade. Its time has come."[43]

After Udall's Parkinson's disease was revealed in 1980, speculation arose before every election whether he would seek reelection. Even his brother Stewart urged him to retire in 1984.[44] At one point, he said that he might retire. "I don't want to leave office by the box—pine box or the ballot box."[45] Toward the end of his career, he told friends he wanted to complete thirty years of House service. His remaining elections were easy victories in the newly carved-out district, including one in 1982 over Roy B. Laos III, a Tucson city councilman. In that election, Udall's staff discovered that although the district was heavily Hispanic, only 5 percent were registered to vote. By election day, 20 percent were registered, Kenski said.[46]

In the mid-1980s, Udall was being referred to as an elder statesman. As such, it gave him the right to reflect on his career. In 1985, he looked at what might have been. "If you gave me the choice of public offices that I would like," he said, "No. 1 would be the White House, No. 2 would be the [House] speaker, No. 3 probably would be the [U.S.] Supreme Court."[47]

In the mid-1980s Udall became embroiled in controversy between two of the great loves of his life: the University of Arizona and environmentalists. It was a battle he wanted to avoid, and tried to avoid. "I'd rather not be in the center of the fight," Udall said.[48] It rages still today.

The university wanted to build seven observatories atop a "sky island" called Mount Graham, a four-hour drive from Tucson in southeastern Arizona. The 10,720-foot mountain was an ideal site for the $200-million project because of its clean air and lack of light pollution. It was hoped the scopes would turn Tucson into an astronomy center of global importance and enhance the university's reputation.

Environmentalists used one of their favored tactics when they wished to protect an area from development: the Endangered Species Act. Tiny red squirrels lived on the mountain and development would threaten them and their habitat, and only about a hundred or so of the eight-ounce rodents were left in the world, they said. Udall sought a compromise that would allow the telescopes and the squirrels to live side by side. Udall aide Mark F. Trautwein said Udall remarked that "the one thing we could not do was support an exemption" from the act. He called the act "the Holy Grail of the environmental movement." At the same time, there was no proof that the scopes would hurt the squirrels.

Trautwein said he received calls from astronomers calling him a "stupid idiot" and asking: "Who cares about squirrels?" He also received calls from biologists who called him a "stupid idiot" and asked: "Who cares about scopes?" Trautwein called it an example of the "hypocrisy and selfishness of science and scientists."[49]

Trautwein said that because of Udall's health he was incapable of waging a campaign to protect the Endangered Species Act. His health had not affected his judgment, but "he might have been able to bring more personal vigor to try to resolve the issues better," he said. Udall was tired, physically broken, and thinking about his legacy, Trautwein said. "His taste for bruising battles and controversies was not great." Once, Udall told Trautwein: "Mark, you've got to get me out of this."

A lobbying firm hired by the university asked Trautwein to urge Udall to pressure the U.S. Fish and Wildlife Service into approving the telescopes. "I said that I would take it to Mo and that it was inconceivable that he would do it. We just don't do that. It was an article of faith in the office that you do not interfere in the appropriate decision making, particularly the decision-making process of federal agencies. It was simply wrong and inappropriate." He said one of the lobbyists became abusive and said, "Oh, come on Mark, we all know that's how Washington works." Trautwein replied, "That's [not] how we work."

Finally, Trautwein went to Udall and said that the controversy "would go on forever if you don't stop the scopes." Udall replied, "Well, I think the controversy will be intense but brief."[50] Udall did not want to exert pressure on a federal agency for a political decision. The issue, he said, "is where it ought to be, in the hands of the experts."[51]

In the end, Trautwein said, everyone lost. Even though the university received approval to build three telescopes, its reputation was badly damaged. "It earned it with remarkable arrogance and shortsightedness," he said. "The environmentalists were late, ineffective, strident, pompous, behaved badly." And the Arizona congressional delegation resorted "to the power politics that people find distasteful," he said.[52]

Stephen E. Emerine, a university spokesman during the controversy, noted in 1999 that there were five times more squirrels on Mount Graham in the 1980s than the environmentalists claimed and that the population had increased since the telescopes were built.[53]

In 1985, Udall left the Post Office and Civil Service Committee, where he had served for twenty-four years, to join the Foreign Affairs Committee, a new challenge for the sixty-three-year-old congressman. He toured the Soviet Union for ten days in September 1986 to look at environmental conditions, particularly in Siberia. The trip was to lay the groundwork for a bilateral environmental meeting scheduled for November during which the two countries would discuss whaling, toxic waste, and other environmental issues.

Udall's enormous popularity in the House, especially among younger members, who thought of him as a folk hero, helped him pass legislation to protect his interests. Hedrick Smith, in his 1988 book *The Power Game,* noted how Udall's popularity helped him foil an attempt by some House members to halt subsidies for public power in some western states. Udall sponsored a bill to continue the subsidies, but Barney Frank, a Massachusetts Democrat, and other liberals wanted hydroelectric power to be priced at market rates. The bill was before Udall's Interior Committee. "The environmentalists were with us; the old system was wasting water. It was bad economics," Frank said. "I talked to some of the guys on the floor. I said, 'Look, on all the merits of the bill you should be with us.' And they said, 'But how can we vote against Mo?' It was a fairly close vote but we lost. We were opposing Mo Udall, and we love Mo. We lost because of Mo—a good example of personality affecting politics."[54]

Sibling rivalry broke out again between Mo and Stewart in early 1986 when Stewart, sixty-six, thought about running for a seat in Congress from a Phoenix-area district. He said, "When I started thinking about running for Congress, I fantasized that a maverick with my background might gain an audience and have influence on events."[55] Stewart said he had not discussed his plans with Mo, adding, he "would probably try to talk me out of it."[56] When Stewart did ask him, Mo was against the idea. "I was furious," Stewart said. He said he wrote him a letter saying that they were "coming to the end of the game" and that they should not be competing anymore. Stewart said Mo wrote him a letter of apology.[57] Stewart decided against running, saying that "it was foolish to think that one angry old-timer could make a difference."[58]

Among the more significant environmental legislative efforts Udall accomplished as House Interior Committee chairman was expansion of the Arizona wilderness area he helped conserve in 1964 after years of acrimonious debate in Congress. In 1984, Congress passed the Arizona Wilderness Act, which set aside 1 million acres in Udall's home state with the bipartisan support of a longtime colleague and fellow Arizonan.

The bill's passage revealed a story about the closeness of Mo Udall and Barry Goldwater. When Udall wrote the bill, he wanted Goldwater to sponsor a similar one in the Senate, despite the fact that Goldwater was a friend of miners, cattlemen, and developers. He called Goldwater to ask for a meeting. Goldwater invited him to his office. "It was extraordinary," Trautwein said. "His going to Barry showed respect, deference." After some small talk, Udall asked him to sponsor the bill in the Senate. "Sure, Mo," Goldwater said. "I'd be glad to." Goldwater's bill had several sections that could be cut so it would pass, but it essentially was what Udall wanted, Trautwein said. "The trust and confidence that these two men had in one another, which had been built up over [their] lifetimes . . . that

[one] would not embarrass the other, that the other man's word was his bond was an extraordinary lesson to me," Trautwein said.[59]

In 1990, Congress passed the Arizona Desert Wilderness Act, another Udall bill, which protected 1.4 million acres in the southern and western sections of the state from development.

Udall also arranged for the Buenos Aires Wildlife Refuge, 116,000 acres of grasslands, mountains, and wetlands 60 miles southwest of Tucson that was home to the masked bobwhite bird. The land was owned by a Mexican national and was sought by a Japanese conglomerate that wanted to build a resort. Udall was vilified in the press, particularly by the *Arizona Republic,* Trautwein said. He said that the land purchase to create the refuge was the result of "the courage of one man who wanted to do the right thing."[60]

In 1987, Congress made certain that the sun would rise and set on the Udall brothers. A point of land on Guam was named Point Udall after Mo; it was the place the sun rose each day. A few years before, a point on the Virgin Islands had been named Point Udall in honor of Stewart; it was the first place the sun set in the United States.[61]

As Udall's health slipped, some House members became concerned about his performance as Interior Committee chairman. Udall had selected Democrat George Miller of California as his heir apparent, but Miller was careful to avoid usurping any of Udall's power.

In 1987, Udall slipped up on an issue because of his weakened condition. He failed to oppose a proposal to roll back mineral royalty rates after years of trying to get higher ones. "It was one of those things that got missed because he can't do everything he used to be able to do," a lobbyist said.[62]

Stewart said that in 1988, House Speaker Jim Wright wanted Mo to share power with Miller. They requested that Stewart negotiate the arrangement. "Mo wouldn't hear of it," Stewart said.[63]

Trautwein said he never thought Miller tried to force Udall out. He said Miller was concerned about the committee's ability to function.[64] S. Lee McElvain, the Interior Committee's retired counsel, wondered how well Miller's style would go over. "Udall basically was able to work out a compromise, to work together with the minority to get things accomplished," McElvain said. "The new school is a little bit harder-line—sort of, we got the votes, so we'll do it the way we want to do it."[65]

Udall received a traumatizing blow on August 13, 1988, when his wife, Ella, committed suicide. Ella's death compounded Udall's health struggles. Trautwein called it a "devastating emotional experience for Mo."[66] A year later, on August 6, he married Norma Gilbert, who had helped him through his grief. Aide Bob Neuman said Udall probably would have retired in 1988 had not Ella committed suicide. After he remarried he decided to run again in 1990.[67]

Udall asked some of his closest friends and advisers whether he should run again during a Tucson meeting in 1989. Among the participants were Jim McNulty, longtime friend George Rosenberg, and Arthur A. Chapa, an attorney and onetime head of Udall's Tucson office. Wright told them before the meeting that they should urge Udall to step down, but none did. One Udall aide, Prior Pray, told Udall with tears streaming down his face that he should retire. No one else urged him to retire, Wright said.[68]

In 1990 when he announced he would seek his fifteenth full term, he told Tucson-area Democrats that his health would not prevent him from serving one more time. "I stand before you with a painful old back, Parkinson's disease, arthritis, and one eye, and I can tell you, considering the alternatives I feel pretty good. And, if any of you should run into Dr. John Parkinson, please ask him what the hell is going on." He said he wanted another term because he had environmental issues that needed attention. He told the group that he was not what he was in years past, but his experience "makes me better than the man I was when I first went to Washington."[69]

That speech marked one of the few times Udall visited the district in later years. Former aide Thomas C. Duddleston said that beginning in 1986 or 1987, Udall returned to the district two or three times a year, and after his 1990 reelection perhaps not at all.[70]

When Udall was hospitalized in early January 1991, Miller, a burly former high school football player with a macho bluster, served as acting chairman, even installing his own committee staff director while Udall was in the hospital.[71] Representative Ben Nighthorse Campbell accused Democratic leaders of treating Udall shabbily. He said they "rolled Mo right out" as chairman and fired his staff. Said Cy Jamison, director of the U.S. Bureau of Land Management: "They knocked Udall out, and he didn't deserve it. . . . I personally think they should have found a more graceful way to do this to a longtime chairman."[72]

Aide Matt James said Udall's life was Congress. "He deeply loved the institution and public policy." He still was working Saturdays. "He couldn't imagine not working, not being involved in the process." He would miss a day or two at the office on occasion, and his staff had to remind him to take his medication.[73] A student intern, Diane M. Targovnik, the daughter of his physician, often helped Udall find one of the ten or fifteen pairs of glasses he kept in his office because he was continually misplacing them.[74]

Udall aide Trautwein agreed with others that Udall stayed in office too long. "No question about it," he said. At the same time, he added: "Even in his diminished state, he could accomplish things that no one else could do."[75] James said Udall could do "more in one call than most people could do at all."[76] Senator Ted Kennedy supported him as well. "He's better than 95 percent of his colleagues, and the only appropriate comparison of his abilities is against himself," Kennedy said.[77]

Trautwein said the staff, including Roy Jones and Stanley Scoville, took over a lot of Udall's duties. "I think we did things the way Mo wanted them done," he said. "That's a monument to him. You knew what Mo wanted done and how he wanted it done and you were going to be faithful to that. There wasn't any question."[78]

Later Udall said that after he served his last term, he and his wife, Norma, wanted to visit some of the nation's national parks. "I would like to pitch a tent and stay for a while," he said. He also said he wanted to see Central Arizona Project water delivered to Tucson: "I've spent a lot of time on that effort and my parents always taught me to finish what I start."[79]

He would not finish his term. A fall at his home hospitalized him and forced his resignation on May 4, 1991.

THE PRICE THEY PAID

The public and private lives of Mo Udall were a study in contrasts. As a politician he encountered defeats, certainly, but they paled in comparison to the significance of his accomplishments. In private life, it was a different story: His first wife divorced him, his second wife committed suicide, and his third marriage was interrupted by the fall that left him silent for most of the nearly eight years preceding his death. Relations with his six children were tenuous at best.

Friend Jim McNulty said he "paid a terrible domestic price, wives, kids . . . and not from intentional neglect but in terms of the greater good and the bigger picture he had to do this and he had to do that."[1]

His brother Burr said: "My biggest complaint is how he treated his children. Anybody who has children, you owe them a duty to, one, support them, which he did, and, two, to be there to help and counsel and that part he never did."[2] Said Bruce Wright, his administrative assistant from 1981 through 1986, "He always cared about his kids, but he had trouble carving time out for them."[3] Writer Larry L. King, the onetime congressional aide who helped Udall organize his first office, added: "Politics is a disease if they are ambitious, and Mo was ambitious. He was not a chairwarmer. You don't have as much time for your family and wife as you should have."[4]

Myra MacPherson chronicled the ups and downs—mostly downs—of political families in a 1975 book called *The Power Lovers*. It is an account of more than 200 interviews that describe the impact of the public life upon the private. MacPherson recounts how the family assumes a subordinate position to the demands of the job, must live in a fishbowl, and must present the picture of happiness regardless of the reality. The voters expect no less, she wrote.[5]

Most likely, Mo Udall simply did what came naturally. Without thought, he seemed to follow the example of his parents. They had raised him in a rural, Mormon culture, but Mo lived his adult life in urban settings and in a totally different era. In St. Johns, the husband provided and the wife supported and nurtured. With his own family, Mo provided and expected his wives to support and nurture. America was changing, however, and first wife Pat, pulled in many intellectual directions, was, according to her children, a feminist before feminism. Second wife Ella sought to maintain her individuality and struggled to gain the attention of her workaholic husband. Interestingly, years later, in separate interviews, Mo described both women as "spirited."

His sister Eloise Whiting recalled a mid-1960s "good, long talk" with her brother following the divorce. She quoted Mo as saying: "If I could have had my choice, I would have married a Mormon girl and raised my children Mormon." Brother-in-law Warren Whiting explained that Mo had lived in areas with minimal Latter-day Saints population,[6] but it must be noted that Mo did not attend Mormon services.

Pat said, "Mo worked enormously hard. I remember fighting for weekends with the kids, then giving up Saturday and fighting for Sundays."[7] Years later, Udall hinted that the loss of an eye may have triggered his focus on work. In a proposal for a book about his 1976 presidential bid, Udall recalled encounters with a Philadelphia boy and an Ohio University basketball player, each of whom had lost one eye. Udall suggested that a description of the meetings might provide a springboard to "let me flash back and tell a little bit about the loss of my eye, what it did to me, the Mo Udall overachiever in high school and at the University, and how it shaped my life. And how it might have been used to give me identity when I needed it in the early stage."[8]

The record is clear that work consumed Mo. As a military man, his letters suggest nearly around-the-clock activity. As a law student, he also played intercollegiate basketball and served as student body president. As a lawyer, he went to his office early and stayed late. As a congressman, his children recall that when they visited Washington during the summers after the divorce, he would often drop by the office "for a few minutes" that usually turned into hours. To his children, it became known as "swinging by the O."[9]

Udall was aware of the danger of workaholism but perhaps was oblivious to his own obsession. In mid-1986, years after his own children were grown, he advised graduating law students: "The law is a jealous mistress. I remember going down to the bank building in the town where I practiced one Sunday morning, waiting to pick up a friend. Coming to work that Sunday were about five of the most successful lawyers in town. I learned later that they never went to a concert or took a walk or went on a hike or did anything on Sunday except go to work. My advice is to leave some time for yourself. Workaholics will not inherit the next world. The law is tough on your family. Give them a break."[10] It was advice he did not follow.

Pat and Mo Udall settled in Tucson as though they intended to stay. He had begun the practice of law in the spring of 1949 and they set out to establish their family. Mark Emery was born on July 18, 1950, followed by James Randolph (Randy) on October 29, 1951; Judith King (Dodie) on December 22, 1952; Anne Jeannette on July 5, 1954; Bradley Hunt on April 28, 1957; and Katherine Lee on January 26, 1959. Again, the similarity to the Levi-Louise family: six children, three boys and three girls. One difference is that the births spanned fewer than nine years; those of Louise and Levi covered more than thirteen years.

Pat and Mo started in a modest university-area home. As the number of children and his income increased, the size and quality of their homes improved. They moved in mid-1954 to the upscale Colonia Solana neighborhood and then in mid-1960 to the lower foothills of the Catalina Mountains.

"We always ate dinner together," Pat said. "We had a round table with a big lazy Susan in the center, and we would spin it around so people could serve themselves."

Pat said she thought she brought to their marriage "an incredible love of the outdoors" and a knowledge of things Indian. In addition to owning Yellow Cab of Denver, a Denver bus company, and a package delivery service, her father, Roe Emery, had operated five hotels as part of his Rocky Mountain Transportation Company. He visited the Navajo,

Hopi, and Zuni reservations in search of Indian artifacts and rugs to sell in hotel curio shops, and she often traveled with him.

She recalled that "almost all of our [family] activities were outdoors, hiking, camping." Later, after the divorce, Pat took all six children on a summer-long trip on the unpaved Alaskan Highway and on a Christmas trip down the unpaved Baja California highway. It was during this period that youngest daughter Kate referred to her as "Sam the Indian Guide." It was a name she liked, and ultimately adopted. Some of the children still call her "Sam." In turn, Mark, Randy, and Brad usually refer to their father as "Mo."

Pat and Mo liked to fly. "We did a lot of flying together," she said. "We were very noncompetitive in flying. I'd pilot for an hour, and he would pilot for an hour. Back in those days you could dump pamphlets from the air, and I seem to remember doing that for his campaigns."

Pat had learned to fly without her husband's knowledge. "I guess I wanted to surprise Mo," she said. "We had two kids and I was pregnant." One day after she had soloed without Mo's knowledge, she took him to the airstrip, got into the plane with the instructor and taxied out. The instructor then climbed out and sent her off alone, telling Mo: "She's the most remarkable, natural flier there ever was." That was, in fact, only the beginning for her. She and a friend won the 1977 Powderpuff Derby, the last of that cross-country flying event ever held. She still maintains an instructor's license, although she does not fly.

The Udalls made plenty of friends around town, but Pat recalled that Mo was not good at small talk or cocktail party talk. "He became known for his humor," she said. "It broke barriers. He was modest, but self-absorbed."[11]

Mo and Pat maintained some distance between themselves and his parents. In retrospect, Pat thinks she treated her in-laws poorly, although "when Mom Udall came, we lived by her standards," she said. "Dad Udall took me aside and told me I was OK even though I was never a Mormon. I was terrified of my mother-in-law. I was a totally stupid daughter-in-law. She was very good to me."

The Udalls took strong positions when they disagreed. "When we fought, we had good fights," Pat said. "We didn't know how to resolve them. My way was to say 'go away' and he did."

Years later, Mo said: "My marriage had been rocky and shaky all

through the '50s. Pat was a very spirited person. She was intensely interested in all kinds of things, but was sort of unsteady, and went from one
interest to another."[12]

Pat had opposed a 1954 run for Congress but supported her husband's successful 1961 bid to replace his brother Stewart. When the
election was won they drove to Washington in a station wagon. Each of
the children was assigned a number and they changed seats every two
hours.

Despite her acquiescence to Mo's running for Congress, Pat said, "I
kept my kids out of politics. I wanted them to be normal." She found,
too, that she missed the West. Then came the unexpected—she developed rheumatoid arthritis. "I was one really nailed cookie," she recalled.
"I was bedridden with six kids under the age of nine. I had climbed
mountains [including the 14,255-foot Long's Peak in Colorado] and now
I could hardly walk."[13]

Stewart's wife, Lee, remembered, "Pat spent an enormous amount
of time with her children. At times she was almost totally house-bound. I
remember her initiating projects she could do with the children on her
bed. Once Pat and Mark constructed a ham radio together on her bed."[14]

In March 1964, Pat Udall and the children returned to their home
in the Catalina Foothills where Tucson's dry climate might be friendlier
to Pat's arthritis. Indeed, the disease ultimately went into remission. Mo,
of course, continued to do his job in Washington. "We didn't know how
to communicate about this," Pat said. "I was in a wheelchair, pure un-
adulterated hell. What now? Why? In those days, a politician seeking
psychiatric help was disgraceful. In this day and age you seek counseling
and hopefully prevent a divorce. I have always regretted it. I think I just
plain burned out. I had six kids and the damn rheumatoid arthritis. Mo
didn't know how to deal with it. I was so low I didn't even think a lawyer
would help me. I am so ashamed of the divorce."[15]

Pat Udall filed for divorce on November 19, 1965. The sixteen-and-
a-half-year marriage was terminated on January 10, 1966, by superior
court judge Jack G. Marks, once a law partner of Udall's. Pat was awarded
$150 a month for each child, and Mo was granted reasonable visitation
rights. Mo Udall was not present and did not contest the action. In a statement from Washington, he said: "My wife has determined to seek a divorce because of irreconcilable conflicts in our lives and personalities. . . .

We are parting amicably and with great respect and esteem for each other. . . . I intend to remain in Congress as a single man."[16]

Mo Udall remained single until December 1, 1968, when at forty-six he married Ella Royston Ward, thirty-nine, who had been hired by the House Post Office and Civil Service Committee at Mo's request several years earlier.[17] Judge Marks, who had signed the divorce decree almost three years earlier, conducted the ceremony at the home of Alice and Burr Udall in Tucson.[18]

Pat remarried three times in fairly rapid order, describing the unions as "total disasters. I was a total disaster, stupid, dumb," she said. "For about seven years, up was down, round was square, in was out." Her first remarriage was to the twenty-one-year-old son of a friend. Her new husband sought a deferment from Vietnam War service. She wrote Mo and the deferment was granted; the marriage lasted eight months. In retrospect, she called her deferment request "a total disgrace."

Years later, with Mo's approval, she resumed use of the Udall name, and the two became good friends again. Mo and Ella took Pat to the airport in 1983 when she left for a four-year Peace Corps assignment in Nepal. She was working in Washington for the Peace Corps when Ella died and helped out at Mo's home in the early hours after the death. Pat and Ella had scheduled a lunch for the following Saturday.

Ella was born in 1929, the daughter of Edmund and Kathleen Royston of Loudon County, Virginia. She attended elementary school, high school, and business school in the District of Columbia. She worked in secretarial and administrative positions in private business, including four years with the Washington office of Kaiser Industries.[19] She had been married twice, to Vincent Fabrizio, a musician, and to G. Richard Ward, a former Kaiser Industries executive. She had one son, Vincent "Buster" Fabrizio Jr.

Ella became "Tiger" to Mo and others. "I call it a term of endearment," she said in a 1975 interview. "Mo has told somebody that when he upsets me I pounce, but that's not true." Her husband, in the same article, was quoted as saying he chose the name "because she's spirited, and when she wants to do something she's very tenacious . . . and also because of her other side, because she's cuddly, warm, and lovable.[20]

Ella and Rosemarie King, wife of writer Larry King, were close friends, and the four spent time together at Ocean City, Maryland, and

Rehoboth and Bethany Beach, Delaware. "Rosemarie and Ella and I would sit on the beach and smoke grass, and Mo would run eight, ten, twelve miles," King recalled. Rosemarie died in 1972 at the age of forty-three after a seven-year battle with cancer, and "Mo and Ella saw me through it," he said. "I might have flipped out if it hadn't been for Mo and Ella."

King said he had advised Udall against marrying Ella, suggesting she was "volatile, unpredictable, and carries some baggage." Mo did not hold grudges, he said, but "Ella had enough for everybody. I always liked her, but booze made her mean. I saw her snap at him for no reason. He was so solicitous of her, and she snapped a lot."[21]

When Udall sought the presidential nomination, he suggested that his wife ask King how to handle media interviews. King responded with a letter to "Dear Potential First Lady. . . . From what you told me on the phone, I think you're handling it right in saying that your parents wanted to send you to college but you married young, had a baby, and after your divorce went to work first for Kaiser Industries and then came to Capitol Hill. . . . As for the Richard Ward thing, I do not believe I would volunteer it: if asked, however—and eventually you probably will be—I'd say something like, 'That was a painful experience, one of those human mistakes lonely people fall prey to. It was short, and it ended, I hope, without anyone being hurt too badly and without it being anybody's fault.' And the less said after that, the better. I don't think anybody much will push it if you present it in those terms."[22]

The Ward marriage was kept secret at the start of the presidential campaign, and Mo Udall later explained, "She doesn't like talking about the marriage. She has been afraid someone would bring it up because she thinks it makes her look unstable to have had so many husbands.[23]

King also wrote: "Now, if I were a mean reporter and had done some research on you, Miz Ella, I might be inclined to ask if you drink to excess, if it isn't true you have a flash temper, and that through a combination of these you've made some enemies you haven't spoken to in years. I'm not sure anybody will do that, but *if* they do I would consider responding something like this: 'There may have been a time, when I was unhappy, that I drank a bit much but I'm glad that's over. I am strong-willed, I guess, and perhaps I've offended a few people by excessive candor or by standing up for myself. But I don't keep any "enemies list" and I'd rather talk about my friends.'" He concluded: "Cool it on the juice before or during public appearances. Afterwards, call me up and we'll get dronk *[sic]* and talk dirty. Love on you, Miz Ella, and on Mr. Mo."[24]

King married Washington lawyer Barbara Blaine in 1978 and said Ella had difficulty accepting that relationship: "Maybe she thought I was untrue to the memory of my first wife." Subsequently, only Mo responded to invitations to dine at the King home, and King said: "He would come over and make excuses for why Ella couldn't come." In later years, King said Udall's Parkinson's symptoms became more intense. "I hated to see that. He shouldn't even have been driving. He would stumble on curbs." Ultimately, King "quit inviting him because I was afraid he would kill himself."[25]

The Mo-Ella marriage was tumultuous. On several occasions, she kicked him out of the house. Longtime friend Rosemary Cribben recalled that she once saw Ella throw all of Mo's clothes onto the driveway, and that at one point, Udall rented an apartment for himself.[26] Another friend, Diane Rennert, recounted a similar memory.[27]

The three women were confidantes from 1977 until about ten years later, when Rosemary and Diane said Ella cut them off without explanation. Rosemary had been friendly with Ella since the late 1960s when they met in the House of Representatives beauty shop, she as an employee of Representative Wayne Hays, an Ohio Democrat, and Ella as a congressman's new wife. Diane joined the duo after meeting Mo and Ella through her job as a lobbyist for the Association of American Publishers. Both traveled with Ella and the Udalls on political and pleasure trips.

Rosemary, Diane, and others described Ella as bright, warm, funny, down-to-earth, with a big heart. She was a voracious reader with an emphasis on biographies. She had "a very loving relationship" with son Vince and they often traveled together. She created her own circle of friends rather than relying on organizations such as the Congressional Wives Club.

Diane called Ella "very mercurial in a lot of ways," using the nursery rhyme words: " 'When she was good, she was very, very good, and when she was bad, she was horrid.' She was warm and generous and bright and funny. And then she could turn on a dime and just be totally different . . . almost like a Dr. Jekyll and Hyde." She could be "mean and taxing and just unpleasant. Ella was a friendship that took a lot of work."[28]

"Ella had many engaging personal qualities," said sister-in-law Lee Udall, Stewart's wife. "She was outrageously up-front and you always knew where you stood with her. Besides being physically attractive, she had a sharp mind and a wonderful sense of humor. She was an avid reader and had a love of literature and theater."[29]

Iris Jacobson Burnett, who traveled with Ella during the early part of the 1976 presidential campaign, remembered: "People were not kind to her. It was not easy to be kind to her because she was not an easy person. I felt an affection for her for a lot of different reasons, not the least of which was that she was one of the funniest people I have ever met. She was really one of the most compassionate people and one of the most insecure people I had ever encountered, and she loved Mo and he loved her. . . . the insecurities came from the fact that all their friends were Mo's friends, all their life was Mo's life."[30]

Marian S. Goodman, who worked for Udall on both the Post Office and Interior Committees, recalled that she never put on airs, adding: "Going to congressional fund-raising receptions was not her cup of tea. She'd rather go to New York City and go to a show or an Italian restaurant."[31]

Staff members—both congressional and presidential campaign—generally described Ella as hard to get along with and demanding. Onetime top aide Bruce Wright called her "my best buddy" at the outset of his time on the Hill. He said she was a warm, funny individual "when she wasn't drinking and was confident of herself . . . when she was uncertain and drinking, she was nasty as could be."[32]

Rennert had spent ten years as a Senate aide, and subsequently visited senators and representatives in her capacity as a lobbyist. "She was the terror of the office," she said. "I've known others where you have a wife problem, but nothing like Ella. She could just strike terror . . . she was outrageous, she was demanding and abusive. All of that was just her way of grabbing the attention. She didn't give staffers a chance."[33]

Udall knew of the conflicts between Ella and staff members, but he chose not to intervene. In notes prepared for a possible book on the 1976 campaign, he wrote: "There ought to be a chapter or section of conflicts between staff and wife. How Ella reacted to this. Some of the lessons that I've learned. A good starting point is Myra MacPherson's book [The Power Lovers], which has an excellent discussion from other campaigns."[34]

Goodman said, "The point is that people just tended to forget that she needed some respect and acknowledgment as well as Mo did."[35]

Mo's son Randy called "politics a prison sentence" for Ella. "Mo might have been a wonderful romantic suitor," he said, "but the focus was Washington, a pile of papers on his desk, the law."[36]

Iris Burnett said Ella disliked Arizona. "She was not one for subtleties," Burnett said. She called Arizona "Kitty Litter Land. It was not her favorite place."[37]

The 1970s and early 1980s were a time of easy access to tranquilizers—some physicians prescribed them over the phone. Ella consulted three or four doctors, and Rennert recalled: "She managed to get pills all the time I knew her. I'm sure that that combined with the alcohol elevated a lot of the behavior."

Ella isolated herself for prolonged periods of time. Cribben called it a "hibernation," saying Ella would spend up to two months in the house, much of the time in bed and most of the time reading. While she hibernated, Cribben said, "she also spent hours on the phone—she was desperate for outside contact." Rennert called such periods "cocooning" and remembered them as lasting four to five days.

Neither woman challenged Ella about her addictions. "I think we talked about an intervention at one point," Rennert said, "but if it had gone through, I would have remembered being there. Mo was never going to take the lead on that." Cribben said she and Rennert talked to Mo about a confrontation on more than one occasion. "Mo may have agreed once," she said, "but there was no action."

Rennert also said Ella used to embarrass her husband in public—"not sometimes; a lot, a lot"—but that he never responded in negative fashion. "He might have been just confrontation-averse. There were occasions where it was just really appalling what she would do in public to Mo, but I never saw Mo raise his voice or try to discipline her in any way. I think she felt inferior, and so her acting out was a way to express this. She absolutely loved him. I think he loved her. I never had occasion to doubt that." Cribben called Ella's displays "desperate attempts to get attention" from her workaholic husband.[38]

Daughter Anne viewed Ella's "public embarrassment" of her father in another fashion. She spoke at Ella's funeral and referred to it as humor, saying: "She would wait for a crowded elevator. Then she would turn to Dad and say: 'Congressman, don't forget your appointment with the psychiatrist today.'"[39] Daughter Judith, better known as Dodie, disagreed: "I just used to really resent when she would hurt Dad or when she would be mean to him or when she would do these elevator things or when she would be bad to staff or when she would do anything that would put my father in a bad light."[40]

Mo's Parkinson's disease began to show itself more and more in the mid-1980s, and Ella's caretaking responsibilities intensified. "By 1984, he couldn't button his shirt or tie his tie," said Perry Baker, who ran Udall's Phoenix office. "He was stiff and his head bobbed. He was tired and stiff all the time. His mind was always good."[41] Life was becoming more difficult, but as Iris Burnett put it: "Nothing was going to keep him down. He was going to pursue what he wanted to pursue."[42]

The load on Ella increased. "During the months before Ella's death, she was often depressed. She worried about Mo's health, about his continuing to drive, and she was exhausted just taking care of him," said Lee Udall. "Many times I tried to convince her to have live-in help so she could pursue her own interests and even travel a bit, but she always said neither of them wanted to give up their privacy. She called me—we were living in Phoenix at the time—the night before she died. She was exhausted and distraught and talked about the future in terms of 'tunnel vision.' "[43]

Sometime on the morning of Saturday, August 13, 1988, Ella Udall, fifty-nine, had given her husband his medication, and he had gone back to sleep. Still dressed in her nightclothes, she went to the kitchen and turned on the stove to warm food for their poodle, Cokie. Mo Udall awakened about 10 A.M. He found his wife in their car with the engine running in the garage of their McLean, Virginia, home. She was pronounced dead at Fairfax Hospital at 11:03 A.M. A coroner's report found death by carbon monoxide poisoning. "We are ruling it as a suicide," said Judy Duff, a spokeswoman for the Fairfax County Police Department.[44]

Others doubted that she intended to kill herself. Rather, they suggested, she simply was seeking her husband's attention and had counted on him for a rescue. They noted, too, that a garage window was open, and that normally it remained closed.[45]

Mo's relationship with his third wife, Norma Gilbert, began with a chance encounter in 1970 and moved into marriage after she helped him relocate and adjust in the days following Ella's death.

Daughter Dodie noted that with Ella and Norma "there was sort of this component of kind of helping him do his work and that is one of the ways you became important to him." With Ella, she said, "it was not just a relationship, but she was roped into taking care of the kids, too. Because he was such a workaholic that was one of the ways you could spend time with him. He didn't have the free time." Before marrying Mo, Ella used to take time off from work to care for his visiting children while Mo stayed on the job. "And Ella was fixing him dinner," Dodie said.[46]

Like Ella Udall, Norma Gilbert had worked on Capitol Hill, first as a lobbyist and then as an Interior subcommittee staffer. She grew up in southwest Los Angeles, attended UCLA, worked as an aide to a state senator, and wrote a column for a chain of nine San Fernando Valley newspapers. She became a political activist in the late 1950s and applied to be a Golden Girl at the 1960 Democratic National Convention in Los Angeles. She and actresses Jan Sterling and Mercedes McCambridge were among the 200 selected, and she was assigned to assist the Nebraska delegation headed by Governor Frank Morrison.

She worked off and on for Alan Cranston, the onetime Democratic senator from California, and headed for Washington in 1970 after her first marriage broke up. She encountered Mo early one morning as she walked in the Cannon House Office Building. Coming toward her, she recalled, were four men, including Udall, in a shaggy, brown jacket. "He looked at me and said, 'Hi.' I thought, 'My God, here I am in Washington and Morris Udall said hi to me.'" In January 1971, they both attended a fund-raising event for the Consumer Federation of America. Afterward, she was talking to another congressman about getting a ride, but he was headed elsewhere. "Mo said, 'I'm going back to the Hill and I'll give you a ride' . . . and that's how I got to know him. And after that I somehow would see him at a lot of different places."

Norma ultimately went to work as a lobbyist for Motorola, a major Arizona employer. That brought her into additional contact with Udall, and she said they ate lunch about once a month in the Hill cafeteria. She described their friendship as one of "professional buddies." In the early 1980s, she quit Motorola to try to survive on her own. She found it difficult, and when she sought a new employer she was advised that she was fifty and "they were hiring young cuties with skirts way up there and the long hair."

She told Udall, and he referred her to his Interior Committee. She landed a staff job on the Insular and International Affairs Subcommittee headed by Ron de Lugo, a nonvoting Democrat from the Virgin Islands.

Norma was visiting in California when Ella died. She read about the death and wrote a sympathy note. "When I came back," she recalled, "he suggested I be given time to help him move." She found a Crystal City, Virginia, apartment, then helped select a cleaning woman and a law student "to do his buttons and help him shave." While living alone, she said, Udall had fallen one night and lay on the floor for hours.

She helped him with his dinners and once as they ate together, she said Mo told her: "You know, I think I love you." Norma thought a moment, then responded, "You know, I think I love you, too." She elaborated, "He had been out of the picture for me and when he said that, I looked at him in a different way. It's like you took a window shade and it popped up."

Norma, fifty-six, and Mo, sixty-seven, were married on August 6, 1989, in the House chapel with thirty-eight people in attendance. "He was such a man of the House; it was the only place that seemed appropriate," Norma said. "It was a very hot day," she recalled. "He was tired and kind of stooped. When Jim Ford [the House chaplain] asked him the question, he answered so strongly: 'I do, yes I do.' There was a tear trickling down his cheek."[47] Speaker Tom Foley was best man. Representative James H. Scheuer, a New York Democrat, and his wife, Emily, held a reception at their home. They honeymooned for a week in the Watermill, Long Island, home of actor Cliff Robertson, a friend since the 1976 presidential campaign.[48]

On Sunday afternoon, January 6, 1991, seventeen months into their marriage, Mo and Norma were alone at home watching a Washington Redskins football game on television. Mo announced that he was tired and was going to take a nap. They planned to go to a movie afterward. He started up the stairs. He had climbed only four or five steps when he lost his balance and fell backward, striking his head. She called 911 for help.[49] Mo was hospitalized. The voice of visionary public policy and gentle humor would not be heard again.

In its absence, as their father lay silently for nearly eight years with a feeding tube in his stomach, his six children were left to contemplate their feelings toward the individual the sons tend to call Mo and the daughters refer to as both Mo and Dad. They expressed those feelings in separate interviews.[50]

Second son Randy compared his father to "Icarus—the guy flying to the sun. Mo was like a moth. The light was his own ambition, and he was consumed. Too much was never enough. He was like someone never really able to take the track shoes off. He was always running."

All of the children's pre-divorce memories are vague. "I don't remember him being around much," said Mark, who was fifteen when his parents broke up. He said most of his memories were of his siblings and his mother. Anne, who was ten when the divorce occurred, said Mo taught her to ride a bicycle and carried her on his shoulders into the deep end of the family swimming pool. Still, she said, "I have more memories of Dad being available after the divorce than I do before. He was very, very driven, very driven by his work."

Following the divorce, Mo made monthly trips to Tucson. Occasionally, visits with the children were difficult because of parental conflict. The get-togethers usually were event-oriented: bowling, miniature golf, a movie, dinner at a steakhouse or a Mexican food restaurant. Kate recalled going to University of Arizona football games with her father and spending her time there reading a book. Brad and Dodie remembered climbing 7,730-foot Baboquivari Peak with their father.

The summer visits to Washington generally lasted about two weeks and were accomplished in groups of two or three. Anne and Kate talked fondly about Ella. "It was as fun to be with Ella as it was with Dad," Anne said. "She was bright; she was witty; she was a survivor. She really had gone through a lot in her life. She was very accepting of me during some rough times. I have great memories of hanging out with her." Said Kate: "Tiger was great, great to me. Tiger and I could do sort of 'girl things.'"

Contact between Mo and his children became less regular after they finished high school.

Mark attended Williams College in Massachusetts, and spent some weekends at his father's home in 1968, 1969, and 1970. "Not a lot of visits," he said, "not that ongoing contact."

Anne attended Vassar and made frequent visits to Washington. "I saw a lot of him," she said. "I never really remember talking to him much about my career choices or dilemmas and I think he was a very shy man. I know a lot about him, but I don't know how much intimacy was established with him in terms of conversation between him and me. He wasn't a man that was particularly verbose, but he was someone who cared and cared deeply about his children and really was proud of them. I do feel there were things that he didn't do that I would have liked him to do that were about being a father. . . . He missed my Ph.D. graduation [from the University of Arizona] because of a vote on the House floor, which was really painful for me. It still is. I really regret that. But then there were other things that he didn't miss. He was there for Dodie's wedding and gatherings when Randy had his firstborn."

There had been a switch when Dodie graduated from the University of Arizona. Her father was the graduation speaker, but she did not attend. "I was not shooting at Dad at all," she said. "I think it was my sort of saying this degree doesn't really mean much to me. Dad was pretty low-key about those kinds of things. He didn't let me know it was anything of importance to him. He probably told me, 'It's fine, whatever you decide to do.'"

Intimacy was hard to come by for any of the children. "We never had the kind of intimacy where we would sit down," Randy said. Both Mark and Anne recalled that their conversations tended to focus on politics and sports. Mark described his father as "very private; he didn't want to pry."

Youngest son Brad deferred his admission to Stanford to work on the presidential campaign and said: "I used to always tell people the conventional wisdom is that you never see your father, but I saw him more during the campaign than I ever saw him growing up. It was the only time I ever got to spend good, quality time with him."

Despite their lack of time with their father, Anne and Kate used the same phrase: "I adored him," each said. Kate added, "I am so sorry I didn't ever have a relationship with him. He was really uncomfortable with his feelings. He felt as awkward as I. At times, I tried not to be alone with him." Anne said, "I believe, as much as I believe anything, that one cannot achieve as much as Mo has achieved and be as equally committed to family and friends."[51]

Dodie considered herself close to her father but lamented his unwillingness to offer advice. "If you as a father say you can do whatever you want with your life . . . one side of me says that's really wonderful and supportive, but there's another side of me that says, You know gosh darn it, I wish Dad had said, 'But you know, maybe law school would be neat—go give it a try.' Maybe just a little bit more direction. Not pushy. If I had had a little more self-directed support from him, rather than this supposedly unconditional love, maybe I could have done some different things. But he always said that to all of us—'whatever you do is fine.' "

What Dodie viewed as a lack of direction, Mark saw as an advantage. Mark worked part of the presidential campaign but then went off to Alaska. "He respected my decisions," he said. "There was no resentment. He knew I had to find my own way."

Washington Post columnist Richard Cohen once suggested that "greatness and parenting are antithetical to each other. Political greatness presupposes an almost obsessive devotion to a cause. . . . Even the children of politicians that no one would call great testify to childhoods where their parent's career came first—everything from prolonged absences to the anxiety of growing up in a fishbowl as a constantly smiling bit player in someone else's show. The awful truth is that when it comes to time and attention, the people we would most like as president we would least like as parents."[52]

In a letter to Cohen, who had not mentioned Udall, daughter Anne wrote: "One can't do both—excel at parenting and politics. It is simply not possible. On a more philosophical level, I think this statement is true in any profession—not just politics. Can one be a renowned writer or actor or doctor without sacrifice to other priorities? I think not. Politics is a fishbowl, but many of the issues are the same, regardless of the circumstance."[53]

"It's interesting," Brad said. "None of the kids have gone out in the world to make money. We all have brains and could do that if we wanted. But all of us have decided that what we do and how we do it is more important than how much we make."

The six Udall offspring inherited their parents' height—their mother, Pat, too, was tall, five-foot-nine when she married Mo. All completed college. All found their way. All still use the name Udall.

Mark, formerly executive director of Outward Bound in Colorado, was elected to the U.S. House of Representatives in 1998; he and his wife, Margaret Fox, an attorney for the Sierra Club, have two children. Randy is a writer and director of the Community Office for Resource Efficiency in Aspen and lives with his wife, Leslie Emerson, and their three children in Carbondale, Colorado. Dodie taught at private schools in Carbondale, Denver, and Boulder for nine years before quitting to raise a family and work part time in the Boulder water resources engineering firm established by her husband, Benjamin Harding; they have two sons. Anne taught the gifted and disabled in Tucson for about eleven years and now is assistant superintendent for curriculum and instruction in the Charlotte-Mecklenburg school system. Brad is executive director of the Eagle Valley Land Trust; he and his wife, Jane, live in Avon, Colorado. Kate is an assistant professor of voice and drama at West Virginia University.

LIVING WITH PARKINSON'S

*N*ews Director Bob Richardson produced a 1978 documentary for Tucson television station KVOA on the future of the Grand Canyon. He included a Colorado River trip, and at one point Mo Udall took a helicopter to meet the river runners. "It was classic Mo as he walked from the helicopter," Richardson recalled. "Tall, erect, smiling, happy."

Two years later, in October 1980, Richardson happened to review the documentary. A day or two later, he saw Udall, who was back home campaigning against Republican Richard Huff. "He wasn't the same," Richardson said. "He was shuffling his feet." Richardson checked in with Perry Baker, Udall's press aide in Tucson. "Is there a problem with the congressman?" he asked. Baker, who knew better, responded in the negative. Two weeks later, Richardson encountered Udall again and "Mo was demonstrably slower." He decided something was amiss and spoke again to Baker. This time he received a different response. Baker replied: "We'll get back to you."[1]

Udall had told some staff members about a year earlier that he had Parkinson's, according to Baker.[2] Administrative assistant Bruce Wright had known since 1978. His father was a Parkinson's victim, and when Mo had difficulty opening a bag of potato chips en route to a campaign appearance, Wright raised the question. Mo decreed that Wright could tell no one unless asked the direct question: Does Udall have Parkinson's?[3]

Udall later explained his silence this way: "I'm basically an honest politician, but in this instance I had determined to give myself some privacy, for God's sake. I decided I had done enough for openness in government, opening up my income taxes and other things. But in this, I simply made a decision to leave it alone."[4]

The morning after Richardson contacted Baker the second time, Wright and Baker met with Mo, wife Ella, and daughters Dodie and Anne. Wright remembered meeting in the Udalls' Redondo Towers apartment, adding that Ella was ironing and Mo was "just really frightened. I had never seen him that way before."[5]

Dodie, then twenty-eight, kept a personal journal, and several days earlier, on Monday, October 13, had written: "The hardest part of all of this is watching Dad—it is so hard at times to play the game, to pretend all is well. Everyone notices that he is no longer as sharp, as agile. Yet we cover it up—we hold our breath and cross our fingers. I love that man."[6]

After the apartment meeting Udall conducted a routine news conference, and then Wright and Baker told Richardson that Mo had Parkinson's. They agreed that he would go live on Channel 4 that night, make the announcement, and submit to questioning by Richardson.

The statement prepared for that October 16 appearance read: "For the past five years I have suffered from a mild case of Parkinson's disease. The symptoms vary, but in my case involve some tremors, muscular stiffness, and a tendency to slump the shoulders. This is not fatal. The cause is unknown and no cure is known. It can be controlled by different kinds of medicine and has been in my case controlled by a mild medication." Udall said he also suffered from an arthritic condition in the lower back, and added: "I find that none of these developments affect me while I continue to lead an active life. I enjoy playing golf, jogging, swimming, and I keep my garden in reasonably good shape."[7]

In her journal ten days after her father's televised statement, Dodie wrote: "Lots and lots of thoughts about Dad. He has lost or hidden his desire, enthusiasm for campaigning and as a result could lose. Parkinson's is fearful for him and I don't know how and if, he is dealing with it well."[8]

Udall had received only 52 percent of the votes in his 1978 reelection, but three weeks after the Parkinson's announcement, he triumphed with 58 percent. The revelation had not ended his career.

Election victories continued to come easily thereafter, and the disease seemed to have little negative impact with the voters. He faced a primary challenge in 1986 from state senator Luis A. Gonzales. Udall complained that his opponent had instigated a whispering campaign that he had a "terminal illness" that was muddling his mind, but Gonzales denied the accusation. It made little difference. Udall won handily.[9]

In his 1980 announcement, Udall said he had suffered a mild case of Parkinson's for five years, thus dating the illness to 1975. Family members, however, later fixed the diagnosis year at 1977. The 1975 reference may have been to his bout with pneumonia in Phoenix, a situation physician Jerome Targovnik described as "totally independent" and absolutely not a precursor to the Parkinson's.[10]

Nonetheless, two 1976 incidents may have been Parkinson's related. His friend Democratic representative David Obey of Wisconsin said Udall scheduled a campaign stunt shoot-around with a member of the Milwaukee Bucks of the National Basketball Association, and "Mo missed basket after basket after basket," Obey recalled. His usual coordination was absent, and Obey quoted him as saying: "I don't understand it; it's the worst I've ever done."[11]

Udall remembered feeling the first rigidity in his legs "just before the Ohio primary [in June]. I had leg muscles that would just tie up." Udall said he suffered "a little of the characteristic tremor, but this I just attributed to getting older."[12]

The cause of Parkinson's has yet to be pinpointed, but research has indicated that the disease may be genetic. His sister Inez also was a victim and was experiencing some of the characteristic stiffness when she died October 2, 1992, at the age of seventy-six. An uncle and an aunt also had been diagnosed with Parkinson's.

Parkinson's is a progressive neurological disorder with no cure. It is named after an English physician, James Parkinson, who originally described it in 1817 and called it "shaking palsy." The disease results from degeneration of nerve cells in the brain that produce a chemical known as dopamine, which helps control muscle activity. Common symptoms include tremors; rigidity, which occurs without warning; the loss of spontaneous and automatic movement (called bradykinesia), which can deprive the individual of the ability to perform routine tasks such as knotting a tie, buttoning clothing, pulling a zipper, shaving, or combing hair; and postural instability, which creates a forward or backward lean and causes patients to fall easily. The instability also induces a stooped posture in which the head bows and the shoulders droop. Some patients speak softly or in a monotone; some slur their words. Handwriting can become cramped and spidery. The early symptoms are slight tremors, a reduction in speech volume, and the "masked face," a lack of facial expression of which the patients are unaware.[13]

The "mask" affected Udall in a variety of ways, including the delivery of his famed humor. "You think your facial muscles are expressing love or pain or joy or laughter or whatever, but they're not," he said. "To others, your face is expressionless. Looking back at those old pictures in '75 and '76, I can see that developing. It got back to me that people were saying, 'He doesn't look right. He looks tired. He's been drinking too much.' But it was that mask. Sometimes I use a lot of deadpan humor, but it wasn't going over because I thought I was putting expression into it; but it really was deadpan, even when I didn't want it to be."[14]

Mo Udall ultimately displayed all of the symptoms, but in the beginning it was pretty much business as usual. As he always had when he encountered difficulty, Udall simply moved ahead with his life. He did not pause long to feel sorry for himself.

In a 1981 statement prepared for *People* magazine, he offered this advice to other Parkinson's patients: "Just refuse to consider yourself crippled. Don't submit to it. Running, for instance, is important to me. I run every day. If I'm in a hotel room, I'll do a hundred laps around the room or run in place. I've got a chinning bar at home, and as long as I can lift my 200 pounds up to that bar, I can't be in very bad shape. . . . If you've got a motion or a skill, don't let them take it away from you. Because the minute you say this arm shakes worse than the other and I can't play golf, or I'm not going to be able to do these kinds of things, you're quitting and it will overtake you."[15]

Three years later, he discussed the subject with *Arizona Republic* political writer Joel Nilsson, saying, "Yes, sometimes I think, 'Why the hell me? Why did I get Parkinson's?' On the other hand, you've got to look around and see the good things, the good cards that have been dealt: growing up in a little town in Arizona with a father and mother who inspired me to do good; playing professional basketball; being in the military; seeking a presidential nomination. I've got six good kids and not a bum one in the bunch. Life's been awfully good to me in many, many ways and I take the good with the bad."[16]

By all accounts, Udall's condition began to change in the years 1984 and 1985. Years before when the disease had been identified, he had begun treatment with Dr. Thomas N. Chase at the National Institute of Neurological Disorders and Stroke in Bethesda, Maryland. The two arranged early-morning appointments, and Chase recalled that Udall would be waiting, newspaper in hand, when the physician arrived. "I come in grumpy," Chase said, "and he would say, 'Tom, you need a joke.' He always put me at ease. He never lost his ability to connect."[17]

Not all the Bethesda visits were so pleasant.

Bob Neuman worked for Udall from 1974 to 1979 in the congressional office and on the Interior Committee, then returned as administrative assistant in October 1985. He remembered only a shuffle from the late 1970s, but found the situation startlingly different upon his return. "In 1985, he was given a strict regimen of diet and exercise and medication, which he abused," Neuman said. "He did not do it. He'd go to the gym to sleep. He'd feel something come on and take a little bit more medicine. He would OD on some of this stuff. Then he'd have to detox. It was a normal process, which he hated. He'd go back to the National Institutes of Health—he was taking some stuff that was experimental—and he'd have to sit there for a couple days and take nothing. It was frightening. The whole scope of the Parkinson's would come out. It was horrible. I would go out and visit him. He was just haggard and grizzled and gray. It was just awful. He hated that more than anything. He didn't want anyone to see him."[18]

Nonetheless, in an interview that same year, Udall said: "I don't feel lucky in having gotten the damn thing, but I feel lucky that in my case it is not as disabling as it is to a lot of people. My father . . . preached values of independence, taking things as they come. I think of my misfortune and then when I see people my age with Parkinson's who cannot walk or talk, I just feel fortunate."[19]

Udall drove himself to work until January 1988, when press secretary Erik R. Barnett took over. "He didn't stop driving [completely] until maybe 1990," said Barnett. "Mo always said, 'It is man's God-given right to get up on Sunday and drive to the hardware store.' "[20]

His attitude remained positive. "You can talk a great, optimistic game, like I do," he said, "or you can sit around and say 'I can't stand it,

I'll hurt the rest of my life,' and you probably would. I've stretched this thing out 14 years now, and I figure I can go on a few more."[21]

Udall remained legislatively productive and influential, and in 1988 he was honored at the Democratic National Convention in Atlanta. Neuman accompanied him, and noted that stress and heat aggravate Parkinson's "and both were in abundance there. Mo was having trouble just getting dressed." Udall went to an Arizona reception and he was "clearly physically having problems—he wasn't able to talk; he was having involuntary movement with his hands. A lot of people who hadn't recognized how bad things were became immediately acquainted with it," Neuman said.

Udall made a brief appearance at the convention, and later Neuman was alerted by the young man who served as Mo's valet and driver. Mo was in distress; an ambulance was called. "The trick here," Neuman said, "was to get an ambulance to take him out of the hotel, immediately next to the convention, get him to the hospital and diagnosed and treated without anyone knowing about it. And we did that." Ella had not wanted Udall to make the trip, Neuman said, adding: "I think he missed her and that added to the stress. We took a private plane and went home."[22] Four weeks later, Ella Udall was dead.

Interior Committee staffer Norma Gilbert helped Udall find an apartment, and Barnett began picking him up at about 7:30 A.M. for a ten- to thirteen-hour day that concluded between 5:30 and 8 P.M. Udall kept a case of Budweiser in an office closet, Barnett recounted, and he always drank a warm one on the way home.[23]

Early in 1988, Udall said: "This disease won't kill you, but it can sure make you miserable. I have a way of just pounding away on things and not giving up. Parkinson's is just another one of those things. If you're lucky you can lead a pretty normal life even with 'Parko.' It takes devotion from your family. You don't want to be a burden, but you have to have a family that's supportive."[24]

Even when the tremors, the head bobbing, the shuffle, the stoop, and slurred speech became more and more pronounced in the late 1980s, Udall retained his self-deprecating sense of humor.

Matt James, Udall's last administrative assistant, said that occasionally when Mo used his hands as animation, he would make a point and finish talking, but a hand and forearm would remain upright. Mo would see it, James said, turn, pull it down, and say: "Thank you, Dr. Strangelove," a reference to one of the roles Peter Sellers played in the 1964 movie of that name.[25]

In 1990, rumors were circulating of a Democratic primary challenge from Maricopa County supervisor Edward L. Pastor. The supervisors arrived in March for their annual Washington lobbying visit. A meeting was scheduled for 11 A.M. because "the rhythm of his medications" made Udall best from 10 A.M. to 2 P.M. The session began routinely with Udall doing the talking. All was amiable, then Mo got "funny serious" and said, "Now, which one of you sons of bitches is going to run against me?" He looked right at Pastor and everyone burst into laughter.[26] Pastor did not run that year, but he was chosen to succeed Udall in the 1991 special election.

Mark Trautwein, Udall's top environmental aide, recounted a more tense moment that Udall converted to laughter. The Arizona congressional delegation and some staffers were meeting to iron out last-minute problems on the second Arizona wilderness bill. They sat in a circle with Trautwein directly across from Udall. Parkinson's patients "lose consciousness of their posture," Trautwein noted. "He could be hunched over with his head down between his knees and talking and on this occasion that's what was happening. He was sitting on the edge of the chair and hunched way forward and he was talking and he just fell off the chair onto the floor onto his hands and knees."

Everyone looked at Trautwein, but he did nothing. He explained that he knew Udall would have been angry if anyone tried to help. "He always tried so hard not to give in to this," he said. Trautwein could not recall Udall's exact words, but they were something like "the chairman has left his chair." Everyone laughed, and the tension eased. "Very painfully," Trautwein said, "he picked himself up and put himself back in the chair and we went on with the meeting . . . a whole room of people not acknowledging it had happened."[27] "He was enormously proud and very determined to work through all this," Trautwein said.[28]

The last half of the 1980s was a difficult time. Udall remained intent on his job: The second Arizona wilderness bill was passed; Indian matters were handled; battles were lost over nuclear waste and telescopes in his home state; and he undertook major trips to Siberia, in 1986, and the

South Pacific, in early 1989. He tired more easily, and his physical appearance attracted more attention and created concern.

Parkinson's often is referred to as "the invisible disease" because many victims isolate themselves as the symptoms intensify. They tend to become self-conscious and concerned that others will stare. Udall did not hide. Pride carried him forward.

Daughter Dodie traveled with him to Alaska in 1983, and it was one of the few times he ever expressed anger toward her. "I must have helped him, put an arm out, to help him down some steps or something like that and when we got to the bottom [away from the others], he lit into me," she said. "He just said, 'Don't you ever do that.' It was his pride . . . his tremendous pride."[29]

Targovnik, his Phoenix physician, accompanied him on the long-distance trips. "His motor was running all the time" on one trip, Targovnik said, adding: "He was showing more of the symptoms. He really started deteriorating. He had the physical problems—the shuffle, stammer, head bobbing, hand control—of Parkinson's."[30]

The public life seemed to get even tougher in 1989.

Michael J. Murphy covered Washington for the now defunct *Phoenix Gazette* from 1989 through 1992. He said Udall "could hold a conversation" in 1989, but not long after that "people started to talk about him losing control at committee meetings." He said Udall would be slumped over in his chair, his nose two inches from the table. "He may have said something, but it was unintelligible."[31]

The *Tucson Citizen* in May 1989 described Udall as "extremely thin and sparse looking. His entire body seems somehow trapped in motionless silence. He struggles for movement, even for speech. When it comes, his voice is barely audible." It added that during a recent interview, "his glasses fell to his lap and it took his shaking hands an eternity to put them back on his head. He doesn't want help."[32]

Udall was hospitalized with another bout of pneumonia in the late spring of 1989, and on May 28, the *Arizona Republic* called for Mo to resign. Mo's first big Arizona defender was the retired Barry Goldwater, who wrote Udall that he would love to have him in Arizona "with me, to be honest with you, but I'd rather have you in Washington doing the things you do for our state." Then in typical Goldwater fashion, he advised: "Tell them to go to hell."[33] Republican Goldwater was putting his mouth where he later would put his money. On May 11, 1990, he sent Udall a $500 reelection campaign check, saying: "I don't care if you keep this a secret or not. I've always supported you, and I think it's time this old Republican quit hiding behind the bush. You've done this state more damn good than anyone I know. I just want to see you stay in the saddle."[34]

On June 11, 1989, the newspaper carried Mo's response, in which he said: "I will know when the time is right for me to step down. Barry Goldwater retired at 78. John Rhodes put in 30 great years in the Congress and retired at 67. I turn 67 next month and certainly do plan to have a life after Congress—and I will know when it is time to move on to that next stage." He also said, "I do have, and will continue to have, Parkinson's disease. It is not a fun illness. It makes me stiff and causes me to lose facial expression. I sometimes think it is a more painful disease for others to witness than it is for me to bear. It is a disease that I will not die from, but I will die with."[35]

The negative news continued with an Associated Press story that described the Interior Committee hearing room portrait that showed Udall "standing tall with his coat slung over his shoulder" and then reported that "the man occupying the chairman's seat across the room no longer mirrors his portrait. He sits stooped in his chair, his hands quivering and his voice barely audible." At the same time, the story quoted Frank Williams, executive director of the American Parkinson Disease Association, of which Udall was honorary chairman, as emphasizing: "They [Parkinson's patients] do not lose their faculties. They watch their body deteriorate day after day."[36]

Norma had helped care for Mo on the South Pacific trip, and they married in the summer of 1989. The new Mr. and Mrs. Udall purchased a three-story Arlington, Virginia, townhouse. A small elevator was available, but Norma said her husband did not like it. "Sometimes," she said, he would lean and cause an automatic stop. He most often climbed the stairway, which had short steps. "He did well on those steps," she said.[37] They hired a live-in male aide to help Mo shower, shave, and dress, and to drive him to work. They set about establishing their life.

Parkinson's and its medication upset natural biorhythms. Mo often awoke at 2 or 3 A.M., and went downstairs to read and perhaps have a bowl of ice cream with Coca-Cola as a syrup. Hallucinating also is a side effect. He thought Norma had a little dog hidden in the house and would go looking for it.[38] Son Mark recalled that his father sometimes talked to a milk carton.[39] Anne Scott, who served as Udall's legislative director and now is a Phoenix consultant, said he once picked up a stapler and treated it as a telephone. "He was good-natured about it," she said.[40]

The Udalls went to movies. They ate out. "He never objected to my feeding him in restaurants," Norma said. "It didn't bother him at all. His humility was, to me, one of his greatest characteristics. There was nothing ostentatious about Morris Udall." Occasionally when they were walking out of a restaurant, he would fall, she said, noting that Parkinson's patients often fall after eating.[41]

Washington Democrat Tom Foley was particularly alert to Mo's physical problems. He had been a poker-playing buddy, and he had cut short his 1969 honeymoon to race home to vote for Mo for Speaker. Foley was sworn in as Speaker on June 6, 1989, and two months later he served as best man for Mo and Norma.

House rules limited the presence of staffers on the floor to those of the leadership and those needed when a bill was being considered. Foley waived the rule for Mo, explaining: "He was at risk of falling and couldn't move without a lot of effort." Members who were friends would come over to help and "he would pull his arm away from them. He resented, resisted, and rejected help," Foley said. "He didn't want to be helped or to be touched. Mo would struggle and shake, try to stand up and fall back for an agonizingly long time and he always refused help."[42]

Udall remained fiercely independent, but after he fell down some steps in 1989, staff members did start accompanying him to the floor, Scott said. He tried to ditch most staffers, but he erroneously thought Scott was pregnant so he was solicitous of her. When he determined she was not pregnant, his attitude changed. Conversation was nil during the ten-minute walks from his office to the floor. "He was very focused," she said.[43]

"You can't exaggerate too much how hard it was for him during the last five years," recalled Foley, now U.S. ambassador to Japan. There was "a year-to-year deterioration that went from the shuffling to more and more incapacitation." Foley said Udall would preside over hearings with "his jaw hunkered a few inches over the desk," and "toward the end, there were fewer wisecracks and less of his wonderful banter." Nonetheless, Foley said, "he kept his mental acuity . . . his mind was fine, although he had difficulty articulating."[44]

The spring of 1990 brought victory for Udall's second Arizona wilderness bill and announcement of his desire to be elected for a sixteenth time, a campaign he said would be his last.

Reporter Joseph Garcia of the *Tucson Citizen* wrote that Parkinson's "has robbed Udall of speech skills and muscle movement others take for granted."[45] Political writer Tom Beal of the *Arizona Daily Star* said: "Bent over by arthritis, his speech slowed and his voice diminished by Parkinson's disease, Mo Udall has gone from being the most sought after speaker in Arizona to being the feeble old congressman whose appearances are painful to behold."[46]

Friend Jim McNulty recalled that he went to see Udall at a Ramada Inn in Tucson just before the election. The room's door was cracked open and McNulty walked in. "He was in the fetal position with a bottle of Budweiser and a straw. That's how he was drinking the beer." A few nights later, Udall walked into the Viscount Inn in a victory march. "That was ghastly," McNulty said, explaining that his former colleague's speech was slurred and soft and people could not understand him, and his head was wagging.[47]

Udall examined other medical options in 1990. He met with Dr. Curtis R. Freed of the University of Colorado Health Sciences Center and with Dr. D. Eugene Redmond Jr., director of the Yale Neural Transplant Program. The subject in both cases was the possibility of a fetal cell tissue transplant. Federal funds could not be used for such surgery, but the programs at both universities were going ahead with private financing.

After the election, Udall, using a pseudonym to avoid publicity, checked into the Denver hospital. "He came to learn and to be evaluated neurologically," Freed said. Two neurosurgeons, a neurologist, and Freed decided that Udall's disease was too advanced and that the transplant would not be helpful to him, Freed recalled.[48] Udall's last letter to Redmond said he was awaiting notification from Yale. The letter was dated November 27, 1990, a little more than a month before he fell.[49]

His last campaign was over, but the future still was rocky. At a

December caucus, Udall was reelected Interior Committee chairman, but the vote was 208–47.[50] The size of the opposition was something new for Udall, who in 1986 had become the first chairman in secret-ballot history to win unanimous election.[51]

Terry Bracy, one of his early aides, a major player in his presidential candidacy, and now head of the Morris K. Udall Foundation, said attempts were made to secure Udall's resignation. He recalled a phone call from Missouri's Richard A. Gephardt, then majority leader under Speaker Tom Foley. "Dick said, 'Terry, what are we going to do about Mo?' I said, 'What do you mean, he's fine.' He said, 'He's not fine . . . the junior people under him are rebelling.'" At Gephardt's urging, Bracy agreed to talk to his friend. As he had on other occasions, Bracy picked up a strawberry milk shake and a hamburger for Udall, and arranged to spend a lunch hour in his office, something he often did anyway. He suggested retirement, and his proposal was rejected. "Keep in mind," Bracy said, "this is only one thing that was going on. There were many contacts being made."[52]

Why did Udall continue? "What Mo knew and had in his life was Congress," administrative assistant Matt James said. "He deeply loved the institution and public policy. Even at the end, he would work on Saturdays. He couldn't imagine not working, not being involved in the process."[53] Former administrative assistant Bruce Wright quoted Mo as saying: "This is how I get myself out of bed." Wright added, "He was a man of the House."[54]

The January 6, 1991, backward fall down four or five steps did what the voters would not do—it destroyed Udall. He suffered four fractured ribs and a broken shoulder blade, but more seriously, Dr. Targovnik said, a cerebral contusion. Targovnik added: "He was on the knife's edge, and that threw him over."[55] The head injury deprived him of his ability to speak. Udall ultimately was taken to the Veterans Administration Medical Center, where he remained in its nursing home wing for the remainder of his life.

California's George Miller, the ranking Democrat, became acting chairman of the Interior Committee as the public wondered and the family considered what would happen next.

General access to Udall was blocked, but Phoenix reporter Michael Murphy visited Udall on April 5, three months after the congressman was hospitalized. "Bent over in a wheelchair near a nurses' station, Udall, clad in a 'Friends of the River' T-shirt, did not respond when questioned about his health," Murphy wrote. "Efforts to talk to Udall further were blocked by a nurse, who said Udall's wife had requested that reporters not be allowed to visit the 68-year-old congressman."[56]

While Udall lay silently, others talked of his resignation. Son Mark, daughter Anne, and sister Elma spent three or four days in Washington in January, and "we were concerned and got a sense that the likelihood of recovery was slim," Mark recalled, saying the family remembered the case of a Maryland congresswoman who spent eighteen months in a coma while retaining the office.[57] On March 21, the hometown *Tucson Citizen* called for Udall's resignation,[58] the same day Anne, Mark, brother Stewart, and administrative assistant James met with Speaker Foley and his wife, Heather, to discuss that subject. They asked Foley to declare the office vacant, and "he said it was beyond his power," Mark said. "He said it was up to the spouse." Wife Norma did not attend that meeting.[59]

Mark and Anne said they subsequently dined with Norma to advise her of their session with Foley. Norma asked for time, according to Mark, and she later recalled: "It was so sudden. We didn't know if he would get better and be able to go back. It was such a short time and the drum beating started so soon. I said, 'Let him have a little sick-leave time.' I didn't know what all the rush was about. January to May was not a long time. I would never stand in the way of retirement, but everything was moving pell-mell."[60]

Nonetheless, on April 5, she delivered a letter to Foley saying "it appears that he may not be able to return to the rigorous demands and duties required of Members of Congress. . . . If discussions between physicians and our family indicate that a marked improvement in his condition is not forthcoming in the near future, we will ask for your assistance in making the necessary arrangements for his resignation and disability retirement."[61]

On April 10, the state's largest-circulation newspaper, the *Arizona Republic* in Phoenix, declared that the silent congressman should resign.

The blockbuster impact came when Lois Romano of the *Washington Post* reported on April 13 that "the staff and children . . . are in conflict with his wife of two years over how soon his congressional seat should be vacated." The story painted the image of an anguished family on one side and a relatively new wife on the other, with the children hiring an Alexandria law firm, while other unnamed Udall associates suggested Norma was hanging on in a desire for prestige and an increased pension benefit.[62]

Anne Udall was interviewed a few days later by Norma Coile of the *Tucson Citizen,* and said: "In any family situation where you have a family member become ill and you have six highly vocal, highly opinionated children; one stepbrother, Vince, from Dad's second marriage; Norma; and all of Mo's brothers and sisters who also fit the highly verbal, highly opinionated mold you're bound to have some disagreement and some discussion about the best possible outcome."[63]

Norma Udall challenged the *Post* story, but the newspaper said it stood by its report. Years later, Norma said: "Every line [in the Romano story] was a lie. The adjectives—'family purse strings,' 'married shortly afterward,' 'anguished friends'—were a lie. It was ghastly. It was planted. He was not in grief at the time when we decided to marry. It was a result of their loving their father and not knowing about me. They meant the best for him; they didn't intend to hurt me. Their father chose me, trusted me, and loved me. He knew the kind of person I was."[64]

The family dispute was resolved by establishing a joint guardianship with brother Burr Udall in Tucson watching over finances and Norma in Virginia watching over Mo personally.

Still to come was the resignation. Norma Udall, press secretary Erik Barnett, and Roy Jones, the number two Interior Committee aide who had become particularly close to Mo during the Alaska conservation effort and was the planner for Mo's foreign trips, went to Mo's room to inform him that he must resign.

"We announced that it was time," Norma said. "He couldn't talk. I kissed him and said, 'I'm sorry but you just have to resign and I'm sending a letter to the Speaker.' They [Erik and Roy] came up and shook his hand. It was a very loving scene, so touching."[65]

"It lasted maybe thirty minutes," Barnett recalled. "It seemed clear that Mo understood. At that time, it was extremely difficult for him to get words out. We all teared up." Jones remembered telling him, "Mo, we are going to ride your coattails till hell freezes over." Said Barnett: "We all laughed, including Mo. He laughed, but not the old guffaw." Jones said he told Mo he loved him, and he thought Mo tried to say, "I love you, too." Jones added that "tears welled up in my eyes."[66]

On April 19, a simple letter was submitted. "Dear Mr. Speaker: I hereby resign the office of Representative for the Second Congressional District of Arizona, effective May 4, 1991. Sincerely." Administrative assistant Matt James affixed Udall's signature.[67]

In an accompanying letter, Norma wrote of "his integrity and decency, his love of the land, and his warm, self-deprecating humor," and said: "More recently, his steadfastness in confronting the effects of a relentless disease holds a lesson for each of us."[68]

A reception was held in Udall's office on the day the resignation took effect. About 500 people, including President and Mrs. Bush, stopped by.

Meanwhile, Morris Udall settled into a single room in the Veterans Administration nursing home. Gradually, his bones mended and his body recuperated somewhat from the damage of the fall, but he did not speak and he could no longer stand. His brother Stewart composed "Elegy at a Brother's Bedside":

> Like the hawks he knew as a boy
> His spirit soared and darted there.
> And now, crushed, we see him supine,
> His face fixed in an empty gaze.
> Our vigil is to no avail.
> Gone is the wit which sped the dance of laughter,
> Gone the lambent lacework of the mind.
> What savage civility impels us to prolong "life" when the
>   fight for life is over?
> When will we allow loving hands to close lives that have
>   closed?[69]

In late September 1991, doctors cleared him for afternoon visits to his home. James Brady, who was wounded in the assassination attempt on President Reagan, lived a few doors away. He and his wife, Sarah, provided their wheelchair-equipped van and male aide to pick up and return her husband, Norma said. The trips included Thanksgiving and Christmas and occurred "every few weeks" into 1992 until doctors told her they were too much of a strain on Mo.[70]

Udall's room was at the end of the hall, away from the traffic and the simply curious. An Indian sand painting was on one wall. A 1948 photograph of Mo in a basketball uniform and poised to pass was visible from his bed. A photograph of Randy's daughter, Ren, playing basketball was on another wall. Mark Udall was elected to Congress shortly before his father's death, and a nearby picture of Mark was captioned: "A leader who listens to you." A guest book contained dozens of salutations, including one from Senator Ted Kennedy, who wrote: "To Mo: Who all the Kennedy brothers admired, respected, and loved."

Udall spent most of his time in a wheelchair or in a $5,000 bed designed to prevent bed sores. When he no longer could swallow, his nutrient level was maintained through a tube. Family, friends, and former aides visited regularly during the first few years. The number gradually declined, with most individuals saying Mo was unaware of their presence. Others maintained they saw signs of recognition.

In the last months of his life, a Band-Aid held a small, straw cross to the wall above his headboard. It had been left by a summer intern in the Udall Foundation's congressional program for Native American college students. It served as a guardian for the man who had devoted much of his life to being a guardian for others.

On December 12, 1998, Morris K. Udall died from heart failure, nearly eight years after entering the Veterans Administration nursing home.[71] He was cremated. His children scattered some of his ashes during a hike in the Catalina Mountains a day after a Tucson memorial service. Other ashes were spread later in the Washington, D.C., area.

THE LEGACY

hen Mo Udall first went to Congress in 1961, he was astounded to learn that Capitol cafeteria employees were without benefits. Udall embarked on a quiet campaign to arrange appropriate perquisites.

"Dad took it on because it was the right thing to do," daughter Anne said.[1]

In the early 1970s, Udall and Democratic representatives Patricia Schroeder of Colorado and Charles G. Rose III of North Carolina failed to win House approval of workplace harassment rules, so they created a voluntary organization operated by three members and three staffers. It provided employees with a place to complain, and about 100 members of Congress agreed to subject themselves to policing by what they called the House Fair Employment Practices Committee. It was the forerunner of a permanent office instituted when his friend Tom Foley became Speaker.[2]

These two little-known actions demonstrate that Udall was not just another politician who stayed a long time or who sought headlines or about whom the phrase "unsuccessful presidential candidate" might qualify for a trivia contest response.

Still, fame is fleeting, and a book inquiry to a major chain bookstore in Tucson brought forth the question: "How do you spell that name?" At a 1999 gathering of the Morris K. Udall Foundation Scholarship winners, only about one-third of the seventy-five recipients said they had heard of Udall before applying for the college financial aid that bears his name.

The individual whom friends called "the best man never nominated for president" died on December 12, 1998, leaving a legislative and humanitarian legacy that seems to stretch upward like his six-foot-five frame. New words of praise were written and spoken after his death, but some that sounded at the time of his resignation seem to be worth repeating.

Jessica Tuchman Mathews, who had been Udall's issues specialist and the highest-ranking woman in any of the 1976 presidential campaign organizations, quoted Udall's friend David Obey as saying that Mo's symbolic run for Speaker "gave heart to an entire generation" and broke the back of the seniority system. "Later," she wrote, "came reforms of the committee system, a sunshine rule that opened markup sessions to public scrutiny, creation of an ethics committee, and a host of other improvements. His civility and unfailing decency and his commitment to extracting the best from the political process proved infectious. Colleagues found themselves following his lead out of sheer respect and affection."

Mathews, now president of the Carnegie Endowment for International Peace, also recalled Udall's love of the environment and his philosophy that "a nation that does not love and respect its land . . . does not respect itself."[3]

ABC news anchor Peter Jennings described Udall as "what a public servant should be."[4] *Washington Post* political reporter David Broder wrote that "for a whole generation of congressmen, Udall became a mentor and a model."[5]

Indeed, as the 2000 election approached, two of his former colleagues, Republican senator John McCain of Arizona and former Democratic senator Bill Bradley of New Jersey, were unsuccessfully contesting for their party's presidential nomination. Both held Udall in high esteem.

McCain credits Udall with taking him under his wing and giving him responsibility for Native American matters. McCain was a regular visitor when Udall was hospitalized, even when it was unlikely that Udall knew he was there.

Udall first met Bradley when he spoke in England while Bradley was a Rhodes Scholar at Oxford in 1967. A year later, Bradley visited Udall in his office to seek advice about whether to attend law school or play professional basketball. Udall urged him to choose the NBA and then seek a career in public service, advice Bradley followed. Udall aide Terry

Bracy said Udall's and Bradley's political philosophies were close and approached in a similar manner.

The Udall legislative record was significant.

The Alaska Native Land Claims Settlement Act of 1980, perhaps his best-known accomplishment, doubled the size of the national park system and tripled the size of the national wilderness system. The Surface Mining Control and Reclamation Act of 1977 forced the cleanup of hundreds of thousands of acres and elevated environmental protection to near equal status with financial gain. The Campaign Finance Acts of 1971 and 1974 set contemporary standards and began an election cleansing that still seeks perfection. Indian-related bills established gaming as a tribal revenue source, helped settle water rights, improved child welfare, and protected religious and burial rites. Two wilderness bills—the Arizona Wilderness Act of 1984 and the Arizona Desert Wilderness Act of 1990—protected land in his own state.

His impact on the environment led colleagues to name Room 1324 of the Longworth House Office Building in his honor. It is where the Resources Committee—the new name for Interior—conducts its hearings. The room is 30 feet by 49 feet with a ceiling height of 20 feet. Visitors enter at the rear side, and a 1984 painting of a vigorous and rugged-looking Udall, coat slung over his shoulder, greets them from the wall across the way.

Not all of his legislative action stood the test of time. He later questioned the quality of the postal reform. The Nuclear Waste Management Policy Act of 1982 failed to guarantee a scientific process that could designate a burial ground for high-level nuclear waste. He pulled back from a proposed revision of the 1872 law that covers hard-rock mining. The Central Arizona Project that carries water to drier parts of the state remains a target of environmental critics, and Udall in later years voiced his own doubts about its negative impact on the land.

Udall played a major role in structural reform of the House he loved, and he was one of the first congressmen to make public his own income tax documents. His openness paused only when he delayed announcement that he was a victim of Parkinson's disease.

One of his legacies is the graceful way he invoked humor after a defeat, a trait seldom seen in this era of increasing political incivility. Even as he campaigned for what he said would be his final term, Udall said the House and Senate were becoming much too serious. "It's too intense. There's a bigger audience; there are more things you have to be careful about."[6]

His humor and civility won friends and few, if any, enemies. Even an old adversary, House Republican Don Young of Alaska, who now heads the Resources Committee, said Udall "was an exceptionally good chairman. He was very fair. Mo wasn't a zealot. He was a realist, and he had a better understanding of the people than the government agencies. He worried about how people would be affected."[7]

Udall often borrowed from political satirist Will Rogers, and on the wall of his office he had posted this aphorism attributed to Rogers: "We come here for just a spell and then pass on. So get a few laughs and do the best you can. Live your life so that whenever you lose, you are ahead."[8]

Udall also loaned his name and occasionally his presence to the American Parkinson Disease Association, serving as its honorary chairman and appearing in its public service announcements on TV. He said he wanted "to get the word out that it's not hopeless . . . to help people like you and me who discovered we had a disease we didn't know anything about that would change our lives in many ways."[9] The impact of Parkinson's also spurred daughter Anne to join others to lobby against the federal ban on government-funded research aimed at treating diseases by transplanting human fetal tissue. Privately funded research indicated that such transplants could help Parkinson's patients.[10] President Bill Clinton lifted the ban early in his first administration, saying: "This is for you, Mo."[11]

As Udall lay silent in his nursing-home room for years, friends remembered him in different ways. In early 1993, more than 1,800 people turned out in Tucson to raise funds for the American Parkinson Disease Association and the Morris K. Udall Fund for Excellence in Public Policy at the University of Arizona. Mark Russell headlined the program. Barry Goldwater called Udall "the finest member of the congressional delegation we've ever had."[12]

On one occasion, first lady Hillary Rodham Clinton dropped in to see him.[13] In 1996, President Clinton selected Udall as one of eleven recipients of the Presidential Medal of Freedom. "Morris Udall represents everything a lawmaker should be," Clinton said. "His work is a gift to all Americans."[14]

His colleagues so respected Udall that in 1992 they created a foundation in his name. The law noted that Udall "has had a lasting impact on this nation's environment, public lands, and natural resources, and has instilled in this nation's youth a love of the air, land, and water." The act also called him "a champion of the rights of Native Americans and Alaska Natives," and said he had "used his leadership to strengthen tribal self-governance."[15] It was only the fourth congressional foundation ever established. The others honor fellow Arizonan Barry Goldwater and Presidents Harry S. Truman and James Madison.

The Tucson-based Morris K. Udall Foundation is run by executive director Christopher L. Helms, a onetime Udall staffer. Friend and former aide Terry Bracy is chair of the board of trustees. Daughter Anne Udall is vice chair, and former aide Matt James and widow Norma Udall are board members.

The foundation centers its work on environmental matters and Native American affairs, with particular attention to Indian health care and environmental conflict resolution. It annually awards seventy-five scholarships to college juniors and seniors planning careers in the environment or Native American health care and tribal public policy. It also places about a dozen Native Americans in Capitol Hill and White House offices each summer; awards dissertation grants to doctoral students; sponsors national conferences; supports research at the University of Arizona's Morris K. Udall Center for Studies in Public Policy, which was established in 1987; and has begun a "Parks in Focus" program to take inner-city children on trips to national parks. The foundation also provides funding for maintenance of the Morris K. Udall Papers at the University of Arizona Library.

The foundation's responsibility expanded in 1999 when the U.S. Institute for Environmental Conflict Resolution began operation under its auspices. As conceived by Senator McCain, the institute "would provide a neutral place inside the federal government, but outside 'the beltway,' for both public and private interests to resolve disputes involving the environment, public lands, and natural resources."[16] It is the kind of agency that Udall might have wished for when he was trapped between environmentalists and the University of Arizona in the fight over Mount Graham telescopes.

The depth of personal feeling about Udall was demonstrated in

Tucson and Washington, D.C., after his death on December 12, 1998. A hometown memorial service was conducted on January 16, 1999, and more than 1,500 people turned out to appreciate his accomplishments, to laugh at his jokes, and to honor his integrity and civility. In Washington on March 4, 1999, about 500 people paid their respects in much the same manner.

In Tucson, nearly two dozen individuals spoke, each with a favorite joke to include, most of them "Mo specials," and most of them old hat to the audience. Nonetheless, laughter filled the University of Arizona auditorium. "I don't need new jokes," Udall once said. "I need new audiences." Even with old friends, his stories as told by others contained the Mo zing.

It was more of the same in Washington, with members of Congress and the administration playing significant roles. Some of the jokes were the same, and the laughter remained.

A pair of new congressional faces mixed in with the old at both memorial services. Son Mark was elected to the U.S. House of Representatives from the Boulder area of Colorado, and nephew Tom, son of Stewart, was elected from the northern part of New Mexico. Mo Udall had campaigned for Tom years earlier when Tom made an unsuccessful run for the House. The two Democrats, both outdoorsmen and environmentalists, also sought and won appointment as members of the Resources Committee.

The Udall Foundation uses the maxim "dedicated to civility, integrity, and consensus" on its literature, the words intended to describe in short form one aspect of the legacy of Morris K. Udall, and two former staff members talked about the extension of that motto.

Mark Brand, who worked in the 1976 presidential campaign and again in the consideration of a 1984 presidential bid, said, "It is myopic to cite his conservation or other legislative efforts. The biggest legacy is the people he got involved in the system and what change they have brought. It was the quality of the people who gave up a year or two of their lives."[17]

Erik Barnett, his last press secretary, noted that Udall's impact is still being felt, saying that Mo had employed hundreds of full-time staffers who, "almost unanimously, acknowledge the profound influence Udall had on their lives." He said the group included lawyers, doctors, journalists, teachers, and "a cadre of public servants working at the local, state, and federal level. It is from this group of people that Udall's next accomplishments will come. It is in these people that Udall instilled the ideal that public service is an honorable profession. You serve yourself better, Udall taught us, if you serve your community or state or country. It was not the benefits of power which we learned from Udall, but the benefits of public service."

Barnett noted that Udall "spoke from his heart when he quoted his father as saying, 'You won't get wealthy in public service, but you'll be able to look back on an honorable career.' "[18]

NOTES

Abbreviations: "interview with the authors" refers to the interviews conducted by Donald W. Carson and James W. Johnson for this book; "Oral History Project" refers to the interviews conducted by Peter L. Steere and Julie Ferdon for the Morris K. Udall Oral History Project; "Arizona Bar Foundation" refers to the interviews conducted by James F. McNulty Jr. and Virginia Kelly for the Arizona Bar Foundation. The details of these interviews appear in the bibliography.

An online source for selected aspects of the Morris K. Udall Papers at the University of Arizona Library is http://dizzy.library.arizona.edu/branches/spc/udall.

INTRODUCTION
1. Wilhelm and Wilhelm, *St. Johns Arizona Stake,* pp. 346–347.
2. Eloise Udall Whiting interview, Oral History Project.
3. Stewart L. Udall interview with the authors, July 18, 1998.
4. Terrence L. Bracy interview with the authors.
5. Stewart L. Udall interview with the authors, June 24, 1998.
6. Mark Shields, "Mo Udall's Monuments," *Washington Post,* April 23, 1991.
7. Ibid.
8. Reuss, *When Government Was Good,* p. 167.

CHAPTER 1. END OF A DREAM
1. Larry Liebert, "The Hopefuls," *San Francisco Chronicle,* January 20, 1983.
2. Marvin S. Cohen interview with the authors.

CHAPTER 2. MORMON PIONEERS
1. Ben MacNitt, "Mo Udall Album," *Arizona Daily Star,* February 1, 1976.
2. Morris K. Udall speech at the Heard Museum, Phoenix, Arizona, Febru-

ary 18, 1971, Morris K. Udall Papers, Special Collections, University of Arizona Library, Tucson.

3. Pat Bryant, "Udall's Sister Recalls Family Joys and Tears," *Richmond Times-Dispatch,* May 13, 1976.

4. Stewart L. Udall, "Human Values and Hometown Snapshots: Early Days in St. Johns," *American West* magazine, May–June 1982, p. 27.

5. Ibid., p. 28.

6. Udall and Nelson, *Arizona Pioneer Mormon,* p. 15.

7. Ibid., p. 66.

8. Ibid., p. 68.

9. Ibid., p. 77.

10. Speech by Levi S. Udall at the Arizona Museum, Phoenix, April 7, 1946, copy in Levi S. Udall Papers, Special Collections, University of Arizona Library, Tucson.

11. Udall and Nelson, *Arizona Pioneer Mormon,* p. 71.

12. Ben MacNitt, "Mo Udall Album," *Arizona Daily Star,* February 1, 1976.

13. Ellsworth, *Mormon Odyssey,* p. 46.

14. Pauline Udall Smith, *Memoirs,* p. 5.

15. Chanin and Chanin, *This Land,* p. 80.

16. David King Udall journal, David King Udall Papers, Special Collections, University of Arizona Library, Tucson.

17. Stewart L. Udall, "Human Values and Hometown Snapshots: Early Days in St. Johns," *American West* magazine, May–June 1982, p. 27.

18. Ibid.

19. Memorandum from Morris K. Udall to his son Randy, April 28, 1971, Morris K. Udall Papers, Special Collections, University of Arizona Library, Tucson.

CHAPTER 3. THEY STOOD ON HIS SHOULDERS

1. Morris K. Udall interview, Arizona Bar Foundation.

2. Udall and Nelson, *Arizona Pioneer Mormon,* p. 189.

3. Chanin and Chanin, *This Land,* p. 122.

4. Levi S. Udall Papers, Special Collections, University of Arizona Library, Tucson.

5. Orien W. Fifer Jr., "Stewart Udall Leader as Boy," *Arizona Republic,* January 19, 1961.

6. From historical timeline provided courtesy Elma Udall.

7. Orien W. Fifer Jr., "Stewart Udall Leader as Boy," *Arizona Republic,* January 19, 1961.

8. From a eulogy entitled "A Modern Western Cicero" given by Dix W.

Price at Levi S. Udall's funeral, Morris K. Udall Papers, Special Collections, University of Arizona Library, Tucson.

9. Elma Udall interview, Oral History Project.

10. From a eulogy entitled "A Modern Western Cicero" given by Dix W. Price at Levi S. Udall's funeral, Morris K. Udall Papers, Special Collections, University of Arizona Library, Tucson.

11. Maggie Savoy, "Udall's Mother Proud of Courageous Son," Associated Press in *The News and Observer* (Raleigh, North Carolina), April 23, 1962.

12. Clay Thompson, "Always a Leader, Always a Prankster," *Phoenix Gazette,* April 20, 1991.

13. Elma Udall interview, Oral History Project.

14. Joseph Stocker, "Why Udall Wants to Run," *The Nation,* February 15, 1975, p. 172.

15. Ibid.

16. Memorandum from Morris K. Udall to his son Randy, April 28, 1971, Morris K. Udall Papers, Special Collections, University of Arizona Library, Tucson.

17. Chanin and Chanin, *This Land,* p. 123.

18. Thompson, *Never President,* p. 123.

19. Stewart L. Udall interview with the authors, January 16, 1998.

20. Memorandum from Morris K. Udall to his son Randy, April 28, 1971.

21. From historical timeline provided courtesy Elma Udall.

22. Chanin and Chanin, *This Land,* p. 124.

23. Maggie Savoy, "Udall's Mother Proud of Courageous Son," Associated Press in *The News and Observer* (Raleigh, North Carolina), April 23, 1962.

24. From Levi S. Udall's Arizona Supreme Court opinion, July 22, 1948, Levi S. Udall Papers, Special Collections, University of Arizona Library, Tucson.

25. Maggie Savoy, "Udall's Mother Proud of Courageous Son," Associated Press in *The News and Observer* (Raleigh, North Carolina), April 23, 1962.

26. Ibid.

CHAPTER 4. GROWING UP

1. Elma Udall, undated memorandum, Morris K. Udall Papers, Special Collections, University of Arizona Library, Tucson.

2. Letter from Morris K. Udall to his mother, Louise Lee Udall, from Saipan, March 1, 1946.

3. Louise L. Udall, recollection written for her family, January 13, 1946, Morris K. Udall Papers, Special Collections, University of Arizona Library, Tucson.

4. Morris K. Udall, *Too Funny,* p. 89.

5. Louise L. Udall, recollection written for her family, January 13, 1946, Morris K. Udall Papers, Special Collections, University of Arizona Library, Tucson.

6. Ibid.

7. Elma Udall interview, Oral History Project.

8. Transcript of interview with Morris K. Udall by Abe Chanin, undated, but probably mid-1970s, courtesy Abe Chanin.

9. D. Burr Udall interview with the authors.

10. Letter from Louise L. Udall to family and friends, January 23, 1930, Morris K. Udall Papers, Special Collections, University of Arizona Library, Tucson.

11. Statement written by Louise L. Udall the week of her thirty-fourth wedding anniversary, June 1948, Morris K. Udall Papers, Special Collections, University of Arizona Library, Tucson.

12. Stewart L. Udall, "Human Values and Hometown Snapshots: Early Days in St. Johns," *American West* magazine, May–June 1982, pp. 27, 29.

13. Stewart L. Udall, written response to authors' question, January 19, 1998.

14. Chanin and Chanin, *This Land,* pp. 121–122.

15. Bert Farr interview with the authors.

16. Calvin H. Udall, presentation to the Morris K. Udall Foundation Scholarship winners, August 8, 1998.

17. Stewart L. Udall, "Human Values and Hometown Snapshots: Early Days in St. Johns," *American West* magazine, May–June 1982, p. 31.

18. Memorandum from Morris K. Udall to Stewart L. Udall, January 7, 1974, courtesy Stewart L. Udall.

19. Stewart L. Udall, "Human Values and Hometown Snapshots: Early Days in St. Johns," *American West* magazine, May–June 1982, p. 32.

20. Ibid.

21. D. Burr Udall interview, Oral History Project.

22. Elma Udall interview, Oral History Project.

23. Ibid.

24. D. Burr Udall interview, Oral History Project.

25. Warren G. Whiting interview with the authors.

26. Eloise Udall Whiting interview, Oral History Project.

27. Elma Udall interview, Oral History Project.

28. Eloise Udall Whiting interview, Oral History Project.

29. Transcript of interview with Morris K. Udall by Abe Chanin, undated, but probably mid-1970s, courtesy Abe Chanin.

30. Chanin and Chanin, *This Land*, p. 123.

31. Jay Hall, "Mrs. Udall Proud of All Six Children," *Tucson Daily Citizen*, December 6, 1969.

32. Warren G. Whiting interview, Oral History Project.

33. Chanin and Chanin, *This Land*, p. 122.

34. Ibid., pp. 122–123.

35. Stewart L. Udall interview with the authors, July 18, 1998.

36. Letter from Morris K. Udall to his mother, Louise Lee Udall, in St. Johns, undated from Lake Charles, Louisiana, courtesy Elma Udall.

37. Elma Udall interview with the authors.

38. D. Burr Udall interview with the authors.

39. Elma Udall interview with the authors.

40. Morris K. Udall, *Too Funny*, pp. 87–88.

41. D. Burr Udall interview, Oral History Project.

42. Morris K. Udall, *Too Funny*, p. 89.

43. Chanin and Chanin, *This Land*, p. 122.

44. "High School Notes," *St. Johns Herald-Observer*, September 9, 1939.

45. Morris K. Udall, *Too Funny*, p. 87.

46. Calvin H. Udall interview with the authors.

47. Morris K. Udall, "High School Notes," *St. Johns Herald*, April 2, 1938.

48. Morris K. Udall, *Too Funny*, p. 85.

49. Morris K. Udall, "What's on Your Mind?" *St. Johns Herald-Observer*, September 23, 1939.

50. Warren G. Whiting interview with the authors.

51. Calvin H. Udall interview with the authors.

52. Virgene Jarvis Farr interview with the authors.

53. Eloise Udall Whiting interview with the authors.

54. Transcript of interview with Morris K. Udall by Abe Chanin, undated, but probably mid-1970s, courtesy Abe Chanin.

55. Chanin and Chanin, *This Land*, p. 122.

56. Robert W. Pickrell interview with the authors.

57. George F. Genung interview with the authors.

58. Ibid.

59. George Miller interview with the authors.

60. George F. Genung interview with the authors.

61. Morris K. Udall, transcript from taped C-SPAN program with Barry M. Goldwater, May 7, 1985, Morris K. Udall Papers, Special Collections, University of Arizona Library, Tucson.

CHAPTER 5. OFF TO THE MILITARY

1. Letter from Morris K. Udall to family in St. Johns, undated, from Fort Douglas, Utah, courtesy Elma Udall.

2. Memorandum from Morris K. Udall to his son Randy, April 28, 1971, Morris K. Udall Papers, Special Collections, University of Arizona Library, Tucson.

3. Letter from Morris K. Udall to family in St. Johns, undated, from Fort Douglas, Utah, courtesy Elma Udall.

4. Letter from Morris K. Udall to family in St. Johns, November 19, 1942, from Fort Douglas, Utah, courtesy Elma Udall.

5. Letter from Morris K. Udall to family in St. Johns, December 10, 1942, from Fort Douglas, Utah, courtesy Elma Udall.

6. Ibid.

7. Letter from Morris K. Udall to family in St. Johns, December 20, 1942, from Fort Douglas, Utah, courtesy Elma Udall.

8. Letter from Morris K. Udall to family in St. Johns, December 29, 1942, from Fort Douglas, Utah, courtesy Elma Udall.

9. Letter from Levi S. Udall to Stewart L. and Morris K. Udall, January 4, 1943, from St. Johns, courtesy Elma Udall.

10. Letter from Morris K. Udall to family in St. Johns, January 5, 1943, from Fort Douglas, Utah, courtesy Elma Udall.

11. Morris K. Udall, *Too Funny*, p. 94.

12. Letter from Morris K. Udall to family in St. Johns, April 1943, from Fargo, North Dakota, courtesy Elma Udall.

13. Letter from Morris K. Udall to Levi S. Udall in St. Johns, May 1943, from Fargo, North Dakota, courtesy Elma Udall.

14. Letter from Morris K. Udall to Louise L. Udall in St. Johns, June 17, 1943, from Fargo, North Dakota, courtesy Elma Udall.

15. Letter from Morris K. Udall to family in St. Johns, undated, from Tampa, Florida, courtesy Elma Udall.

16. Morris K. Udall, *Too Funny*, p. 94.

17. Ibid., p. 95.

18. Letter from Morris K. Udall to Louise L. Udall in St. Johns, undated, from Lake Charles, Louisiana, courtesy Elma Udall.

19. Letter from Morris K. Udall to family in St. Johns, November 14, 1943, from Lake Charles, Louisiana, courtesy Elma Udall.

20. Letter from Morris K. Udall to family in St. Johns, December 12, 1943, from Lake Charles, Louisiana, courtesy Elma Udall.

21. Ibid.

22. Letter from Morris K. Udall to Louise L. Udall in St. Johns, undated, from Lake Charles, Louisiana, courtesy Elma Udall.

23. Letter from Morris K. Udall to family in St. Johns, December 12, 1943, from Lake Charles, Louisiana, courtesy Elma Udall.

24. Letter from Morris K. Udall to family in St. Johns, July 6, 1944, from Lake Charles, Louisiana, courtesy Elma Udall.

25. Letter from Morris K. Udall to family in St. Johns, January 2, 1944, from Lake Charles, Louisiana, courtesy Elma Udall.

26. Letter from Morris K. Udall to family in St. Johns, March 24, 1944, from Lake Charles, Louisiana, courtesy Elma Udall.

27. Letter from Morris K. Udall to family in St. Johns, May 30, 1944, from Lake Charles, Louisiana, courtesy Elma Udall.

28. Letter from Morris K. Udall to family in St. Johns, undated, from Lake Charles, Louisiana, courtesy Elma Udall.

29. Letter from Morris K. Udall to Louise L. Udall in St. Johns, May 7, 1944, from Lake Charles, Louisiana, courtesy Elma Udall.

30. Letter from Morris K. Udall to family in St. Johns, April 1, 1945, from Lake Charles, Louisiana, courtesy Elma Udall.

31. Letter from Morris K. Udall to Louise L., Elma, and Eloise Udall, undated, from Lake Charles, Louisiana, courtesy Elma Udall.

32. Letter fragment from Morris K. Udall to Stewart L. Udall, Spring 1946, from Saipan, courtesy Elma Udall.

33. Ibid.

34. Letter from Brigadier General F. W. Boye Jr., deputy chief of legislative liaison, to Representative Morris K. Udall, September 19, 1962, Morris K. Udall Papers, Special Collections, University of Arizona Library, Tucson.

35. Morris K. Udall, *Too Funny,* p. 97.

36. Letter from Morris K. Udall to family in St. Johns, March 24, 1944, from Lake Charles, Louisiana, courtesy Elma Udall.

37. Letter from Morris K. Udall to family in St. Johns, undated, from Lake Charles, Louisiana, courtesy Elma Udall.

38. Letter from Morris K. Udall to family in St. Johns, undated, from Fort Sam Houston, Texas, courtesy Elma Udall.

39. Letter from Morris K. Udall to Louise L. Udall, Mother's Day 1945, from Lake Charles, Louisiana, courtesy Elma Udall.

CHAPTER 6. SEEING THE WORLD

1. Letter from Morris K. Udall to Louise L. Udall in St. Johns, July 1945, from Kearns, Utah, courtesy Elma Udall.

2. Letter from Morris K. Udall to family in St. Johns, September 13, 1945, written aboard the U.S.S. *Baxter,* courtesy Elma Udall.

3. Letter from Morris K. Udall to family in St. Johns, November 1945, from Iwo Jima, courtesy Elma Udall.

4. Letter from Morris K. Udall to Levi S. Udall in St. Johns, November 6, 1945, from Iwo Jima, courtesy Elma Udall.

5. Letter from Morris K. Udall to family in St. Johns, Christmas 1945, from Guam, courtesy Elma Udall.

6. In his 1988 book, *Too Funny to Be President,* Udall said he had written President Franklin D. Roosevelt with a plea for an end to military segregation. We were unable to locate a copy of such a letter in the Morris K. Udall Papers at the University of Arizona or in the archives of either President Roosevelt or President Harry S. Truman, who ordered an end to military segregation in July 1948.

7. Letter from Morris K. Udall to National Planning Committee of the American Veterans Committee in New York City, March 15, 1946, from Saipan, courtesy Elma Udall.

8. Letter from Morris K. Udall to Levi S. Udall in Phoenix, March 6, 1946, from Saipan, courtesy Elma Udall.

9. Letter from Morris K. Udall to D. Burr Udall in St. Johns, February 2, 1946, from Saipan, courtesy Eloise Udall Whiting.

10. D. Burr Udall interview with the authors.

11. Morris K. Udall, "Mormon Settlement in Arizona," speech given at the Heard Museum, Phoenix, Arizona, February 18, 1971, Morris K. Udall Papers, Special Collections, University of Arizona Library, Tucson.

12. Marvin Borodkin interview with the authors.

13. Morris K. Udall, transcript from taped C-SPAN program with Barry M. Goldwater, May 7, 1985, Morris K. Udall Papers, Special Collections, University of Arizona Library, Tucson.

14. Larry L. King interview with the authors.

CHAPTER 7. THE TUCSON YEARS

1. Robert W. Pickrell interview with the authors, September 22, 1998.

2. Charles E. Ares interview with the authors.

3. Stewart L. Udall interview with the authors, March 7, 1999.

4. Abe Chanin, *Wildcats,* p. xii.

5. Marvin Borodkin interview with the authors.

6. Abe Chanin, *Wildcats,* p. xiii.

7. Greg Hansen, "A Century of Tucson Sports—10 Who Made a Differ-

ence: Fred W. Enke," *Arizona Daily Star,* June 6, 1999; Fred W. Enke interview with the authors.

8. Stewart L. Udall interview with the authors, July 18, 1998.

9. James F. McNulty Jr. interview with the authors.

10. Ibid.; Virgil Carson, "Talent and Drive Mark Mo Udall's Top Record," *Arizona Wildcat,* December 5, 1947; Douglas D. Martin, *Lamp in the Desert,* p. 222.

11. Morgan Maxwell Jr. interview with the authors.

12. Letter from Morris K. Udall to Levi S. Udall in Phoenix, September 29, 1948, from Denver, courtesy Elma Udall.

13. Morris K. Udall interview, Arizona Bar Foundation.

14. Morris K. Udall, March 14, 1977, statement written for proposed *Esquire* magazine article on prominent Americans and their first jobs, Morris K. Udall Papers, Special Collections, University of Arizona Library, Tucson.

15. Harry Farrar, "Old Nugget to Seek Biggest Prize of All," *Denver Post,* December 1, 1974.

16. Morris K. Udall, undated letter to Levi S. Udall, probably in February 1949, Morris K. Udall Papers, Special Collections, University of Arizona Library, Tucson.

17. Morris K. Udall interview, Arizona Bar Foundation.

18. "Newsmakers," *Newsweek,* January 5, 1981, p. 29.

19. Patricia E. Udall interview with the authors.

20. Stewart L. Udall interview with the authors, July 18, 1998.

21. Bonnie Henry, "Tucson Self-Service Gas Pioneer Dies at 83," *Arizona Daily Star,* January 17, 1999.

22. Stewart L. Udall interview with the authors, March 7, 1999.

23. From the *Arizona Daily Star:* "Harassed Indian Barber Will Force Test Suit of State Law," December 21, 1949; "Jury Disagrees in Barber Case," March 11, 1950; "Indian Barber's Trade Enjoined," March 28, 1950.

24. Morris K. Udall, notes on speech to Pima County Bar Association, April 8, 1983, Morris K. Udall Papers, Special Collections, University of Arizona Library, Tucson.

25. Charles E. Ares interview with the authors.

26. Morris K. Udall, *Too Funny,* pp. 102–103.

27. Charles E. Ares, "Morris K. Udall, Arizona Lawyer," *Arizona Law Record,* Fall 1991, pp. 7–9.

28. "Udall to Enforce Gambling Statute," *Arizona Daily Star,* November 18, 1953.

29. Morris K. Udall, *Too Funny,* p. 104.

30. Morris K. Udall interview, Arizona Bar Foundation.

31. Chanin and Chanin, *This Land,* pp. 126–127.

32. Patricia E. Udall interview with the authors.

33. Letter from Stewart L. Udall to his uncle Don T. Udall, November 7, 1953, courtesy Stewart L. Udall.

34. Stewart L. Udall interview with the authors, July 18, 1998.

35. "Udall to Seek Judgeship of Fourth Court," *Arizona Daily Star,* May 2, 1954.

36. "Stewart Udall Candidate for Lower House," *Arizona Daily Star,* June 17, 1954.

37. Stewart L. Udall interview with the authors, July 18, 1998.

38. Ibid., February 25, 1999.

39. Vince Davis, "Problems You Run into When Seeking Votes," *Arizona Daily Star,* July 18, 1954.

40. Consensus based on numerous interviews conducted by the authors, including S. Thomas Chandler, James F. McNulty Jr., and Charles E. Ares.

41. Patricia E. Udall interview with the authors.

42. Morris K. Udall interview, Arizona Bar Foundation.

43. S. Thomas Chandler interview with the authors.

44. J. Daniel O'Neill interview with the authors.

45. Marvin S. Cohen interview with the authors.

46. Stanley G. Feldman interview with the authors.

47. Charles E. Ares interview, Oral History Project.

48. S. Thomas Chandler interview, Oral History Project.

49. Stewart L. Udall interview with the authors, July 18, 1998.

50. Stanley G. Feldman interview with the authors.

51. Charles E. Ares interview with the authors.

52. S. Thomas Chandler interview with the authors.

53. Chanin and Chanin, *This Land,* p. 127.

54. Don Carson, "Congressional Candidates Exchange Hot Words at Press Club," *Arizona Daily Star,* March 22, 1961.

55. Shadegg, *Arizona Politics,* p. xix.

CHAPTER 8. THE OUT-OF-TOWNERS

1. Morris K. Udall, *Education,* p. 23.

2. Ibid., p. 18.

3. Morris K. Udall interview with Ross R. Rice, November 30, 1972, for the Carl Hayden Project at Arizona State University, Tempe, Arizona, transcript in the Arizona State University Library.

4. Morris K. Udall, *Education,* p. 17.

5. Memorandum written February 26, 1997, by Stewart L. Udall to Peter L. Steere, archivist, Special Collections, University of Arizona Library, Tucson.

6. Morris K. Udall, *Education,* p. 294.

7. Morris K. Udall, *Too Funny,* p. 106.

8. Larry L. King interview with the authors.

9. Roger K. Lewis interview with the authors.

10. Richard C. Olson interview with the authors, October 24, 1998.

11. Ward Sinclair, "Udall," in *The Citizen's Guide to the 1976 Presidential Candidates,* Capitol Hill News Service, 1976.

12. Ibid.

13. Ibid.

14. John B. Gabusi interview with the authors, September 14, 1998.

15. Morris K. Udall, *Education,* pp. 4–5.

16. Larry L. King interview with the authors.

17. Hedrick Smith, *Power Game,* p. 54.

18. Morris K. Udall, "The Congressional Primer," *Washington Post,* January 23, 1977.

19. Morris K. Udall, *Education,* pp. 24–25.

20. Morris K. Udall interview by Jack Murphy, NASA director of public affairs, on C-SPAN, May 7, 1985, transcript in Morris K. Udall Papers, Special Collections, University of Arizona Library, Tucson.

21. Morris K. Udall, *Education,* p. 294.

22. Morris K. Udall, *Too Funny,* p. 106.

23. Morris K. Udall, *Education,* p. 294.

24. Ibid., p. 18.

25. Arthur Hadley, "Can a Congressman from a Small State out West . . . ?" *The Atlantic,* December 1974, p. 20.

26. *Addresses and Special Orders,* p. 174.

27. Morris K. Udall, *Too Funny,* p. 107.

28. William E. Kimble interview with the authors.

29. Morris K. Udall, *Too Funny,* p. 108.

30. Morris K. Udall, *Education,* p. 23.

31. Ibid., p. 329.

32. Morris K. Udall interview with Ross R. Rice, November 30, 1972, for the Carl Hayden Project at Arizona State University, Tempe, Arizona, transcript in the Arizona State University Library.

33. Richard C. Olson interview with the authors, October 24, 1998.

34. Morris K. Udall interview with Ross R. Rice, November 30, 1972, for the Carl Hayden Project at Arizona State University, Tempe, Arizona, transcript in the Arizona State University Library.

35. Ibid.

36. Ibid.

37. Ibid.

38. Terrence L. Bracy, "Losing and Winning: Lessons of the Gentleman from Arizona," *Arizona Daily Star,* December 15, 1998.

39. Larry L. King, "The Road to Power in Congress," *Harper's,* June 1971, p. 40.

CHAPTER 9. A RISING STAR

1. Morris K. Udall, *Education,* p. 103.

2. Daniel Epstein, "Morris K. Udall, Democratic Representative from Arizona," in *Citizens Look at Congress,* Ralph Nader Congressional Project, Washington, D.C., August 1972, p. 3.

3. Letter from Morris K. Udall to William A. Small Jr., September 6, 1962, Morris K. Udall Papers, Special Collections, University of Arizona Library, Tucson.

4. William E. Kimble interview with the authors.

5. Daniel Epstein, "Morris K. Udall, Democratic Representative from Arizona," in *Citizens Look at Congress,* Ralph Nader Congressional Project, Washington, D.C., August 1972, p. 9.

6. John B. Gabusi interview with the authors, September 21, 1998.

7. "Health Warning Required on Cigarette Packs," *Congressional Quarterly Almanac,* 1965, p. 351.

8. "Cigarette Ads Rapped by Udall," *Arizona Daily Star,* September 28, 1963.

9. "Senate, House Differ on Approaches to Reform of Nation's Land-Use Laws," *The National Journal,* July 22, 1972, p. 1200.

10. "Senate Holds Hearings on Birth Control," *Congressional Quarterly Almanac,* 1965, p. 314.

11. "Limitation of Family Size Urged by Rep. Mo Udall," *Arizona Daily Star,* August 1, 1969.

12. Letter from Morris K. Udall to Ernest Gruening, Morris K. Udall Papers, Special Collections, University of Arizona Library, Tucson.

13. Robert A. Neuman, a tribute contained in "Memories of Mo," prepared for the November 10, 1990, dedication of the Morris K. Udall Center for Studies in Public Policy at the University of Arizona.

14. Chanin and Chanin, *This Land,* pp. 127–128.

15. Morris K. Udall, "The High Cost of Being a Congressman," *Playboy,* November 1967, p. 1 (reprint).

16. Ibid., p. 2 (reprint).

17. Daniel Epstein, "Morris K. Udall, Democratic Representative from Arizona," in *Citizens Look at Congress,* Ralph Nader Congressional Project, Washington, D.C., August 1972, p. 12.

18. Morris K. Udall, "The High Cost of Being a Congressman," *Playboy,* November 1967, p. 6 (reprint).

19. Morris K. Udall, "Is Congress Sick? II: Needed, a Transfusion of Democracy," *Congressman's Report,* February 7, 1964, Morris K. Udall Papers, Special Collections, University of Arizona Library, Tucson.

20. "Congressional Disclosure of Income and Other Information," *Congressional Record,* January 10, 1967, p. 77.

21. Ibid.

22. Morris K. Udall, "The High Cost of Being a Congressman," *Playboy,* November 1967, p. 2 (reprint).

23. "Udall: A Long Campaign for Recognition," *Congressional Quarterly,* November 22, 1975, p. 2534.

24. Ibid.

25. Henry S. Reuss interview with the authors.

26. Evelyn Dubrow interview with the authors.

27. Morris K. Udall, *Education,* p. 332.

28. *Guide to the Congress of the United States: Origins, History and Procedure,* Congressional Quarterly, Inc., Washington, D.C., 1976, p. 610.

29. Ibid., p. 611.

30. Ibid., p. 612.

31. Robert W. Kastenmeier and Thomas S. Foley interviews with the authors.

32. Andrew J. Glass, "Uncommitted Democrats Hold Key to Choice of New House Majority Leader," *The National Journal,* January 9, 1971, p. 72.

33. John B. Gabusi interview with the authors, September 21, 1998.

34. Terrence L. Bracy, "Losing and Winning: Lessons of the Gentleman from Arizona," *Arizona Daily Star,* December 15, 1998.

35. Frank Joseph, "Administration Victorious in Long Fight for Basic Reform of Postal System," *The National Journal,* July 4, 1970, p. 1434.

36. Ibid.

37. John B. Gabusi interview with the authors, September 21, 1998.

38. James W. Johnson, "Mo's Quick, Clean Wit," *Tucson Monthly,* September 1998, p. 39.

39. Letter from Morris K. Udall to O. L. Parris, April 10, 1969, Morris K. Udall Papers, Special Collections, University of Arizona Library, Tucson.

40. Christopher Swan, "America's Dwindling Number of Newspaper 'Voices,'" *Christian Science Monitor,* January 2, 1986.

41. Statement by Morris K. Udall, May 8, 1978, Morris K. Udall Papers, Special Collections, University of Arizona Library, Tucson.

42. Christopher Swan, "America's Dwindling Number of Newspaper 'Voices,'" *Christian Science Monitor,* January 2, 1986.

43. Morris K. Udall, "Representative Udall Adds Newspapers to Bill Seeking Review of 'Critical Industries,'" *Typographical Journal,* May 1977.

44. James E. Cook, "The Enigma of Mo Udall," *Arizona,* June 20, 1971, p. 12.

45. Ibid., p. 15.

CHAPTER 10. CAUGHT ON A TREADMILL

1. Al Bradshaw Jr., "Udall Tells Reason for Meeting," *Arizona Daily Star,* September 23, 1966.

2. "The Vietnam Conflict," testimony presented at an informal congressional hearing, Tucson, October 10, 1966, Morris K. Udall Papers, Special Collections, University of Arizona Library, Tucson.

3. Al Bradshaw Jr., "Anti-War Feeling Boils at Hearing," *Arizona Daily Star,* October 11, 1966.

4. Morris K. Udall, "Vietnam: This Nation Is Caught on a Treadmill," *Reveille,* July 1967, p. 12.

5. Morris K. Udall, *Education,* p. 342.

6. Morris K. Udall, "Vietnam: This Nation Is Caught on a Treadmill," *Reveille,* July 1967, p. 12.

7. Morris K. Udall, *Too Funny,* p. 122.

8. Stewart L. Udall, *Myths of August,* p. 16.

9. Letter from Morris K. Udall to Lyndon B. Johnson, October 18, 1967, White House Central Files, Lyndon B. Johnson Library, Austin, Texas.

10. Memorandum from Walter W. Rostow to Lyndon B. Johnson, October 21, 1967, White House Central Files, Lyndon B. Johnson Library, Austin, Texas.

11. Morris K. Udall, *Education,* p. 342.

12. Stewart L. Udall interview with the authors, July 18, 1998.

13. Morris K. Udall, *Too Funny,* p. 120.

14. Charles E. Ares interview with the authors.

15. Morris K. Udall, *Too Funny,* p. 120.

16. Richard C. Olson interview with the authors, October 24, 1998.

17. Morris K. Udall, *Education,* p. 50.

18. Stewart L. Udall interview with the authors, July 18, 1998.

19. Thompson, *Never President,* p. 124.

20. Morris K. Udall, *Education,* p. 50.

21. Charles E. Ares interview with the authors.

22. Lynda Cuqua, "Lawmaker Reverses Position," *Arizona Daily Star,* October 23, 1967.

23. John W. Finney, "Rep. Udall Splits with Administration over War," *New York Times,* October 23, 1967.

24. "Udall Says Mail Backs His Stand," *Tucson Daily Citizen,* October 30, 1967.

25. "Udall's Gamble," *The New Republic,* November 18, 1967, p. 10.

26. Morris K. Udall, *Education,* p. 342.

27. Ibid. p. 341.

28. Stewart L. Udall interview with the authors, July 18, 1998.

29. Press release, May 4, 1970, Morris K. Udall Papers, Special Collections, University of Arizona Library, Tucson.

30. Letter from Ronald L. Ridenhour to the Congress of the United States, March 29, 1969, Morris K. Udall Papers, Special Collections, University of Arizona Library, Tucson.

31. Roger K. Lewis interview with the authors.

32. Richard C. Olson interview with the authors, October 24, 1998.

33. Ben Cole, "Udall Staff Members Had Part in My Lai Probe," *Arizona Republic,* December 5, 1969.

34. Mary McGrory, "Ronald Ridenhour's Dilemma," *Washington Star,* March 29, 1970.

35. Laurence Stern, "Udall Says Rivers Aided Mylai Probe," *Washington Post,* December 4, 1969.

36. Letter from Colonel Raymond T. Reid to Morris K. Udall, April 24, 1969, in "Pinkville Chronology," Morris K. Udall Papers, Special Collections, University of Arizona Library, Tucson.

37. Laurence Stern, "Udall Says Rivers Aided Mylai Probe," *Washington Post,* December 4, 1969.

38. Ben Cole, "Udall Staff Members Had Part in My Lai Probe," *Arizona Republic,* December 5, 1969.

39. Memorandum from Roger K. Lewis to Morris K. Udall, August 11, 1969, Morris K. Udall Papers, Special Collections, University of Arizona Library, Tucson.

40. Richard C. Olson interview with the authors, October 24, 1998.

41. Mary McGrory, "Ronald Ridenhour's Dilemma," *Washington Star,* March 29, 1970.

42. Memorandum from Richard C. Olson to Roger K. Lewis, August 29, 1969, Morris K. Udall Papers, Special Collections, University of Arizona Library, Tucson.

43. Roger K. Lewis memorandum in "Pinkville" file, August 8, 1969, with handwritten addition on January 26, 1970, Morris K. Udall Papers, Special Collections, University of Arizona Library, Tucson.

44. Mary McGrory, "Ronald Ridenhour's Dilemma," *Washington Star,* March 29, 1970.

45. "Pinkville Chronology," January 29, 1970, Morris K. Udall Papers, Special Collections, University of Arizona Library, Tucson.

46. Richard C. Olson memorandum, undated, Morris K. Udall Papers, Special Collections, University of Arizona Library, Tucson.

47. Morris K. Udall, "The Ballot Box Marked 'U.S. Mail,'" April 28, 1970, Morris K. Udall Papers, Special Collections, University of Arizona Library, Tucson.

CHAPTER 11. THE REFORMER

1. Morris K. Udall, "Congressional Comeback: A Slumbering Giant Awakens," *Congressman's Report,* April 9, 1973, Morris K. Udall Papers, Special Collections, University of Arizona Library, Tucson.

2. Morris K. Udall, "Is Congress Sick? Needed: A Transfusion of Democracy," *Congressman's Report,* February 21, 1964, Morris K. Udall Papers, Special Collections, University of Arizona Library, Tucson.

3. Ibid.

4. Ronald M. Peters Jr., *The Speaker,* p. 22.

5. Morris K. Udall, *Education,* p. 242.

6. Ibid., p. 244.

7. Ibid., p. 245.

8. Ibid., p. 248.

9. Ibid., p. 249.

10. Ronald M. Peters Jr., *The Speaker,* p. 160.

11. Ibid., p. 161.

12. Terrence L. Bracy, "Losing and Winning: Lessons of the Gentleman from Arizona," *Arizona Daily Star,* December 15, 1998.

13. Terrence L. Bracy interview with the authors.

14. "Rotation of Chairmanships," *Congressional Quarterly Almanac,* 1965, p. 597.

15. Morris K. Udall, *Education,* p. 111.

16. Jacobs, *A Rage for Justice,* p. 147.

17. Morris K. Udall, *Education,* p. 112.

18. Terrence L. Bracy interview with the authors.

19. Ibid.

20. Morris K. Udall, *Too Funny,* p. 112.

21. Morris K. Udall, *Education,* pp. 255–256.

22. Morris K. Udall, *Too Funny,* p. 113.

23. Ibid.

24. Morris K. Udall, *Education,* p. 252.

25. Hamilton, *Adam Clayton Powell, Jr.,* p. 18.

26. Morris K. Udall, *Education,* p. 254.

27. "Five Major Committees to Have New Chairmen," *Congressional Quarterly,* January 13, 1967, p. 51.

28. Morris K. Udall, *Too Funny,* pp. 113–114.

29. Morris K. Udall, *Education,* p. 257.

30. Haygood, *King of the Cats,* p. 348.

31. Morris K. Udall, *Education,* pp. 348–349.

32. Ibid., p. 259.

33. "Powell Loses Chairmanship; Seat in Doubt," *Congressional Quarterly,* January 13, 1967, p. 47.

34. Ibid.

35. Haygood, *King of the Cats,* p. 351.

36. Morris K. Udall, *Education,* pp. 253–254.

37. Ibid., pp. 260–261.

38. Morris K. Udall, *Too Funny,* p. 117.

CHAPTER 12. CHALLENGING THE LEADERSHIP

1. Morris K. Udall memorandum for "Files," February 27, 1969, Morris K. Udall Papers, Special Collections, University of Arizona Library, Tucson.

2. John W. Finney, "McCormack, [77], Faces Increasing . . . ," *New York Times,* December 22, 1968.

3. Ibid.

4. Janet Hook, "Bolling and Udall: Last of a Breed," *Congressional Quarterly,* May 11, 1991, p. 1234.

5. Letter from Morris K. Udall to John W. McCormack, November 27, 1968, Morris K. Udall Papers, Special Collections, University of Arizona Library, Tucson.

6. Letter from John W. McCormack to Morris K. Udall, December 10, 1968, Morris K. Udall Papers, Special Collections, University of Arizona Library, Tucson.

7. Green, Fallows, and Zwick, *Who Runs Congress?* p. 74.

8. Ronald M. Peters Jr., *The Speaker,* p. 188.

9. Morris K. Udall, "Memorandum for File," December 20, 1968, Morris K. Udall Papers, Special Collections, University of Arizona Library, Tucson.

10. Morris K. Udall, *Education,* p. 296.

11. Morris K. Udall letter, "Dear Democratic Colleagues," December 26, 1968, Morris K. Udall Papers, Special Collections, University of Arizona Library, Tucson.

12. Memorandum from Morris K. Udall to Carl B. Albert, undated, Morris K. Udall Papers, Special Collections, University of Arizona Library, Tucson.

13. Memorandum from Morris K. Udall to Stewart L. Udall, "Speakership Contest," January 2, 1969, Morris K. Udall Papers, Special Collections, University of Arizona Library, Tucson.

14. "Teddy Cracks the Whip," *Newsweek,* January 13, 1969.

15. Morris K. Udall, *Education,* p. 297.

16. Andrew J. Glass, "Congressional Report: Uncommitted Democrats Hold Key to Choice of New House Majority Leader," *The National Journal,* January 9, 1971, p. 72.

17. Morris K. Udall, *Education,* p. 342.

18. "The House Edges Forward," *New York Times,* January 3, 1969.

19. Morris K. Udall, "Some Postmortem Thoughts on the Speaker Contest," January 3, 1969, Morris K. Udall Papers, Special Collections, University of Arizona Library, Tucson.

20. Ibid.

21. Ibid.

22. Morris K. Udall, *Education,* pp. 342–343.

23. Ibid.

24. O'Neill, *Man of the House,* p. 147.

25. Larry L. King, "The Road to Power in Congress," *Harper's,* June 1971, p. 41.

26. James Deakin, "McCormack Facing Rebellion," *St. Louis Post-Dispatch,* January 17, 1970.

27. Larry L. King, "The Road to Power in Congress," *Harper's,* June 1971, p. 41.

28. Marjorie Hunter, "M'Cormack Says He Will Not Seek New House Term," *New York Times,* May 21, 1970.

29. Larry L. King, "The Road to Power in Congress," *Harper's,* June 1971, p. 42.

30. Andrew J. Glass, "Congressional Report: Uncommitted Democrats Hold Key to Choice of New House Majority Leader," *The National Journal,* January 9, 1971, p. 69.

31. O'Neill, *Man of the House,* p. 257.

32. Larry L. King, "The Road to Power in Congress," *Harper's,* June 1971, p. 48.

33. Ibid., p. 48.

34. Ibid., pp. 48–49.

35. Ibid., p. 57.

36. Andrew J. Glass, "Congressional Report: Uncommitted Democrats Hold Key to Choice of New House Majority Leader," *The National Journal,* January 9, 1971, p. 72.

37. Morris K. Udall memorandum, "Some Further Reflections on My Defeat," January 21, 1971, Morris K. Udall Papers, Special Collections, University of Arizona Library, Tucson.

38. Larry L. King, "The Road to Power in Congress," *Harper's,* June 1971, p. 60.

39. Barry, *Ambition,* p. 25.

40. Larry L. King, "The Road to Power in Congress," *Harper's,* June 1971, p. 60.

41. January 20, 1971, editorial in the *New York Times* with a typewritten note, Morris K. Udall Papers, Special Collections, University of Arizona Library, Tucson.

42. Andrew J. Glass, "Congressional Report: Uncommitted Democrats Hold Key to Choice of New House Majority Leader," *The National Journal,* January 9, 1971, p. 189.

43. Larry L. King, "The Road to Power in Congress," *Harper's,* June 1971, p. 63.

44. Memorandum, "Draft," from John B. Gabusi to Morris K. Udall, undated, Morris K. Udall Papers, Special Collections, University of Arizona Library, Tucson.

45. James E. Cook, "The Enigma of Mo Udall," *Arizona,* June 20, 1971, p. 14.

46. Morris K. Udall, *Too Funny,* p. 118.

CHAPTER 13. THE CENTRAL ARIZONA PROJECT

1. Morris K. Udall, "Central Arizona Project: Tapping Arizona's Last Water Hole," *Congressman's Report,* May 21, 1963, Morris K. Udall Papers, Special Collections, University of Arizona Library, Tucson.

2. Stewart L. Udall interview with the authors, July 18, 1998.

3. Morris K. Udall, "The CAP Is Signed—This Is Next Year," *Congressman's Report,* October 10, 1968, Morris K. Udall Papers, Special Collections, University of Arizona Library, Tucson.

4. Central Arizona Project Web site, www.cap-az.com/about_CAP/histcap.htm.

5. McMillan, *McFarland Papers,* pp. 230–231.

6. Johnson, *Central Arizona Project,* p. 124.

7. Morris K. Udall, "Central Arizona Project: Tapping Arizona's Last Water Hole," *Congressman's Report,* May 21, 1963, Morris K. Udall Papers, Special Collections, University of Arizona Library, Tucson.

8. Letter from Stewart L. Udall to Carl T. Hayden, June 12, 1963, Morris K. Udall Papers, Special Collections, University of Arizona Library, Tucson.

9. Morris K. Udall, "Arizona's Water Fight: Which Path Leads to Victory?" *Congressman's Report,* July 12, 1963, Morris K. Udall Papers, Special Collections, University of Arizona Library, Tucson.

10. Ibid.

11. "Water for Thirsty Southwest," *Business Week,* August 31, 1963, pp. 20–21.

12. Charles Coate, "The Biggest Water Fight in American History: Stewart Udall and the Central Arizona Project," *Journal for the Southwest,* Spring 1995, p. 81.

13. Rice, *Carl Hayden,* p. 135.

14. Ibid., p. 86.

15. Morris K. Udall, *Education,* p. 157.

16. Morris K. Udall, *Too Funny,* p. 46.

17. Reisner, *Cadillac Desert,* p. 255.

18. Stewart L. Udall interview, Oral History Project.

19. Morris K. Udall, *Too Funny,* pp. 50–51.

20. Reisner, *Cadillac Desert,* p. 295.

21. Morris K. Udall, *Too Funny,* p. 52.

22. Morris K. Udall, "The Facts about Grand Canyon and Dams," *Public Power,* July 1966, p. 46.

23. Charles Coate, "The Biggest Water Fight in American History: Stewart Udall and the Central Arizona Project," *Journal for the Southwest,* Spring 1995, p. 99.

24. Morris K. Udall, *Too Funny,* p. 52.

25. Ibid.

26. Reisner, *Cadillac Desert,* p. 297.

27. Byron Eugene Pearson, "People above Scenery: The Struggle over the Grand Canyon Dams, 1963–1968," doctoral dissertation, 1998 (Department of History, University of Arizona, Tucson), p. 206.

28. Ibid.

29. Ibid., p. 207.

30. Cohen, *Sierra Club,* p. 361.

31. Byron Eugene Pearson, "People above Scenery: The Struggle over the Grand Canyon Dams, 1963–1968," doctoral dissertation, 1998 (Department of History, University of Arizona, Tucson), p. 209.

32. Cohen, *Sierra Club,* p. 361.

33. Morris K. Udall, "The Facts about Grand Canyon and Dams," *Public Power,* July 1966, p. 23.

34. Russell Martin, *Glen Canyon,* p. 266.

35. Morris K. Udall, *Too Funny,* p. 62.

36. Phil Kurz, "Interior to Feel Firmer Touch after Udall's Gentle Hand," *Congressional Quarterly,* April 27, 1991, p. 1053.

37. Morris K. Udall, "Flooding the Grand Canyon: A Phony Issue," *Congressional Record,* June 9, 1966, Morris K. Udall Papers, Special Collections, University of Arizona Library, Tucson.

38. Ibid.

39. Byron Eugene Pearson, "People above Scenery: The Struggle over the Grand Canyon Dams, 1963–1968," doctoral dissertation, 1998 (Department of History, University of Arizona, Tucson), p. 213.

40. Charles Coate, "The Biggest Water Fight in American History: Stewart Udall and the Central Arizona Project," *Journal for the Southwest,* Spring 1995, p. 87.

41. Ibid., p. 88.

42. Ibid.

43. Ibid., p. 94.

44. Byron Eugene Pearson, "People above Scenery: The Struggle over the Grand Canyon Dams, 1963–1968," doctoral dissertation, 1998 (Department of History, University of Arizona, Tucson), p. 215.

45. "Congress Fails to Pass Colorado River Basin Measure," *Congressional Quarterly Almanac,* 1966, p. 673.

46. Charles Coate, "The Biggest Water Fight in American History: Stewart Udall and the Central Arizona Project," *Journal for the Southwest,* Spring 1995, pp. 91–92.

47. Ibid., p. 100.

48. August, *Vision in the Desert,* p. 263.

49. Charles Coate, "The Biggest Water Fight in American History: Stewart Udall and the Central Arizona Project," *Journal for the Southwest,* Spring 1995, p. 92.

50. Morris K. Udall, *Education,* p. 155.

51. Robert Dean, "Dam Building Still Had Some Magic Then," *Pacific Historical Review,* February 1, 1997, p. 97.

52. Charles Coate, "The Biggest Water Fight in American History: Stewart Udall and the Central Arizona Project," *Journal for the Southwest,* Spring 1995, p. 101.

53. Fradkin, *River No More,* p. 253.

54. Charles Coate, "The Biggest Water Fight in American History: Stewart

Udall and the Central Arizona Project," *Journal for the Southwest,* Spring 1995, p. 93.

55. Byron Eugene Pearson, "People above Scenery: The Struggle over the Grand Canyon Dams, 1963–1968," doctoral dissertation, 1998 (Department of History, University of Arizona, Tucson), p. 233.

56. Morris K. Udall, "The CAP Is Signed—This Is Next Year," *Congressman's Report,* October 10, 1968, Morris K. Udall Papers, Special Collections, University of Arizona Library, Tucson.

57. Byron Eugene Pearson, "People above Scenery: The Struggle over the Grand Canyon Dams, 1963–1968," doctoral dissertation, 1998 (Department of History, University of Arizona, Tucson), p. 234.

CHAPTER 14. FINISHING THE JOB

1. "Statement of Congressman Morris K. Udall, Departmental Water Projects Review Team," *Congressional Record,* March 21, 1977, p. 1.

2. Bill Richards, "Udall Presses for Huge Project," *Washington Post,* March 20, 1977.

3. Ibid.

4. J. Dicken Kirschten, "Draining the Water Projects Out of the Pork Barrel," *The National Journal,* April 9, 1977, pp. 540–548.

5. Ibid.

6. Bill Richards, "Udall Presses for Huge Project," *Washington Post,* March 20, 1977.

7. Fradkin, *River No More,* p. 10.

8. Bill Richards, "Udall Presses for Huge Project," *Washington Post,* March 20, 1977.

9. Wiley and Gottlieb, *Empires in the Sun,* p. 57.

10. "Arizona Officials Sacrifice Dam for Water Project," *The National Journal,* March 26, 1977, p. 483.

11. Ibid.

12. Fradkin, *River No More,* pp. 10–11.

13. Sheila Caudle, "New Interior Secretary Watt Worries Mo on Environment," *Tucson Citizen,* June 3, 1981.

14. "Watt May Block Aqueduct unless Udall OKs GOP Issues," *Tucson Citizen,* June 26, 1981.

15. Ibid.

16. David S. Broder, "Watt Tells of Making Threat to Udall," *Washington Post,* August 19, 1981.

17. John H. Jennrich, "Watt, Center of Controversy, Pushes Access to Federal Land," *Oil & Gas Journal,* September 28, 1981, p. 137.

18. "Udall Reiterates Watt: 'A Tragedy for the Country,' " news release, August 19, 1981, Morris K. Udall Papers, Special Collections, University of Arizona Library, Tucson.

19. Ben Cole, "Angry Udall Denies Watt Has 'Cowed' Him," *Arizona Republic,* August 20, 1981.

20. J. J. Casserly, "Feud with Udall Over; Watt OKs Tucson Aqueduct," *Arizona Republic,* September 12, 1981.

21. "A Statement from Congressman Morris K. Udall," news release, October 10, 1983, Morris K. Udall Papers, Special Collections, University of Arizona Library, Tucson.

22. Henry C. Kenski Jr. interview with the authors.

23. Remarks by Morris K. Udall at the CAP dedication, November 15, 1985, Morris K. Udall Papers, Special Collections, University of Arizona Library, Tucson.

24. Robert Dean, "Dam Building Still Had Some Magic Then," *Pacific Historical Review,* February 1, 1997, p. 81.

25. David S. Broder, "Can Emmett McLoughlin Defeat Mo Udall, Ron Asta, the No-Growth Movement and . . . ," *Tucson Daily Citizen,* July 5, 1975.

26. Frances Gendlin, "A Talk with Mo Udall," *Sierra* magazine, July/August 1982.

27. "Udalls Prod Environmentalists to Tackle Growth Water Issues," *Arizona Daily Star,* April 14, 1987.

28. "The Grand Plans of Congressman Udall," *Sierra* magazine, May/June 1989.

29. Stewart L. Udall interview, Oral History Project.

30. "Original CAP Plan Didn't Include Urban Growth," *Tucson Citizen,* November 13, 1999.

31. Ibid.

32. Stewart L. Udall, *Quiet Crisis,* p. 208.

33. Robert Dean, "Dam Building Still Had Some Magic Then," *Pacific Historical Review,* February 1, 1997, p. 98.

CHAPTER 15. THE HUMOROUS MO

1. James W. Johnson, "Mo Udall's Clean, Quick Wit," *Tucson Monthly,* September 1998, p. 37.

2. E-mail from R. Kent Burton to Donald W. Carson, May 19, 1998.

3. Rhodes Cook, "Mo Udall Takes Politics with a Grain of Humor," *Congressional Quarterly,* August 18, 1990, p. 2698.

4. Larry L. King interview with the authors.

5. Marian Christy, "Laughter Is Udall's Medicine," *Boston Globe,* February 17, 1988.

6. E-mail from Anne Scott to James W. Johnson, July 13, 1999.

7. Morris K. Udall, "Mo Udall: Humor Helps," *Washington Post,* February 24, 1983.

8. Morris K. Udall, *Too Funny,* p. xiii.

9. J. Randolph Udall interview with the authors.

10. John B. Anderson interview, Oral History Project.

11. Morris K. Udall, "Mo Udall: Humor Helps," *Washington Post,* February 24, 1983.

12. Morris, K. Udall, *Too Funny,* p. xvi.

13. James W. Johnson, "Mo Udall's Clean, Quick Wit," *Tucson Monthly,* September 1998, p. 38.

14. Ibid.

15. Aaron Latham, "Will Rogers Is Running for President," *New York* magazine, December 1974, p. 91.

16. James W. Johnson, "Mo Udall's Clean, Quick Wit," *Tucson Monthly,* September 1998, p. 39.

17. Myra MacPherson, "Mo Udall, Triumph of the Good Guy," *Washington Post,* December 29, 1985.

18. Donald W. Carson, notes taken at March 4, 1999, memorial service for Morris K. Udall, Washington, D.C.

19. MacPherson, *Power Lovers,* p. 241.

20. Morris K. Udall, "Mo Udall: Humor Helps," *Washington Post,* February 24, 1983.

21. As told to James W. Johnson, September 28, 1998.

22. Ibid.

23. Told at a Saints and Sinners dinner in Washington, D.C., March 9, 1978.

24. Morris K. Udall, *Too Funny,* p. 92.

25. Ibid., p. 83.

26. Ibid., p. 216.

27. Morris K. Udall, "Mo Udall: Humor Helps," *Washington Post,* February 24, 1983.

28. Rhodes Cook, "Mo Udall Takes Politics with a Grain of Humor," *Congressional Quarterly,* August 18, 1990, p. 2698.

CHAPTER 16. MO'S AUDACITY

1. Morris K. Udall speech to the National Press Club, February 9, 1983, Morris K. Udall Papers, Special Collections, University of Arizona Library, Tucson.

2. From a draft of an introduction to an unfinished book by Morris K. Udall on the 1976 presidential campaign, undated, Morris K. Udall Papers, Special Collections, University of Arizona Library, Tucson.

3. Martin Schram, "Udall Won't Seek Presidency in '84; Time, Financial Constraints Cited," *Washington Post,* February 10, 1983.

4. Charles E. Ares interview with the authors.

5. Joseph Stocker, "Why Udall Wants to Run," *The Nation,* February 15, 1975, p. 173.

6. Witcover, *Marathon,* p. 139.

7. Henry S. Reuss interview with the authors.

8. David R. Obey interview with the authors.

9. Terrence L. Bracy interview with the authors.

10. A joint statement by House members, November 27, 1974, Morris K. Udall Papers, Special Collections, University of Arizona Library, Tucson.

11. Janet Hook, "House to White House: How Tough a Trail?" *Congressional Quarterly,* May 10, 1986, p. 1028.

12. James M. Perry, "And Now, the Man Who . . . Mo Udall!" *National Observer,* October 12, 1974.

13. Janet Hook, "House to White House: How Tough a Trail?" *Congressional Quarterly,* May 10, 1986, p. 1025.

14. David S. Broder, "The House Gets No Respect," *Washington Post,* December 6, 1987.

15. Janet Hook, "House to White House: How Tough a Trail?" *Congressional Quarterly,* May 10, 1986, p. 1028.

16. From a draft of an introduction to an unfinished book by Morris K. Udall on the 1976 presidential campaign, undated, Morris K. Udall Papers, Special Collections, University of Arizona Library, Tucson.

17. Arthur Hadley, "Can a Congressman from a Small State out West . . . ?" *The Atlantic,* December 1974, p. 19.

18. "Udall: A Long Campaign for Recognition," *Congressional Quarterly,* November 22, 1975, p. 2538.

19. Barry Farrell, "Morris Udall: Playing by Winners' Rules," *The Progressive,* December 1975, p. 26.

20. Memorandum from John B. Gabusi to Stewart L. Udall, January 1975, Morris K. Udall Papers, Special Collections, University of Arizona Library, Tucson.

21. Memorandum from Morris K. Udall to his staff, February 11, 1975, Morris K. Udall Papers, Special Collections, University of Arizona Library, Tucson.

22. Witcover, *Marathon,* p. 203.

23. Joseph Stocker, "Why Udall Wants to Run," *The Nation,* February 15, 1975, p. 172.

24. Notes made by Morris K. Udall for an unfinished book on the 1976 presidential campaign, September 8, 1976, Morris K. Udall Papers, Special Collections, University of Arizona Library, Tucson.

25. Marilyn Evans, "Mo's Race Stays in the Family," *Tucson Citizen,* October 23, 1980.

26. Ibid.

27. Notes made by Morris K. Udall for an unfinished book on the 1976 presidential campaign, September 8, 1976, Morris K. Udall Papers, Special Collections, University of Arizona Library, Tucson.

28. Ibid.

29. John B. Gabusi interview with the authors, September 21, 1998.

30. Hadley, *Invisible Primary,* p. 19.

31. Ibid.

32. Mike Barnes, "Udall for President: No Laughing Matter," *Democratic Review,* June/July 1975, p. 17.

33. James R. Dickenson, "Udall Seeks Poker Chips," *Washington Star-News,* October 2, 1974.

34. Ibid.

35. Milton Viorst, "Take Mo Seriously," *Washington Star-News,* May 30, 1974.

36. Hadley, *Invisible Primary,* p. 21.

37. Robert A. Neuman interview with the authors.

38. Iris Jacobson Burnett interview with the authors.

39. Robert A. Neuman interview with the authors.

40. Iris Jacobson Burnett interview with the authors.

41. Edward F. Coyle interview with the authors.

42. Iris Jacobson Burnett interview with the authors.

43. Hadley, *Invisible Primary,* p. 20.

44. Ibid., p. 21.

45. Memorandum from Terrence L. Bracy to Stewart L. Udall, Morris K. Udall, and John B. Gabusi, December 30, 1974, Morris K. Udall Papers, Special Collections, University of Arizona Library, Tucson.

46. Aaron Latham, "Will Rogers Is Running for President," *New York* magazine, December 1974.

47. Memorandum from Terrence L. Bracy to Stewart L. Udall, Morris K. Udall, and John B. Gabusi, December 30, 1974, Morris K. Udall Papers, Special Collections, University of Arizona Library, Tucson.

48. Mike Barnes, "Udall for President: No Laughing Matter," *Democratic Review,* June/July 1975, p. 17.

49. Memorandum from Stewart L. Udall to Morris K. Udall, January 19, 1975, Morris K. Udall Papers, Special Collections, University of Arizona Library, Tucson.

50. Mike Barnes, "Udall for President: No Laughing Matter," *Democratic Review,* June/July 1975, p. 17.

51. Memorandum from Stewart L. Udall to Morris K. Udall, January 19, 1975, Morris K. Udall Papers, Special Collections, University of Arizona Library, Tucson.

52. Myron S. Waldman, "Udall's Plan: Look Liberal, Talk Moderate," *Arizona Republic,* February 16, 1975.

53. Memorandum from Terrence L. Bracy to Morris K. Udall, March 4, 1975, Morris K. Udall Papers, Special Collections, University of Arizona Library, Tucson.

54. David S. Broder interview, Oral History Project.

55. "Where's Franklin Fitzgerald Jones?" *Time* magazine, August 25, 1975, p. 17.

56. Mike Barnes, "Udall for President: No Laughing Matter," *Democratic Review,* June/July 1975, p. 17.

57. Iris Jacobson Burnett interview with the authors.

58. Memorandum from John B. Gabusi to Stewart L. Udall and Stanley Kurz, March 31, 1975, Morris K. Udall Papers, Special Collections, University of Arizona Library, Tucson.

59. Memorandum from Stewart L. Udall to Morris K. Udall, June 24, 1975, Morris K. Udall Papers, Special Collections, University of Arizona Library, Tucson.

60. "From House to White House—Udall Aims for the Big Jump," *U.S. News & World Report,* August 18, 1975, p. 40.

61. Terrence L. Bracy interview with the authors.

62. Robert A. Reveles interview with the authors.

63. Medical reports of the presidential candidates, *Medical World News,* February 9, 1976.

64. Jerome H. Targovnik interview with the authors, October 16, 1998.

65. Memorandum from Bonnie Kell to Morris K. Udall, August 30, 1976, Morris K. Udall Papers, Special Collections, University of Arizona Library, Tucson.

66. E-mail message from Terrence L. Bracy to James W. Johnson, July 27, 1999.

67. Ibid.

68. Notes made by Morris K. Udall for an unfinished book on the 1976 presidential campaign, September 8, 1976, Morris K. Udall Papers, Special Collections, University of Arizona Library, Tucson.

69. Ibid.

70. Edward F. Coyle interview with the authors.

71. Report on media brainstorming session, November 14, 1975, Morris K. Udall Papers, Special Collections, University of Arizona Library, Tucson.

72. Schram, *Running for President*, p. 17.

73. Confidential memorandum from Jack Quinn to Morris K. Udall, November 19, 1975, Morris K. Udall Papers, Special Collections, University of Arizona Library, Tucson.

74. Memorandum from Curtis B. Gans to Morris K. Udall, November 24, 1975, Morris K. Udall Papers, Special Collections, University of Arizona Library, Tucson.

75. Terrence L. Bracy interview with the authors.

76. Chanin and Chanin, *This Land*, p. 129.

77. Terrence L. Bracy interview with the authors.

78. Medical reports of the presidential candidates, *Medical World News*, February 9, 1976.

79. Elizabeth Drew, "Our Far-Flung Correspondents," *The New Yorker*, December 1, 1975, pp. 54–118.

80. E-mail from Terrence L. Bracy to James W. Johnson, July 27, 1999.

81. "A House Is Not a Home," *Newsweek*, December 8, 1975.

82. Memorandum from Stewart L. Udall to Morris K. Udall, undated, Morris K. Udall Papers, Special Collections, University of Arizona Library, Tucson.

83. "Udall: The Sage," *Time*, April 12, 1976.

84. Gold, *PR as in President*, p. 154.

85. Douglas E. Kneeland, "Udall Seeking to Outstrip 'Liberal Pack,' " *New York Times*, January 1, 1976.

CHAPTER 17. SECOND-PLACE MO

1. "Udall Denies He Seeks Fannin's Senate Seat," *New York Times*, December 31, 1975.

2. Ben Cole, "Udall Links Loss to Forecast of Brokered Convention," *Arizona Republic*, June 12, 1976.

3. Memorandum from Roger K. Lewis to Morris K. Udall, February 27, 1976, Morris K. Udall Papers, Special Collections, University of Arizona Library, Tucson.

4. Schram, *Running for President*, p. 15.

5. James W. Johnson, "Mo's Quick, Clean Wit," *Tucson Monthly,* September 1998, p. 37.

6. Palmer, *New Hampshire Primary,* p. 17.

7. Moore and Fraser, *Campaign for President,* p. 84.

8. Chanin and Chanin, *This Land,* p. 129.

9. Davis, *Presidential Primaries,* p. 84.

10. Witcover, *Marathon,* p. 229.

11. From a draft of an introduction to an unfinished book by Morris K. Udall on the 1976 presidential campaign, undated, Morris K. Udall Papers, Special Collections, University of Arizona Library, Tucson.

12. Palmer, *New Hampshire Primary,* p. 17.

13. Brereton, *First in the Nation,* p. 181.

14. Palmer, *New Hampshire Primary,* p. 109.

15. Witcover, *Marathon,* p. 239.

16. John B. Gabusi interview with the authors, September 21, 1998.

17. George Will, "The Loneliness of the Long-Distance Liberal," *Newsweek,* May 3, 1976.

18. Stroud, *How Jimmy Won,* p. 247.

19. Schram, *Running for President,* p. 19.

20. Lasky, *Jimmy Carter,* pp. 186–187.

21. Gerry Gersten, "Udall," *New Times,* February 20, 1976.

22. Stewart L. Udall interview with the authors, July 18, 1998.

23. Gerry Gersten, "Udall," *New Times,* February 20, 1976. ˙

24. Davis, *Presidential Primaries,* p. 216.

25. "Shooting from Left Center," *Time,* March 15, 1976, p. 15.

26. "It's a Democratic Dogfight," *U.S. News & World Report,* March 15, 1976, p. 13.

27. Ken Bode, "The Primary Portents," *The New Republic,* March 27, 1976, p. 4.

28. Schram, *Running for President,* p. 112.

29. Ibid., p. 113.

30. Witcover, *Marathon,* p. 276.

31. Schram, *Running for President,* p. 114.

32. Jack Quinn interview with the authors.

33. Witcover, *Marathon,* p. 286.

34. Fred R. Harris interview with the authors.

35. Stroud, *How Jimmy Won,* p. 282.

36. David R. Obey interview with the authors.

37. Reuss, *When Government Was Good,* p. 172.

38. Schram, *Running for President,* p. 118.

39. Patterson, *Mass Media Election,* p. 46.

40. Morris K. Udall, *Too Funny,* p. 30.

41. Reuss, *When Government Was Good,* p. 172.

42. Memorandum from Jessica Tuchman to Morris K. Udall, April 16, 1976, Morris K. Udall Papers, Special Collections, University of Arizona Library, Tucson.

43. Outline for an unfinished book by Morris K. Udall on the 1976 presidential campaign, undated, Morris K. Udall Papers, Special Collections, University of Arizona Library, Tucson.

44. Witcover, *Marathon,* p. 276.

45. Moore and Fraser, *Campaign for President,* p. 90.

46. Notes made by Morris K. Udall for an unfinished book on the 1976 presidential campaign, September 8, 1976, Morris K. Udall Papers, Special Collections, University of Arizona Library, Tucson.

47. Schram, *Running for President,* p. 118.

48. Palmer, *New Hampshire Primary,* p. 110.

49. Peter Goldman, "Carter's Trip of the Tongue," *Newsweek,* April 19, 1976, p. 14.

50. Memorandum from Peter Hart to Morris K. Udall, undated, but probably about March 17, 1976, Morris K. Udall Papers, Special Collections, University of Arizona Library, Tucson.

51. Schram, *Running for President,* p. 126.

52. *Addresses and Special Orders,* p. 67.

53. David R. Obey interview with the authors.

54. Ibid.

55. Mark Shields interview with the authors.

56. "Udall: The Sage," *Time,* April 12, 1976, p. 16.

57. Peter Goldman, "Carter's Trip of the Tongue," *Newsweek,* April 19, 1976, p. 14.

58. Schram, *Running for President,* pp. 147–148.

59. Moore and Fraser, *Campaign for President,* p. 104.

60. Witcover, *Marathon,* p. 207.

61. Schram, *Running for President,* p. 148.

62. Morris K. Udall memorandum for book project file and book editor Helen Braun, August 12, 1976, Morris K. Udall Papers, Special Collections, University of Arizona Library, Tucson.

63. Schram, *Running for President,* p. 148.

64. "Udall Gets Mayor's Apology," *Arizona Daily Star,* August 6, 1976.

65. David R. Obey interview with the authors.

66. Peter Goldman, "Can Anyone Stop Carter?" *Newsweek,* May 31, 1976.

67. Schram, *Running for President,* p. 173.

68. McGovern, *Autobiography,* p. 264.

69. Daniel Chu, "Ol' Second-Place Mo," *Newsweek,* June 7, 1976, p. 21.

70. Terry Bracy, "Udall—Private Citizen," *Arizona Daily Star,* July 12, 1976.

71. Schram, *Running for President,* p. 176.

72. Ben Cole, "Udall Links Loss to Forecast of Brokered Convention," *Arizona Republic,* June 12, 1976.

73. Morris K. Udall, "Yes, the Press Has Been Fair," undated paper, Morris K. Udall Papers, Special Collections, University of Arizona Library, Tucson.

74. Edward F. Coyle interview with the authors.

75. Morris K. Udall, *Too Funny,* p. 43.

76. Witcover, *Marathon,* p. 344.

77. Memorandum from Morris K. Udall to Robert A. Neuman on political humor, October 15, 1976, Morris K. Udall Papers, Special Collections, University of Arizona Library, Tucson.

78. Daniel Chu, "Ol' Second-Place Mo," *Newsweek,* June 7, 1976, p. 21.

79. Notes made by Morris K. Udall for an unfinished book on the 1976 presidential campaign, September 8, 1976, Morris K. Udall Papers, Special Collections, University of Arizona Library, Tucson.

80. Thompson, *Never President,* p. 125.

81. News release, July 16, 1976, Morris K. Udall Papers, Special Collections, University of Arizona Library, Tucson.

82. Davis, *Presidential Primaries,* p. 113.

83. Ibid., p. 205.

84. Richard Reeves, *Convention,* pp. 8–9.

85. Anne Udall, "A Daughter's Fond Memories," *Arizona Law Record,* Fall 1991.

86. Martin Nolan, " 'Bridesmaid' Udall Leaves Them Cheering," *Boston Globe,* July 15, 1976.

87. David Espo, "Mondale Hoping Udall Will Show Hart the Way," Associated Press, June 12, 1984.

88. From a copy of a speech by Morris K. Udall releasing his delegates, July 14, 1976, Morris K. Udall Papers, Special Collections, University of Arizona Library, Tucson.

89. Drew, *American Journal,* p. 305.

90. Outline for an unfinished book by Morris K. Udall on the 1976 presidential campaign, undated, Morris K. Udall Papers, Special Collections, University of Arizona Library, Tucson.

91. Memorandum prepared by Morris K. Udall for a book on the 1976 presidential campaign, August 30, 1976, Morris K. Udall Papers, Special Collections, University of Arizona Library, Tucson.

92. Memorandum from Maria Carrier to Stewart L. Udall, November 17,

1975, Morris K. Udall Papers, Special Collections, University of Arizona Library, Tucson.

93. "Humor for New York," undated, Morris K. Udall Papers, Special Collections, University of Arizona Library, Tucson.

94. Larry L. King, "Unbowed Udall," *Washington Post,* July 14, 1976.

95. Outline for an unfinished book by Morris K. Udall on the 1976 presidential campaign, undated, Morris K. Udall Papers, Special Collections, University of Arizona Library, Tucson.

96. Ibid.

97. Edward F. Coyle interview with the authors.

98. Chanin and Chanin, *This Land,* p. 132.

99. Morris K. Udall memorandum to "Files," November 19, 1976, Morris K. Udall Papers, Special Collections, University of Arizona Library, Tucson.

100. King, *Of Outlaws,* p. 210.

CHAPTER 18. KEEPING THE HOPES ALIVE

1. Adam Clymer, "Kennedy Leads Carter 53% to 40% as Democrats' 1980 Choice in Poll," *New York Times,* May 7, 1978.

2. Morris K. Udall endorsement of Senator Ted Kennedy for the 1980 Democratic presidential nomination, December 18, 1979, Morris K. Udall Papers, Special Collections, University of Arizona Library, Tucson.

3. Charles Stafford, "An Untold Story of Campaign '80," *St. Petersburg Times,* February 16, 1981.

4. Ibid.

5. "Udall Said to Have Rejected Notion of Running with Anderson," Associated Press, May 8, 1980.

6. Bisnow, *Diary of a Dark Horse,* p. 235.

7. Warren Weaver Jr., "Master of Art of Compromise," New York Times Biographical Service, August 1980.

8. Tom Raum, "Democratic Keynoter Sees His Role as Party's Conciliator," Associated Press, August 11, 1980.

9. Ibid.

10. Warren Weaver Jr., "Master of Art of Compromise," New York Times Biographical Service, August 1980.

11. Ward Sinclair, "Keynoter Udall: Reformer and Mediator," *Washington Post,* August 11, 1980.

12. Steve Meissner, "Udall Not Running, Period—But . . . ," *Arizona Daily Star,* July 11, 1982.

13. "Udall Says He's Physically Fit Except for 'Terminal Indecision,' " *Washington Post,* December 4, 1982.

14. Donald M. Rothberg, "Rep. Udall Cites 'Political Realities': Won't Enter '84 Race for President," *Philadelphia Inquirer,* February 10, 1983.

15. Curtis Wilkie, "Anatomy of a 'Wrenching' Choice," *Boston Globe,* February 10, 1983.

16. Ibid.

17. Terrence L. Bracy interview with the authors.

18. "Udall: A Matter of Health," *New York Times,* December 9, 1982; memorandum from Bruce A. Wright to Morris K. Udall, December 9, 1982, Morris K. Udall Papers, Special Collections, University of Arizona Library, Tucson.

19. John DeWitt, "Udall Nears Decision on Presidency," *Arizona Daily Star,* January 6, 1983.

20. Chris Collins, "For Udall, It All Boiled Down to a Single Word: No," *Tucson Citizen,* February 9, 1983.

21. Steve Meissner, "Udall Keeping His Plans a Secret," *Arizona Daily Star,* January 9, 1983.

22. Marvin S. Cohen interview with the authors.

23. Martin Schram, "Mo Weighs 'Presidentialitis,' Parkinson's," *Tucson Citizen,* January 27, 1983.

24. Perry G. Baker interview with the authors, February 4, 1999.

25. Curtis Wilkie, "Anatomy of a 'Wrenching' Choice," *Boston Globe,* February 10, 1983.

26. Chris Collins, "For Udall, It All Boiled Down to a Single Word: No," *Tucson Citizen,* February 9, 1983.

27. Howell Raines, "Udall Says He Will Not Seek Presidential Nomination in 1984," *New York Times,* February 10, 1983.

28. From a collection of typed excerpts from stories that appeared in newspapers or syndicates, Morris K. Udall Papers, Special Collections, University of Arizona Library, Tucson.

29. Richard DeUriarte, "Udall Opens Favorite Son Campaign," *Arizona Republic,* July 4, 1983.

30. "Udall Withdraws '84 Favorite-Son Presidential Candidacy," *Arizona Daily Wildcat,* February 3, 1984.

31. Jake Henshaw, "Udall's '76 Presidential Campaign Recalled by Washington Backers," *Tucson Citizen,* October 28, 1985.

CHAPTER 19. SAVING THE ENVIRONMENT

1. Jacobs, *A Rage for Justice,* pp. 330–331.

2. Roy S. Jones Jr. interview with the authors, October 17, 1998.

3. Austin and Borrelli, *Strip Mining of America,* p. 8.

4. Donald A. Crane interview with the authors.

5. John F. Seiberling interview, Oral History Project.

6. "Strip-Mining Bill OK'd; Veto Vowed," New York Times News Service, *Arizona Daily Star,* December 14, 1974.

7. "Strip Mining Bill Cleared, Faces Veto," *Congressional Quarterly,* December 21, 1974, p. 3383.

8. "Ford Will Veto Strip-Mine Bill; Udall Outraged," Associated Press, *Arizona Daily Star,* May 20, 1975.

9. Morris K. Udall, text of closing floor speech on strip-mine override, June 10, 1975, Morris K. Udall Papers, Special Collections, University of Arizona Library, Tucson.

10. "Rules Committee Kills Strip Mining, Clears Synfuels," *Congressional Quarterly,* September 18, 1976, p. 2503.

11. Loretta Neumann interview with the authors.

12. Donald A. Crane, written response, July 26, 1999.

13. Rochelle L. Stanfield, "Lit by Mo's Wit," *The National Journal,* May 16, 1987, p. 1276.

14. Ben A. Franklin, "Decade after Strip Mine Law: Successes and Some Setbacks," *New York Times,* August 3, 1987.

15. Charles H. Callison, "It's High Time to Scuttle the Giveaway Mining Law," *The Living Wilderness,* January 1979, p. 4.

16. J. C. Martin, "Udall Gives Defense of Mine Bill," *Arizona Daily Star,* April 14, 1971.

17. Morris K. Udall, "The Mining Law of 1977; H.R. 5806: For a Healthy Mining Industry," May 24, 1977, Morris K. Udall Papers, Special Collections, University of Arizona Library, Tucson.

18. Ibid.

19. Ibid.

20. R. Kent Burton, written response, February 22, 1999.

21. Christina Collins, "Udall Papers Miss Deadline; Udall Says They Don't Exist," *Tucson Citizen,* January 12, 1978.

22. C. J. Hansen, "Mo Udall and the Miners," *Pay Dirt,* May 1991, p. 16B.

23. Stewart L. Udall interview with the authors, July 18, 1998.

24. R. Kent Burton, written response, February 22, 1999.

25. C. Stanley Sloss interview with the authors.

26. Morris K. Udall, "Statement on Nuclear Power," April 8, 1976, Morris K. Udall Papers, Special Collections, University of Arizona Library, Tucson.

27. Henry R. Myers interview with the authors.

28. Paul Parshley interview with the authors.

29. Ibid.

30. Victor Gilinsky interview with the authors.

31. Henry R. Myers and Paul Parshley interviews with the authors.

32. Victor Gilinsky interview with the authors.

33. Morris K. Udall, "Nuclear's Future Hinges on 'Public Confidence,'" *Business Week,* December 25, 1978, p. 66.

34. Andrea Dravo interview with the authors.

35. Rochelle L. Stanfield, "Behind the Hill's Nuclear Brawl," *The National Journal,* October 17, 1987, p. 2610.

36. Linda Keene, "Nuclear-Waste Site Delay Is Endorsed by House Unit," States News Service, July 1, 1987.

37. Andrea Dravo interview with the authors.

CHAPTER 20. ALASKA'S CROWN JEWELS

1. John F. Seiberling interview, Oral History Project.

2. Morris K. Udall, *Too Funny,* pp. 75–76.

3. "Carter Acts to Preserve Alaskan Wilderness," *Congressional Quarterly Almanac,* 1978, p. 725.

4. Julius Duscha, "How the Alaska Act Was Won," *The Living Wilderness,* Spring 1981, pp. 4–9.

5. Hammond, *Bush Rat Governor,* p. 244.

6. Peter Barnes, "Unfreezing Alaska," *The New Republic,* September 11, 1971, p. 15.

7. Morris K. Udall, memorandum to House colleagues, October 15, 1971, Morris K. Udall Papers, Special Collections, University of Arizona Library, Tucson.

8. Don Young interview with the authors.

9. John F. Seiberling interview with the authors.

10. "Well-Organized Environmental Lobby," *Congressional Quarterly Almanac,* 1979, p. 666.

11. John F. Seiberling interview with the authors.

12. "Carter Acts to Preserve Alaskan Wilderness," *Congressional Quarterly Almanac,* 1978, p. 727.

13. Loretta Neumann and C. Stanley Sloss interviews with the authors.

14. Lloyd Meeds, Loretta Neumann, and C. Stanley Sloss interviews with the authors.

15. John F. Seiberling interview, Oral History Project.

16. Roy S. Jones Jr. interview with the authors, October 21, 1998.

17. "Carter Acts to Preserve Alaskan Wilderness," *Congressional Quarterly Almanac,* 1978, p. 729.

18. Ibid., p. 735.

19. Ibid., p. 736.

20. Ibid., p. 740.

21. Dennis Farney, "House Panel Chairmen, Their Powers Reduced, Use Guile, Persuasion," *Wall Street Journal,* May 3, 1979.

22. Years later in an August 7, 1998, interview with Julie Ferdon of the Morris K. Udall Oral History Project, Anderson said he became a co-sponsor only because his friend wanted a Republican name on the bill to make it bipartisan. "I deserve no credit," Anderson said, adding that he never even went to Alaska.

23. Roy S. Jones Jr. interview with the authors.

24. Ibid.

25. "House Passes Alaska Bill but Senate Stymied," *Congressional Quarterly,* 1979, p. 677.

26. "Congress Clears Alaska Lands Legislation," *Congressional Quarterly,* 1980, p. 580.

27. Ibid., p. 583.

28. Ibid.

29. Ibid., p. 584.

30. Mark F. Trautwein interview, Oral History Project.

31. William Kronholm, "Environmentalists Yield on Alaska Lands Bill," Associated Press, November 12, 1980.

32. James M. Perry, "This Fella from Arizona," *Audubon,* November 1981, pp. 64–73.

33. William Kronholm, "Environmentalists Yield on Alaska Lands Bill," Associated Press, November 12, 1980.

34. Kathy Koch, "Alaska Lobbying: Using the Silver Spoon," *Congressional Quarterly,* August 9, 1980, p. 2297.

35. William Kronholm, "Conservationists Unwilling to Take Chances with New Congress," Associated Press, November 12, 1980.

36. Frances Gendlin, "A Talk with Mo Udall," *Sierra* magazine, July/August 1982, pp. 23–26.

37. Hammond, *Bush Rat Governor,* p. 244.

38. Julie E. Kitka, president of the Alaska Federation of Natives, remarks at a Washington, D.C., memorial service for Morris K. Udall, March 4, 1999.

39. James W. Johnson, "Mo's Quick, Clean Wit," *Tucson Monthly,* September 1998, pp. 35–39.

40. Morris K. Udall, *Too Funny,* pp. 69–70.

CHAPTER 21. A FRIEND TO THE INDIAN

1. Stewart L. Udall, memorial service eulogy for Morris K. Udall, January 16, 1999, Tucson.

2. John McCain, "Mo Udall: True Friend of Indian Tribes," *Arizona Daily Star*, May 3, 1991.

3. Patricia E. Udall, written response, July 12, 1999.

4. Morris K. Udall, "The American Indians and Civil Rights," speech given at American University, October 4, 1965, Morris K. Udall Papers, Special Collections, University of Arizona Library, Tucson.

5. Franklin D. Ducheneaux interview with the authors.

6. Franklin D. Ducheneaux remarks in *Addresses and Special Orders*, pp. 79–81.

7. Colman McCarthy, "Reopening the Drain on Indians' Legacy," *Washington Post*, July 16, 1996.

8. Franklin D. Ducheneaux interview with the authors.

9. Ibid.

10. Morris K. Udall, "The Navajo and the Hopi: No Villains, Only Victims," *Washington Post*, June 23, 1986.

11. Mark Sullivan, "Hopi Leader, U.S. Official Criticize Plan," States News Service, *Arizona Daily Star*, May 9, 1986.

12. Mark Sullivan, unheadlined story, States News Service, June 5, 1986.

13. "Navajos on Hopi Land Won't Face Eviction," Associated Press, *Arizona Daily Star*, April 1, 1997.

14. Vickie Chachere, unheadlined story, States News Service, September 13, 1988.

15. Deborah Sliz interview with the authors.

16. Emily Benedek, "Thy Will Be Done," *Arizona Trend*, November 1988, pp. 36–43.

17. Mark Sullivan, unheadlined story, States News Service, October 3, 1985.

CHAPTER 22. THE CONSENSUS BUILDER

1. Ward Sinclair, "Keynoter Udall: Reformer and Mediator," *Washington Post*, August 11, 1980.

2. Myra MacPherson, "Mo Udall, Triumph of the Good Guy," *Washington Post*, December 29, 1985.

3. Ward Sinclair, "Keynoter Udall: Reformer and Mediator," *Washington Post*, August 11, 1980.

4. Ehrenhalt, *Politics in America*, p. 54.

5. Joseph A. Davis, "The Grand Plans of Congressman Udall," *Sierra* magazine, May/June 1989, p. 87.

6. Ibid., p. 91.

7. Matt James interview with the authors.

8. Robert L. Dolezal, "Quarter of a Century," *Tucson Weekly*, September 30, 1987, p. 6.

9. Patricia S. Schroeder interview with the authors.

10. Anne Scott interview with the authors.

11. Davidson and Oleszek, *Congress and Its Members,* p. 69.

12. Ibid., p. 116.

13. Four-page fund-raising letter, "Dear Friend," undated, Morris K. Udall Papers, Special Collections, University of Arizona Library, Tucson.

14. Bill Shaw, "Udall Showing Teeth, Muscle in Re-election Bid," *Arizona Daily Star,* September 2, 1978.

15. Jack W. Germond and Jules Witcover, "Udall: An American Winner," *Courier-Journal* (Louisville, Kentucky), April 24, 1991.

16. "The Great Congressional Power Grab," *Business Week,* September 11, 1978, p. 91.

17. Jack W. Germond and Jules Witcover, "Carter Had Good Reasons for Making Udall More Welcome," *Washington Star,* May 4, 1978.

18. James M. Perry, "This Fella from Arizona," *Audubon,* November 1981, pp. 64–73.

19. "Movers and Shakers in the Capitol," *U.S. News & World Report,* January 14, 1980, p. 40.

20. *Washingtonian,* October 1980; October 7, 1980, campaign literature, Morris K. Udall Papers, Special Collections, University of Arizona Library, Tucson.

21. Martin Tolchin, "Udall Re-election Imperiled by Newest Constituents," *New York Times,* October 30, 1980.

22. Ehrenhalt, *Politics in America,* p. 56.

23. Martin Tolchin, "Udall Re-election Imperiled by Newest Constituents," *New York Times,* October 30, 1980.

24. Ranney, *American Elections of 1980,* p. 289.

25. Helen Dewar, "Udall Facing the Toughest Challenge in His 20-Year House Career," *Washington Post,* October 15, 1980.

26. Henry C. Kenski Jr. and Bruce A. Wright interviews with the authors.

27. Henry C. Kenski Jr. interview with the authors.

28. Ranney, *American Elections of 1980,* p. 289.

29. April 24, 1980, campaign literature, Morris K. Udall Papers, Special Collections, University of Arizona Library, Tucson.

30. Helen Dewar, "Udall Facing the Toughest Challenge in His 20-Year House Career," *Washington Post,* October 15, 1980.

31. Letter from Barry M. Goldwater to George W. Elkins, April 16, 1980, Morris K. Udall Papers, Special Collections, University of Arizona Library, Tucson.

32. "Arizona District Plan Splits Udall's District," *New York Times,* December 4, 1981.

33. Ibid.

34. Tom Miller, *Arizona,* p. 214.

35. "Udall Is Deciding between Two Districts," *New York Times,* January 17, 1982.

36. Norma Coile, "Immigration Amendment Draws Heavy Fire," *Tucson Citizen,* June 20, 1984.

37. J. Daniel O'Neill interview with the authors.

38. Norma Coile, "Mo, McNulty See Hispanics," *Tucson Citizen,* July 3, 1984.

39. Ibid.

40. Norma Coile, "Udall, McNulty Hear Hispanics but Defend Vote," *Tucson Citizen,* July 12, 1984.

41. Isabel G. Garcia interview with the authors.

42. Anne Scott interview with the authors.

43. Morris K. Udall statement, October 17, 1986, Morris K. Udall Papers, Special Collections, University of Arizona Library, Tucson.

44. Stewart L. Udall interview with the authors, February 11, 1999.

45. Bruce A. Wright interview with the authors.

46. Henry C. Kenski Jr. interview with the authors.

47. Steve Meissner, "Setbacks Haven't Kept Mo Udall from Outstanding Career in Congress," *Arizona Daily Star,* June 16, 1985.

48. "Udall Caught in the Middle," *Tucson Citizen,* July 25, 1990.

49. Mark F. Trautwein interview with the authors.

50. Mark F. Trautwein interview, Oral History Project.

51. Anne Hazard, "Udall Cites 'Unfinished Business' before Last Swearing In," States News Service, January 3, 1991.

52. Mark F. Trautwein interview with the authors.

53. Stephen E. Emerine, "Owl Is Not at Risk," letter to the editor, *Arizona Daily Star,* July 8, 1999.

54. Hedrick Smith, *Power Game,* p. 54.

55. Stewart L. Udall, "Why I Won't Run for Office in Alice-in-Wonderland Time," *Los Angeles Times,* June 3, 1986.

56. "Stewart Udall Is Considering Run for Congress," *Arizona Daily Star,* March 16, 1986.

57. Stewart L. Udall interview with the authors, March 7, 1999.

58. Stewart L. Udall, "Why I Won't Run for Office in Alice-in-Wonderland Time," *Los Angeles Times,* June 3, 1986.

59. Mark F. Trautwein interview, Oral History Project.

60. Ibid.

61. "Bill Would Name Point in Guam after Mo Udall," *Arizona Daily Star,* May 16, 1987.

62. Rochelle L. Stanfield, "Behind the Hill's Nuclear Brawl," *The National Journal,* October 17, 1987, p. 2610.

63. Stewart L. Udall interview with the authors, February 11, 1999.

64. Mark F. Trautwein interview with the authors.

65. Phil Kurz, "Interior to Feel Firmer Touch after Udall's Gentle Hand," *Congressional Quarterly,* April 27, 1991, p. 1051.

66. Mark F. Trautwein interview, Oral History Project.

67. Robert A. Neuman interview with the authors.

68. Bruce A. Wright interview with the authors.

69. Morris K. Udall, speech to the Democrats of Greater Tucson, April 9, 1990, Morris K. Udall Papers, Special Collections, University of Arizona Library, Tucson.

70. Thomas C. Duddleston interview with the authors.

71. Ellen Gamerman, "House Interior Panel Head Plays Hardball," *Phoenix Gazette,* January 2, 1993.

72. Ellen Miller, "Udall Treated 'Shabbily,' Colo. Congressman Says," *Arizona Daily Star,* February 17, 1991.

73. Matt James interview with the authors.

74. Diane M. Targovnik interview with the authors.

75. Mark F. Trautwein interview with the authors.

76. Matt James interview with the authors.

77. Emily Benedek, "Thy Will Be Done," *Arizona Trend,* November 1988, p. 36.

78. Mark F. Trautwein interview, Oral History Project.

79. Diane Duston, "Leaving Job to Others, but First One More Term," Associated Press, June 4, 1990.

CHAPTER 23. THE PRICE THEY PAID

1. James F. McNulty Jr. interview, Oral History Project.

2. D. Burr Udall interview, Oral History Project.

3. Bruce A. Wright interview with the authors.

4. Larry L. King interview with the authors.

5. MacPherson, *Power Lovers.*

6. Eloise Udall Whiting and Warren G. Whiting interviews with the authors.

7. Patricia E. Udall interview with the authors.

8. Morris K. Udall, book proposal to Helen Braun, August 13, 1976, Morris K. Udall Papers, Special Collections, University of Arizona Library, Tucson.

9. Judith K. "Dodie" Udall, Anne J. Udall, and Katherine L. Udall interviews with the authors.

10. Morris K. Udall, "new draft" of a commencement address to the American University's Washington College of Law, May 18, 1986, courtesy R. Kent Burton.

11. Patricia E. Udall interview with the authors.

12. Chanin and Chanin, *This Land,* p. 127.

13. Patricia E. Udall interview with the authors.

14. Lee Udall, written statement to the authors, March 21, 1999.

15. Patricia E. Udall interview with the authors.

16. "Rep. Udall's Wife Seeks Divorce," *Arizona Daily Star,* November 20, 1965.

17. Richard C. Olson interview with the authors, July 21, 1999.

18. "Rep. Udall Announces Marriage," *Arizona Daily Star,* December 3, 1968.

19. Taken from a profile prepared for the 1976 presidential campaign, Morris K. Udall Papers, Special Collections, University of Arizona Library, Tucson.

20. Louise Sweeney, "Morris Udall's Candid Reluctant 'Tiger,' " *Christian Science Monitor,* November 28, 1975.

21. Larry L. King interview with the authors.

22. Larry L. King, letter to Ella Udall, December 18, 1974, courtesy Larry L. King.

23. Maxine Cheshire, "Concerning Foreign Gifts, Marriages," *Washington Post,* May 2, 1976.

24. Larry L. King, letter to Ella Udall, December 18, 1974, courtesy Larry L. King.

25. Larry L. King interview with the authors.

26. Rosemary Cribben interview with the authors.

27. Diane Rennert interview with the authors.

28. Ibid.

29. Lee Udall, written statement to the authors, March 21, 1999.

30. Iris Jacobson Burnett interview with the authors.

31. Marian S. Goodman interview with the authors.

32. Bruce A. Wright interview with the authors.

33. Diane Rennert interview with the authors.

34. Morris K. Udall, "Some Miscellaneous Observations for 1976 Book Project," July 19, 1976, Morris K. Udall Papers, Special Collections, University of Arizona Library, Tucson.

35. Marian S. Goodman interview with the authors.

36. J. Randolph Udall interview with the authors.

37. Iris Jacobson Burnett interview with the authors.

38. Diane Rennert and Rosemary Cribben interviews with the authors.

39. Sean Griffin, "From the Lip: Mo Known for Zinging Politics, Self with Wit," *Phoenix Gazette,* August 22, 1988.

40. Judith K. "Dodie" Udall interview with the authors.

41. Perry G. Baker interview with the authors, December 12, 1998.

42. Iris Jacobson Burnett interview with the authors.

43. Lee Udall, written statement to the authors, March 21, 1999.

44. Tom Shields, "Suicide of 'Mo' Udall's Wife Leaves Her Friends Mystified," *Tucson Citizen,* August 15, 1988; Lois Romano, "Ella Udall, Congressman's Wife, Found Dead at McLean Home," *Washington Post,* August 14, 1988; "Autopsy Confirms Carbon Monoxide Poisoning Killed Congressman's Wife," *Washington Post,* August 15, 1988.

45. Based on numerous interviews conducted by the authors, including former aides Robert A. Neuman and Anne Scott, presidential campaign companion Iris Jacobson Burnett, and friends Diane Rennert and Rosemary Cribben.

46. Judith K. "Dodie" Udall interview with the authors.

47. Norma G. Udall interview with the authors, October 19, 1998.

48. Cliff Robertson interview with the authors.

49. Norma G. Udall interview with the authors, October 19, 1998.

50. Based on interviews by the authors with Mark E. Udall, J. Randolph Udall, Judith K. "Dodie" Udall, Anne J. Udall, Bradley H. Udall, and Katherine L. Udall.

51. Anne J. Udall, speech to the Tucson Literary Club, October 21, 1991, Morris K. Udall Papers, Special Collections, University of Arizona Library, Tucson.

52. Richard Cohen, "Who Pays for Greatness," *Washington Post Magazine,* September 11, 1988, p. 17.

53. Letter from Anne J. Udall to Richard Cohen, September 20, 1988, courtesy Anne J. Udall.

CHAPTER 24. LIVING WITH PARKINSON'S

1. Robert Richardson interview with the authors.

2. Perry G. Baker interview with the authors, December 12, 1998.

3. Bruce A. Wright interview with the authors.

4. Joel Nilsson, "Parkinson's Disease Slows, but Does Not Impair Udall," *Arizona Republic,* February 12, 1984.

5. Bruce A. Wright interview with the authors.

6. Judith K. "Dodie" Udall, personal journal, October 13, 1980, courtesy Judith K. Udall.

7. Morris K. Udall statement, October 16, 1980, Morris K. Udall Papers, Special Collections, University of Arizona Library, Tucson.

8. Judith K. "Dodie" Udall, personal journal, October 26, 1980, courtesy Judith K. Udall.

9. Jackie Rothenberg, "Udall Talk Ends in an Uproar," *Arizona Daily Star,* September 2, 1986.

10. Jerome H. Targovnik interview with the authors, April 7, 1999.

11. David R. Obey interview with the authors.

12. Joan McQueeny Mitric, "A Personal Campaign for Mo Udall," Maturity News Service, *Orange County Register* (Anaheim, Calif.), March 9, 1988.

13. "Parkinson's Disease: Hope through Research," National Institute of Neurological Disorders and Stroke, Bethesda, Maryland.

14. Morris K. Udall, rough draft of statement prepared for *People* magazine, November 9, 1981, Morris K. Udall Papers, Special Collections, University of Arizona Library, Tucson; "A Onetime Presidential Candidate Out-Campaigns a New Foe: Parkinson's Disease," *People* magazine, December 1981.

15. Ibid.

16. Joel Nilsson, "Parkinson's Disease Slows, but Does Not Impair Udall," *Arizona Republic,* February 12, 1984.

17. Thomas N. Chase interview with the authors.

18. Robert A. Neuman interview with the authors.

19. Myra MacPherson, "Triumph of the Good Guy," *Washington Post,* December 29, 1985.

20. Erik R. Barnett interview with the authors.

21. Emily Benedek, "Thy Will Be Done," *Arizona Trend,* November 1988, p. 36.

22. Robert A. Neuman interview with the authors.

23. Erik R. Barnett interview with the authors.

24. Joan McQueeny Mitric, "A Personal Campaign for Mo Udall," Maturity News Service, *Orange County Register* (Anaheim, Calif.), March 9, 1988.

25. Matt James interview with the authors.

26. Ibid.

27. Mark F. Trautwein interview, Oral History Project.

28. Mark F. Trautwein interview with the authors.

29. Judith K. "Dodie" Udall interview with the authors.

30. Jerome H. Targovnik interview with the authors, April 7, 1999.

31. Michael J. Murphy interview with the authors.

32. Joseph Garcia and Mary Benanti, "Mo: Who Said 'Retire'?" *Tucson Citizen,* May 6, 1989.

33. "Goldwater Says 'Nuts' to Calls for Udall's Resignation," *Arizona Daily Star,* June 4, 1989.

34. Letter from Barry M. Goldwater to Morris K. Udall, May 11, 1990, Morris K. Udall Papers, Special Collections, University of Arizona Library, Tucson.

35. Morris K. Udall, "Udall: Unfinished Agenda Keeps Me from Retiring," *Arizona Republic,* June 11, 1989.

36. Diane Duston, "Morris Udall: Ravaged by Disease, but Still Tough," Associated Press, June 15, 1989.

37. Norma G. Udall interview with the authors, July 24, 1999.

38. Ibid., October 20, 1998.

39. Mark E. Udall interview with the authors.

40. Anne Scott interview with the authors.

41. Norma G. Udall interview with the authors, October 20, 1998.

42. Thomas S. Foley interview with the authors.

43. Anne Scott interview with the authors.

44. Thomas S. Foley interview with the authors.

45. Joseph Garcia, "Looking Bad or Not, He's Running," *Tucson Citizen,* April 10, 1990.

46. Tom Beal, "Udall Still Tells Stories—It's Just Hard to Hear Them," *Arizona Daily Star,* April 15, 1990.

47. James F. McNulty Jr. interview, Oral History Project.

48. Curtis R. Freed interview with the authors.

49. Letter from Morris K. Udall to Dr. D. Eugene Redmond Jr., November 27, 1990, Morris K. Udall Papers, Special Collections, University of Arizona Library, Tucson.

50. Jeff Herr, "Pressure to Quit Catches Up with Udall," *Arizona Daily Star,* April 19, 1991.

51. Dinah Wisenberg, unheadlined story, States News Service, June 11, 1987.

52. Terrence L. Bracy interview with the authors.

53. Matt James interview with the authors.

54. Bruce A. Wright interview with the authors.

55. Jerome H. Targovnik interview with the authors, April 7, 1999.

56. Michael Murphy and Mike Padgett, "Udall Might Retire, Wife Says in Letter," *Phoenix Gazette,* April 6, 1991.

57. Mark E. Udall interview with the authors.

58. "Time Has Come for Morris Udall to Leave Office," *Tucson Citizen,* March 21, 1991.

59. Mark E. Udall interview with the authors.

60. Norma G. Udall interview with the authors, October 20, 1998.

61. Karen Foerstel, "If Condition of Arizonan Does Not Improve Shortly, He Will Leave Hill, Wife Tells Speaker," *Roll Call,* April 11, 1991.

62. Lois Romano, "Udall Family Split over Resignation," *Washington Post,* April 13, 1991.

63. Norma Coile, "One Big Family," *Tucson Citizen,* April 18, 1991.

64. Norma G. Udall interview with the authors, October 20, 1998.

65. Ibid.

66. Erik R. Barnett (October 31, 1998) and Roy S. Jones Jr. (October 21, 1998) interviews with the authors.

67. Matt James interview with the authors.

68. Letter from Norma G. Udall to House Speaker Thomas S. Foley, April 19, 1991, Morris K. Udall Papers, Special Collections, University of Arizona Library, Tucson.

69. Courtesy Stewart L. Udall.

70. Norma G. Udall interview with the authors, July 24, 1999.

71. Ibid., February 4, 2000.

CHAPTER 25. THE LEGACY

1. Anne J. Udall, speech to Morris K. Udall Foundation Scholarship winners, Tucson, August 7, 1999.

2. Patricia S. Schroeder interview with the authors.

3. Jessica Tuchman Mathews, "As Good as American Politics Can Be," *Washington Post,* April 21, 1991.

4. Peter Jennings, ABC News, April 19, 1991.

5. David S. Broder, "Udall's Triumph," *Washington Post,* April 24, 1991.

6. Rhodes Cook, "Mo Udall Takes Politics with a Grain of Humor," *Congressional Quarterly,* August 18, 1990, p. 2698.

7. Don Young interview with the authors.

8. Letter from Norma G. Udall to Speaker Thomas S. Foley, April 19, 1991, Morris K. Udall Papers, Special Collections, University of Arizona Library, Tucson.

9. Cindy Hubert, "Udall Brings Encouragement to Sufferers of Parkinson's Disease with His Own Story," *Arizona Daily Star,* February 16, 1984.

10. Liz Hunt, "Another Udall Works the Halls of Congress," *Washington Post,* July 25, 1991.

11. Jeff Barker, "Mo Udall's Life Frozen in Time," *Arizona Republic,* August 2, 1998.

12. Mary Jo Pitzl, " 'Mo' Recalled Fondly with Jokes, Tributes," *Arizona Republic,* February 8, 1993.

13. Karen Foerstel, "Still Hospitalized, Udall Gets an Early Birthday Surprise: A Visit by First Lady," *Roll Call,* June 3, 1993.

14. "11 Receive Medal of Freedom," Associated Press, September 10, 1996.

15. Public Law 102-259, 102d Congress, March 19, 1992.

16. Annual report, 1998, the Morris K. Udall Foundation.

17. Mark J. Brand interview with the authors.

18. Erik R. Barnett, "Udall Alumni Will Carry on Legacy of Public Service," *Tucson Citizen,* May 23, 1991.

BIBLIOGRAPHY

INTERVIEWS

The following interviews were conducted by Donald W. Carson and James W. Johnson (an asterisk indicates that the interview was conducted via telephone). They are identified in the notes as "interview with the authors."

Ares, Charles E. Professor of law, University of Arizona College of Law. Tucson, September 4, 1998 (Carson and Johnson).

Baker, Perry G. Public affairs consultant. Phoenix, December 12, 1998; *February 4, 1999; *August 5, 1999 (Carson).

Barnett, Erik R. Assistant district attorney for the Commonwealth of Virginia. Alexandria, October 31, 1998 (Carson).

Borodkin, Marvin. Attorney, Tucson, November 13, 1998 (Carson).

Bracy, Terrence L. Lobbyist, Bracy Williams & Co. Washington, D.C., October 19, 1998 (Carson and Johnson).

Brand, Mark J. Public relations specialist, MRA Brand Strategic Communications. Boulder, Colorado, *June 16, 1999 (Carson).

Broder, David S. Political columnist for the *Washington Post.* Washington, D.C., March 2, 1999 (Carson).

Burnett, Iris Jacobson. Co-founder and chairman of Count Me In for Women's Economic Independence. Washington, D.C., October 29, 1998 (Carson).

Burton, R. Kent. Public affairs specialist with the federal government. Washington, D.C., October 6, 17, and 31, 1998 (Carson).

Carrier, Maria L. Retired political consultant. Washington, D.C., October 15, 1998 (Carson).

Chandler, S. Thomas. Attorney. Tucson, June 22, 1998 (Carson and Johnson).

Chapa, Arthur A. Attorney. Tucson, June 3, 1999 (Carson and Johnson).

Chase, Thomas N. Physician. Washington, D.C., March 4, 1999 (Carson).

Cohen, Marvin S. Attorney. Phoenix, April 16, 1999 (Carson and Johnson).

Cole, Ben R. Retired Washington, D.C., reporter/columnist for Pulliam newspapers. Arlington, Virginia, *November 1, 1998 (Carson).

Conconi, Chuck. Editor at large of *Washingtonian* magazine. Washington, D.C., October 23, 1998 (Carson and Johnson).

Coyle, Edward F. Executive director, Radio Fair America. Washington, D.C., October 20, 1998 (Carson and Johnson).

Crane, Donald A. Corporate representative, W. R. Grace & Company. Washington, D.C., October 12, 1998 (Carson).

Cribben, Rosemary. Political consultant and fund-raiser. Washington, D.C., March 3, 1999 (Carson).

Dravo, Andrea. Advertising executive. Bethesda, Maryland, *July 17, 1999 (Carson).

Drinan, Rev. Robert F., S.J. Former Democratic representative from Massachusetts and current professor of law, Georgetown University. March 22, 1999, written responses (Carson).

Dubrow, Evelyn. Retired labor lobbyist. Washington, D.C., *April 1, 1999 (Carson and Johnson).

Ducheneaux, Franklin D. Indian affairs lobbyist. Washington, D.C., October 9, 1998 (Carson).

Duddleston, Thomas C. Retired reporter and editor. Tucson, January 18, 1998 (Carson and Johnson).

Enke, Fred W. Farmer. Casa Grande, Arizona, *June 10, 1999 (Carson).

Farr, Bert. Retired independent insurance agent. St. Johns, Arizona, July 17, 1998 (Carson and Johnson).

Farr, Virgene Jarvis. Homemaker. St. Johns, Arizona, July 17, 1998 (Carson and Johnson).

Feldman, Stanley G. Associate justice, Arizona Supreme Court. Tucson, April 21, 1999 (Carson and Johnson).

Foley, Thomas S. U.S. ambassador to Japan. Washington, D.C., *June 19, 1999 (Carson and Johnson).

Fox, Morley. Retired water lobbyist. Washington, D.C., March 4, 1999 (Carson).

Freed, Curtis R. Physician; professor and division head, University of Colorado Health Sciences Center. Denver, *July 8, 1999 (Carson).

Gabusi, John B. Vice chancellor for enrollment services, Pima Community College. Tucson, September 14 and 21, 1998 (Carson and Johnson).

Garcia, Isabel G. Pima County legal defender. Tucson, *July 14, 1999 (Carson).

Genung, George F. Retired high school basketball coach. Tucson, October 15, 1998 (Johnson).

Gilinsky, Victor. Nuclear energy consultant. Santa Monica, California, *July 16, 1999 (Carson).

Goodman, Marian S. Former Udall staff member. Washington, D.C., March 1, 1999 (Carson).

Greenberg, Garry. Former TV newsman. Tucson, August 26, 1998 (Carson).

Harris, Fred R. Professor of political science, University of New Mexico. Albuquerque, *June 7, 1999 (Carson and Johnson).

Harrison, Gilbert A. Former editor of *New Republic* magazine. Scottsdale, Arizona, December 12, 1998 (Carson).

Heap, Anona. At ninety-four years of age, the oldest woman in St. Johns, Arizona. St. Johns, May 13, 1998 (Carson and Johnson).

Heap, Wallace. Retired construction supervisor. St. Johns, Arizona, May 13, 1998 (Carson and Johnson).

Hodge, Wavell. Physician; medical director, Veterans Administration Nursing Home, District of Columbia. Washington, D.C., October 19, 1998 (Carson and Johnson).

James, Matt. Strategic communications director, Cisco Systems, San Jose, California, February 19, 1999 (Carson).

Jones, Roy S., Jr. Attorney. Washington, D.C., October 17 and 21, 1998 (Carson and Johnson).

Kastenmeier, Robert W. Former Democratic representative from Wisconsin. Arlington, Virginia, *October 30, 1998 (Carson).

Kell, Bonnie C. Associate, Ogilvy Public Relations Worldwide. Washington, D.C., October 16, 1998 (Carson).

Kenski, Henry C., Jr. Associate professor of communication, University of Arizona, and regional director for southern Arizona for U.S. senator Jon Kyl, Republican. Tucson, December 16, 1998 (Carson and Johnson).

Kimble, William E. Retired attorney. Tucson, December 11, 1998 (Carson and Johnson).

King, Larry L. Writer. Washington, D.C., October 21, 1998 (Carson and Johnson).

Lewis, Roger K. Retired newspaper reporter and editor. Sun Lakes, Arizona, December 16, 1997 (Carson and Johnson).

Matheson, Mac C. Retired insurance and real estate agent. Mesa, Arizona, December 19, 1998 (Carson and Johnson).

Mathews, Jessica Tuchman. President, Carnegie Endowment for International Peace. Washington, D.C., March 3, 1999 (Carson).

Maxwell, Morgan, Jr. Real estate broker. Tucson, *February 17, 1999 (Johnson).

McNulty, James F., Jr. Attorney. Tucson, November 21, 1997 (Carson and Johnson).

Meeds, Lloyd. Attorney and former Democratic representative from Washington state. Washington, D.C., *February 10, 1999 (Carson).

Miller, George. Retired painting contractor and former mayor of Tucson. Tucson, December 11, 1998 (Carson).

Murphy, Michael J. Public information director, Arizona Department of Health. Phoenix, January 29, 1999 (Johnson).

Muys, Jerome C. Attorney. Washington, D.C., October 29, 1998 (Carson).

Myers, Henry R. Physicist. Peaks Island, Maine, *January 7, 1998 (Carson and Johnson).

Neuman, Robert A. Lobbyist, Neuman & Company. Washington, D.C., October 19, 1998 (Carson and Johnson).

Neumann, Loretta. Freelance writer. Washington, D.C., *May 15, 1999 (Carson and Johnson).

Ninemi, Gwen. Retired teacher. Tucson, *December 14, 1998 (Johnson).

Obey, David R. Democratic representative from Wisconsin. Washington, D.C., March 1, 1999 (Carson).

Olson, Richard C. Author. Fairfax, Virginia, October 24, 1998; *July 21, 1999 (Carson and Johnson).

O'Neill, J. Daniel. Attorney. Tucson, December 15, 1997 (Carson and Johnson).

Owens, Wayne. President, Center for Middle East Peace and Economic Cooperation, and former Democratic representative from Utah. Washington, D.C., March 2, 1999 (Carson).

Parshley, Paul. Director, Northern American Power Group, Cambridge Energy Research Associates. Cambridge, Massachusetts, *February 15, 1999 (Carson and Johnson).

Pickrell, Robert W. Attorney. Phoenix, September 22 and 28, 1998 (Carson and Johnson).

Quinn, Jack. Partner, Arnold & Porter. Washington, D.C., *January 20, 1999 (Carson).

Rennert, Diane. Retired lobbyist. Phoenix, April 2, 1999 (Carson and Johnson).

Reuss, Henry S. Former Democratic representative from Wisconsin. Belvedere, California, *January 21, 1999 (Carson and Johnson).

Reveles, Robert A. Retired vice president for government affairs, Homestake Mining Co. Gold Canyon, Arizona, December 19, 1998 (Carson and Johnson).

Richardson, Robert. Executive producer, KVOA-TV, Tucson, *February 8, 1999 (Carson).

Robertson, Cliff. Actor. New York City, *February 19, 1999 (Johnson).

Rosenberg, George. Retired *Tucson Citizen* managing editor. Tucson, November 13, 1998 (Carson and Johnson).

Russell, Mark. Political satirist. Washington, D.C., *October 15, 1998 (Carson).

Scates, Karen T. President and chief executive officer, Kids Voting USA. Tempe, Arizona, February 19, 1999 (Carson).

Schroeder, Patricia S. President and chief executive officer, Association of American Publishers Inc. Washington, D.C., March 1, 1999 (Carson).

Scott, Anne. Public affairs consultant. Phoenix, July 12, 1999 (Carson and Johnson).

Seiberling, John F. Former Democratic representative from Ohio. Akron, Ohio, *August 5, 1999 (Carson).

Shields, Mark. Syndicated newspaper columnist, moderator for CNN's *Capitol Gang*, and public television analyst. Washington, D.C., March 2, 1999 (Carson).

Sliz, Deborah. Senior government affairs professional, Morgan Meguire, Washington, D.C., March 2, 1999 (Carson).

Sloss, C. Stanley. Senior legislative counsel for Representative Mark E. Udall. Washington, D.C., *May 15, 1999 (Carson and Johnson).

Steiger, Sam. Former Republican representative from Arizona and now mayor of Prescott. Prescott, Arizona, *January 9, 1998 (Johnson).

Strand, Dolores Jackson Briney. Former Udall staff member. Tucson, September 28, 1998 (Carson and Johnson).

Targovnik, Diane M. Arizona State University law student. Phoenix, October 16, 1998 (Johnson).

Targovnik, Jerome H. Physician. Phoenix, October 16, 1998; *April 7, 1999 (Carson and Johnson).

Trautwein, Mark F. Freelance editor. San Anselmo, California, *July 19, 1999 (Carson and Johnson).

Udall, Anne J. Assistant superintendent, Charlotte-Mecklenberg Schools. Roadside rest area near Marion, North Carolina. October 27, 1998 (Carson).

Udall, Bradley H. Executive director, Eagle Valley Land Trust. Eagle, Colorado, August 4, 1998 (Johnson).

Udall, Calvin H. Attorney. Phoenix, August 26, 1998 (Carson).

Udall, D. Burr. Attorney. Tucson, April 3, 1998 (Carson and Johnson).

Udall, Elma. Retired State Department aide. Albuquerque, June 17, 1999 (Carson and Johnson).

Udall, Gwen. Retired teacher. St. Johns, Arizona, May 13, 1998 (Carson and Johnson).

Udall, J. Randolph. Director, Community Office for Resource Efficiency. Aspen, Colorado, July 29, 1998 (Johnson).

Udall, Judith K. "Dodie." Former teacher. Boulder, Colorado, November 25, 1998 (Carson).

Udall, Katherine L. Assistant professor, West Virginia University. Morgantown, West Virginia, October 22, 1998 (Carson and Johnson).

Udall, Keith. Retired school administrator. St. Johns, Arizona, May 13, 1998 (Carson and Johnson).

Udall, Lee. Homemaker. Tucson, March 7, 1999 (Carson and Johnson).

Udall, Mark E. Democratic U.S. representative from Colorado. Boulder, Colorado, November 25, 1998 (Carson).

Udall, Norma G. Retired lobbyist and congressional aide. Arlington, Virginia, October 19 and 20, 1998; *July 24, 1999; *February 4, 2000 (Carson and Johnson).

Udall, Patricia E. Former Peace Corps administrator. Boulder, Colorado, July 16, 1998 (Carson).

Udall, Stewart L. Author, historian, attorney, former secretary of the interior, and former Democratic U.S. representative from Arizona. Santa Fe, New Mexico, *January 16, 1998; *February 4, 1998; *June 24, 1998; July 18, 1998; *February 11 and 25, 1999; March 7, 1999; November 11, 1999 (Carson and Johnson).

Whiting, Eloise Udall. Homemaker. Albuquerque, July 17, 1998 (Carson and Johnson).

Whiting, Warren G. Retired mechanical engineer. Albuquerque, July 17, 1998 (Carson and Johnson).

Whitten, Leslie H. Retired syndicated columnist. Silver Spring, Maryland, *October 30, 1998 (Carson).

Wright, Bruce A. Associate vice president for economic development, University of Arizona. Tucson, December 17, 1998 (Carson and Johnson).

Young, Don. Republican U.S. representative from Alaska. Washington, D.C., October 7, 1998 (Carson).

TAPED INTERVIEWS

The following interviews were conducted by Peter L. Steere and Julie Ferdon for the Morris K. Udall Oral History Project, Morris K. Udall Papers, Special Collections, University of Arizona Library, Tucson. Interviews from this source are identified in the notes as "Oral History Project."

Anderson, John B. Tucson, August 7, 1998 (Ferdon).

Ares, Charles E. Tucson, June 9, 1998 (Ferdon).

Broder, David S. Washington, D.C., March 5, 1999 (Ferdon).

Chandler, S. Thomas. Tucson, July 2, 1998 (Ferdon).

Ford, Gerald R. Palm Springs, California, March 25, 1999 (Ferdon).

McNulty, James F., Jr. Tucson, July 9, 1998 (Ferdon).

Rhodes, John J. Scottsdale, Arizona, March 25, 1999 (Ferdon).

Seiberling, John F. Akron, Ohio, September 11, 1998 (Ferdon).

Trautwein, Mark F. San Anselmo, California, July 31, 1998 (Ferdon).

Udall, D. Burr. Tucson, October 15, 1998 (Ferdon).

Udall, Elma. Albuquerque, May 15–16, 1996 (Steere).

Udall, Stewart L. Santa Fe, New Mexico, October 24, 1996 (Steere).

Whiting, Eloise Udall. Albuquerque, May 17, 1996 (Steere).

Whiting, Warren G. Albuquerque, May 17, 1996 (Steere).

TRANSCRIPTS OF INTERVIEWS

The following interviews were conducted by James F. McNulty Jr. and Virginia Kelly for the Arizona Bar Foundation Oral History Project: Arizona Legal History, University of Arizona College of Law. Interviews from this source are identified in the notes as "Arizona Bar Foundation."

Ares, Charles E. Tucson, May 10, 1988 (McNulty).

Chandler, S. Thomas. Tucson, May 3, 1988 (McNulty).

Truman, Alice N. Tucson, March 5, 1994 (Kelly).

Udall, Morris K. Tucson, March 28, 1989 (McNulty).

BOOKS

Addresses and Special Orders Held in the U.S. House of Representatives and the Senate Presented in Honor of Hon. Morris K. "Mo" Udall (House Document 102-149, May 2, 1991). Washington, D.C.: U.S. Government Printing Office, 1993.

Arnold, Ron. *At the Eye of the Storm: James Watt and the Environmentalists.* Chicago: Regnery Gateway, 1982.

Ashby, LeRoy, and Rod Gramer. *Fighting the Odds: The Life of Senator Frank Church.* Pullman: Washington State University Press, 1994.

August, Jack L., Jr. *Vision in the Desert: Carl Hayden and Hydropolitics in the American Southwest.* Fort Worth: Texas Christian University Press, 1999.

Austin, Richard C., and Peter Borrelli, eds. *The Strip Mining of America.* New York: Sierra Club, 1971.

Baker, Ross K. *The New Fat Cats: Members of Congress as Political Benefactors.* New York: Priority Press, 1989.

Barry, John M. *The Ambition and the Power.* New York: Viking, 1989.

Bennett, James T., and Thomas J. Dilorenzo. *Official Lies: How Washington Misleads Us.* Alexandria, Va.: Groom Books, 1992.

Bernstein, Irving. *Guns or Butter: The Presidency of Lyndon Johnson.* New York: Oxford University Press, 1996.

Bisnow, Mark. *Diary of a Dark Horse: The 1980 Anderson Presidential Campaign.* Carbondale: University of Illinois Press, 1983.

Bolling, Richard. *House Out of Order.* New York: E. P. Dutton, 1964.

Brereton, Charles. *First in the Nation: New Hampshire and the Premier Presidential Primary.* Portsmouth, N.H.: Peter E. Randall Publishers, 1987.

Broder, David S. *Changing of the Guard.* New York: Simon and Schuster, 1980.

Brower, David R. *For Earth's Sake: The Life and Times of David R. Brower.* Salt Lake City: Peregrine Smith Books, 1990.

——. *Work in Progress.* Salt Lake City: Peregrine Smith Books, 1991.

Carter, Jimmy. *Keeping Faith: The Memoirs of Jimmy Carter.* New York: Bantam Books, 1982.

Carter, Rosalynn. *First Lady from Plains.* Fayetteville: University of Arkansas Press, 1984.

Chanin, Abe. *They Fought Like Wildcats.* Tucson: Midbar Press, 1979.

Chanin, Abe, and Mildred Chanin. *This Land, These Voices.* Flagstaff, Ariz.: Northland Press, 1977.

Chelf, Carl P. *Congress in the American System.* Chicago: Nelson-Hall, 1977.

Cohen, Michael P. *The History of the Sierra Club, 1892–1970.* San Francisco: Sierra Club Books, 1988.

Corbett, Doris R. *Outstanding Athletes in Congress.* Washington, D.C.: U.S. Capitol Historical Society, 1977.

Corrado, Anthony. *Creative Campaigning:* PACs and the Presidential Selection Process. San Francisco: Westview Press, 1992.

Davidson, Roger H., and Walter J. Oleszek. *Congress and Its Members.* Washington, D.C.: Congressional Quarterly Press, 1981.

Davis, James W. *Presidential Primaries: Road to the White House.* Westport, Conn.: Greenwood Press, 1980.

Drew, Elizabeth. *American Journal.* New York: Random House, 1977.

Ehrenhalt, Alan. *Politics in America: Members of Congress in Washington and at Home.* Washington, D.C.: Congressional Quarterly Press, 1981.

——. *The United States of Ambition: Politicians, Power and the Pursuit of Office.* New York: Times Books, 1991.

Ellsworth, Maria S. *Mormon Odyssey: The Story of Ida Hunt Udall, Plural Wife.* Urbana: University of Illinois Press, 1992.

Fleming, Harold C. *The Potomac Chronicle.* Athens: University of Georgia Press, 1996.

Fradkin, Philip L. *A River No More.* Tucson: University of Arizona Press, 1981.

Gibbons, William Conrad. *The U.S. Government and the Vietnam War.* Princeton, N.J.: Princeton University Press, 1995.

Glad, Betty. *Jimmy Carter in Search of the Great White House.* New York: W. W. Norton, 1980.

Goff, John S. *Arizona Civilization.* Phoenix: Hooper Publishing Corp., 1968.

Gold, Vic. *PR as in President.* Garden City, N.Y.: Doubleday, 1977.

Goldberg, Robert Alan. *Barry Goldwater.* New Haven, Conn.: Yale University Press, 1995.

Goldwater, Barry M. *Goldwater.* New York: Doubleday, 1988.

Green, Mark J., James M. Fallows, and David R. Zwick. *Who Runs Congress?* 3d ed. New York: Viking Press, 1979.

Hadley, Arthur T. *The Invisible Primary.* Englewood Cliffs, N.J.: Prentice Hall, 1976.

Hall, Bill. *Frank Church, D.C. & Me.* Pullman: Washington State University Press, 1995.

Hamilton, Charles V. *Adam Clayton Powell, Jr.: The Political Biography of an American Dilemma.* New York: Atheneum, 1991.

Hammond, Jay. *Tales of Alaska's Bush Rat Governor.* Fairbanks, Alaska: Epicenter Press, 1994.

Harris, Fred R. *Potomac Fever.* New York: W. W. Norton, 1977.

Hass, Garland A. *Jimmy Carter and the Politics of Frustration.* Jefferson, N.C.: McFarland, 1992.

Haygood, Wil. *King of the Cats: The Life and Times of Adam Clayton Powell.* New York: Houghton Mifflin, 1993.

Hollander, Zander, ed. *The Pro Basketball Encyclopedia.* Los Angeles: Corwin Books, 1977.

Iverson, Peter. *Barry Goldwater, Native Arizonan.* Norman: University of Oklahoma Press, 1997.

Jacobs, John. *A Rage for Justice.* Berkeley: University of California Press, 1995.

Jamieson, Kathleen H. *Packaging the Presidency.* New York: Oxford University Press, 1992.

Johnson, Rich. *The Central Arizona Project: 1918–1968.* Tucson: University of Arizona Press, 1977.

Jones, Charles O. *The United States Congress: People, Place, and Policy.* Homewood, Ill.: Dorsey Press, 1982.

Jones, Rochelle, and Peter Woll. *The Privileged World of Congress.* New York: Free Press, 1979.

King, Larry L. *Of Outlaws, Con Men, Whores, Politicians and Other Artists.* New York: Viking Press, 1980.

———. *None but a Blockhead: On Being a Writer.* New York: Viking Press, 1986.

Lasky, Victor. *Jimmy Carter: The Man and the Myth.* New York: Richard Marek Publishers, 1979.

Laycock, George. *Alaska: The Embattled Frontier.* Boston: Houghton Mifflin, 1971.

Leydet, François. *Time and the River Flowing.* San Francisco: Sierra Club, 1964.

MacPherson, Myra. *The Power Lovers.* New York: Putnam, 1975.

Martin, Douglas D. *The Lamp in the Desert.* Tucson: University of Arizona Press, 1960.

Martin, Russell. *A Story that Stands Like a Dam: Glen Canyon and the Struggle for the Soul of the West.* New York: Henry Holt, 1989.

Mayhew, David R. *Congress: The Electoral Connection.* New Haven, Conn.: Yale University Press, 1974.

McClintock, James M. *Mormon Settlement in Arizona.* Tucson: University of Arizona Press, 1985.

McCombs, Maxwell, Edna F. Einsiedel, and David H. Weaver. *Contemporary Public Opinion: Issues and the News.* Hillsdale, N.J.: Lawrence Earlbaum Associates, 1991.

McCullough, David. *Truman.* New York: Simon and Schuster, 1992.

McGovern, George. *The Autobiography of George McGovern.* New York: Random House, 1977.

McGuire, Thomas R., William B. Lord, and Mary C. Wallace, eds. *Indian Water in the New West.* Tucson: University of Arizona Press, 1993.

McMillan, James E. *The Ernest W. McFarland Papers: The U.S. Senate Years, 1940–52.* Prescott, Ariz.: Sharlot Hall Museum Press, 1995.

Melder, Keith. *Hail to the Candidate: Presidential Campaigns from Banners to Broadcasts.* Washington, D.C.: Smithsonian Institution Press, 1992.

Miller, Tom. *On the Border: Portraits of America's Southwestern Frontier.* Tucson: University of Arizona Press, 1985.

———, ed. *Arizona: The Land and the People.* Tucson: University of Arizona Press, 1986.

Miller, William "Fishbait." *Fishbait: The Memoirs of the Congressional Doorkeeper.* New York: Warner Books, 1977.

Mitchell, Donald C. *Sold American: The Story of Alaska Natives and Their Land.* Hanover, N.H.: University Press of New England, 1997.

Moore, Jonathan, and Janet Fraser. *Campaign for President: The Managers Look at '76.* Cambridge, Mass.: Ballinger Publishing, 1977.

Morehouse, Barbara J. *A Place Called Grand Canyon.* Tucson: University of Arizona Press, 1996.

Morris, Kenneth. *American Moralist.* Athens: University of Georgia Press, 1996.

Nash, Roderick, ed. *Grand Canyon of the Living Colorado*. San Francisco: Sierra Club, 1970.

O'Neill, Tip. *Man of the House: The Life and Political Memoirs of Speaker Tip O'Neill*. New York: St. Martin's Press, 1987.

Orren, Gary R., and Nelson W. Polsby. *Media of Momentum: The New Hampshire Primary and Momentum Politics*. Chatham, N.J.: Chatham House Publishers, 1987.

Palmer, Niall A. *The New Hampshire Primary and the American Electoral Process*. Westport, Conn.: Praeger, 1997.

Pare, Madeline Ferri. *Arizona Pageant: A Short History of the 48th State*. Tempe: Arizona Historical Foundation, 1967.

Patterson, Thomas E. *The Mass Media Election: How Americans Choose Their President*. New York: Praeger, 1980.

Peters, Charles. *How Washington Really Works*. Reading, Mass.: Addison-Wesley, 1980.

Peters, Ronald M., Jr., ed. *The Speaker: Leadership in the U.S. House of Representatives*. Washington, D.C.: Congressional Quarterly, 1995.

Ranney, Austin. *The American Elections of 1980*. Washington, D.C.: American Enterprise Institute for Public Policy Research, 1981.

Reeves, Andre E. *Congressional Committee Chairmen: Three Who Made an Evolution*. Lexington: University of Kentucky Press, 1993.

Reeves, Richard. *Old Faces of 1976*. New York: Harper and Row, 1976.

———. *Convention*. New York: Harcourt Brace, 1977.

Reisner, Marc. *Cadillac Desert: The American West and Its Disappearing Water*. New York: Penguin Books, 1986.

Reuss, Henry S. *When Government Was Good: Memories of a Life in Politics*. Madison: University of Wisconsin Press, 1999.

Rhodes, John J. *I Was There*. Salt Lake City: Northwest Publishing, 1995.

Rice, Ross. *Carl Hayden: Builder of the American West*. New York: University Press of America, 1994.

Rothman, Hal K. *Reopening of the American West*. Tucson: University of Arizona Press, 1998.

Runte, Alfred. *National Parks: The American Experience*. Lincoln: University of Nebraska Press, 1979.

Sabato, Larry L. *PAC Power: Inside the World of Political Action Committees*. New York: W. W. Norton, 1984.

Safire, William. *Safire's Washington*. New York: Times Books, 1980.

Schram, Martin. *Running for President 1976*. New York: Stein and Day Publishers, 1977.

Shadegg, Stephen C. *Arizona Politics: The Struggle to End One-Party Rule.* Tempe: Arizona State University Press, 1986.

Smith, Hedrick. *The Power Game.* New York: Random House, 1988.

Smith, Pauline Udall. *The Memoirs of Pauline Udall Smith.* Published by her family, November 1993. Two copies available in the University of Arizona Library.

Solomon, John S., III. *Congress and the New Politics.* Boston: Little, Brown, 1969.

Stern, Philip M. *The Best Congress Money Can Buy.* New York: Pantheon Books, 1988.

Stroud, Kandy. *How Jimmy Won.* New York: William Morrow, 1977.

Thompson, Kenneth W. *Statesmen Who Were Never President.* Lanham, Md.: University Press of America, 1997.

Udall, David King, and Pearl Udall Nelson. *Arizona Pioneer Mormon.* Tucson: Arizona Silhouettes, 1959.

Udall, Jesse Addison. *Jesse A. Udall.* Orem, Utah: Remember When, 1981.

Udall, Louise. *Me and Mine: The Life Story of Helen Sekaquaptewa.* Tucson: University of Arizona Press, 1969.

Udall, Morris K. *Education of a Congressman: The Newsletters of Morris K. Udall,* Robert L. Peabody, ed. New York: Bobbs-Merrill, 1972.

———. *Too Funny to Be President.* New York: Henry Holt, 1988.

Udall, Morris K., and Donald G. Tacheron. *Job of a Congressman.* New York: Bobbs-Merrill, 1966.

Udall, Stewart L. *The Quiet Crisis.* New York: Avon Books, 1963.

———. *The Quiet Crisis and the Next Generation,* 2d ed. Salt Lake City: Peregrine Smith Books, 1988.

———. *The Myths of August.* New York: Pantheon Books, 1994.

Volger, David J. *The Politics of Congress,* 2d ed. Boston: Allyn and Bacon, 1977.

Watkins, T. H. *The Grand Colorado: The Story of a River and Its Canyons.* Palo Alto, Calif.: American West Publishing, 1969.

Weaver, David, Doris A. Graber, Maxwell E. McCombs, and Chaim E. Eyal. *Media Agenda-Setting in a Presidential Election: Issues, Images, and Interest.* New York: Praeger, 1981.

White, Tracy. *Power in Congress.* Washington, D.C.: Congressional Quarterly, 1987.

Wiley, Peter Booth, and Robert Gottlieb. *Empires in the Sun: The Rise of the New American West.* New York: Putnam, 1988.

Wilhelm, C. LeRoy, and Mabel R. Wilhelm. *A History of the St. Johns Arizona Stake.* Orem, Utah: Historical Publications, 1982.

Wilkinson, Charles K. *Crossing the Next Meridian: Land, Water and the Future of the West.* Washington, D.C.: Island Press, 1992.

Witcover, Jules. *Marathon: The Pursuit of the Presidency 1972–1976.* New York: Viking, 1977.

Wooten, James. *Dasher: The Roots and the Rising of Jimmy Carter.* New York: Summit Books, 1978.

Worster, Donald. *Rivers of Empire.* New York: Oxford University Press, 1985.

Wright, Jim. *Balance of Power.* Atlanta: Turner Publishing, 1996.

Zaslowsky, Dyan, and T. H. Watkins. *These American Lands: Parks, Wilderness, and Public Lands.* Washington, D.C.: Island Press, 1994.

INDEX

nation of, 253–54; tobacco industry and, 70; Tucson law practice of, 50–56; at University of Arizona, 23–25, 40, 44–48; Vietnam War and, 76, 82–92; women and, 210

Udall, Norma G., 234, 260; and Mo, 221, 222, 233–35, 245, 249, 252, 253, 254

Udall, Patricia J. (nee Emery), 49, 204, 226; and family, 224, 225–27; and 1954 congressional election, 53–54, 61, 66, 67, 73, 160, 227; and Mo, 224, 227, 228; remarriage of, 228

Udall, Pearl, 38

Udall, Ren, 255

Udall, Stewart L.: as advisor to Mo, 66, 88, 216; Central Arizona Project and, 120–21, 124, 125–27, 135; as competitor of Mo's, 22, 52, 219; as confidant of Mo's, 84, 89, 108; in Congress, 52–53, 58, 60, 61, 94, 219; describing Mo, xvi, 19, 47, 87, 144, 189; early life of, 9, 11, 13, 16–19, 22–24; education of, 27, 45, 47; and the environment, 7, 122, 183, 193–94; law practice of, 50–51; local politics and, 53; military correspondence from Mo, 32–40 passim; and Mo's health, 252, 254; and Mo's presidential campaign of 1976, 152–53, 154, 156, 158, 163–69 passim, 172; Point Udall (Virgin Islands) named for, 220; political influence of, xiii, 49–50, 60, 67, 177; as secretary of the interior, x, 60–61, 83, 118

Udall, Tom, 261

underground mining, 186–89

University of Arizona, 9, 44, 217, 260

U.S. Institute for Environmental Conflict Resolution, 260

Vander Jagt, Guy, 212

Vietnam War, 76, 82, 84, 90, 92, 93, 84, 163

Viorst, Milton, 149

Voting Rights Act of 1965, 72

Waldie, Jerome R., 72, 107

Wallace, George C., 144, 147, 149, 154, 162, 167

Wallop, Malcolm, 186

Walsh, James A., 79

Ward, Ella Royston. See Udall, Ella

Ward, G. Richard, 228

Washingtonian, 212

Washington Redskins, 213, 235

Watson, Albert W., 98

Watt, James G., 131–32

Whiting, Eloise (nee Udall), 4, 9, 18, 23, 28, 224

Whiting, Warren G., 18, 19, 224

Wicker, Tom, 136

Wilderness Society, 62, 121, 195

Wilkins, Roger, 136

Williams, Frank, 248

Williams, John Bell, 98

Wilson, Bryce H., 51

Windsor, Merrill, 47

Wolff, Lester L., 107

Wong, Tunney, 54

Wright, Bruce A., 179, 181, 213–15, 221, 223, 231, 240–41, 251

Wright, James C., Jr., 114, 182, 212, 220

Wurf, Jerry, 176

Young, Andrew, 145, 167

Young, Coleman, 168–69

Young, Don, 195, 197, 198, 259

Young, Robert, 127, 134

Zarb, Frank G., 185

ABOUT THE AUTHORS

Donald W. Carson, a former newspaper reporter and editor, is professor emeritus and former head of the University of Arizona journalism department. Carson spent three summers as a Fulbright Scholar in Ecuador and has lectured in Mexico, Costa Rica, Bolivia, Colombia, and Sweden.

James W. Johnson, a former newspaper reporter and editor, is a professor of journalism at the University of Arizona, where he has taught for the past twenty-two years. He is the co-author of *One Step from the White House: The Rise and Fall of Senator William F. Knowland.*